Red-Hot Rivals

FERRARI vs MASERATI

Rivals

Epic clashes for supremacy

Red-Hot Rivals

FERRARI vs MASERATI

Rivals

Epic clashes for supremacy

KARL LUDVIGSEN

For Simon Michael Ludvigsen Gaines

First published in February 2008

A catalogue record for this book is
available from the British Library

ISBN 987 1 84425 412 5

Library of Congress control no 2007922006

Published by Haynes Publishing,
Sparkford, Yeovil, Somerset BA22 7JJ, UK
Tel: 01963 442030 Fax: 01963 440001
Int. tel: +44 1963 442030 Int. fax: +44 1963 440001
E-mail: sales@haynes.co.uk
Website: www.haynes.co.uk

Haynes North America Inc.,
861 Lawrence Drive, Newbury Park,
California 91320, USA

Page layout by G&M Designs Limited,
Raunds, Northamptonshire

Printed and bound in Britain by
J. H. Haynes & Co. Ltd, Sparkford

CONTENTS

RED-HOT RIVALS

PREFACE

Ironically it was the unification of Ferrari and Maserati under common ownership that prompted this book about their rivalry on the race track. With both marques under the same roof, America's Ferrari-dedicated *Forza* magazine began dipping its toes into stories about Maseratis. Its readers not only tolerated this but also expressed interest in learning more about the Trident's cars, both current and historic.

In reply to one reader, *Forza* editor Jacqueline Jouret said, 'We won't be running stories about pre-Ferrari Masers, but stories that include both marques are a distinct possibility. The Ferrari-Maserati rivalry of the 1950s certainly provides plenty of material!'

I was no stranger to that rivalry. I had seen the Mondials race the A6GCSs, the Monza versus 300 S battles, the 450 S beating the 335 S at Sebring and the 'Birdcages' tackling the Testa Rossas. At Monza in 1958 I'd watched Moss in the bellowing Eldorado take on Musso, Hawthorn and Phil Hill in the formidable Ferrari 412 MI. I was both friend and colleague of Chris Amon in 1967 when he raced for the Prancing Horse against the surprisingly effective Trident-powered Coopers.

In short, as a contributor to *Forza* I felt obliged to step into the breach. I e-mailed Jackie that I'd be happy to tackle stories on the rivalry. I set out the idea of casting it in terms of the rival models of each marque. Then, in September of 2002, I even mooted the idea of developing a series of articles into a book. At an early stage I alerted Mark Hughes at Haynes to this possibility, with the result that you now hold in your hands. It exists thanks to the initiative of Jackie Jouret, her successor at *Forza* Aaron Jenkins and their intrepid publisher Tom Toldrian.

Depicting the rivalry model-by-model inevitably leads to some chronological overlap. I hope the reader will excuse this, as it seems the best way to show how the antagonists fared in the different categories in which they competed. I've also taken the opportunity to describe the main technicalities of the vehicles involved. This can easily be skipped over by readers less interested in the nuts and bolts. I hope, in such an instance, it will be because the saga of the rivalry's two decades is stirring in its own right.

This story has accreted in my grey matter over the decades since it began in the late 1940s. I owe thanks to many who have helped me understand how the rivalry progressed during the years, not least Adolfo Orsi and Alfieri Maserati, respectively grandson and nephew of the protagonists of the same names. Writings and interviews by the much-missed Piero Casucci have been helpful, as have the researches of leading historian Gianni Cancellieri. Only by virtue of his preoccupation with other themes have I had a chance to get to grips with this one.

The bibliography gives an insight into the wide range of sources that were consulted during the writing. Among these special attention must be drawn to the works of Gianni Rogliatti, Joel Finn and Doug Nye, researchers and authors who have given these great Italian cars the attention that they deserve. Antoine Prunet, Keith Bluemel, Alexis Callier, Peter Sachs, Tony Willis and Marcel Massini are among the red-car experts who have corrected and/or elucidated. Any errors of commission or omission remain mine alone.

At Maserati Ermanno Cozza has been very helpful over the years, while at Ferrari I am grateful for the assistance provided by Antonio Ghini, Riccardo Andreoni and Stefania Martinelli. Images are principally from the Ludvigsen Library, thanks especially to photographers Rodolfo Mailander, Edward Eves, Max Le Grand and Stanley Rosenthall. Gerhild Drücker-Gotschke kindly provided the stunning endpaper images by her late, great husband. They show the epic Ferrari/Maserati batle in the 1957 German Grand Prix.

The team required to put a book like this together includes Mark Hughes, Flora Myer and Steve Rendle at Haynes; to them and their colleagues very many thanks. Gratitude is owed as well to Mike Holland in the Ludvigsen Library and to Norman Kent, master at extracting visual value from dubious negatives. Gil Pearson has helped with transcriptions. No support is more essential to a project of this kind than that of my wife Annette, to whom I express my deepest love and appreciation.

The reader is entitled to ask whether the author of a book about a rivalry favours one side or the other. I hope it doesn't show, but I'd have to confess to an affection for Maserati. In the 1960s I was the proud owner of a 1952 A6GCS, a rare twin-cam transitional model. I had great fun racing it in events of the VSCCA, of which I am proud to be an honorary member. Also one of the most memorable episodes of my editorship of *Car and Driver* was a drive in Gaston Andrey's SCCA-champion 'Birdcage' at Thompson Raceway. What a car!

In compensation, productive contacts with Ferrari have tipped the balance toward neutrality. On a recent visit to Maranello I saw the plans for a new museum in Modena to be centred on Enzo

Ferrari's former residence. Sensationally, appropriately, it will celebrate both of the city's grand sporting cars. As its prospectus states, it will 'unite two marques characterised by ferocious rivalry'. As this book demonstrates, that is if anything an understatement.

Karl Ludvigsen
Hawkedon
Suffolk
December 2007

For the April 1961 debut issue of Car and Driver, *of which he was then editor, Karl Ludvigsen track-tested the Type 61 Maserati being raced at the time by his friend Gaston Andrey. He found it a stunningly well-balanced racing car.*

Origins of a rivalry

Outstanding Italian journalists covered the intense rivalry between Ferrari and Maserati in the two decades from 1947 to 1967. Among them were Corrado Millanta, 'Johnny' Lurani and Giovanni Canestrini. Yet others in the front line of reporting on their Red-Hot Rivalry were foreigners. Hans Tanner was Swiss, Graham Gauld Scottish, Jesse Alexander and Pete Coltrin American and Rodolfo Mailander half-German. They had the distinct advantage of being neutrals in the bitter war between two makers of racing cars based in and around the Northern Italian city of Modena.

'Modena in the 1950s was a very exciting place to work,' Romolo Tavoni told Gauld, 'as there was great rivalry between Maserati and Ferrari. Indeed, the rivalry was so great that the Via Emilia, the old Roman road which runs through the centre of the city, became the boundary. The Ferrari offices and service departments were only about 500 metres from the Maserati factory on either side of this road. If you worked on the north side of the Via Emilia, you were a Maserati man, and if you worked on the south side, you were a Ferrari man.

'At the height of the rivalry,' Tavoni continued, 'it was generally known that if you worked for Ferrari you would never be employed by Maserati and vice

The spirit of the 1930s, in which the rivalry between Maserati and Ferrari flourished, was exemplified by the start at Donington on 5 October 1935. Nino Farina's Maserati V8RI (16) burned rubber next to the ex-Ferrari Alfa Romeo Type B of Raymond Sommer (8). Behind them was another Maserati (12) and a Bugatti (1). A sister ex-Ferrari Alfa won.

The charismatic Alfieri Maserati, third of the six brothers to arrive, was the driving force behind the family's racing-car production. Their first business was registered in December 1914.

For the free-formula races of the early 1930s the Maseratis concocted their 4.0-litre 16-cylinder Type V4. It upped the world record for the flying 10 kilometres by a dozen miles per hour, at Cremona on 28 September 1929.

versa.' In fact Tavoni disproved this adage by switching from Maserati to Ferrari to become secretary to Enzo himself and later his racing manager. This narrative will reveal others who crossed the Via Emilia, including engineers Valerio Colotti, Vittorio Bellentani and Alberto Massimino, racing manager Nello Ugolini and coachbuilder Medardo Fantuzzi.

Drivers too negotiated the Via Emilia. One such was Piero Taruffi, who found it 'easy for anyone working in Modena who severs his connection with one of these two manufacturers to find a job with the other, especially so when the reasons for the disagreement are well known and understood.' In 1949 notable defections from Maserati to Ferrari were Alberto Ascari and Gigi Villoresi. Juan Fangio went in the other direction in 1957 to win a fifth World Championship on Maserati after his previous year's Ferrari-mounted fourth. Vividly John Surtees made the transition in 1966, becoming the first and only man to win championship Grands Prix for both rivals in a single season.

Known to the Romans as the Via Aemilia, the die-straight Via Emilia slashes calf-high across the boot of Italy from Rimini on the Adriatic coast north-west through Forli, Faenza, Imola, Bologna, Modena, Reggio Emilia and Parma to Piacenza, on the doorstep of Milan. It is a major trade artery of the region of Emilia-Romagna, which is traversed as well by the Po River and bordered on the south by the foothills of the Apennines. Mutina to the Romans, Modena is the capital of the province of the same name. It rests at an important crossroads between Verona in the north and Livorno on the Gulf of Genoa.

No stranger to conflicts, Roman colony Mutina was sacked by Attila's Huns and then, in the 13th century, became one of the arenas of battle between the Guelfs, loyal to Rome, and the Ghibellines, allied with the German emperors. Stability came in the 14th century under the Guelf-leaning Este dynasty with its base at Ferrara, north of Bologna. Modena became their stronghold in 1598. With one Napoleonic interruption the Estensi ruled Modena until 1859, when the province became part of the kingdom of Italy. Its medieval defences are still evident in the pentagonal plan of the city's partly moated centre.

That year of Modena's union with Italy saw the birth of Alfredo Ferrari a dozen miles north of its capital city. Marrying a girl from Forli, down the Via Emilia, he set up a metalworking shop in Modena. A structural engineer, Alfredo produced railway gangways and sheds – appropriately for a family whose name in Italian is the equivalent of 'Smith'. In this Ferrari was drawing on the city's tradition of crafts skills in metal and leather. In February of 1898 Alfredo and Adalgisa celebrated the birth of their second son, Enzo Anselmo. In 1903 the five-year-old was a delighted passenger in the family's first car, a French de Dion-Bouton.

Railway engineering was also the *métier* of Piacenza's Rodolfo Maserati. Marrying Carolina, he moved west to Voghera, where the couple had six surviving sons. Carlo and Bindo were born in 1881 and 1883. Alfieri arrived in 1887, Mario in 1890,

Ettore in 1894 and the youngest, Ernesto, in the same year as Enzo Ferrari, 1898.

Of the six Maserati brothers only Mario would not be obsessed by machinery and automobiles. As an artist, however, he made an important contribution to the cars that his brothers would build. He designed their emblem, featuring the trident wielded by Neptune in a famous statue in the heart of Bologna. In that city the Officine Alfieri Maserati was registered on 1 December 1914 to build and repair racing cars. After the war it moved to Bologna's Pontevecchio district, where ringleader Alfieri was joined by brothers Ernesto, Bindo and Ettore. The eldest, Carlo, was felled by pneumonia when not yet 30.

Deciding that they could do better on their own account than with the Diattos they were racing, in the mid-1920s the Maserati brothers built straight-eight 1½-litre racing cars under their own name. Two Tipo 26 Maseratis retired early in the 1926 Italian Grand Prix, one euphoniously piloted by Emilio Materassi. In 1930 Maserati shifted into high gear. Its new 2½-litre 26M won at Rome (Luigi Arcangeli), Montenero (Fagioli) and Pescara, Monza and San Sebastian (Varzi), marking a new presence at the top of Grand Prix racing.

To be confident of having a car for any occasion the Maserati brothers also built a 4.0-litre V16 named the 'V4', uniting two of their 2.0-litre straight eights. In a straight line it was a prodigy, as the V4 proved in the hands of Umberto Borzacchini at Cremona in September of 1929. Its average speed over a 10km stretch, six miles, was a rousing 152.9mph. This was a world record for the distance and 14mph faster than the best that a racing Alfa Romeo could do. The Maserati record was a decisive poke in the eye for Alfa's sales

representative in Modena, Enzo Ferrari. Nevertheless he attended the celebratory dinner given for the Maserati brothers by the Automobile Club of Bologna.

Following the car as his star, Ferrari had done well. With both his father and brother dying in 1916, young Ferrari was forced into the world of work, first of all in the workshop of the Modena Fire Brigade. He also had to survive the war, which he ended in poor health after succumbing to the flu epidemic of 1918.

By 1932 the Maserati brothers produced an even more potent version of their twin-eight, the 16-cylinder 4.9-litre Type V5. Luigi Fagioli (left) piloted this at Monza on 11 September 1932 in a dramatic battle against Tazio Nuvolari in an Alfa Romeo like the one fielded by the Scuderia Ferrari.

Nattily attired here in three-piece tweed, Vittorio Jano left Fiat to join Alfa Romeo to design its world-beating eight-cylinder P2 Grand Prix car. Enzo Ferrari made the initial contact that led to Jano's move from Turin to Milan.

Driving a sports Alfa Romeo stripped of its wings, a cheerful Enzo Ferrari placed fifth against outright racing cars – including a Maserati – in the 192-mile Pozzo Circuit race near Verona on 2 June 1929.

Having set up the Scuderia Ferrari in 1929, the eponymous Enzo posed in proprietorial style next to the Alfa Romeo that Achille Varzi would drive in the 1930 Mille Miglia. Varzi finished second with the best Maserati 46th.

Demobbed and turned down for a job with Fiat, Ferrari found work in Turin as a tester for a company converting old vans into sports cars. He then moved to CMN[1] in Milan to work as a test driver. He also raced for CMN in the 1919 Parma-Berceto hillclimb and in the Targa Florio, in which he finished ninth.

In 1920, with the assistance of his friend Ugo Sivocci, Ferrari joined Alfa Romeo. Driving an Alfa, Enzo placed second in the 1920 Targa Florio only 12 minutes behind the winner after eight and a half hours of racing. In 1921 he was fifth in the Targa and second in the 1921 Circuit of Mugello.[2] In 1923 after retiring in the Targa and at Mugello he won the Circuito del Savio at Ravenna.[3] Among those impressed by his form, which included the fastest lap, were the parents of Francesco Baracca, an Italian flying ace who lost his life in the war. They suggested that Ferrari carry the heraldry that marked out the fighters in Baracca's squadron: a prancing horse.

His successes led to Alfa Romeo's appointment of Enzo Ferrari to its official team for the 1924 Grand Prix de l'ACF at Lyons. Driving a P2, he was to join Louis Wagner, Giuseppe Campari and his role model, Antonio Ascari, at the wheel of one of these first-line cars. The new straight-eight P2 was the work of Vittorio Jano, who left Fiat to join Alfa after an initial contact by Ferrari. Thus this race was of great significance to Enzo. This may have accounted for his sudden pre-race decision not to drive – described by some as 'a nervous breakdown'.

---

1 *Costruzioni Meccaniche Nazionali.*

2 Ferrari had raced an Isotta-Fraschini at Mugello in 1920. Much later Ferrari's company would buy a circuit built at Mugello and develop it for both testing and racing. Mugello certainly held positive memories for Enzo Ferrari.

3 Following Ferrari over the line was Edoardo Weber, driving a Fiat 501. Weber would later become a celebrated manufacturer of racing carburettors.

Competing only occasionally thereafter, Ferrari concentrated on his responsibilities at Alfa, where he acted as the right arm of Giorgio Rimini, aide to company chief Nicola Romeo. Enzo's Alfa Romeo distributorship in Modena was an additional benison. But Ferrari, in his own words an 'agitator of men', had another idea. It matured at the Automobile Club of Bologna's celebratory dinner for Borzacchini's speed in the Maserati V4. There he dined in the company of textile-making brothers from Ferrara, Augusto and Alfredo Caniano, who, with Mario Tadini, were enthusiastic amateur racers.

With their backing and that of Alfa Romeo and Pirelli, Enzo set up the Scuderia Ferrari in 1929, *Scuderia* simply meaning 'team'. Baracca's prancing horse, on a shield added by Ferrari, became its emblem.[4] Soon a capacious headquarters workshop was acquired on Modena's Viale Trento e Trieste. Racing Alfa Romeos, attracting seasoned experts as well as amateurs, Ferrari had as his main rivals not only the agile cars of Ettore Bugatti but also the maturing products of the Maserati brothers.

This was the spark that fired the Red-Hot Rivalry. Finding Ferrari's ageing Alfas not up to the job, star driver Achille Varzi defected to Maserati during the 1930 season. Enzo replaced him with the fast-rising Tazio Nuvolari, only to have the Mantuan desert him to drive Maseratis in 1933, a defection that historian Gianni Cancellieri called 'a bombshell'.

The *Fratelli* Maserati were becoming a nagging thorn in the side of Ferrari's new enterprise, so

much so that Enzo considered buying a trio of Maseratis for his Scuderia, only to abandon the idea. That he entertained such an acquisition served to put the wind up his client Alfa Romeo, which stepped up its own racing-car development under Vittorio Jano.

---

4 The shield did not actually appear on the cars until 1932, when it adorned the bonnets of two Alfas entered by the Scuderia in the Spa 24-Hour Race on 9 July.

Hatless Count Carlo Felice Trossi stood between two of the Maserati brothers during preparations for a bench test of a 6CM 1500 engine. Trossi defected from the Scuderia Ferrari to drive Maseratis successfully.

Uniquely in Europe, the Bologna-based Maserati brothers had set themselves up strictly to build racing cars for their own use and for sale. Said Ernesto, 'We began with a very small shop and just a few basic machine tools. But we had very good workers, the best. Little by little we grew and our equipment improved.' It seemed a daring idea, but in fact their strict specialisation helped the Maseratis survive Italy's sharp 1926 depression, a slump that wiped out all save the nation's strongest auto makers.

In 1938 Adolfo Orsi (left) explained to Tazio Nuvolari the opportunities he would enjoy with the new car that the Maserati brothers were building with his backing. But having left the Scuderia Ferrari, Nuvolari would race for Auto Union instead.

For 1934 the Maseratis introduced their 3.7-litre six-cylinder Type 6C 34 to meet the demands of the new Grand Prix formula. On 14 October it was Tazio Nuvolari's mount in the 80-mile race in the city centre of Modena. The early laps saw a duel with Achille Varzi in a Scuderia Ferrari Alfa, but Nuvolari was quickly past on his way to a decisive victory for the Trident. Maserati rubbed salt into the wound of defeat by delivering a bale of hay to the Scuderia Ferrari with the mocking note: 'For your horses …' It took the intervention of Vittorio Jano and Alfa Romeo to restore Nuvolari to the Prancing Horse stable for 1935.

To challenge not only the big-engined Maseratis but also the new German racing cars of 1934, the Scuderia Ferrari first dipped its toe in the waters of car manufacture with the 'Bimotore', built at the beginning of 1935. This had two straight-eight 3.2-litre Alfa Romeo engines, one in the usual position and the other behind the driver, giving the impressive total of 540hp. A key Ferrari ally in building two such cars was Luigi Bazzi, who would remain Enzo's faithful car-development lieutenant into the 1960s.

By the mid-1930s Ferrari's Scuderia was transformed into an engineering-racing division of Alfa Romeo, taking over the competition function entirely in 1933. With this more businesslike orientation the interests of the founding Canianos were bought out by Count Carlo Felice Trossi, himself a driver of considerable merit. Ferrari represented Alfa almost exclusively in racing from 1933 until his Scuderia was acquired by Alfa Romeo in March 1938 so that the company could set up its own racing unit, Alfa Corse. In November of that year Ferrari left Alfa Romeo under terms that prevented his competing with them in racing for four years.

For the first time in many years Enzo Ferrari found himself at arm's length from racing. To his frustration he had to suffer a spectacular resurgence by Maserati. After Alfieri's premature death in 1932 the Bologna company regrouped under Ernesto's presidency, with Bindo playing an increased role. Although 1934 and '35 were profitable years, thanks to the popularity of Maserati's 1.5-litre *Voiturettes*, Italy's war in Ethiopia siphoned off racing-car customers in 1936. Prospects for 1937 were grim.

Bologna-based journalist and editor Corrado Filippini naturally took an interest in the fate of his home town's world-famous racing-car builders. He knew that in Modena Adolfo Orsi, a shrewd self-made businessman, was building a commercial empire that included scrap-metal processing, electrical equipment, farm machinery, the trolley-

In his splendid works-entered 8CTF Maserati, Count Trossi took the early lead in the Coppa Ciano at Livorno on 7 August 1938, ahead of three Mercedes-Benz racers. First his brakes and then his engine failed, however.

In the German Grand Prix on 23 July 1939, German driver Paul Pietsch placed his works Maserati 8CTF amongst the silver cars on the grid, briefly held the lead and finished an excellent third after 312 miles on a damp Nürburgring.

This 8CTF Maserati, with its single exhaust pipe instead of twin pipes, was victorious at Indianapolis in both 1939 and 1940, driven by Wilbur Shaw. A faulty wire wheel denied them a third success in 1941.

car concession and a Fiat dealership. Cementing his relationship with Modena, for a spell he was chairman of the city's football club.

That the Maseratis had a strong and underexploited brand name, also associated with a small spark-plug business, commended them to Adolfo Orsi. With Filippini as intermediary Orsi acquired a controlling majority of Maserati shares. Ernesto, Ettore and Bindo agreed to provide their services to the company for a period of ten years.

Versatile as well as jovial, Alberto Massimino engineered both cars and engines for Ferrari, then for Maserati and finally for Ferrari, crossing the demarcation line of the Via Emilia more than once.

This fresh backing helped the brothers lay down a magnificent supercharged straight-eight racing car of 3.0-litres, the 8CTF, for the new Grand Prix formula commencing in 1938. Although German cars still dominated, the handsome 8CTF was able to lead Grands Prix briefly in 1938 and '39. More importantly, an 8CTF acquired by Mike Boyle and tended by ace mechanic Cotton Henning won the 500 miles of Indianapolis in 1939 and 1940, driven by Wilbur Shaw. This was the first success for a foreign car in the world's richest race since a Peugeot victory in 1919.

'The Indianapolis race was highly popular in Italy,' wrote Ferrari biographer Brock Yates, 'and the one event that Enzo Ferrari openly stated he wanted to win. Surely it was galling for him to read of the lavish praise being heaped on the Maserati brothers, especially during a period when his racing fortunes were at such a low ebb.' At the end of 1939 the Maserati Trident was flaunted in his face when Adolfo Orsi moved the racing-car operation from Bologna to new facilities on Modena's Viale Ciro Menotti. On the north side of the Via Emilia this was the continuation of the Viale Trento e Trieste. A Trojan steed was wheeled into the stables of the Prancing Horse.

In 1944 the revitalised Maserati operation attracted the skills of engineer Alberto Massimino, who had joined Scuderia Ferrari in 1938 from Fiat to help build a *Voiturette* for Alfa Romeo, the eight-cylinder Type 158. Massimino was the principal

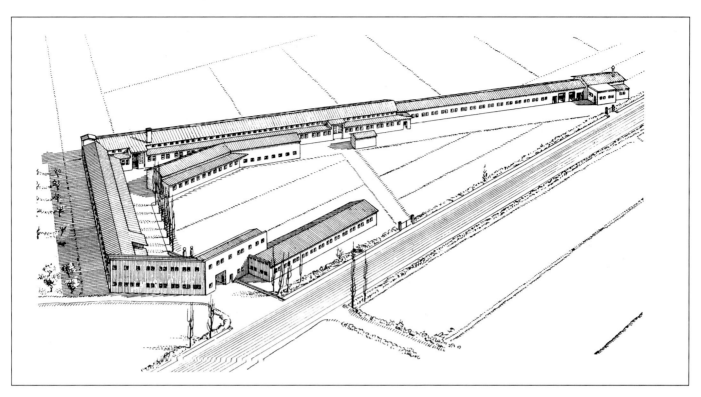

designer of the two Fiat-based cars that Ferrari produced under his company name, Auto-Avio Costruzioni, to compete in the 1940 Mille Miglia. Further thoughts of racing-car building were interrupted on 10 June 1940, when Italy entered the Second World War.

At first Ferrari turned the skills of his 40-strong staff toward the production of small engines for training aircraft, with Massimino's help in co-operation with Rome's National Aeronautic Company. Then he heard from Corrado Gatti, a Turin machine-tool dealer, that fine hydraulically controlled grinders from Jung in Germany were much in demand but difficult to get. After meticulously copying the German originals, whose patent protection was invalid in Italy, Ferrari switched his production to the precision grinders in support of the war effort.

To conform with an industrial decentralisation edict, in 1943 Ferrari moved his plant from Modena

Erected in 1943, Enzo Ferrari's factory surrounded a courtyard on the west side of the road running north to Modena (toward the upper right), and the small town of Maranello nearby (to the lower left).

Having both purchased and produced machine tools, Enzo Ferrari had acquired excellent facilities during the war, which he soon turned to the manufacture of sports and racing cars.

Origins of a rivalry **17**

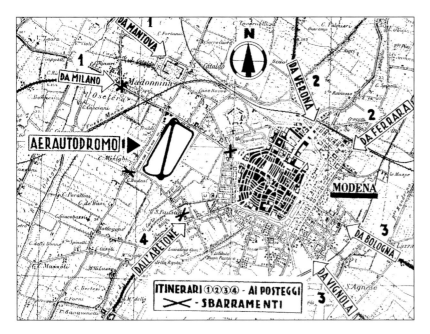

Modena's Aerautodromo was west of the centre of the old city, its north-east side flanking the Via Emilia that was the demarcation line between Ferrari to the south and Maserati to the north.

to a small town some ten miles to the south, Maranello, where he had some land and a small stone summer house. A friend there helped him acquire additional acreage on both sides of the main north-south highway, the Via Abetone Inferiore leading to the Abetone Pass. On the west side of the road he established a machine-tool factory of 40,000 square feet which soon was employing between 140 and 160 workers. In spite of its remote location the factory suffered air-raid damage in November 1944 and February 1945.

Ferrari didn't let the hostilities pass without thinking about motor racing. During the war, he said, 'I had always continued to make plans for racing cars and when we got out of the storm I quickly got rid of the machine tools.' In fact he continued to produce his Jung-pattern grinders for a few years to provide financing for his car-building effort. In 1945 – at the age of 47 – he established Auto Costruzioni Ferrari, a new company with the mission of building cars and taking part in competitions.

Although his Maranello factory was well equipped to make all the major components of a car's engine, drive line and suspension, Enzo Ferrari relied on outside suppliers for important parts of his automobiles. Until he set up his own foundry in 1954, castings came from Bologna's Alessandro Calzoni. Also in Bologna was Weber, whose carburettors fed all Ferraris. Its founder, Edoardo Weber, was a close colleague of Ferrari until his disappearance in the last months of the war.

Maserati too was a customer for these key racing-car components. Ball bearings came from Turin's RIV, while Britain's Vandervell supplied vital engine bearings. Magneti Marelli delivered electrical components, Fren-Do brake linings, Cogne special steels, Borrani wheels, Houdaille shock absorbers, Mondial pistons, Livia valves, Gilco frames, Regina roller chains, Rejna chassis springs and Champion spark plugs. Among the suppliers were names that would remain part of

When Argentineans Juan Manuel Fangio (right) and Oscar Galvez (centre) visited Europe in 1948 it was natural that they would see Adolfo Orsi to discuss the purchase of racing cars. In 1949 Fangio drove Maseratis.

the Ferrari and Maserati stories for more than half a century.

In the last pre-war years the Maserati brothers – daily commuters from their homes in Bologna – built their final racing cars and then developed electric trucks and vans for the Orsis to meet wartime needs. With the help of Massimino, from 1944 they began work on the new six-cylinder car that they foresaw as the basis of their peacetime production for both road and racing. Enzo Ferrari could only grit his teeth when the rattling windows of his flat above the works at Viale Trento e Trieste signalled the roaring passage of a Maserati prototype on its way to tests on the Via Abetone Inferiore.

Thus did Modena on the Emilian plain become a thriving centre of racing-car design, manufacture and development. From 1949 the city made its dual-purpose Aerautodromo available for races and testing. Other racing-mad locals, like Fiat dealer Vittorio Stanguellini, got into the act. And from Modena the competition cars of Ferrari and Maserati went out into the world to demonstrate Italy's dominance of this arcane discipline, spurred by one of the most intense rivalries that auto racing has ever known.

Having had a good war, Adolfo Orsi was well placed to resume automotive activity in peacetime. When racing was revived the first important Grand Prix successes fell to Maseratis. This was galling to Enzo Ferrari, said Brock Yates: 'Ferrari considered the Orsis interlopers on his turf and below his station. Moreover, their products were aimed at the same clientele of gentlemen drivers, which qualified them as commercial enemies of the first order. As for the Maserati brothers, he viewed them as legitimate competitors on the race track but was never close to them personally.' With this as background, said Yates, the implacable rivals 'were locked in a struggle for bragging rights in Modena.'

Added frisson was given to the rivalry by the contrasting characters of its protagonists. 'There was always a clear distinction in Modena between the two,' said Omer Orsi's son Adolfo. 'Everyone knew Ferrari's ways – a tough regime – while Maserati was run on business lines.' 'I liked Maserati,' recalled Romolo Tavoni. 'It was a family environment. Adolfo Orsi was more a friend, almost a father, than a chairman. His son Omer was a true gentleman.' This contrasted with the imperious style of Enzo Ferrari, unchallenged master of his Maranello domain.

In addition to its fine sports cars Modena's exports include its balsamic vinegars and sparkling red Lambrusco wines, of which it is justly proud. Belying its international impact, however, Modena remains unpolished and inward-looking. This

attribute of the city's character contributed to the fervour of its citizens' support for Ferrari or Maserati. Wrote historians Franco Zagari and Luigo Orsini, 'The rivalry was intensified by the environmental conditions typical of Modena, a city of genuinely provincial character, where there lingered a perennial air of challenge accompanied by a taste for off-colour jokes.' This hothouse atmosphere, they said, further fostered Modena's 'stimulating confrontation' between the two racing-car makers.

The pages that follow provide many examples of vigorous competition between the Trident and the Prancing Horse. One episode, however, is worth relating in advance. During preparations for the 1955 Grand Prix at Spa it was reaffirmed to Belgian Paul Frère that 'what dominated Ferrari's policies during the 1950s was the rivalry with Maserati.' Frère recalled 'team manager Nello Ugolini briefing us – Farina, Trintignant and myself – on the morning of the 1955 Belgian Grand Prix and making his recommendation: "We know that the Mercedes will be very difficult to beat, but our main target is to beat the Maseratis." On that occasion we did, Farina taking third place and myself fourth.' Mission accomplished.

CHAPTER TWO

125 F1 vs 4CLT/48

The great racing rivals first tested their relative skills and strengths in the 1940s with new and improved supercharged Formula 1 cars that were diametrically opposite in design yet closely competitive. Of the two, Ferrari had the most to prove.

The first clash between Ferrari and Maserati in Formula 1, at the apogee of the sport, took place far from Modena. The 1948 Italian Grand Prix was staged at Piedmont's Turin on 5 September. This was only the second season of the new Formula 1, or Formula A as it was originally dubbed. Ingeniously it pitted cars with 4½-litre unsupercharged engines – eligible under the 1938–39 Grand Prix rules – against the supercharged 1½-litre cars that were raced before the war in a smaller *Voiturette* category. Between them enough of both such racing cars existed to give post-war racing a head start.

Juan Fangio's first major race in Europe was the San Remo GP on 3 April 1949. Driving number 18, a blue and yellow San Remo Maserati, he raced from the start against Raymond Sommer's 125 F1 Ferrari, which retired.

Although an Alfa Romeo was leading the wet 1948 Italian Grand Prix, behind it the Red-Hot Rivals were going at it hammer and tongs. Luigi Villoresi's Maserati 4CLT/48 here led Raymond Sommer in the first Formula 1 Ferrari on its debut. They finished second and third in the order shown.

Their 4CL of 1939 was the basis for the post-war successes of the Maserati brothers. Key features were its torsion-bar front suspension, oil tanks under the driver's seat and 16-valve four-cylinder engine with single blower.

Many of the supercharged 1½-litre racers were Maseratis. In the winter of 1938 the Maserati brothers put together everything they'd learned from their earlier *Voiturette* models to design and build a new car, the 4CL. It was a four with four valves per cylinder. Apart from Mercedes-Benz in the 1930s, the use of a four-valve head was unusual. Also radical for the year of the 4CL's introduction was its use of 'square' cylinder dimensions of 78 x 78mm for 1,498cc. Heads and blocks were cast as a single 'monobloc' unit, avoiding problems with head gaskets at high supercharge pressures. Two twin-cylinder blocks of iron were mounted on a magnesium crankcase that carried a massive crankshaft in three main bearings.

Bindo Maserati announced the new Type 4CL in January 1939, mentioning that it would be available with both single- and two-stage supercharging. Like other recent Maseratis it had torsion-bar independent front suspension, channel-steel frame and a live rear axle sprung by trailing quarter-elliptics. In 1939 Maserati built nine 4CLs, some for customers and some for its own use as a factory team. Hidden away during the war, most of these were still available to racers when hostilities ceased.

As the quickest car available to private teams post-war, the 4CL attracted such drivers as Tazio Nuvolari in his last Grand Prix appearances, Raymond Sommer, Gigi Villoresi, Reg Parnell – Britain's best driver in the 1940s – Siam's Prince Bira and Giuseppe 'Nino' Farina. From 1946 through '47 Maserati made 15 more 4CLs.

In the late spring of the latter year the Maserati brothers, having ended their ten-year commitment to the Orsis, left the firm. Ernesto and Bindo ceased commuting to Modena and remained in Bologna, establishing OSCA there at the end of 1947 to produce sports-racing cars and single-seaters, as we will see in Chapter 4. Leaving behind their name, for spark plugs as well as cars, the brothers received some compensation at the time of the divorce.

Continuity in this crucial transition was afforded by the young Omer Orsi, who had taken Maserati's car activity under his wing. Assisting him were engineers Osvaldo Gorrini as overall technical director, Alberto Massimino as planner and designer, and Vittorio Bellentani in charge of the workshops.

A gift from the Maseratis to the new regime was a revised chassis for the 4CL with a stiffer and

lighter tubular frame that also served as an oil reservoir. Dubbed the 4CLT (T for *tubolare* or tubular), it was first raced by Villoresi in South America at the beginning of 1947 and then by Alberto Ascari at Reims in July the same year.

The Orsi team brought to fruition the two-stage supercharging that Bindo had promised before the war. Instead of a single large Roots-type blower pumping air into the engine, this compressed air in two stages, first in a large Roots-type blower and then in a smaller one. A two-stage system did not necessarily give higher boost pressure, but before the war it had been proven by Mercedes-Benz and Auto Union to reduce substantially the amount of horsepower needed to drive the blowers. Mixture came from a big Weber carburettor feeding the first blower.

This new engine, developing a reliable 240–250bhp at 6,000rpm on methanol-based fuel and capable of 260bhp at 7,000, deserved an improved chassis. This was laid out by Albert Massimino and readied for the 1948 season. He sharply lowered the car's profile with a new tubular frame, and forged upper wishbones that operated inboard coil springs for a cleaner front suspension.[1] Retained was the live rear axle sprung by trailing quarter-elliptic leaf springs and controlled by a torque tube and radius arms.

With its high unsprung weight and vulnerability to torque reaction, its live rear axle was a retrograde feature of the Maserati, one which it shared with the 4½-litre French Talbot-Lagos that were among its rivals. 'Their roadholding and braking is said by drivers to be far and away better than that of any other Maserati yet built,' *The Motor* nevertheless reported, 'and although the engine tends to throw out a great deal of oil, mostly over the pilot, the unit seems to be reliable.'

Thus was created the 4CLT/48, handsomely bodied by Modena artisan Medardo Fantuzzi in a lower, more rounded style that was extremely appealing. This was important, because Maserati's

1 This elegant design foreshadowed the upper wishbones designed to work as rocker arms to inboard coil springs and dampers that Lotus introduced in the 1960s.

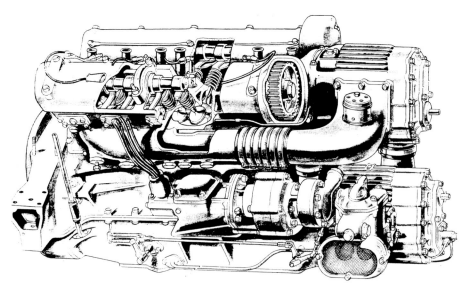

A large Weber carburettor fed the lower, larger primary blower of the 4CLT/48's two-stage boosting system. Finger-type followers were interposed between its cam lobes and valve stems.

minor event they won easily, Ascari leading his team-mate. In recognition the new car was nicknamed the 'San Remo' model, a tag that remained with it. The dominant team and car in 1948 was Alfa Romeo with its works-entered Type 158, known as the 'Alfetta' or 'little Alfa' for the *Voiturette* derivation that it shared with the 4CLT/48. 'The Maserati people themselves are confident that this new model is a real playmate for the 158 Alfa Romeo,' wrote *The Motor*'s correspondent, 'and have been expecting great things from it.'

Meanwhile another 'playmate' for the Alfetta was being created ten miles south of the Viale Ciro Menotti. When Enzo Ferrari and Gioachino Colombo schemed together in 1945 – as described in the next chapter – to design the first Ferrari car, the Type 125, they gave it a V12 engine of only 1,497cc (55 x 52.5mm). With a 60° angle between its banks, the engine had a chain-driven single overhead camshaft for each cylinder bank, operating inclined overhead valves – two per cylinder – by rocker arms. Both block and heads were of aluminium, the heads being conventionally detachable. When Colombo left in November 1945 to return to Alfa Romeo, helping them revive the Type 158 that he'd originally designed, Giuseppe Busso took over Ferrari's car development.

Ferrari himself admitted that it had been a bold decision for him to choose a 12-cylinder engine to

post-war policy was to concentrate on selling cars to customers rather than to enter a works team. From 1947 its principal partner was the Scuderia Ambrosiana, named for St Ambrose, patron saint of its home city of Milan. Maserati worked closely with the Scudiera, but it was the latter's responsibility to engage drivers, enter cars and carry out routine preparation.

Ambrosiana arranged the entries of its two stars, the established Gigi Villoresi and up-and-coming Alberto Ascari, for the San Remo Grand Prix on that city's streets on 27 June 1948. Both drove the new 4CLT/48 models. Against an indifferent field in this

For the 19th Italian Grand Prix, held in Turin's Valentino Park on 5 September 1948, Ferrari introduced its first Formula 1 car, the 125 F1 (right). It scooted away from the start, driven by forceful Raymond Sommer.

power his first cars. Twelves had been prominent in pre-war racing but not with engines as small as 1,500cc. Expert opinion held at the time that these tiny twelves would be temperamental and unreliable and would lead Ferrari to regret his rash decision.

Indeed, taming them was not easy. The V12 had the potential to rev high with its tiny pistons, but bearing materials weren't up to the job. For several years Ferrari racing engines had to use needle-type connecting-rod bearings to stand the stress. Only when Britain's Tony Vandervell made his multi-layer thin-wall bearings available could ordinary plain bearings be relied upon. Enzo Ferrari openly acknowledged the debt he owed to Vandervell.

With its 1½-litre capacity the twelve was obviously tailored to the new Formula 1. Such ambitions were initially set aside at Maranello while Giuseppe Busso expanded the V12 to 2.0-litres to create the Type 166 for sports-car racing. But Busso did give some thought to a Formula 1 version of the engine, so when Gioachino Colombo agreed to return to Maranello in September 1947 he found evidence of his efforts on both a single-seater car and its engine. Colombo's return meant Busso's departure – to Alfa Romeo – so it was up to Colombo to respond to Ferrari's desire to bring his F1 programme up to speed. He did this with the help of a younger assistant new to Ferrari, Aurelio Lampredi.

By November 1947 Gioachino Colombo had laid out a design for the '125 G.P.C' as he initially called the car that later became known as the 125 F1. It married the V12 engine to an integral five-speed gearbox (the Maserati and Alfa had four speeds), which drove to a chassis-mounted differential. From this swung separate universal-jointed half shafts to each rear wheel, braced by radius arms. Rear springing was by torsion bars and front suspension was by unequal-length wishbones with a transverse leaf spring. These were mounted on a twin-tube frame not unlike that of the rival Maserati.

Driven from the front accessory case of the V12 was a single Roots-type blower, fed by a Weber carburettor. Its output was delivered down the centre of the vee to six cylinders on each side. Reports at the time spoke of a scheme to add two more superchargers, the idea being that these would comprise the first stage of a two-stage system, but the single-cam V12 never raced with more than one blower. Initially it developed 225bhp at 7,000rpm.

Colombo's first layout of the 125 F1 showed a 92in wheelbase, but when the first cars were built during 1948 they were much shorter at only 85in. 'They presented quite a new aspect of Grand Prix

The 125 F1 Ferrari had a 1.5-litre V12 engine with a separate camshaft-driven magneto for the spark plugs on each bank. Compressed mixture came from a single-stage Roots-type supercharger at the front.

design,' commented Denis Jenkinson, 'for they were exceedingly small.' Jenkinson said that they first appeared with wheels of only 15in, while the Maserati had 17in wheels in front and 16in at the rear and the Alfetta 17in front wheels and 18in rears.

Initially Colombo calculated a dry weight of only 1,160lb for his design. As finally produced, he said, it weighed 1,280lb dry. This contrasted sharply with the 1,500lb of the 4CLT/48. For the latter, with the much longer wheelbase of 98.4in, Maserati published a weight of 1,390lb – attractive to potential customers – but its real heft was considerably greater. Ferrari, in contrast, quoted 1,540lb dry for its 125 F1. It saw no point in revealing what it considered to be an important advantage of its new design.

In power-to-weight terms the cars were remarkably close, with 352bhp per ton for the Ferrari against 347 for the Maserati. These were the ratios for the cars less fuel and driver; Ferrari expected that its lighter car allied with a lower boost pressure and more efficient induction would deliver better fuel economy than either the Maserati or Alfa, both of which needed to be refuelled during longer races – sometimes twice. With less weight of fuel needing to be carried, this had the potential to

Behind Jean-Pierre Wimille's leading Alfa Romeo, Sommer in the new Ferrari – leading here – had a race-long battle at Turin in September 1948 with the Maserati 4CLT/48 of Luigi Villoresi.

give the little Ferrari race-winning pace in spite of its seemingly modest specification.

The Italian Grand Prix at Turin would tell the story. In the last days of August 1948 the new car's prototype was taken there to be driven in the traffic-free early-morning hours over the 2¼-mile circuit in Turin's Valentino Park next to the Po River. Its tester was Nino Farina, whom Ferrari esteemed as an evaluator but whose fees were so high that he could only be used sparingly for such tasks. Improvements were incorporated in the first car –

given to Prince Bira for the race – and in the two newer Ferraris raced by Farina and fast Frenchman Raymond Sommer.

'From the outset' of the Turin doings, wrote Denis Jenkinson, 'it became fairly obvious that these new Grand Prix Ferraris had not been brought to the race only partially completed, as many Grand Prix cars are.' Although three Alfas were entered, only two could shoulder into the four front-row places. Villoresi qualified his Maserati in 2:20.0 while Sommer was only a tick slower at 2:20.4 in the new Ferrari, both quicker than the third Alfa. Farina was in the second row and Bira in the fifth.

Contrasting with the dry and sunny practice, the 224-mile race was run on 'a very English day of steady rain and grey skies which hung low over the hills flanking the River Po,' reported Rodney Walkerley in *The Motor*. While Jean-Pierre Wimille easily took the win in his Alfetta, the battle behind him made this the 'finest post-war race' according to Walkerley. Villoresi and Sommer went at it hammer and tongs in their Modenese rivals. Of the Ferraris it was said that 'they cornered faster than any other car on the course although their front wheels appeared to cant over astonishingly under the strain.' Farina's canted terminally when he hit a curb, while Bira suffered transmission failure in his hard-used prototype.

Both leading protagonists were delayed – Villoresi by a change of plugs and Sommer by brake adjustment and a slow refill – and ended up chasing each other hard right to the final flag.

At the 1949 San Remo start, Fangio was closely chased by his Argentine team-mate Benedicto Campos in another 4CLT/48, Prince Bira's similar car right on his tail, with Felice Bonetto's Ferrari on the outside. Fangio went on to win.

Villoresi's Maserati finished second just five car lengths ahead of Sommer in third. 'So ended a tremendous race,' said Walkerley. 'For the first time the Alfas could not arrange their finishing order. The new Ferrari covered itself with glory on its first appearance and the new Maserati proved itself again to be a vast step forward in this factory's design.' The Red-Hot Rivalry had been forged – with a vengeance.

Ferrari and Maserati clashed twice more in 1948. The first occasion was a big one: the Monza Grand Prix on the full Monza road circuit on 17 October, over a 313-mile distance that made it the equivalent of a major international race. On this fast track the four Alfas filled the four front-row places. Qualifying in the second row were our rivals as follows:

Sommer	Ferrari	2:08.0
Farina	Ferrari	2:08.2
Villoresi	Maserati	2:09.0
Ascari	Maserati	2:10.2

Ferrari sold one of his 1948 cars to Briton Peter Whitehead, here ahead of Villoresi's 4CLT/48 and Bob Ansell's 4CM in the 176-mile road race on the Channel Island of Jersey on 28 April 1949. Villoresi placed sixth and Whitehead seventh.

Gigi Villoresi's 125 F1 (left) and Juan Fangio's 4CLT/48 (centre) squared off at the start of the Belgian Grand Prix on 19 June 1949. The Ferrari placed second to Louis Rosier's unsupercharged 4.5-litre Talbot-Lago.

An exciting field took the start of the Swiss Grand Prix at Bern on 3 July 1949. The leading Ferrari of Alberto Ascari (right) and the Maserati of Prince Bira were chased by Talbot-Lagos and more Maseratis.

As was his habitual race-winning style, Alberto Ascari in his 125 F1 Ferrari jumped in front at the start of the 1949 Swiss GP, chased by Bira's San Remo Maserati. Ascari dominated over the race's 180 miles to claim Ferrari's first Grand Prix victory.

The fiery Sommer gave early battle to the Alfas but after a few laps had to retire with an attack of asthma, attributed to his inadvertent ingestion of methanol at a race earlier in the year. Oddly, Ferrari fielded no relief driver to take over his healthy car. Farina later retired with gearbox trouble, as did Villoresi. Ascari survived to chase the four Alfas home with his Maserati.

The streets of Barcelona provided another fast track for the Grand Prix of Peña Rhin on 31 October over a distance of 194 miles. With the Alfas absent, the Spanish grid's front row was shared by the same quartet of makes that filled the second row at Monza, this time with Bira standing in for the unwell Sommer. A third Ferrari was provided to local man José Pola, who found it a bit of a handful and eventually blew up its engine. Bira led early but had to retire, as did Nino Farina in the other Ferrari. Villoresi was the winner with Reg Parnell in another San Remo Maserati behind him.

In 1948 Maserati and Ferrari faced each other in three Grands Prix. In all three they were close in speed, with the Ferraris showing a fractional advantage, while the seasoned Maseratis proved

more raceworthy, either winning outright or leading the Ferraris home. This pattern was repeated in the races over the winter in Argentina, where the Maseratis held the upper hand in spite of some of the Ferraris racing with engines of 2.0 supercharged litres in these *Formule Libre* events.

In the cars sent to South America, Gioachino Colombo tried out new rear-suspension designs using transverse leafs instead of torsion bars to spring the Ferrari's swing axles. For 1949 he also extended the wheelbase 7in to 92in to improve his car's balance and biddability. Drivers less adaptable than Bira, Sommer and Farina found the 1948 model a real handful. The 125 F1 'needed a great deal of driving,' said Denis Jenkinson, adding that 'care was needed to avoid spinning the car completely round, especially on wet roads. Another peculiar trait … was a tendency to yaw when going in a straight line, which the Italians had commented upon when they first tried the cars.' This was a consequence of the swing-axle rear suspension in concert with the short wheelbase.

In 1949 the experienced English racer Raymond Mays drove a modified 1948 125 F1 at Silverstone

Other protagonists in the 1949 Swiss Grand Prix were Toulo de Graffenried's Maserati 4CLT/48 (ahead here) and Gigi Villoresi's works-entered 125 F1 Ferrari. They placed seventh and second respectively.

During his drive to an historic victory for Ferrari in the 1949 Swiss Grand Prix at Bern, Ascari lined up to lap Anton Branca in a Maserati 4CL, the model that was a forerunner of the 4CLT/48.

In the 1949 season the battle between Maserati and Ferrari moved to centre stage in Europe's Grand Prix clashes because Alfa Romeo absented itself from the field for the full season. This wasn't immediately obvious; as late as March pundits were speculating about Alfa's drivers and hopes were high for an appearance at the Italian GP in September. But they didn't show, leaving the way clear for the Modenese firms to fight it out with interference from the 4½-litre French Talbot-Lagos, which could run through a long race non-stop while the supercharged cars needed refuelling.

The season began at San Remo on 3 April with a two-heat race adding up to 187 miles. While Ferrari's protagonist was Raymond Sommer, Maserati had a powerful new ally in the Argentine Auto Club, which had bought two 4CLT/48s to be driven in Europe by Benedicto Campos and, more importantly, by Juan Manuel Fangio. Although the latter was pipped by a fifth of a second for pole by Bira in a similar car, Fangio reversed the order in the race results while Sommer – who shared the three-car front row – retired.

Another new player was Briton Peter Whitehead, who was entered by the Ferrari factory in a 176-mile race at St Helier on the Channel Island of Jersey on 24 April in a 1948-model 125 F1 that he'd acquired. Whitehead, who had retired at San Remo, qualified six seconds off Villoresi's pole time of two minutes flat in Jersey. All the main actors hit problems in a wet race, so the result, with Villoresi sixth and Whitehead seventh, was inconclusive. The Englishman was again Ferrari's sole defender

Maseratis, two of which were leading, and Ferraris – one here on the outside of the turn – figured in the first-ever Dutch Grand Prix, held at the seaside circuit of Zandvoort on 31 July 1949. Villoresi's Ferrari was the winner ahead of Farina's Maserati.

and found it daunting: 'At this stage of Ferrari's history the marque's engine performance was notoriously much in advance of the several factors contributing to controllability and I must say that I have never had a more frightening ride than the [GP Ferrari] gave me on May 14, 1949. Any attempt to take corners with the power on resulted in the tail chasing the front wheels …' This was a judgement with which Enzo Ferrari would not necessarily have disagreed. He later admitted that he believed at that time that sheer engine power accounted for 80 per cent of success in racing.

'Perhaps,' he reflected, 'in designing this car as in the years that followed I underestimated the importance of the chassis.'

After two heat races, three Maseratis and a Ferrari made up the front row for the start of the final in the International Trophy at Silverstone on 20 August 1949. Alberto Ascari (number 8) won in his Ferrari 125 F1.

in the 300-mile British Grand Prix at Silverstone on 14 May, which saw him pitted against five San Remo Maseratis. The newest, that of Swiss Baron Emmanuel de Graffenried, was the winner.

Dramatic changes were evident when the entries were posted for the Belgian Grand Prix on 19 June. Entered in Ferraris were the former stars of the Scuderia Ambrosiana, Gigi Villoresi and Alberto Ascari. The proximate cause of their switch from Maserati to Ferrari was the closing of the Viale Ciro Menotti works from February to June of 1949. Problems in the Orsis' enterprises forced the shuttering of Maserati and the layoff of its staff.

At that early stage, as well, in the absence of the Maserati brothers the more experienced Villoresi was impatient with what he saw as indecision by the Orsis, with Adolfo too remote and Omer not yet in full command. Vittorio Bellentani did his best to hold things together in the hiatus, but the temporary closing inevitably curtailed the support that Maserati could give to the teams racing its cars.

The Ferraris, in contrast, were improved. Engine output was nearer 250bhp, close to that of the 4CLT/48 in spite of continued use of a single Roots blower, with drivelines that were now more reliable. Suspension was much better, thanks to development work conducted in parallel with the same chassis powered by an unblown 2.0-litre V12 for Formula 2 racing. The transverse rear spring was now specially mounted to give an anti-roll effect.

In the 316-mile Belgian race on the great Spa circuit the fastest lap was set by a 4CLT/48, that of Nino Farina, who had gone over to the Maserati camp. At the finish, however, Ferraris filled second through fourth places behind a winning Talbot-Lago, which had gone through non-stop. With Maserati's doors again open, Farina had a brand-new San Remo model for the Swiss Grand Prix on 3 July. On the demanding roads through Bern's forest park he put it on pole with a time of 2:50.4. Next best was Bira in a similar car at 2:53.2, with the best Ferrari third with Ascari's 2:54.7. Farina also set fastest lap in the race but struck problems and retired.

Although the Swiss race was relatively short, at 181 miles, and although the Ferraris had additional fuel tankage in their cowls since Spa, their thirst was such that Ascari had to make one stop for more methanol blend on his way to victory. The up-and-coming Alberto, once a protégé of Villoresi but now more than his equal, scored Ferrari's first victory in a major national Grand Prix. He was followed home by Villoresi, while the best-placed Maserati was Bira's in fifth. The tables were beginning to turn away from the Trident and toward the Prancing Horse.

This reversal was redressed in the next contest, the 309-mile French Grand Prix on the fast Reims circuit on 17 July. Only Villoresi's factory Ferrari arrived, backed up by Whitehead's private V12 – both of them given further improvements. Villoresi was on pole and the Englishman came close to giving Ferrari another win, only to have his gearbox seize in fourth of his five ratios, relegating him to third after setting fastest lap. A Talbot won and

Ascari scampered away from Silverstone's International Trophy grid in the final, chased by the Maseratis of Prince Bira (15), Reg Parnell (16) and Nino Farina (30), who finished only two seconds behind winner Ascari.

Bira's Maserati was second. Bira and de Graffenried were now driving 4CLT/48s prepared by Enrico Platé's Scuderia Platé.

The Dutch Grand Prix on 31 July showed that the ascension of Ferrari was not to be denied. Yet another rear-suspension change moved the transverse leaf to a lower position. The Ferrari 'was far steadier on the corners in the wet,' said one observer at the Zandvoort track, 'while the Maserati rear end tended to buck around.' The high unsprung weight of the 4CLT/48's rear axle was increasingly a handicap. The added power of the Ferrari was transmitted through both rear tyres, as *The Motor* reported: 'Ascari went up the hill behind the pits with tyres almost on fire with spin-and-acceleration; never saw such smoke off a racing tyre in all my days.'

Nevertheless the Farina/Maserati combination was fastest in practice, a fifth of a second quicker than Villoresi, who was a tenth faster than Ascari. Run in two 65-mile heats followed by a 104-mile final, the Dutch race saw a victory for Villoresi's Ferrari followed home by the Maseratis of de Graffenried, Bira and Farina in that order. Another heats-and-final race was held at Silverstone on 20 August. The International Trophy drew a strong turnout of the Italian teams, which practice times showed were closely matched. Maseratis won both heats with the Ferraris prudently second. Ascari won the final, but only by holding off the fiery Farina, whose Maserati bounced off hay bales en route to finishing only two seconds behind the winning Ferrari.

That the pairing of Nino Farina with the San Remo Maserati still had the power to sting was demonstrated on the streets of Lausanne, Switzerland. In a 182-mile race on 27 August the Turin-based driver started from pole and shrugged off the Ferraris of Ascari and Villoresi to score a convincing victory. This augured well for the Italian Grand Prix at Monza on 11 September, but there Farina drove a much-modified 4CLT/48 from the Scuderia Milan that was fast enough to qualify on the front row but fatally unreliable.

Ferrari brought to Monza a completely new model, its ambitious G.P.49 with two-stage supercharging of a new V12 with twin overhead cams for each cylinder bank. Mounted in a chassis with a 93.7in wheelbase, this Colombo creation was credited with 305bhp at 7,500rpm. Although clearly faster than an older Ferrari driven there by Raymond Sommer, it was beset by maladies that included severe overheating. Nevertheless Alberto Ascari nursed it to a victory that he considered his most satisfying yet. A non stopping Talbot was second in the 313-mile race and Maseratis were third and fourth, with Sommer's Ferrari fifth.

A coda to the 1949 season was the Czechoslovakian Grand Prix, run over 20 laps of a harrowing 11-mile road course at Brno. No fewer than seven Maseratis were faced by the single Ferrari of Peter Whitehead. Several of the 4CLT/48s crashed out early and by the finish none was left, handing the victory to Whitehead's 125 F1 ahead of a Talbot and a 2.0-litre unblown Ferrari.

With its ups and downs this Alfa-free season was difficult to assess. It is best judged by applying to it the point system that came into use in 1950 with the introduction of the World Championship. Counting the British, Belgian, Swiss, French, Dutch and Italian races as qualifying events and crediting all the finishes down to fifth place, the final points tally is 49 for Ferrari – with three wins – and 36 for Maserati, with only a win in the British race to its credit. Ferrari was in the ascendant, but in view of its plant closure and its loss of Ascari and Villoresi – no small divestiture, that – Maserati acquitted itself creditably.

For the first-ever World Championship in 1950 the Orsis put Maserati forward bravely with a press launch at which eight Formula 1 cars were lined up for inspection. Bringing total San Remo production to 20, two new cars were given the 4CLT/50 designation to mark improvements that included a built-up crankshaft allowing one-piece connecting rods and roller big-end bearings. Horsepower edged upward toward 280 and weight was removed.

But in 1950 the Maseratis were eclipsed both by the return of Alfa Romeo – which dominated – and by Ferrari's dramatic abandonment, during the year, of the supercharged engine to pursue the unblown 4½-litre alternative. Not until 1951 would this bring Ferrari victories over Alfa, which provided the World Champion's mount in both 1950 and '51.

Together with Alfa Romeo, Ferrari and Maserati built the best of the last road-racing cars with mechanically driven superchargers. High-pressure induction would return, but with exhaust-driven turbochargers. For the moment, newcomer Ferrari had gained the upper hand over its Modenese rival. But Maserati would fight back – and vigorously – with both sports cars and Grand Prix cars. In this it would have the help of none other than Gioachino Colombo, developer of the supercharged Ferraris. This was a rivalry with legs.

With his Ferrari the only Maranello representative in the field for the 176-mile Jersey Road Race on 13 July 1950, Peter Whitehead won ahead of Reg Parnell's San Remo Maserati, chasing him here.

CHAPTER THREE

166 SC vs A6GCS

Both Ferrari and Maserati burst out of the chocks in 1947 with new 1½-litre sports-racing cars. Moving up to 2.0 litres during that year, they clashed head-on in memorable sports-car battles in 1948. After that, Ferrari's radical V12 pulled it ahead of Maserati's six.

In their first sports-car encounter, both lost. Instead of battling to the death, Ferrari and Maserati were trounced over 62 miles, at Piacenza on 11 May 1947, by Righetti's humble Stanguellini-prepared Fiat 1100. Maserati could hold its head a bit higher after placing its car second overall and first in the 1,500cc class. And Ferrari, in the first-ever race entry of its 125, could take comfort from the fact that its car started from pole and was retired while in the lead by a banal fuel-pump failure. This was but the first of the many encounters that would see the world's best drivers at the wheels of Maserati

Somewhere on Lake Garda's ten-mile circuit Bruno Ruffo was applying pressure to the 166 SC Ferrari of Antonio Stagnoli in October 1950. Next to the stripped Ferrari the A6GCS Maserati's low build was evident.

Maranello's 166 SC exemplified the dual-purpose character of the 2.0-litre Ferraris and Maseratis of the late 1940s. It often wore cycle wings to compete as a sports car and could easily be stripped, as here, to race in Formula 2.

With a temporary body, painted to heighten night visibility without headlamps, the A6 prototype was subjected to testing by Ernesto Maserati on the roads around Modena and Bologna during the war. Ernesto's son Alfieri is posed engagingly.

and Ferrari sports-racers in the difficult years just after the war.

Both companies started their sports-car wars with 1½-litre cars, for quite different reasons. Ferrari created his V12 with Formula 1 racing in mind and only secondarily as a sports-car engine. With Formula 1 catering in those days for supercharged 1½-litre engines, his choice was made for him. Maserati, on the other hand, conceived its new six-cylinder 1½-litre engine for a series-built road car. Hitherto, the Modena company had never enjoyed a production-car base for its activities, but now the company's owners, Adolfo Orsi and his son Omer, encouraged the Maserati brothers in their development of a 1½-litre road car. Soon, of course, it would be raced as well.

By the end of the 1947 season both companies would move up to the 2.0-litre class, where some of their most memorable battles would be fought. 2.0-litre sports cars were popular at home in Italy, were they contended for national championship honours both in races and in the very popular hillclimbs. In addition they were just the job for the great races, the Mille Miglia and Targa Florio, that were being revived. Another magnet for 2.0-litre cars was the new Formula 2 (originally Formula B) that took effect in 1948. Open to out-and-out racing cars, this attracted a breed of sports car that could also be converted into an open-wheeled racer. Ferrari and Maserati would both enter this attractive new arena.

Preoccupied as they were after the war with the resuscitation and production of their 4CL racing cars, the Maserati brothers made relatively slow headway with their 1½-litre road car, a concept that dated back as far as 1941. That's when Ernesto Maserati began working on a sports version of his 6CM racing car, a supercharged 1,500cc twin-cam six-cylinder single-seater that he and his brothers had produced in rewarding numbers from 1936 to 1939.

By mid-1943 Ernesto had defined a new concept for the engine of his planned sports Maserati. Instead of twin overhead cams it would have a more compact and less costly chain-driven single overhead camshaft. Ernesto began his new model's designation with the letter 'A', in honour of his deceased brother Alfieri, and followed it with '6' for its cylinder count. The first A6, a magnificent Pininfarina-bodied 1½-litre coupé, was displayed at Geneva in March 1947.

With its rough provisional body the A6 prototype had taken to the roads around Modena during the war and was still circulating in 1946. Joining it were two Maserati-based sports-racers conceived by privateers eager to get back into the sport. Both used carburetted 1½-litre 6CM twin-cam engines, live rear axles sprung by quarter-elliptics, and parallel-wishbone independent front suspension. Guido Barbieri's car had a channel-steel frame and an ultra-low full-envelope body. Built with the help of Ernesto Maserati and Alberto Massimino, it was an official factory project – albeit powered by an engine that belonged to driver Gigi Villoresi.

Although the other 6CM-based car was less official, it foreshadowed future sports Maseratis with its adaptation of the traditional grille. Hammered out by Medardo Fantuzzi, its slab-sided body covered a light tubular chassis frame. This car was built at the initiative of Mario Angiolini, whose robust build betrayed his former role as goalkeeper with the Modena soccer team. Both cars were open roadsters.

Maserati motivation was a feature of another car that featured in the 1947 season. This was a special built by Rinaldo Tinarelli, marrying a Fiat 1100 chassis with a pre-war 1½-litre Maserati twin-cam engine running without its usual supercharger. It differed from the others in having cycle-winged bodywork. Its main asset during 1947 was the presence in its cockpit of Giovanni Bracco, a

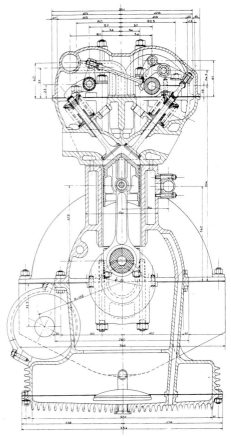

Geneva's Salon in 1947 saw the debut of the A6 Maserati, powered by this 1.5-litre in-line six. Its single overhead camshaft operated the inlet valves through finger followers, pushrods and rocker arms. Rockers opened the exhausts directly.

In the centre of Piacenza's grid on 11 May 1947 was the 6CM-based Maserati special of Mario Angiolini, who placed third in the 62-mile race. He was flanked by a BMW and (on the left) the Ferrari 125 S, making its first competition appearance.

Enzo Ferrari chose Gioachino Colombo to be the architect of his new company's first engine. Before the war Ferrari had worked with Colombo in the design of Alfa Romeo's Type 158 Voiturette, now his rival in Formula 1.

Salient features of the 1.5-litre V12 powering the Ferrari 125 S were its single overhead camshafts, opening the valves through rocker arms, and its hairpin valve springs from motorcycle practice. This was a radical conception for the straitened post-war era.

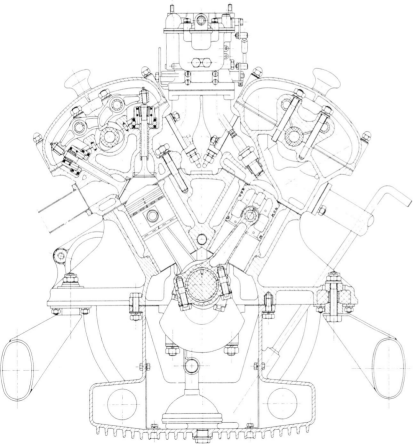

splendid driver who was just beginning to come into his own.

Facing these sports-racing Maseratis in 1947's 1½-litre class was the first Ferrari. Its engine was – of all things – a V12. Twelves as such were not rare. But 12-cylinder engines as small as 1½-litres, the original size of the first Ferrari engine, were extraordinarily rare. In 1925 Itala built a 1½-litre V12 racing car (and, indeed, also a 1.1-litre version) but never competed with it. In 1927 a 1½-litre Fiat 12-cylinder engine with side-by-side geared crankshafts was successful in the one and only Grand Prix race it entered, at Milan. Fiat then withdrew from racing. In 1939–40 Auto Union drew up plans for a 1½-litre V12 but built only a single-cylinder test engine. The Alfa Romeo Type 512, a flat-opposed 1½-litre 12-cylinder, was secretly tested in the early 1940s but never raced.

This was the state of play in August 1945 when Enzo Ferrari and former Alfa engineer Gioachino Colombo met at Modena to discuss the design of a new car that should be adaptable to the 1½-litre supercharged category of Formula 1 and should also serve as the basis of a production sports car. Both were familiar with Alfa Romeo's Type 158 eight-cylinder racing car, which they had designed and built. Britain's ERA was a six and Maserati had powerful four-cylinder engines. They agreed to surpass these rivals with a power unit that was novel for its category: a twelve.

This choice of a 12-cylinder layout for such a small engine ultimately endowed the first Ferrari with demonstrable advantages in both performance and reliability. Careful design, such as using only a chain-driven single overhead camshaft for each cylinder bank, helped keep such a complex engine from being prohibitively costly. In sports-racing form it was capable of revving to 7,000rpm – very fast for that time.

'You had to pay very close attention to the revs with this engine,' said Franco Cortese, the first man to race it. 'It was a somewhat different engine, one that went up to speed very quickly. If you were used to normal fours and sixes, this twelve was like an electric motor. It revved so easily that you always had to be on your guard. You had to drive with your head … and with your eye on the tachometer.

'It was Ferrari who chose the 12-cylinder,' added Cortese. 'It was an *idée fixe* with him, and one for which he was heavily criticised. Several forecast, "He's a nutcase. It will eat his money and finish him." In particular the Maserati brothers were highly critical. But if he'd made a four, or a six or even an eight, Ferrari wouldn't have enjoyed the great success he's had.' His V12 first ran on 26 September 1946.

Ferrari installed his radical engine in a chassis that was conventional with one notable exception: he fitted a five-speed gearbox. Hitherto only out-and-out Grand Prix cars – and precious few of them – had five speeds forward. Gioachino Colombo's choice of five forward speeds was a breakthrough for the first Ferrari. Not until the early 1950s would Spain's Pegaso offer a five-speed transaxle in its cars. But Colombo was aware of the high-revving potential of the V12 engine he was designing and wanted a transmission that would have the versatility needed to exploit his engine to the full.

The Ferrari transmission was laid out like a conventional four-speed gearbox, with direct drive on fourth gear. Its fifth speed was an overdrive, using an additional pair of gears placed at the extreme rear of the case. This basic transmission was used on all Ferrari two-seaters until 1952, when a stronger four-speed transmission was introduced to cope with engines that had grown in cubic capacity in the meantime.

Dubbed the Type 125, after the displacement in cubic centimetres of one of its cylinders, this first Ferrari had a frame of oval-section tubes. These kicked up over the live rear axle and its semi-elliptic springs and carried independent suspension by wishbones in front. Ferrari prepared two types of bodies for it: one a full envelope design, called the 125 S, and the other a cycle-winged version, officially the 125 SC but nicknamed the 'cigar' for its narrow tubular body. Weight was 1,430lb and available power was 118bhp at 6,800rpm from an engine that measured 55 x 52.5mm for 1,497cc. Road trials of the new model began on 12 March 1947.

Only two months after this new Ferrari first ran, it was raced. 'We raced every Sunday to prove the car,' said Franco Cortese. 'Against the Maseratis, more than others. But we had an advantage. The Ferrari was a more modern machine, indeed exceptional for those days.' Modern it was indeed, and Maserati's opposition was highly provisional at best. But the six-cylinder cars from Modena's Viale Ciro Menotti would have a few surprises for Ferrari.

For both companies the 1947 season started with the race at Piacenza mentioned above. Two Ferraris should have started, but one was damaged during pre-race testing by the impetuous Nino Farina. The quick and reliable Franco Cortese put its 125 S sister on pole and led the race but retired, leaving first and second places in the 1,500cc class to the Maseratis of Guido Barbieri and Mario Angiolini. The following Thursday, 15 May, was unlucky for footballer Angiolini, who turned turtle and was injured in the twisty Sassi-Superga

hillclimb in the hills east of Turin. Giovanni Bracco won with his Fiat-Maserati.

The next Ferrari-Maserati contest was on 25 May over 85 miles at Rome's Caracalla Baths. The first-ever Ferrari victory was scored by Cortese, with Barbieri's Maserati second. Opinions differ about the 34-mile race at Vercelli on 1 June, in which the 1,500cc class was won by either Cortese (Ferrari) or Barbieri (Maserati). At Vigevano on 15 June Cortese was untroubled by Maseratis and easily won in the sports category. The following weekend saw the big event of the year, the Mille Miglia, in which Cortese's 125 SC retired with gearbox problems and a new Maserati appeared – of which more later.

As part of his sequential-weekend proving of the 125, Cortese had an easy race to victory over 89 miles at Varese on 29 June. On the next two weekends at Forli and Parma respectively the great Tazio Nuvolari drove for Ferrari. He won the 1,500cc class in the first and won outright at Parma over 60 miles, with Cortese's 125 second and Barbieri's Maserati third.

Maserati didn't figure in the 53-mile race at Florence on 20 July, where Ferdinando Righetti was rewarded for his giant-killing drive at Piacenza in May with the wheel of a 125. He placed third in the sports category while Cortese retired the other

Franco Cortese, who had driven for Ferrari's Scuderia since 1932, piloted the envelope-bodied 125 S in its first race at Piacenza in May 1947. He led easily until retired by a fuel-pump failure only three laps from the finish.

Cortese's stripped 125 SC 'cigar' was surrounded by Cisitalia single-seaters at the start of a race for Formula cars in Rome's Caracalla district on 5 June 1947. The Ferrari was lying second when it retired with steering trouble.

On 16 August 1947, the start of a 321-mile race for sports cars at Pescara on the Adriatic, Cortese's 125 S is seen on the left; he placed second. On the right was Enrico Beltrachini's Auto Avio Costruzioni Type 815, one of the two cars built by Enzo Ferrari for the 1940 Mille Miglia. The former property of Alberto Ascari, it retired at Pescara.

Ferrari. In the last race for the Ferrari 125, at Livorno on 24 August, Nuvolari retired early. Cortese should have raced the other one but it was badly damaged in a road accident that cost Ferrari's technical lieutenant Luigi Bazzi three broken ribs and a broken leg.

Meanwhile the Maseratisti had not been idle. The 10th of August saw them at two venues. Guido Barbieri was at Cascine for a race in which he failed to figure while Giovanni Bracco took his Fiat-Maserati to the 20-mile Aosta-Gran San Bernardo hillclimb, which he won. At Pescara on 16 August Felice Bonetto raced the rebuilt Angiolini Maserati to a second place in his category. Barbieri took his car to Venice for a race on a 2.4-mile circuit on the roads of the city's Lido on 14 September, where he finished first in the 1,500cc sports category. He scored a similar success in the race on the streets of Modena on 28 September.

Totting up the 1947 season's results in the events counting for the Italian championship, Cortese and Barbieri each won three qualifying

Right: Giovanni Cavara's drawing of Maserati's 2.0-litre A6GCS engine, introduced in 1947, showed its seven main bearings, high-domed pistons and chain drive to the overhead camshaft. Inlet-valve actuation was now by a long tappet and rocker arm.

Below right: Nicknames 'Monofaro' and 'Cyclops' came easily to the 1947 A6GCS Maserati, with a single headlamp in the centre of its grille. This greatly eased the conversion from sports car – as shown – and outright racer.

contests. Bracco won another with his Fiat-Maserati. This made it a pretty good year for Maserati; when all the points were scored the 1,500cc class champion was Guido Barbieri for Maserati. Though the Ferraris had shown their potential, they were too new to finish consistently.

Thus ended the rivalry between Ferrari and Maserati in the 1.5-litre sports category. During 1947 both made it clear that they were stepping up their challenge by developing 2.0-litre cars in preparation for 1948. Maserati was the first to show its hand. Its entry for the '47 Mille Miglia was a low, sinister-looking coupé powered by a 2.0-litre version of its A6 engine. It retired in the thousand-mile race and again at Varese on the following weekend, both times driven by Gigi Villoresi. These were the only outings for the enclosed-body version of a new model that was to gain many successes for Maserati.

From the 66 x 72.5mm dimensions of the 1,488cc A6, the 2.0-litre was expanded internally to 72 x 81mm to displace 1,979cc (the coupé's engine was at a preliminary stage of 72 x 80mm and 1,955cc). In parallel Maserati was developing a 2.0-litre road-car engine, which it called the A6G, the 'G' standing for *ghisa* for its cast-iron block. Added to this for the new racing model was 'C' for *corsa* and 'S' for *sport*, meaning sports-style bodywork and road equipment, thus creating the A6GCS model name. 'G' was kept, although the new engine's block was fitted with dry cylinder liners; certainly some blocks were cast in aluminium instead of iron.

Atop the block was a detachable aluminium cylinder head with hemispherical combustion chambers. Its two valves per cylinder were inclined at 32° for the inlets and 39° for the exhausts, giving an included angle of 71°. Ernesto Maserati chose an unusual solution for his engine's valve gear. A single camshaft ran above the exhaust valves and opened them through rocker arms. The cam's inlet-valve lobes pressed against short tappets which in turn opened the inlets through rocker

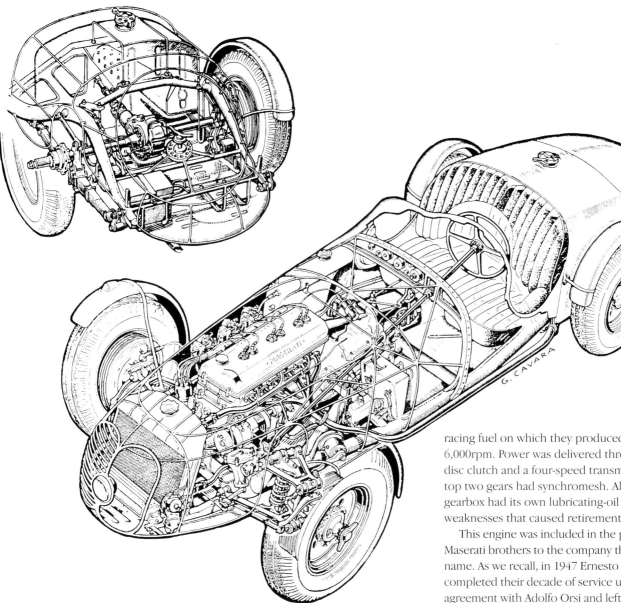

Alberto Massimino played a key role in fashioning the A6GCS from the ingredients left to the Orsis by Ernesto Maserati. Its engine and propeller shaft were offset to the right in order to seat the driver as low as possible.

arms. In some versions of the design a finger-type follower and pushrods operated the inlet valves.

A triple-roller chain drove the camshaft from the nose of the crankshaft. Adjacent to it was a single-roller chain that powered an accessory package at the engine's right front. This included the oil-pressure pump and the Marelli ignition, angled to the right and driven by a skew gear. While the first such engines had wet sumps with a front-mounted oil cooler, the A6GCS was soon given dry-sump oiling with a reservoir mounted in the cowl to the right of the footwell. A vee belt drove the generator along the left side of the block and, in tandem, the water pump.

Initially the engine was fed by three horizontal single-throat Weber carburettors, each supplying two cylinders through a Y-pipe. Toward the end of the A6GCS's lifetime twin-throat Webers were supplied to give each cylinder a venturi. The very high compression ratio of 11.0:1 was possible because the engines burned a methanol-based

racing fuel on which they produced 130bhp at 6,000rpm. Power was delivered through a single-disc clutch and a four-speed transmission whose top two gears had synchromesh. Although the gearbox had its own lubricating-oil pump, it had weaknesses that caused retirements in early races.

This engine was included in the patrimony of the Maserati brothers to the company that bore their name. As we recall, in 1947 Ernesto and Bindo completed their decade of service under their agreement with Adolfo Orsi and left to build a new base in Bologna. Under Adolfo's son Omer a new team took over, with Alberto Massimino the lead designer. Continuity was assured by the continued presence at Modena of Guerino Bertocchi, whose Trident tenure reached back to riding as mechanic in the class-winning Maserati in 1931's Mille Miglia. He was aptly described as 'the soul of the company'.

Setting aside the 1947 Mille Miglia coupé, in that summer of '47 Omer Orsi's squad decided to exploit the materiel that Ernesto had bequeathed them by using it as the basis of a new open sports-racing car. They conceived it with sketchy bodywork that could be raced, without wings, as a 2.0-litre Formula 2 car or with cycle wings as a sports car. The utter simplicity of a single headlamp in the middle of its grille won the new Maserati its '*Monofaro*' and 'Cyclops' nicknames.

Ingeniously, Massimino offset the engine and gearbox to the right of the A6GCS chassis – at the cost of cramping the 'passenger' side – so the engine's mass would balance that of the driver. The drive shaft was displaced laterally to let the driver sit

well down between it and the outer rail of the steel-tube frame. This contributed to one of the A6GCS's most striking features: its ultra-low driving position. The live rear axle was located by radius rods above semi-elliptic leaf springs while the parallel-wishbone front suspension was sprung by coils.

Over a tubular framework Medardo Fantuzzi fashioned a functional yet handsome aluminium body for the A6GCS. A token door was fitted on the right below a tonneau cover, while the driver's side was cut down to give full freedom to flailing elbows. Maserati made three such two-seaters in 1947 and would build four in 1948, four more in 1949, three in 1950 and later two more, for a total of 16 chassis.

Enzo Ferrari had not been idle in the meantime. Giuseppe Busso, who had been charged with the technical development of the new Ferrari after

The A6GCS Maserati had a token door on the right-hand side to meet sporting rules. Ultra-low, it flaunted sleek Fantuzzi bodywork. Minimal clearance to the cycle wings hinted at stiff springing.

Gigi Villoresi showed off the ground-hugging lines of Maserati's A6GCS as he drove his works entry to second place in the race through Modena's city-centre streets on 28 September 1947.

Colombo's departure, was tasked with the V12's enlargement to 2.0-litres. 'Work started at a frenetic pace after the first race at Piacenza,' said Busso. 'We prepared the increase of displacement to 2.0-litres. We approached it in stages, first with the 159, whose engine was fired up at the end of July, and later with the 166, which gave its first sneezes at the end of November.' Busso's 'frenetic pace' had to accelerate after Luigi Bazzi was sidelined by his road-crash injuries.

From the original proportions of 55 x 52.5mm the bore and stroke were enlarged to 59 x 58mm to bring capacity to 1,903cc. With each cylinder displacing 159cc, this provided the '159' designation of the engine with which – like Maserati – Ferrari would move by stages from 1.5 to 2.0-litres. Rated at 125bhp, the Type 159 first raced in the 321-mile event at Pescara on 16 August, fitted in an envelope-bodied chassis. Cortese took it to second place overall.

The first clash between Maserati and Ferrari with 2.0-litre cars took place on home territory: the streets of Modena on 28 September. This was the launch event for the new A6GCS, driven by Gigi Villoresi and the rising young talent Alberto Ascari. Against them were ranged two 159s: the 'cigar' of Cortese and the envelope-bodied car of Righetti.

When the race had to be stopped because of an accident after one-third distance – a little over 40 miles – the Maseratis were running one-two with Ascari in the lead. Cortese set fastest lap but retired, victim of a bad spark-plug choice, and Righetti finished fifth. Guido Barbieri's class-winning Maserati was fourth overall.

That this was a serious encounter for hometown bragging rights was rubbed in after the race. Romolo Tavoni, then working for Maserati, remembered the aftermath: 'The next day Bertocchi had the cars parade by the nearby Scuderia Ferrari, then take the road to Maranello and then pass repeatedly in front of Ferrari, simulating a test drive.' Short though the race had been, it was sublimely decisive for the Trident and a promising debut for the new A6GCS.

'It's very obvious that the Maserati represents a serious challenge to the 12-cylinder Ferrari,' mused Corrado Millanta afterwards. 'In any case this first encounter between these two cars of differing conception was extremely interesting. The Ferrari, with its highly subdivided displacement and consequent reduction in cylinder size, stroke/bore ratio less than unity and very high rev range, probably has a few horses more than its adversary. The [Maserati], of classical conception, is likely to

compensate for less power with lighter weight.' Millanta was of the impression that the Ferrari was already at the full 2.0-litres, but in fact it was still five per cent short of that capacity.

Ferrari would have 1947's last word. Over 313 miles in Turin's Valentino Park on 12 October Raymond Sommer drove a cycle-winged 159 SC to a convincing victory against strong international opposition. This included the two A6GCSs from Modena, both of which retired with broken gearboxes after applying enough pressure to keep Sommer honest. As at Modena, they were sufficiently close competitors to suggest a rivalry that would blossom in 1948.

Over the winter all Ferrari's engines were rebuilt to new bigger bores of 60mm, bringing displacement up to 1,968cc. Soon enough the stroke was also lengthened to 58.8mm to create the 166's final displacement of 1,995cc. With a compression ratio of 8.0:1 and triple 32mm Weber twin-throat carburettors it was rated at 130bhp at 7,000rpm. In 1948 this model, known as the 166 SC, competed both with 'cigar'-type bodies and with all-enveloping coupé and spyder coachwork by Allemano to designs by Turin stylist Bruno Ermete, whom Giuseppe Busso had asked to assist after Enzo Ferrari criticised some of the engineer's

own initial efforts. In all Ferrari built eight new cars for the 1948 season, including some for sale to private entrants.

On the big occasions in 1948 it was no contest: in 2.0-litre sports cars, Ferrari bested Maserati. In the Giro di Sicilia, a 670-mile lap of Sicily in April, four Maseratis lined up against three Ferraris. Villoresi led early with his A6GCS but retired, while team-mate Ascari was sidelined early. Salvatore Ammendola took his Maserati to fifth overall and second in class

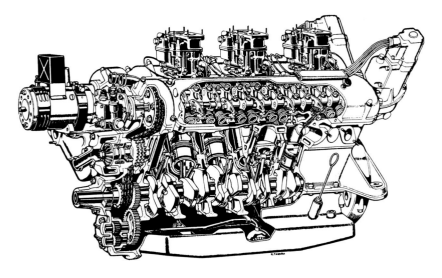

Coupled to a five-speed gearbox that helped the driver make best use of its output, the 2.0-litre Ferrari V12 – here in 166 MM guise – gained a reputation for reliability after Maranello's adoption of Vandervell thin-wall bearings.

coupé. It was his third Mille Miglia victory.

On the more mundane Italian domestic scene the achievements of one performer stood out: Giovanni Bracco in the A6GCS Maserati. In July he won both the Dolomite Trophy over 189 miles – with Villoresi second in a sister car – and the Bolzano-Mendola hillclimb, defeating two Ferraris. Two other hillclimbs fell to Bracco and Maserati, the Biella-Oropa and the Aosta-Gran San Bernardo (class victory). Together with another hillclimb victory in a Ferrari 166 SC at the end of the season, this was enough to make Bracco the Italian champion in the 2.0-litre class.

Another compelling result for Maserati's sports six in 1948 came in the gruelling 317-mile race over the 15.8-mile Pescara road circuit. Seven Ferraris were entered, including a short-wheelbase 'cigar' for Raymond Sommer and a Piacenza-type envelope-bodied 166 SC for Cortese. Maserati had three works entries for Villoresi, Ascari and Bracco. Chased by Villoresi, Ferraris led the early laps under the hot August sun. On the third of 20 laps Alberto Ascari limped into the pits with a broken leaf-spring hanger. He jumped into Bracco's Maserati and by the fourth lap was third behind Sommer's Ferrari and Villoresi's Maserati, maintaining a quick yet steady gait. Both of them obliged him by retiring. Over almost four hours he scored an important win for Maserati.

The 1948 season also saw the Ferrari 'cigars' and Maserati 'Cyclops' stripped for action for the

behind the outright winner, Clemente Biondetti in an Allemano-bodied 166 SC spyder. Another Ferrari was sixth overall and third in class.

Hopes were high for a Maserati fight-back in the Mille Miglia in May. Four cars of each marque started the 1,133 miles. By the mid-point at Rome, two of each remained. One of the Maseratis was Ascari's, which was always in contention, but first his transmission and then his engine failed, while the other also retired. The race was memorable for Tazio Nuvolari's splendid leading drive in a cycle-winged Ferrari, but this broke near the finish and left the win to Biondetti in an Allemano 166 SC

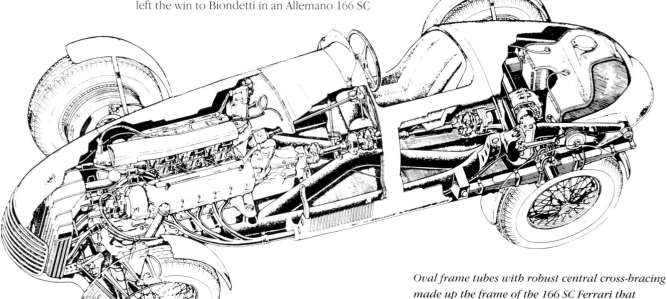

Oval frame tubes with robust central cross-bracing made up the frame of the 166 SC Ferrari that competed in 2.0-litre races from 1948. Enzo must have had second thoughts about the column-mounted gearshift shown in Cavara's drawing.

first time to compete in Formula 2 as 2.0-litre racing cars. In this arena the cars bearing the Trident had little to offer against those with the Prancing Horse. During the season six Formula 2 races had representation from both marques. In none of these could Maserati wrest victory from Ferrari. At Vercelli in May 'Azzi' managed a third for Maserati and at Mantua in June Alberto Ascari was fifth ahead of three of the six Ferraris entered. Ascari set fastest lap in the race at Naples in September but retired.

F2 wins fell to 166 SC Ferraris at Bari (Chico Landi) and at Reims (Sommer). The latter won at Florence in September, but driving a proper single-seater Ferrari instead of the 166 SC in which Biondetti took second place. Florence saw seven Ferraris and five Maseratis take the start. Of the latter both Villoresi and Ascari pressed the Ferraris, but had to retire. Cheeky Frenchman Raymond Sommer even entered his wingless 166 SC in full-fledged Grand Prix races during 1948, his best results being third at Geneva and fourth at San

On 2 May 1948 at Geneva the only cars to defeat Raymond Sommer's 166 SC Ferrari in the city's 146-mile Grand Prix were two supercharged Formula 1 Maseratis. The Maranello machine was entered by Ecurie Inter.

Ecurie Inter entered this 166 SC in the Grand Prix of Monaco on 16 May 1948, the first appearance of a Ferrari in the principality. Prince Igor Troubetskoy crashed out on the 58th of 100 laps.

Clemente Biondetti stood in for an otherwise-engaged Nuvolari to drive this 166 SC Ferrari to second place in a 125-mile race at Stockholm on 30 May 1948. No Maseratis made the trip to Sweden.

Remo, the race that saw Maserati introduce its new 4CLT/48 Grand Prix car for winner Ascari.

1949 saw Ferrari and Maserati tracing different trajectories. Drawing lessons from his 1948 results, Enzo Ferrari huddled with Carrozzeria Touring to create the classic 'Barchetta', designated 166 MM after 1948's Mille Miglia victory. This highly accomplished car cut a swathe through 1949's major contests, winning the Giro di Sicilia, the Mille

Miglia and the 24-hour races at Le Mans and Spa. Clemente Biondetti won the Italian races and Luigi Chinetti the 24-hour events, accompanied by Lord Selsdon (briefly) at Le Mans and Jean Lucas at Spa.

For Maserati in contrast 1949 was a difficult year. Its star works drivers, Gigi Villoresi and Alberto Ascari, defected to Ferrari when financial problems struck the Orsi businesses and forced the closing of the Maserati factory from February until June.

Driving a 166 SC 'cigar' Tazio Nuvolari was leading in the early laps of the 56-mile race at Mantua on 13 June but soon retired, exhausted. The Maseratis of Ascari and Villoresi hit trouble.

Both Ferrari and Maserati put bold faces forward in their racing rivalry, which continued for over two decades. Ferrari featured its aggressive Prancing Horse and egg-crate grille, while Maserati's Trident communicated a powerful message: keep out of my way!

As raced in 1949, Ferrari's Type 125 F1 (right) produced 250bhp from its 1.5-litre V12, fed by the single Roots-type blower at the left. Its chassis (below) had rear swing axles with a transverse-leaf spring, introduced for 1949. The frame-mounted final drive had double reduction gears to lower both the input shaft and the driver's seat.

For the 1949 racing season Ferrari introduced the 166 MM, the Touring-bodied version of the 166 SC. In the early 1950s it triumphed over Maserati in the 2.0-litre class.

Enzo Ferrari's ambitious V12 engine was at the heart of his first creations, starting life as 1.5-litres and quickly moving up to 2.0-litres. This one powered a Type 225 S of 2.7-litres.

A key advantage of the Type A6GCS Maserati was its low centre of gravity, thanks to a design that seated the driver down alongside the drive shaft. It raced with and without its cycle wings.

Two generations of A6GCM Maserati were paddock fellows at Goodwood (right): the 1952 model on the right and the 1953 version. Between them in Trident evolution was the interim-type A6GCS sports-racer (below), with a 1952-type Formula 2 engine in a chassis akin to that of the cycle-winged 'Cyclops'.

The 1954 racing season saw the first clashes between Ferrari's 500 Mondial (left) and Maserati's A6GCS/2000 (below). Early Mondials were bodied by Pininfarina, including two coupés like the one shown. The Maserati's shape was inspired by its designer's experience with Alfa Romeo's 'Flying Disc' sports-racers.

The Type 500 Mondial Ferrari's four-cylinder engine was identical in all major respects to the unit that powered Alberto Ascari to two World Championships, in 1952 and 1953. It was handicapped, however, by being asked to power a chassis shared with the 3.0-litre Type 750 Monza.

Like Ferrari's Mondial, Maserati's Type A6GCS/2000 was propelled by the same engine – in this case an in-line twin-cam six – that the Trident used in its Formula 2 cars. It had a small but significant power advantage over its Maranello rival, albeit with a more peaky power curve.

Under Gioachino Colombo's direction, the first version of Maserati's much-loved 'Aseigiciesse' received a handsome new interpretation of the traditional grille.

No racing car ever made a more glorious sound than the sonorous snarl of the twin pipes of Maserati's 1953 Type A6GCS/2000, adjacent to its left-hand driver position.

Later versions of the Type A6GCS/2000 Maserati had a Trident-filled grille and, in this instance, lateral air venting from the engine room.

Holding the fort with a skeleton staff in the interim, it was all that works manager Vittorio Bellentani could do to service the Grand Prix cars that were in the hands of customers. Significant development of the company's sports-racers was out of the question. Emphasis was placed instead on two prototypes for the planned production run of A6G road cars.

In Italy's domestic competitions Ferrari's hand was strengthened by the mercurial Giovanni Bracco's move from Maserati to the Prancing Horse. He won five hillclimbs with the 166 MM. Circuit successes were scored by Roberto Vallone, who was the Italian champion in his class for 1949. Nevertheless the A6GCS had its moments, thanks mainly to the persistence of Nicola Musmeci. Competing from a Sicilian base he won two hillclimbs and two road races against Ferrari opposition. Musmeci carried on in 1950 to win

Although the Ferraris challenged – here Biondetti passing a Cisitalia in a 166 SC – Bracco's Maserati A6GCS, taken over by Ascari, triumphed in the 317-mile Pescara Grand Prix on 15 August 1948.

In 1948 Ferrari made a proper Formula 2 car by installing its 2.0-litre V12 in a Formula 1 chassis, creating the 166 F2 as acquired by the Argentine Auto Club's team to be raced by Juan Fangio at Reims in 1949.

road races at both Syracuse and Palermo, the latter over 239 miles. Another 1950 Maserati winner was Sonio Coletti in the Giro dell'Umbria.

Musmeci was still winning the odd hillclimb with his Maserati in 1951, including the Monte Pellegrino and Catania-Etna climbs, the latter counting for the Italian championship. In the 2.0-litre class the '51 champion was Ferrari-mounted Antonio Stagnoli, though future star Umberto Maglioli did take victory in the Dolomite Cup with his A6GCS. This was one of the last appearances of these lively Cyclops-eyed sports racers in Italian annals. In sports-car racing they were overwhelmed by the phalanxes of Ferraris, especially those with the new 2.3- and 2.6-litre engines, the Types 195 and 212.

In Formula 2 Ferrari stole a jump on Maserati by installing its 2.0-litre V12 in one of its single-seater GP chassis, with excellent results. This was an entirely *ad hoc* initiative that brought big dividends. This path was not barred to Maserati. In 1950, in fact, the Argentine team competing in Europe installed an A6GCS six in one of its Grand Prix 4CLT/48 chassis. Juan Fangio won with it at Angouleme in June and Roberto Mieres drove it to fourth at Geneva in July. Cylinder-block problems kept the hybrid from starting in the German Grand Prix. In 1951 Maserati would build a not-dissimilar car of its own.

Stripped of their lights and cycle wings, the Ferrari 166 SC and Maserati A6GCS continued to provide useful Formula 2 mounts into the 1950s. Hopes for the Trident were high when the Argentine team entered Maseratis for Fangio and Benedicto Campos in 1949's Rome GP, but both retired. Emilio Romano placed his A6GCS fifth behind two 166 SCs. Maseratis were out in force for the Bari GP but the only one to finish was the reliable Musmeci's, in sixth. Cortese's 166 SC was second in a pack of Ferraris. The Argentines gave up on the A6GCS and switched to single-seater Ferraris, with which Fangio won the Monza GP. The best Maserati was Piero Carini's in sixth place. The 166 SC Ferraris were fading from Formula 2 and being replaced by the single-seater 166 C.

With Ferraris dominating in 1950 the old A6GCS had only a few chances to shine in Formula 2. On Modena's Autodromo a newcomer to F2, Pietro Palmieri, showed a flamboyant driving style and finished fourth in spite of several spins, one of which vaulted him over the hay bales. Palmieri's impetuousness caught up with him at Monza where he started his heat from the front row but soon crashed, breaking his pelvis. Both car and driver were mended in time to place third in the Bologna-Raticosa hillclimb later in 1950.

The presence of only one Ferrari at 1950's Naples GP opened opportunities for the two A6GCS entries. Sesto Leonardi was third in his heat but retired in the final, in which Nicola Musmeci

In 1950 the Argentine team led by Juan Fangio installed an A6GCS six in a 4CLT/48 chassis to create this Formula 2 single-seater. At Angouleme on 11 June two works Ferraris led by Sommer had no answer to Fangio's winning drive.

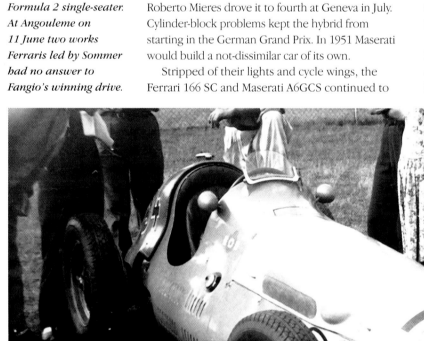

was fourth behind a Ferrari, HWM and OSCA. German publisher Paul Pietsch piloted an A6GCS in the German GP but retired before half-distance with clutch trouble. At Garda's difficult road course in October a lone Maserati was driven by Bruno Ruffo, a double motorcycling champion who was having his first go on four wheels. Over 183 miles Ruffo finished an excellent third behind the inevitable Ferraris. He would continue to compete in Maseratis through the 1950s.

If durability is any measure, the A6GCS scored against the 166 SC with its continued usefulness in Formula 2 races. Entries in 1951 were made by Gino Ughetti, Adolfo Schwelm, Inico Bernabei, Pasquale Placido and Guiseppe Ruggiero, among whom Schwelm's placed sixth in the Rome GP. Of these only Ruggiero would persevere into 1952, when the World Championship was opened up to Formula 2 cars. He would leave his few entries empty-handed.

In the meantime the 166 MM Ferrari was compiling its outstanding record, including class wins in the Mille Miglia in 1950, '51 and '52. To this Maserati had no answer. Since its troubles in 1949 it had never properly gotten to grips with Ferrari's stunning advances. Balancing up 1947 and '48, however, the Emilian rivals could be seen to have been very much at each other's throats. This set an exciting pattern for the future.

On 15 October 1950 Bruno Ruffo finished a plucky third in his Maserati Cyclops behind two Ferraris on the demanding road course adjoining the west side of Lake Garda. Here he passed through the lakeside town of Saló.

As late as 1951 Maserati's A6GCS was still competing in European Formula 2 races. Here leading a battered Ferrari, Adolf Schwelm's Monofaro placed sixth in Rome's Grand Prix on 10 June.

CHAPTER FOUR

375 F1 vs OSCA Type G

At a time when the Viale Ciro Menotti was unable to renew its Grand Prix challenge to Ferrari, the Maserati brothers had no such constraints. Like Enzo Ferrari they saw great potential in the unblown element of the Formula 1 rules.

I n the Grand Prix *corida* Ferrari and Maserati were locking horns with their highly boosted 1½-litre racers through 1949 and into 1950. Swilling their alcohol-based fuels, these supercharged cars had to make several pit stops to complete a 300-mile Grand Prix. Meanwhile the unblown 4½-litre Talbot-Lagos were going through non-stop. Though their long-stroke sixes were far from state-of-the-art, the Talbots suggested that the huge displacement advantage given the unsupercharged engine could be a race winner if exploited with the latest technology.

At the start of the Pescara Grand Prix on 15 August 1951, two unsupercharged Talbot-Lagos (right) flanked three unblown 4.5-litre V12 Ferraris, leaving black lines. The Maserati brothers were also readying an unblown V12 for Formula 1.

A new face among France's racers was willing to give this alternative a try. This was Amédée Gordini, born as Amedeo near Bologna in 1899. Since 1922 Gordini had lived and worked in France. By the 1940s he was building and racing small sports and single-seater cars with the backing of French auto maker Simca and, remarkably, Vietnam's Imperial dynasty.

Gordini's contract with Simca barred him from racing cars with more than the four cylinders offered by the French auto maker. He'd made do with lightly blown versions of his fours, but these were completely uncompetitive. Hankering to field a more ambitious engine in Formula 1, Amédée was encouraged by Guglielmo Carraroli, active as a racing driver through much of the 1930s and now an entrepreneur.

If Gordini arranged to design and build the car outside France, Carraroli assured him, Simca needn't be troubled. And he had just the men to do it: the Maserati brothers. At the end of 1947 they'd established their own company, OSCA, in Bologna to make racing cars after their ten-year contract with Maserati expired.[1] The connection was more than casual: as a youngster Gordini had apprenticed to Alfieri and Bindo Maserati at Isotta Fraschini before leaving Italy.

With Carraroli's help, by early 1949 Gordini had contracted with OSCA to create his car's new engine. Breaking with the supercharged tradition, it would be an unblown 4½-litre unit. At the Italian company the prime movers were Ernesto (51), Ettore (55) and Bindo (66). They agreed on the project's budget and parameters with Amédée Gordini (50). The latter would design and make the chassis in his own workshop. Its chief was Antoine (Antonio) Pichetto, whose pedigree included work on a 12-cylinder Itala racing car of 1927 and Bugatti's four-wheel-drive Type 53. Gordini and Pichetto both influenced the design of the engine, which the Maseratis named 'Type G' in honour of their customer.

They decided on a 12-cylinder engine. Its square dimensions of 78 x 78mm (4,473cc) harked back to successful 1½-litre racing engines made by both parties. Vee angle was 60°, with cylinder centres spaced at 100mm. Wet steel liners were used in an aluminium-alloy block with detachable aluminium heads which were mirror images of each other.

Each cylinder was surrounded by its own set of four studs, adding up to 24 per bank. The block

---

1 OSCA stood for *Officine Specializzate Costruzioni Automobili* or Workshop Specialising in Automobile Construction.

Seen in a 1950 portrait by Rodolfo Mailander, Amédée Gordini was – like Bugatti before him – an Italian manufacturing cars in France. Unlike Bugatti he made his elegantly light Gordinis chiefly for racing.

The cylinder block of the 60-degree vee-twelve that the Maserati brothers built for Gordini was of aluminium with wet steel liners for its bores. Apertures enclosed gear drives to the twin overhead camshafts in each head.

was cut off at the centreline of the steel crankshaft, which was carried by seven 61.4mm main bearings. Two-bolt main-bearing caps were cast integrally with the magnesium sump, which was closed at its bottom end by a simple magnesium plate. A central oil-delivery gallery was integral with the sump as well.

Full-skirted pistons carried two compression rings and one oil ring above the gudgeon pin and one oil ring below. Any need for cylinder offset was avoided by the use of fork-and-blade connecting rods – a unique initiative among post-war automotive vee-twelves. The forked rods were in the OSCA's right bank, blade rods in the left. Bearings for both were white metal applied directly to the rod surface. Journal size for the forked rod was 50.7mm diameter and 42mm width, while the blade rod ran on a journal 60mm in diameter and 17mm wide in the big end of the forked rod. Both rods had I-section shanks and were 151mm long.

A feature of the forked rod was that its four-bolt big end was made in three pieces instead of the usual two. The removable big-end cap was as normal, but its opposing surface, normally part of the rod, was detachable. It mated closely with the main part of the rod at surfaces machined at a 120° vee angle. This allowed the two pieces constituting the big end to be made of nitride-hardenable steel, as was needed because they also supplied the bearing journal for the blade rod. The rest of the rod was made of a steel better suited to durability. The cost of this construction in performance terms was that while the blade rod weighed 530gm, the forked rod was almost twice as heavy at 962gm. Each rod journal had its own pair of counterweights.

A train of spur gears up the front of the Type G OSCA drove its oil pumps, a single water pump with dual outlets, a gearbox with a spiral-bevel

drive to two transverse six-cylinder Marelli magnetos and a fuel pump on its way to turning two overhead camshafts in each bank. Set low, the cams opened inclined overhead valves through short roller-tipped rocker arms, whose two arms were significantly offset. Splayed equally at an included angle of 80°, the valves measured 43mm for the inlets and 36.5mm for the exhausts. The former were fed by three double-throat Weber carburettors on short two-

With cylinder bores mutually opposed, Type G OSCA connecting-rod big ends were of fork-and-blade design. Domed pistons were full-skirted to carry oil rings both above and below their gudgeon pins.

The OSCA Type G twelve's blade rod, on the left, had its bearing on the surface of the big end of the forked rod, on the right. A penalty of the layout was the forked rod's much higher weight.

Aluminium cylinder heads of OSCA's Type G V12 for Gordini had hemispherical combustion chambers with single ignition. Studs in top of head retained camshaft bearings and pivot shafts for short roller-tipped rocker arms to valve stems.

Ferrari engineer Aurelio Lampredi (left) showed piston-ring-maker Gerry Grant his 4.5-litre Grand Prix V12 with triple downdraft carburettors. Lampredi leaned on the special magneto built to fire its 24 spark plugs in the engine's 1952 version.

Through rocker arms, a single central camshaft opened the vee-inclined valves in one cylinder head of Ferrari's 4.5-litre Formula 1 V12. Each valve was closed by a pair of hairpin or rat-trap springs.

cylinder manifolds down the centre of the vee. Magnesium covers for the valve gear were held on by the individual screwed-in pipes that gave access to the spark plugs.

The Maseratis reported to Amédée Gordini that his engine first ran in February of 1950 but was initially 'erratic' between 3,000 and 4,500rpm. After attention to its Webers it held solidly at 4,200rpm and produced an early 215bhp. At the Gordini works Pichetto was busy with its chassis, giving it a five-speed transaxle, inboard rear brakes and independent suspension at all four corners. By July he had completed his layouts.

Gordini's only chance to realise such an ambitious racer was to gain the support of his sponsor Simca. Apprised of the project by a hopeful Amédée, Simca definitively turned it down. Although some funding was provided by His Imperial Majesty Bao Dai of Vietnam it was not enough to allow Gordini to continue. He salvaged something from his investment by basing the design of the twin-cam cylinder head of a new four-cylinder engine on that of the single Type G that he received.

While the Bologna-based brothers regrouped after this setback to their project, their Maranello-based rival was having similar thoughts. A driver

Elegant counter-balancing, by masses tailored to larger and smaller dimensions according to the needs of each throw, characterised the crankshaft of the 4.5-litre Ferrari twelve. Nose sprocket drove triple-roller chain to overhead camshafts.

whom Enzo Ferrari esteemed, Parisian Raymond Sommer, had driven both the unsupercharged 4½-litre Talbots and the early GP Ferraris and, before the war, the Type 158 Alfas as well. His advice to Enzo was that the much better fuel economy of an unblown engine, with adequate power, would be a strong combination. Similar arguments advanced by engineer Aurelio Lampredi were accepted by Ferrari, who was at a dead end with his elaborate and only-marginally-serviceable supercharged G.P.49.

Before Enzo could unleash Lampredi on a new engine project he had to find a way to finance its construction. Turning to his tyre supplier and sponsor Pirelli, he requested and received a grant of some $20,000 for this purpose, £8,000 at the exchange rate prevailing at that time. The amount seemed so trivial to Piero Pirelli that he double-checked to make sure that it was all that Ferrari really needed. Further justifying the investment was the engine's planned suitability to sports-racing and even production Ferraris.

Although he kept the general concept of Gioachino Colombo's V12 design, with its single overhead cams on each bank and rocker arms, Aurelio Lampredi created an engine of his own. He

Here used as a practice car at Geneva on 30 July 1950, this swing-axle chassis provided the debut for Lampredi's new big V12 in 3.3-litre form in the Belgian GP on 18 June. Alberto Ascari made his requirements known.

At Geneva, seen here, and then at Pescara and Monza in 1950 the new big Ferrari V12 showed that it had what it took to lead and win races. A collector duct fed ram-pressurised air to its triple Weber carburettors.

gave roller tips to his rocker arms to give them better durability and enable the cam lobes to be narrow. Symmetrically disposed at a 60° included angle, instead of opposing each other directly, the valves were slightly offset longitudinally to allow their actuating rocker arms to be straighter than would otherwise have been the case. Spark plugs angled in from the sides of the head to cavities in the chamber; the developed 1951 version had two plugs per cylinder. A single triple-roller chain drove both camshafts.

Lampredi expanded the cylinder-centre distance from 90mm to 108mm to provide room for bigger bores, which he fashioned as wet steel cylinders that screwed into the heads. The latter were deep, extending almost two inches below the combustion chambers to form the upper water jacket. The bottom ends of the cylinders were sealed to the crankcase by two O-rings in grooves in their outer surfaces. A Lampredi trademark in the crankcase was his doubling up of its flanks to give added stiffness to an aluminium-alloy casting that was cut off at the crankshaft centreline and enclosed by a deeply finned sump. Racing versions had dry sumps, with a triple-gear scavenge pump, while road applications had wide wet sumps.

'I believe that the best approach is to make small engines and then make them grow,' said Lampredi, who proved it by baptising his new V12 as the 275 F1 at 3,322cc (72 x 68mm) for the Belgian Grand Prix in 1950. This was in fact an experimental outing, using a version of the 275 S sports-car engine tuned for alcohol-based fuel, but its success in powering Alberto Ascari to fifth place in Belgium was encouragement for his unblown-engine project. During that year Lampredi's twelve was enlarged to 4,102cc (80 x 68mm).

Fed by three double-throat 42 DCF Weber carburettors, the new engine was bench-tested by Ferrari stalwart Luigi Bazzi in 4.1-litre form in the summer of 1950. 'Bazzi thought the test bench was out of order,' Lampredi related, 'as the power recorded seemed too high. The test bench was stripped and reassembled twice, until he was

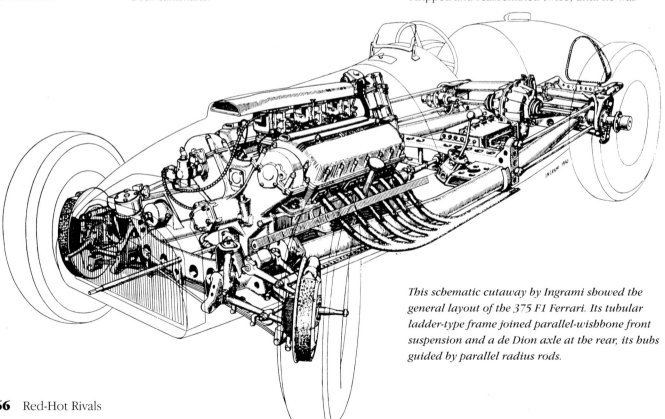

This schematic cutaway by Ingrami showed the general layout of the 375 F1 Ferrari. Its tubular ladder-type frame joined parallel-wishbone front suspension and a de Dion axle at the rear, its hubs guided by parallel radius rods.

convinced that the power reading was correct.' On the special fuel needed by its 12.0:1 compression ratio the 4.1-litre V12 was giving 335bhp at 7,000rpm – more power than any Ferrari yet built.

With the longer stroke of 74.5mm the twelve was opened out to the full allowable capacity of 4,494cc for the last championship race of 1950 at Monza. As the 375 F1 it was now rated at 350bhp at 7,000rpm. In speed it was breathtakingly close to the Alfas and placed second behind one of them after a hammer-and-tongs battle of attrition and car-swapping.

Ferrari's success with an unblown Grand Prix engine didn't go unnoticed in Bologna. While meeting strong demand for their successful small-displacement racers, through the winter of 1950–1 the Maserati brothers continued work on the twelve, now their sole property after Amédée Gordini's defection. In all, four engines were completed of the eight that were originally planned.

Initially the Maseratis claimed 295bhp at 5,600rpm on alcohol fuel with a compression ratio of 11.5:1. Shrewdly they offered the unit as a

This remarkable marriage of an Orsi-era Maserati 4CLT/48 chassis with the Maserati brothers' new Type G V12 created an impressive-looking motorcar in the spring of 1951. The installation, with OSCA-style grille, was made during March.

First appearance of Bira's OSCA-powered Maserati was at Goodwood on 26 March 1951. No Ferraris were in the ten-car field that the Siamese Prince defeated, over 29 miles, to win and set a new lap record at 90.38mph.

Flaunting its pioneering rocker-arm upper wishbones, Bira's Maserati-OSCA set a competitive practice time for the San Remo Grand Prix on 22 April 1951 but damaged its radiator in a scuffle and couldn't challenge the Ferraris.

replacement for the supercharged 1½-litre engines of the 4CLT/48 Maseratis, which by now were distinctly fatigued. They found a customer in Birabongse Bhanudej Bhanubandh, Prince of Siam, who raced as 'B. Bira'.

With incredible speed – only ten days, they claimed – the brothers installed their twelve in Bira's Maserati in the spring of 1951, also giving it an OSCA-styled oval nose with vertical grille bars. Bira won a 12-lap race in its first appearance at Goodwood on Easter Monday, against modest

opposition that included no Ferraris. The prince set a new lap record in spite of his concerns that the car wasn't running as he'd like.

At San Remo on 22 April Bira's Maserati-OSCA faced the Ferrari factory team for the first time. Ascari had a new version of the Maranello V12 with twin plugs per cylinder, identifiable by the staggered positioning of its exhaust downpipes. With dual ignition and larger 46 DCF/3 Webers its power peak was raised to 7,500rpm and its output to 380bhp, to complete what Aurelio Lampredi regarded as his 'real' Formula 1 engine.

Prospects were good for the Maserati-OSCA with the Siamese in the second row, qualifying only a fifth of a second slower than Dorino Serafini in a Ferrari 375 F1. However, Bira was sidelined with radiator damage after an early shunt while Alberto Ascari swept to victory in his dual-ignition Ferrari.

Ferrari passed up next weekend's inaugural Bordeaux Grand Prix. Again Bira was well placed in what was effectively the newest entry, but suffered several pit stops in the 188-mile race. He finally finished fourth behind a winning Talbot-Lago and two private Ferraris. Silverstone's International Trophy in May denied a confrontation with Ferrari when the latter withdrew. Bira was third in his heat behind two Alfa Romeos, in spite of having failed to record a practice time, but finished nowhere in the rained-out final.

Engine problems forced Bira to forfeit his entry in Dundrod's Ulster Trophy in June. In a season that saw intense struggles between the latest

With staggered exhaust pipes showing that it was powered by the latest twin-ignition version of its V12, the Ferrari 375 F1 of Froilan González made haste in the French Grand Prix on 1 July 1951. Ascari took over this car to finish second.

Ferraris and the supercharged Alfa Romeos he elected not to intervene in most of the major championship races. In a heat at Goodwood late in 1951 he again raised the lap record but his engine broke in the final. It also failed on the first lap of the only championship Grand Prix he entered, the Spanish GP at Barcelona in October. There the Maserati-OSCA was next to last on the grid with a time 35 seconds slower than Ascari's Ferrari on pole.[2]

Meanwhile in 1951 the OSCA workshops bravely built two pukka OSCA GP racers around their V12 engines. Though they were commissioned by wealthy amateur racers Luigi Piotti and Franco Rol, their subsidies would by no means cover their costs. Based on a ladder-type frame, the GP car had coil-sprung parallel wishbones in front like those of OSCA sports-racers. The de Dion rear suspension had a single radius arm at each side, requiring an articulated de Dion tube to avoid torsional effects. A Watt linkage located the tube laterally while springing was by torsion bars.

A special rear-mounted four-speed transaxle was constructed for the Type G, as the brothers continued to call the car that was born with a commission from Gordini. The all-indirect gearbox was located under the driver's seat in the same manner as the concurrent Ferrari. The clutch was located at the V12, which by now was producing 320bhp and 340lb-ft of torque according to Ernesto: 'It had balance like an electric motor. And power was there too. It had excellent low-speed

torque. Acceleration was tremendous, too much for the traction even in fourth gear.'

With its generously louvred bonnet and typical OSCA vertical-bar grille the Type G was a

---

2 A June 1952 outing in Ulster's Tourist Trophy, in which it crashed on the first lap, was the final European appearance of Bira's Maserati-OSCA. In 1955 Bira took it to Australia, where he used it at Orange when his Maserati 250 F failed, only to have the unprepared Maserati-OSCA break as well. Through the 1950s it kept racing down under in the hands of Australian owners.

By the end of the 1951 season the Maserati brothers completed their first pukka Type G OSCA. An under-bonnet view showed its twin horizontal magnetos, each serving one cylinder bank, and triple Weber carburettors.

In the 313-mile Italian Grand Prix on 16 September 1951 Franco Rol drove the OSCA Type G to its sole finish in a championship Formula 1 race. Neither the brothers nor their customers had the means to develop their ambitious creation.

purposeful-looking machine in the brothers' style. Its first challenge to Ferrari was in the Italian Grand Prix at Monza on 16 September 1951. Although OSCA had hoped to have both cars ready, one to be a works entry for French veteran Louis Chiron,

When Franco Rol's Type G OSCA was fielded at Turin in April 1952 it was seen to have revised cam-box breathers and a ram-air plenum atop its carburettors. The output had been tweaked to 320 horsepower.

only customer Rol's was raceworthy. Qualified by the gentleman driver a quarter-minute off the pace, it trailed the field to finish ninth and last, 13 laps behind the winning Ferrari and unclassified.

Overhauled, with an airbox above its carburettors and a concave grille, Rol's Type G appeared at Turin for a 156-mile race on 6 April 1952. Piotti's car was entered as well but failed to arrive. From his third-row grid position Franco Rol made a hesitant start and pulled into his pit at the end of a single lap. With the diagnosis of a blown gasket the OSCA was retired.

At Turin Ferraris filled the first five places while Britain's BRM, from which so much was expected, failed to arrive. Nor was the new arrival from OSCA terribly convincing. With Alfa Romeo's withdrawal this shortage of rivals for Ferrari sounded the death knell for the current Formula 1, which had been expected – also by the Maserati brothers – to continue through 1953. Instead championship races for the next two years were run to the 2.0-litre Formula 2.

This was the downbeat conclusion to the Maserati brothers' effort to offer a fresh challenge to historic rival Ferrari.[3] 'It still needed refinement,'

---

3 Both Grand Prix chassis were later rebodied as sports cars, with compression ratios lowered to 8.0:1 and developing 220–240bhp at 5,500rpm on petrol. However, neither was destined to find a buyer who had the wherewithal to complete the development and race preparation of these elaborate cars. The owner of one was Turin's Paolo Cordero di Montezemolo. His nephew, Luca Cordero di Montezemolo, rose to head Ferrari, Maserati and ultimately the Fiat Group in the 21st century.

said Ernesto Maserati of his creation. 'We had spent a fortune on it. We couldn't afford to go on and it just stood. There wasn't the ten million lire to do the job!' This was equivalent to $16,000, not far short of the subsidy that Enzo Ferrari had negotiated from Pirelli for his 4½-litre V12.

'There have been so many projects the successful outcome of which I've been positive,' Ernesto told Griff Borgeson, referring to the Type G. 'But this was at a time when we could do well with 1100s, 1300s and 1400s. We could make money building them and we concentrated on them. We're not terribly full of drive and also we have lacked the material resources, the money. Perhaps we did very wrong.' Resource-constrained though the Maserati brothers were, they would shift gears and offer a challenge to Ferrari in the fertile new field of Formula 2.

For 1952 the Maserati brothers revised Franco Rol's Type G with a concave grille. In its last race, however, on 6 April at Turin, the biggest-ever OSCA retired soon after the start with a failed head gasket.

In its final 1952 guise, as raced that year at Turin, shown, and Indianapolis, the Ferrari 375 F1 was a formidable machine, pictured by Mailander with Ascari driving. After the de facto expiration of the then-current Formula 1, neither it nor the Type G OSCA had many places to play.

CHAPTER FIVE

500 F2 vs A6GCM

The rivalry between Ferrari and Maserati intensified in 1952 and '53 when the World Championship was run to Formula 2. Led respectively by Alberto Ascari and Juan Manuel Fangio, the two factory teams were at each other's throats.

Statistics say that in the Grand Prix seasons of 1952 and '53 Ferrari and Alberto Ascari were the dominant forces, winning two driver World Championships. Ascari won an incredible seven championship GPs in a row, indeed nine if we overlook Indianapolis, which in those days counted for world points. But chasing them every kilometre of the way was Modena neighbour Maserati, which started slowly in 1952 but then accelerated strongly into the 1953 season, which it ended with a famously stunning victory for Fangio. Between them, excepting occasional interference from France's

In one of history's most exciting Grands Prix, at Reims on 5 July 1953, the Ferrari of Mike Hawthorn (16) staged a race-long battle with the Maserati of Juan Fangio (18). The bow-tie-wearing Englishman won by a one-second margin.

Fangio's Maserati, leading Hawthorn's Ferrari at the Nürburgring on 2 August 1953, typified the intensity of the Red-Hot Rivalry during the two years when the World Championship was fought with Formula 2 cars. They finished second and third in the order shown.

Gordini, the two Italians dominated those dramatic years.

Through 1951, prematurely the final year of the original post-war Formula 1 for 1½-litre supercharged cars and 4½-litre unblown engines, both Maserati and Ferrari were competitors in the lesser category, Formula 2, for 2.0-litre unsupercharged cars. While Ferrari took the category seriously, with its V12 engine installed in a proper single-seater chassis, Maserati drivers

had to make do with the A6GCS, a cycle-winged sports-racer that could and did also compete as a stripped racing car. The Maserati's engine showed promise, however. It was an in-line six with inclined overhead valves operated by a single overhead camshaft through rocker arms, a design originated during the war by Ernesto Maserati.

In 1949 the Argentine Auto Club's entries of 4CLT/48 Maseratis in Europe had relished success

In his home Grand Prix at Bern, Switzerland, on 18 May 1952, Toulo de Graffenried took his Maserati-Platé to a sixth-place finish, four laps in arrears. Its origins as a shortened and lightened Type 4CLT/48 were evident.

in the absence of Alfa Romeo, which had taken that season off. In 1950 Alfa returned and snapped up the Argentines' best driver, Juan Fangio. Looking to Formula 2 for a more amenable arena, as previously related the South Americans decided to marry the A6GCS engine with one of their 4CLT/48 Grand Prix cars.

Implemented by Maserati, the swap was impressively easy. The 2.0-litre six with its three twin-throat Weber carburettors plugged neatly into the space left by the supercharged 1½-litre four. Ferrari had done much the same thing in creating its 2.0-litre V12 single-seater, the 166 C that continued to carry the company's banner through 1951.

In Argentine blue and yellow the 2.0-litre Maserati first appeared at the tight 0.8-mile street circuit at Angouleme in France for a 104-mile race on 11 June 1950. It looked much like a 4CLT/48 save for an oval aperture in its grille to accommodate the six's different starter-shaft position (see page 58). Juan Fangio took it to victory ahead of a Gordini and Ferrari at an average speed of only 43.2mph, so tortuous was the track's layout.

At Reims in early July, Froilan González practised with it for a Formula 2 race but chose the team's Ferrari instead. Fellow Argentine Roberto Mieres took the handsome hybrid to fourth place at Geneva at the end of July, behind two Gordinis and a Ferrari. Fangio practised with it at the subsequent German Grand Prix but had to withdraw when its

cylinder block cracked during practice. This unique car wasn't seen again.

Maserati's 4CLT/48 figured in 1952's Formula 2 racing thanks to an initiative taken by Milan's Enrico Platé. Realising that 2.0-litres are not that much different to 1.5, Platé enlisted Maserati's help in enlarging the four four-valve cylinders of his cars with new blocks and crankshafts to increase both bore and stroke. By removing the bulky superchargers he was

Maserati's own creation for the 1952 Formula 2 was the A6GCM single-seater, its twin-cam engine offset slightly to the left to make room for the carburettors and magneto. Its grille continued the traditional contours.

Preparation at the Viale Ciro Menotti showed the tail-mounted fuel tank and tubular bracing of the ladder-type frame of the 1952 A6GCM. In addition to selling its cars, Maserati entered Formula 2 races as a works team from mid-1952.

able to shorten the chassis by 8in and lighten the cars proportionally.

Swiss 'Toulo' de Graffenried and Franco-American Harry Schell were among those who pedalled the Maserati-Platés in the 1952 season, mainly in minor events in which they had a chance to figure when the factory teams were absent. Their nine entries in championship races in 1952 garnered no points at all.

In 1953 Enrico Platé would become a customer for a new Formula 2 car from the Maserati factory, the A6GCM. Its name signified its derivation from the dual-purpose A6GCS, now with 'M' for *monoposto* or single-seater to show that it was a dedicated racing car. Work on it began during the 1950–1 winter under the direction of Vittorio Bellentani to the designs of Alberto Massimino.

At first the A6GCM used the single-cam engine of the A6GCS, from which it also borrowed its coil-sprung parallel-wishbone front suspension.

In Maserati *monoposto* tradition its steering box was atop the clutch housing, operating the linkage through a drag link along the right side of the engine.

A new narrower chassis frame was made, based on twin tubes with a modest superstructure. At the rear a solid axle was located by a radius rod above a trailing quarter-elliptic spring at each side. Like that of the 4CLT/48, though lighter, the live rear axle had a set of step-up gears at the input to its pinion to lower the propeller shaft and, accordingly, the driver. Rolling on 15in Borrani wires, the prototype was bodied by Medardo Fantuzzi with lines that were close kin to those of the 4CLT/48, albeit with a more pear-shaped grille.

These weren't easy times for Maserati, which was still struggling to regain momentum after the forced closing of its factory for much of 1949. Its Formula 1 cars were no longer in demand; its road-car programme was at a standstill; and a big

effort to make two eight-cylinder cars for Indianapolis had foundered when the cars failed to be ready in time. Thus the Orsi family, father and son, weren't in a position to force the pace of the new car's development. The first A6GCM came together in the spring of 1951 and was tested at the Modena Aerautodromo in July by the faithful Guerino Bertocchi and then at Monza by Felice Bonetto. The single-cam engine was used until the car's pukka power unit was ready.

Alberto Massimino was the original author of the twin-cam engine that powered the A6GCM. He based it on the block of the A6GCS, shortening its stroke by 1mm and increasing its bore to dimensions of 72.6 x 80mm for 1,954cc. In retaining a relatively long stroke Massimino had the support of Maserati's Bellentani. Thus maximum-power revs were increased only slightly from those of the A6GCS to 6,500, at which the six developed 160bhp on the alcohol fuel that was compatible with its high 13.5:1 compression ratio. Its mixture was fed by triple Weber 38 DCO3 carburettors.

Cast of aluminium, the engine's block had dry cast-iron cylinder liners. In the hemispherical combustion chambers of the new aluminium head Massimino inclined the inlet valves at 36° and the exhausts at 41°, opening them through finger-type followers. A train of gears up the front of the block drove the twin camshafts, with pairs of gears at the top helping to keep the engine's profile low. Inclined at the front was a magneto to fire the spark plugs. Retained was the robust bottom end with its seven main bearings, newly equipped with dry-sump lubrication. Power was delivered through a multi-disc clutch and four-speed transmission.

After further tests, two of these first full A6GCMs were built and sold to the Brazilian Escuderia Bandeirantes, which entered them in the winter season or *Temporada* of free-formula races in Brazil and Argentina. Nominated by Maserati to demonstrate its new model was motorcycle star Nello Pagani, who had scored some successes for the Trident in the 1940s. Pagani and the underdeveloped A6GCM were not at their best in South America, however. Their best result was fourth on 20 January 1952 at Rio's Gavea circuit, where Pagani was relieved by Felice Bonetto. Neither car nor driver figured well in the rest of the *Temporada*, the Argentine end of which was held on the just-inaugurated road circuit at Buenos Aires.

The South American races were dominated by supercharged 2.0-litre V12 Ferraris, which were only eligible to compete there because the events were open to all comers regardless of capacity or supercharging. Minus its blower, the basic car

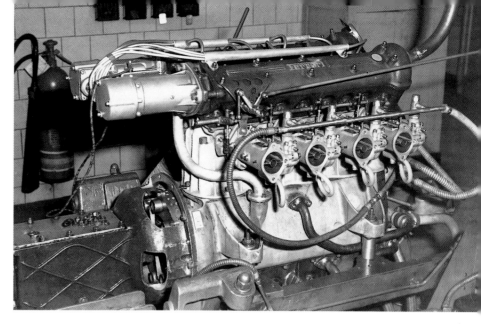

closely resembled the V12 Formula 2 cars that Ferrari had been racing through the 1951 season. For that year's final continental F2 race, at Modena on 23 September, five such Ferraris appeared. Four of them were entered by the team of the Marzotto brothers, wealthy textile producers who were entitled to feel that they had acquired some very quick equipment from Maranello. Even with Froilan González in one of their cars, however, their V12s were beaten by a full lap by a new Ferrari driven by Alberto Ascari. A new era in Formula 2 racing had begun.

Ascari's dominant performance traced its origins back to a Sunday in early June of 1951. Ferrari technical director Aurelio Lampredi was in his office at Maranello, as usual, when Enzo Ferrari made up his mind. The two men had been debating the sort of power unit to build for the coming 1954 Formula 1, which permitted 2½-litre unsupercharged engines. It could serve, in the meantime, as a 2.0-litre F2 unit. They had considered uprating to

Pictured on the Maranello test bench by Rudy Mailander in February 1952, Ferrari's new four was the work of Aurelio Lampredi. In this early version the twin magnetos for dual ignition were camshaft-driven.

Giovanni Cavara's cutaway of Ferrari's 500 F2 four showed its hairpin valve springs, wet cylinder liners screwed into the head and piping to scavenge its dry sump. This late version had front-mounted magnetos.

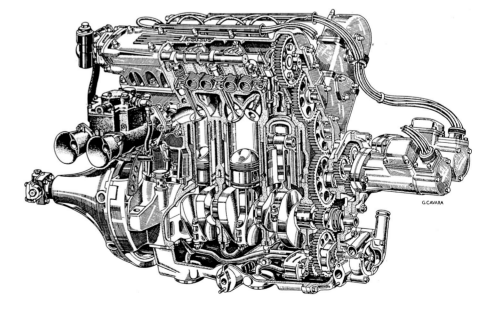

G.CAVARA

2.0-litres their failed supercharged 1½-litre four-cam V12, the work of Lampredi's predecessor Gioachino Colombo. Indeed, they had built and tested such an engine. But this was a weighty solution when lightness and agility were needed. In 1950 John Heath's Alta-engined HWMs had pressed the works team of 2.0-litre Ferrari V12s and had done so with only four cylinders.

Enzo Ferrari appreciated that a four-cylinder engine had torque and weight characteristics that were well suited to the twisty circuits that predominated in European racing. For Ferrari this was a daring concept after the success he'd enjoyed with his twelves. He was well aware that arch-rivals Maserati were developing a six-cylinder engine with a similar aim in view. After mulling it over Ferrari plumped for a four, as he told Lampredi that June morning. The engineer forgot his plans for the Sabbath afternoon. He reached for T-square and triangle and in a few hours had sketched the essentials of the Type 500, destined to be one of Ferrari's most successful engines.

Some have described the 500 as a 'simple' engine. It was anything but. Lampredi lavished all his skill and ingenuity on this, the first Ferrari power unit he designed from scratch. He had been responsible for the unsupercharged 4½-litre F1 engine of 1950–1, but that was a continuation of Colombo's V12 concept and, to boot, also served as a production-car engine. In contrast, he said, 'the 500 was born as a racing car. I did everything possible to improve the engine's design.' It was simple solely in that it had only four cylinders.

The 500's cylinder-head construction unified its head and block in an aluminium alloy casting that extended downward three-quarters of the length of the cylinder. Screwed into this head/block unit, reaching right up to its combustion chambers, were four cast-iron wet cylinders. For the Formula 2 unit Lampredi specified a bore and stroke of 90 x 78mm to give 1,985cc. He disposed the stems of

the two valves per cylinder equally at an included angle of 58°.

Carried over from other Ferrari engines were hairpin-type valve springs, which permitted short and light valves. Above each valve was a steel-tipped light alloy follower with a circular top, into which was set a large-diameter roller. Pressing up against this circular top were two relatively light concentric coil springs whose only task was to keep the roller in steady contact with its cam lobe. The

function of controlling the follower was separated from that of closing the valve.

Each cam follower slid in a thin-wall iron guide which stabilised both its circular top and its stem, into which a hollow steel tip was inserted at the point of contact with the valve stem. The iron guides in turn were set into a magnesium tappet and cam carrier that was bolted to the head.

Attached to the front of the block and crankcase was an aluminium alloy cover which supported the

In his Starlet the star of the 1952 season, Alberto Ascari, showed his class at Silverstone on 19 July 1952 by winning the British Grand Prix with a lap in hand over team-mate Taruffi. The works Maseratis weren't yet ready to respond.

outer ball bearings of the gear drive to the camshafts. The gears were strikingly thin and light to minimise space, weight and rotating mass. Initially the twin Marelli magnetos for the 500's dual ignition were driven from the backs of the camshafts and protruded through the firewall into the cockpit. During 1952 they were relocated to the front of the engine and given their own drive from a gear turned by the crank nose.

The magnetos were an Achilles' heel of the engine, Lampredi said: 'I always used to tell the drivers they could do what they liked with the gears, because no matter what happened the engine would not break. They couldn't rev the engine above 7,500–7,800rpm even when going flat out because of the poor ignition.' Assisting this unburstability was the dry-sump lubrication system built into the engine's separate barrel-shaped crankcase with its five main bearings and rugged steel crankshaft.

During the 1952 season, when the new four developed 165bhp at 7,000rpm, it breathed through four single-throat Weber 45 DOE carburettors. In 1953 twin-throat Weber 50 DCOA carburettors were used. With these, by the end of 1953 the Type 500 (named for the capacity in cubic centimetres of one of its cylinders) produced 185bhp at 7,500rpm on methanol-based Shell Super F fuel with a compression ratio of 13.0:1. Peak torque was an excellent 152lb-ft at 5,700rpm.

As in the V12 Formula 2 Ferraris, the drive went at engine speed to a rear-mounted transaxle under the driver's seat, to the left of which was a gated shift lever for four forward speeds. Behind the differential ran a de Dion tube joining the rear hubs together. It was guided laterally by a frame-mounted vertical slide at its centre and in the fore-and-aft plane by parallel radius rods at each side, as on the bigger 4½-litre F1 Ferraris of 1951. At both front and rear Lampredi sprung with transverse leafs which were carried by two pairs of rollers in such a way that the springs gave an inherent anti-roll effect.

Inherited from the 4½-litre Formula 1 Ferrari of 1951 were new drum brakes designed by Aurelio Lampredi that had a central pivot for each shoe. Instead of being fixed, the pivot acted as an abutment against which the shoe was pressed when the brakes were applied. Each shoe was applied to the drum at both ends by a double-ended hydraulic cylinder. The design's effect was to provide a balanced brake performance, because one part of each shoe was leading and the other part was trailing. It proved to be a stable and consistently powerful brake.

Thus both rivals had new equipment ready for the 1952 Formula 2 season – Ferrari rather more ready than Maserati. For both, the shape of the 1952 season was a surprise. Despairing of being able to assemble decent fields for the then-

current Formula 1, race organisers turned to Formula 2 instead. With the blessing of the international authorities, the World Championships were decided with Formula 2 cars, a status that prevailed during both 1952 and '53. To add to the fun, in 1952 France's race organisers assembled a national Formula 2 championship – to the benefit, they hoped, of their national champion Gordini.

The French were destined to be disappointed, for both 1952 championships were swept by the Type 500 F2 Ferraris. To the surprise of many, who expected the four-cylinder cars to be used only on twisty low-speed tracks, Ferrari parked his V12s in favour of his new fours. For the first World-Championship event, the Swiss GP at Bern on 18 May, two Maseratis were entered for Fangio and González but failed to arrive. Three weeks later, for the non-championship Monza Grand Prix – virtually a command performance – no fewer than five A6GCMs were mustered to face an equal number of four-cylinder Ferraris. While two Maseratis were the cars of the Brazilian Escuderia Bandeirantes, three were sparkling new works machines from Modena assigned to Fangio, González and Bonetto.

Over two hard-fought high-speed heats at Monza totalling 274 miles the Ferraris were dominant, as they would be throughout 1952. The new Maseratis showed their speed, with González

starring before retiring in the first heat and Bonetto running third in the final heat before retiring only a few laps from the flag. Most catastrophically the reigning World Champion, Juan Fangio, crashed on his second lap and suffered a spinal injury severe enough to sideline him for the rest of the season. He'd started from the back of the field after arriving too late to practise, having driven all night from a race in Northern Ireland the previous day. The loss of Fangio's skills was a mortal blow to Maserati's hopes for 1952.

The meticulous craftsmanship of the Maserati brothers was evident in the chassis of their Type F2 OSCA with its coil-spring front suspension and robust twin-tube ladder frame. This was their second car, readied for the 1953 season.

In the Italian Grand Prix at Monza on 7 September 1952 the A6GCM Maserati of Froilan González put the wind up the Ferraris by leading with a part-filled fuel tank, sharing fastest lap with Alberto Ascari and finishing second.

The works Ferraris had a dramatic new look at Monza. Hitherto Maranello's racers had the same distinctive 'egg-crate' or 'chip-cutter' grille as the road cars, a powerful identifying characteristic of the Ferrari automobile. This was still a feature of the first 1952 Type 500 F2s, although their noses were shaped like large open air scoops, within which egg-crate grilles were recessed. Ferrari dropped the other shoe at Monza. There, in a longer and more rounded nose, the latest 500 F2 had a fully open air inlet, an air scoop that would

not have looked out of place on a jet fighter. Instantly every other car – including the A6GCM – looked antiquated.

While the Brazilian sixes made some appearances in the French events and the British Grand Prix, the first works Maserati entry in a 1952 World-Championship race came at the Nürburgring on 3 August for the German Grand Prix. It was a solo entry for Felice Bonetto, whose car's power was quoted as 158bhp. Bonetto started from the third row but suffered a broken rear-spring hanger and spun on his first lap. He was disqualified for receiving outside assistance in getting started. Ferraris filled the first four places at the finish.

A week later at St Gaudens in France both Ferrari and the Brazilian Maseratis arrived for the three-hour Comminges Grand Prix to find a first appearance by a third party to the Red-Hot Rivalry. Marseilles-based Elie Bayol, a reliable OSCA exponent, fired up the latest creation of the Maserati brothers. One of the prettiest Formula 2 cars, it was powered by an in-line six of 1,987cc (76 x 73mm) that was an extrapolation of the successful OSCA twin-cam fours. Credited with 160bhp at 6,500rpm, the six drove through a rear-mounted transaxle akin to that of the 4½-litre Type G. Inboard mounting of its rear brake drums and location of the de Dion tube by lower quarter-elliptic leafs and upper radius rods suggested that the Maseratis had taken a good gander at the previous season's British HWM-Altas.

Trimly bodied and OSCA-grilled, this was rated one of the lighter Formula 2 contenders. At St

Early 1953 found Louis Chiron testing his unpainted OSCA F2 in a private session organised by the Maserati brothers. For the new season, inboard rear brakes were moved outboard on both OSCAs.

Gaudens Bayol it qualified well, only half a second off Nino Farina's pace in a Ferrari. He was running a strong third in the race, mixing it with the works Ferraris, when a pit stop for fuel was needed. A struggle in restarting led to a disqualification from seventh place. Nevertheless it was an impressive debut for OSCA in the hands of a newcomer to Grand Prix racing.

On 7 September the Red-Hot Rivals were out in force for the Italian Grand Prix, to be contested over 313 miles at Monza. Escuderia Bandeirantes now had three cars, driven by Heitel Cantoni, Gino Bianco and veteran Francisco 'Chico' Landi. Landi placed eighth and Cantoni 11th while Bianco retired. Maserati nominated a customer, former OSCA racer Franco Rol, plus González and Bonetto. Ferrari's flag was carried by regulars Alberto Ascari, Nino Farina, Gigi Villoresi and Piero Taruffi, plus Frenchman André Simon. Also present was the Formula 2 OSCA, which Bayol qualified on the heels of the works cars, only to retire with gearbox trouble after the first lap.

While the Ferraris ran non-stop as usual, Maserati decided on mid-race refuelling to allow its cars to start with less of an alcohol-based fuel that provided more power at the price of a higher thirst. This saw the feisty González leap into an early lead, which he held until his mid-race stop. After a (too long) 55-second stop he couldn't catch Ascari, who won with a minute's advantage. Significant, however, was the fact that both drivers shared the fastest lap, set at 116.61mph. Bonetto was fifth, splitting the remaining Ferraris.

A new feature of the A6GCM at Monza had been dual ignition, with two spark plugs in each cylinder.

A second magneto was driven from the back of the exhaust camshaft to double up the spark supply. This provided better ignition with the larger cylinder bore of 75mm, matched with the shorter stroke of 75mm – a 'square' engine. Maximum-power revs were now 7,300 and output was creeping up to the 170bhp level.

After the exciting battle at Monza, expectations were high for the 143-mile Modena Grand Prix on the following weekend. Ferrari had been unopposed by Maserati the year before, but this

time two of the Brazilian team's cars were entered plus two of the latest works sixes for González and Bonetto. The Trident's forces were slashed in half when Bonetto's car, being driven from the factory to the circuit for the race, lost a core plug from its cylinder-block casting and couldn't start. Lined up against the lonely González were Ascari, Villoresi, Farina and Sergio Sighinolfi, with Ascari starting from pole – as usual.

All Modena took sides for one or the other hometown team. Sixty thousand Emilians, each shouting for his favourite, packed the stands along the perimeter road of the combined race track and airport only a mile west of the centre of Modena. They were surprised by two early developments: a quick dash to the pits by González to have a radiator blanking plate removed and the retirement of the highly favoured Ascari. This left Gigi Villoresi to defend the Prancing Horse against González, who was back in the fray in spite of a missing third gear.

'The 60,000 spectators were on their feet shrieking advice,' reported *Autocourse*, as the combatants started on the last ten of 100 laps. Balked by a slower car on his penultimate lap, González was overtaken by Villoresi, who clung to his lead and crossed the line a fraction ahead of the Maserati. 'At that very moment,' said *Autocourse*, 'Lampredi, who had been subjected to much nerve strain during the race, fainted in

the pit.' Both cars and drivers were credited with exactly the same time for the race and both shared the fastest lap. González – considered by many the moral victor – had stayed in the running in spite of having to rev his Maserati to 8,600rpm to bridge his missing third gear. Elie Bayol calmly motored home sixth in his OSCA.

This dramatic ending to the season gave Modena's bench racers plenty to gossip about during the winter. The Ferrari-Maserati rivalry had been brought to thrilling fruition. After the Modena race Enzo Ferrari was quoted as being 'happy about this competition, which made racing more attractive to him and which would urge him to begin gaining practical experience now for the new Formula.' Gigi Villoresi would later remark that this victory marked the one and only time that he was thanked by Ferrari for his efforts on his behalf. Beating a hometown rival at the very gates of Modena – that was a success worth a compliment.

Ferrari's domination of 1952 was shown by Paul Sheldon's calculation of a putative World Championship of makes for the seven qualifying races, which put Ferrari first with 36 points ahead of Gordini with 16, Cooper-Bristols with 12 and Maserati with 6.5, the half-point coming from the shared fastest lap at Monza.

For 1953 the Type 500 F2 required only an overhaul and an increase in its rev limit and power. In contrast, the evolution of Maserati's cars for the

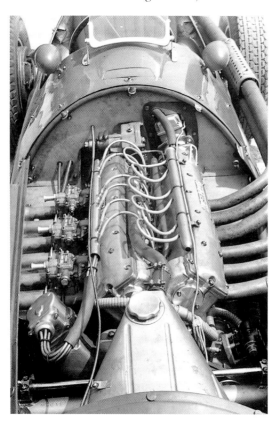

New since the 1952 Italian GP was dual ignition for Maserati's six, which was given more oversquare internals by Gioachino Colombo for the 1953 season. It enjoyed a slight power advantage over Ferrari's four.

The new front brakes for the 1953 edition of Maserati's A6GCM had radial finning designed to centrifuge warm air from the interior of the drum. Anti-roll bars were fitted at both front and rear.

new season was tortuous. Maserati's racing cars received a strong impulse from the arrival in Viale Ciro Menotti in October 1952 of one of the era's outstanding engineers, Gioachino Colombo. A Milanese, Colombo had long been associated with Alfa Romeo, from whom he made a detour after the war to create the first V12 Ferrari. His engagement by Maserati was welcomed by the returning Juan Fangio, who had seen the difference that Colombo made at Alfa Romeo when he returned to that team for 1951.

Colombo found new bodies under construction for A6GCMs that were essentially the 1952 Monza/Modena cars cleaned up. They were rebodied along similar lines and had new bigger radial-finned front brakes, which he was happy to retain. Cars of this type were taken to Argentina for that country's first points-qualifying Grand Prix on 18 January 1953. Ferrari's four-car team was much as before, although Briton Mike Hawthorn had now joined in place of Taruffi. Fangio, González and Bonetto made a strong Maserati entry, with Argentine star Oscar Galvez in a fourth car. Ferrari finished one-two-four, with the inevitable Ascari winning, while Maseratis were third and fifth.

For the first European Formula 2 race of 1953 on 22 March, Ferrari sent two works cars to Syracuse in Sicily. There they encountered privateers that included Louis Chiron in his new blue OSCA. Although born in 1899, the genial French ace still enjoyed the thrill of the chase. His car was akin to Bayol's, although with its rear brakes mounted outboard, a change also made on the earlier OSCA. When all three works Ferraris broke at Syracuse he finished a delighted second, albeit three laps behind a Platé-stable Maserati.

On 6 April both OSCAs were at Pau where they placed fourth and sixth, Bayol ahead of Chiron, behind two Ferraris and a Gordini. The 3rd of May found them on Bordeaux's street circuit with Chiron well qualified in the second row of the grid. He was disqualified for a push start while Bayol placed fifth behind two Ferraris and two Gordinis. A week later Chiron was on the front row of the grid for his heat at Silverstone and placed fifth, only to suffer fuel-tank problems in the International Trophy final. On 16 May he was fifth in the final of the Ulster Trophy, won by Mike Hawthorn's works Ferrari.

Step-up gears in the nose of the 1953 Maserati A6GCM's differential lowered its drive-shaft line to reduce the driver's seating height. Parallel radius rods and A-arm under the centre section guided its live rear axle.

One of Giovanni Cavara's finest cutaways showed the internals of the 1953 Maserati A6GCM with its engine-mounted gearbox shifted by a left-hand lever working through a pivoted rocker arm. Brake air scoops were still like those of the 4CLT/48.

G.CAVARA

Against the works Maserati of Onofre Marimon and the private Type 500 F2 Ferrari of Louis Rosier the OSCA of Elie Bayol pulled off an overall win in the two-heat race at Aix-les-Bains on 26 July. Marimon obliged him by spinning off the circuit while Rosier couldn't match the OSCA's speed. It was Chiron's turn to shine at Sables d'Olonne on 9 August, placing second to Rosier in a two-heat race. These were 1953's high points for the Bologna-built cars. For the Italian GP Bayol's engine had the update of a twin-plug cylinder head but retired, while Chiron finished tenth.

Meanwhile in Modena the Orsis were committing more of their resources to their racing cars. A restructuring of their businesses saw electrical-equipment activity hived off to other family members while Adolfo Orsi and his son Omer took full possession of the auto factory and its associated machine-tool production. With Omer's enthusiastic backing, staunchly supported by Vittorio Bellentani, Gioachino Colombo revised the A6GCMs from stem to stern for the European season.

The Milanese engineer further enlarged the six's bore to 76.2mm and shortened its stroke to 72mm for a capacity of 1,988cc. Still using dry cast-iron cylinder liners in an aluminium block, this bigger bore meant that the cylinders had to be siamesed – no cooling water could run between them. Equipped with larger valves and uprated to triple Weber 40 DCO3 twin-throat carburettors, the six was now credited with 190bhp at 8,000rpm on alcohol-based fuel, a five-horse advantage over the rival Ferrari.

Maserati's six continued to drive through a four-speed box in unit with the engine. While still based on twin tubes, the frame was revised with a more efficient upper structure. Cockpit sides were raised to envelop the driver better while handsome bodywork by Fantuzzi tapered forward to a new oval interpretation of the Maserati grille.

Although the 153-mile Naples Grand Prix on 10 May had a scanty entry of only eight cars, two were of great significance as the first appearance of the definitive 1953 A6GCM. Ascari, Farina, Villoresi and Lampredi clustered around the handsome new cars to ascertain their secrets. In the race Ascari was delayed by throttle problems and Fangio led before Farina forced his way past to claim victory ahead of the Argentine, with his team-mate González third.

The Ferrari's excellence and the Maserati's improvement set the stage for some classic battles

Poised for testing at Modena, the 1953 Type A6GCM Maserati cut a handsome figure with its Fantuzzi bodywork and new interpretation of the Trident grille. The driver enjoyed improved cockpit enclosure.

during the 1953 season. In these Maserati was again disadvantaged by the loss of a key driver: González suffered a fractured vertebra in practice for a sports-car race at Lisbon that knocked him out from August to the end of the year. A newcomer to the team was talented young Argentine Onofre Marimon. Facing them was the Ascari-Farina-Villoresi triumvirate with the addition of a talented Ferrari debutant, Mike Hawthorn. With Juan Fangio and the doughty Felice Bonetto

on the Maserati roster, the strength in depth of both squads ensured that their machinery would show to best advantage.

The record shows that Ferrari held the upper hand over the eight World-Championship races of 1953. The cars from Maranello won all but the final race at Monza, where Fangio seized the victory in dramatic circumstances. The 500 F2 took Alberto Ascari to his second title with 34.5 points (fastest lap shared with González at

At the Nürburgring for the 1953 German GP on 2 August, Maranello's entries posed for Rudy Mailander. The Type 500 F2 of Nino Farina (front) was the race winner with a one-minute margin ahead of Fangio's Maserati.

Replacing the stub exhausts used in 1952 was a scavenging exhaust system for the Ferrari Type 500 F2 in 1953. Instead of the previous individual Weber carburettors the four was now fed by two twin-throat Webers.

A frequent sight in 1953 was a victorious Alberto Ascari, crossing the line in his Ferrari, as here at Buenos Aires on 18 January. That season he won his second consecutive World Championship.

Silverstone) against 28 for Juan Fangio. Had there been a makes championship, Ferrari would have won with 36 points to Maserati's 27, leaving a paltry four for Gordini and nil for OSCA. Including non-championship races, the Ferrari Type 500 F2 won 32 of its 35 starts in 1952–3 – a phenomenal record of success.

In 1953 Maserati kept Maranello honest by seizing pole position for the races in Belgium and Switzerland and recording fastest lap in Belgium,

France, Britain (shared) and Italy. In fact, the Trident gave the Prancing Horse a wake-up poke in the first European event of the season, a 268-mile non-championship race at Syracuse in Sicily. Four works Ferraris easily dominated until – *mirabile dictu* – they all retired. This was one occasion on which Aurelio Lampredi's unofficial rev-limiting system (the shortcoming of his magnetos) failed to prevent engine damage. The delighted winner was Toulo de Graffenried in Enrico Platé's A6GCM

Maserati, followed in second place by Louis Chiron's OSCA.

Two weeks later, on 6 April, the genial de Graffenried won a 17-mile sprint race at England's Goodwood, and on 9 May he won his 42-mile heat at Silverstone's International Trophy races but withdrew from the final in a huff when he was penalised for jumping the start. On 31 May de Graffenried and the A6GCM were winners again in a wet race at the Nürburgring, the 96-mile Eifelrennen. His private Maserati bested the private Ferrari of Kurt Adolff, which finished fourth.

Although fast, the Maseratis were also more fragile than the Ferraris, especially in their vulnerable rear suspension and axles. The live axle, with its high unsprung weight in relation to the light A6GCM, made it a handling handful on less-smooth tracks. Nevertheless on the demanding Spa road circuit in Belgium Fangio put his car on pole, with Ascari and team-mate González alongside. The two Argentines dominated the early running but their cars failed before one third distance.

On the ultra-fast Reims road course on 5 July the two Emilian teams staged a staggering battle of speed and endurance that left onlookers gasping for adjectives. From mid-race to the finish the protagonists were Juan Fangio for Maserati and Mike Hawthorn for Ferrari, passing and repassing not more than a second apart to the end of the 311-mile race, when the Briton was the winner by only one second while González in a Maserati was

1.6 seconds behind the winner. These cars and drivers, wrote Rodney Walkerley, 'gave the shouting spectators what is probably the finest Grand Prix ever run anywhere any time. Fangio tried every trick in the bag but Hawthorn remained quite undaunted and now and then pulled one on Fangio with the utmost goodwill.'

The dramatic Reims race was clear warning – should it be needed – to Ferrari that the boys downtown in Modena were catching up. This was

Wearing a flat cap, Guerino Bertocchi helped push the A6GCM of Froilan González to the grid for the British GP on 18 July 1953. Behind Bertocchi (in sunglasses) was Omer Orsi, who witnessed his car's run to fourth place.

Until his blue and yellow Maserati retired with a fatigued engine, Argentina's Onofre Marimon, leading here, battled fiercely with the Ferrari of Nino Farina in the 1953 British GP at Silverstone. Farina placed third.

Although Ascari was on pole for the 1953 German Grand Prix on 2 August, Fangio's Maserati led into the first turn. Behind Ascari was Hawthorn's Ferrari and the Maseratis of Marimon and Bonetto. Modena ruled the roost.

In the 1953 Swiss GP on 23 August, Fangio put his Maserati on pole and led from the start. Behind him were the Ferraris of Ascari (46), Hawthorn (26) and Villoresi (28) and the Maserati of Marimon (36). In spite of stopping for a change of plugs Ascari was the winner.

the intense character of the 1953 season, which Enzo Ferrari's later secretary Franco Gozzi called 'tenacious and tough'. That Grand Prix year featured many worthy competitors, he recalled, 'but the two giants were Ferrari and Maserati. It was they who were always in the limelight, alternating in the roles of protagonist and antagonist. They were the ones who unleashed the passion of the

fans, then more than at any other time divided in their relentless, fractious duelling.'

Thus expectations were at fever pitch for the final points race of 1953 at Monza on 13 September. Preparing for this vital showdown, Vittorio Bellentani asked young engineer Valerio Colotti, newly arrived from Ferrari, to locate the troublesome live rear axle more precisely. In his

new layout parallel radius rods guided each hub, freeing the leaf springs of any locating function. Lateral guidance was by a wide-based A-arm under the axle, assuring a low rear roll centre for this final version of the A6GCM.

On the fast Monza track, where slipstreaming was standard operating procedure, the Ferraris and Maseratis travelled like a close-coupled train with cars constantly swapping positions. Near the finish the disputants were Ascari and Farina for Ferrari – both craving the prestigious home-country win – and Fangio for Maserati. They were only wheel-widths apart. On the last turn of the last lap Ascari was leading when the flying group encountered a slower Maserati. It was squarely in their way.

'I decided to throw myself toward the outside of the track,' said Ascari. 'The opening was very narrow. In a flash I saw clearly that I would not succeed in passing. But I wanted to risk it in spite of everything. When you race 500km as important as Monza and are so close to success it is impossible to hesitate in front of danger. It is perhaps a madness, a useless risk, but one feels the right and almost the duty to try. So at 105mph I attempted the narrow outside passage. The track was streaked with oil. My Ferrari skidded sideways. Farina, just behind me, braked and swerved. He lost precious time and Fangio, who was third, succeeded in sliding between us and winning.'

Slightly behind, Fangio's view was similar yet different: 'Ascari, who stood between me and the victory I needed so badly, took the final curve very sharply and his Ferrari did a half spin. He was hit by Marimon [in a lapped Maserati]. Farina, whom I had only just overtaken and was breathing down my neck, had to swerve to avoid hitting them. In that split second of danger I was through, winning literally in the 312th mile of a 312-mile race. There was such confusion when we crossed the line that the man didn't put down the chequered flag, so I did another lap with Farina behind me, but all the time I thought they had made a mistake. They say I was almost hysterical that day, and I'm not surprised, although as a rule I'm usually rather calm.'

Rodney Walkerley found Fangio 'dazed with his sudden and unexpected victory, quite unable to speak for emotion after a tremendously hard drive. Reims all over again, with added and undesirable drama in the fall of the curtain.' For the Maserati men it was vindication at last of their intense drive to tackle Ferrari, coming at the end of a gruelling season in the last Formula 2 race that counted for championship points.

Sulking, threatening to withdraw in 1954, Ferrari withheld his cars from the subsequent Modena GP, which was swept by Maserati. Though the Trident's fans had bragging rights for the winter season, they admitted that the Prancing Horse was likely to gallop back strongly in the new Formula 1. As Walkerley wrote after Monza, 'There is undoubtedly something about this motor racing.'

Changing their positions on every lap, this was the slipstreaming 'train' of Modena machinery leading the Italian Grand Prix on 13 September 1953. Here Fangio was ahead of Farina and Ascari and it was in this order that they were credited with the top three places. Marimon, trailing, was awarded 10th place.

CHAPTER SIX

500 Mondial vs A6GCS /2000

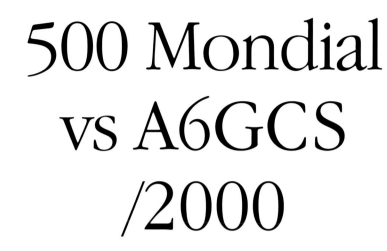

In the midst of the bitter rivalry between Ferrari and Maserati for the World Championship in 1953 with 2.0-litre racing cars, the Red-Hot Rivals squared off in sports-car racing as well. Both built real beauties.

In sports-car racing Ferrari had it all. In 1953 it shrugged off challenges from Jaguar, Aston Martin and Cunningham to win the first-ever instalment of the FIA's World Championship for sports cars. With its big 4½-litre sports-racers and a superb driver cadre Ferrari was king of the heavy metal. Maserati had nothing to offer in response. Indeed, in 1951 and '52 Ferraris were dominant in the popular sports 2.0-litre category as well, the

Italy's enthusiasm for racing 2.0-litre sports cars was exemplified by the all-red field for the inaugural race at Imola's new circuit on 20 June 1954. Umberto Maglioli won in his Mondial (36) with Luigi Musso (8) finishing third in a Maserati.

Pictured at Connecticut's Thompson Raceway on 1 November 1953, this Maserati was a transitional model with an engine of 1952 Formula 2 type in a chassis akin to that of the original A6GCS. It won two races there in the hands of Fritz Koster.

166 MM easily having the measure of the cycle-winged single-camshaft A6GCS.

But things were stirring on Modena's Viale Ciro Menotti. Having spun off the less-interesting parts of their mini-conglomerate, the Orsis began focusing on their auto business. The elements of a twin-cam 2.0-litre production car were laid down, with the potential to make Maserati a significant player in the road-car world for the first time. Also the skills of Alberto Massimino and Vittorio Bellentani gave Maserati a Formula 2 car which, in 1952, kept Ferrari and its new 500 F2 honest, although it was denied success in the World Championship races.

Because Massimino's 2.0-litre twin-cam engine for Formula 2 was derived from Maserati's single-cam six, the two units were interchangeable in one and the same chassis. In fact as we recall the Formula 2 car had first been tested with the single-cam six. Thus it was no great leap of imagination for the Maseratisti to install their F2 engines in A6GCS chassis.

At the end of 1952 they built several such cars, which were widened through the cockpit. Detuned from F2 specification to run on petrol instead of methanol, their engines developed 140bhp at 6,800rpm on an 8.5:1 compression ratio. Some had cycle wings while others were given wings which were faired back into the body. International sports-car rules had outlawed cycle wings and this was Maserati's first response.

Although a faired-wing car was publicised in early 1953 as the first of a new breed of sports Maseratis, especially by US importer Tony Pompeo, it was in fact a transitional machine.[1] Since October

of 1952 a new engineering breeze had been blowing through Maserati in the person of Gioachino Colombo, then a prematurely balding 40. Colombo had long been associated with Alfa Romeo, from whom he made a detour after the war to create the V12 Ferrari. He was with Alfa again in 1951 for Fangio's World Championship, and in 1952 when the Milan firm was exploring dramatic new ovoid cross-sectional shapes for sports-racing cars in co-operation with Carrozzeria Touring. The press dubbed these new-look cars *'Disco Volante'* or 'Flying Saucer' after their curvaceous aerodynamic lines.

Colombo's first priority was to deal with Maserati's Formula 2 car, giving its six-cylinder engine an update with improved combustion-chamber design and oversquare dimensions of 76.5 x 72mm for 1,986cc. Next, with Bellentani's help, he turned to the sports-racer. Interest in the 2.0-litre sports-car category was growing in the early 1950s, especially in Italy, at a time when arch-rival Ferrari was giving it less attention. The Trident's traditional customers were eagerly awaiting a new sports Maserati to take the place of the outdated A6GCS.

Although totally transformed the new car, too, would be an A6GCS – wonderfully sibilant in Italian as *'Aseigiciesse'*. This was the affectionate way Maserati's clients referred to it, although officially it was the A6GCS/2000 or, with a more commercial twist, the 'Sport 2000'. Totally transformed from its antecedent, it showed the influence of Colombo's

---

1 In the 1960s the author was the keeper of one of these interim cars.

*The original
A6GCS/2000 of early
1953 was a masterwork
of Italian design, its
Fantuzzi body
influenced by
Colombo's experience
with Disco Volante Alfa
Romeos. The grille was
a new interpretation
of the traditional
Maserati shape.*

experience with the Disco Volantes, especially in its deeply rounded central cross-section. Final refinements to the shape were made by Maserati's in-house craftsman, Medardo Fantuzzi, who built the first A6GCS/2000 bodies and many more until the job was taken over by Fiandri.

Panelled in aluminium, the result was one of the handsomest sports-racing cars of all time. Its hood sloped astonishingly low between upswept front wings to an oval grille which reinterpreted the Maserati theme with close-spaced vertical bars flanking a central divider. Later grilles would have a bold Trident at their centre. The early cars all had full Plexiglas windscreens, some with a sexy central dip that reflected the positions of driver and passenger. The dash panel was flat and plain, fitted above a cross tube that could intrude on thigh room in a cockpit that was tight for larger drivers. A spare wheel, under a deck lid, and fuel and oil tanks of 27½ and 5 gallons respectively filled the rear compartment.

Fabricated in Milan by Gilco after Maserati made the first ones, the A6GCS/2000's frame was a platform of steel tubes in which the driveline was placed centrally, not offset as it had been in the cycle-winged A6GCS. It was bridged by five crossmembers in all, that at the front being doubled to support the independent suspension. Carried over from the A6GCS, this used coils and unequal-length steel wishbones. New for a Maserati sports-racer was the fitting of anti-roll bars at both front and rear to permit tailoring of its handling.

Rear suspension was close kin to that of the Formula 2 Maserati. A live axle was located by two upper trailing radius rods and a chassis-wide lower A-arm, the apex of which was ball-jointed to the bottom of the differential housing. Rear springing was by trailing quarter-elliptic leaves, shackled to the ends of the axle. While the live rear axle was a weak point of the F2 Maserati, on which it provided a larger proportion of the unsprung versus sprung weight, on the A6GCS/2000 it was more effective. Nevertheless, wheelspin on the inside in tight corners was a fault; from mid-1954 deliveries a limited-slip differential was added to assist traction.

*Late versions of the
A6GCS/2000 Maserati
had bodies by Fiandri
to the original design.
New features were the
Trident-decorated grille
and double curvature
of the windscreen.
Borrani wheels had a
distinctive spoke
pattern.*

*Pictured by Mailander
at Viale Ciro Menotti in
December 1954, this
was the late version of
the A6GCS/2000's frame,
with square-section
crossmembers carrying
its front suspension and
truss-type bracing for
side members.*

Although broadly similar to previous Maserati sixes, the A6GCS/2000's aluminium cylinder block had a new architecture. Instead of being dry, its fine-grained iron cylinder liners were exposed to the cooling water over their topmost 33mm, a thicker portion of the liner that was clamped between head and block. Split on the crankshaft centreline, the block carried its Nitralloy steel crankshaft in seven Vandervell thin-wall bearings. A narrow aluminium casting enclosed the bottom end, its flat sump cover a separate removable

*The front brake of the
Maserati A6GCS/2000
had aluminium leading
and trailing shoes
actuated by a single
double-ended hydraulic
cylinder. The front anti-
roll bar and its linkage
were visible as well.*

casting. Die-cast aluminium pistons carried three compression rings and two oil-control rings, one above and one below the wrist pin.

At the crankshaft nose a set of narrow gears drove the oil pumps and, through a skew gear, one of the distributors for the dual ignition. This was usually coil, although some sixes were magneto-sparked. Another train of gears rose up to drive the twin overhead camshafts. By the ingenious use of compound gears at the top of the gear train, the engine's profile was kept very low at the front to facilitate the A6GCS/2000's low hood line. Through finger-type followers the camshafts opened valves that were inclined at 36° for the inlets, 41° for the exhausts. Their respective diameters were 41.5 and 38mm. Although the design made provision for three coil springs to close each valve, the sports version used only two.

With two spark plugs in each chamber to ensure fast ignition, a second Marelli distributor was driven from the rear of the exhaust camshaft. Induction was through three twin-throat Weber 40 DCO3 carburettors, giving each cylinder its own venturi for optimum inlet tuning. An intermediate gear in the timing chest drove the generator and water pump through twin vee-belts. Cooling water was supplied both to the block and direct to the head to cool the exhaust valves. An adjustable blind to control temperature was in front of the water radiator. In front of that was an oil-cooling radiator.

Maserati initially rated its A6GCS/2000 six at 165bhp at 6,750rpm with a compression ratio of 8.5:1. Power was delivered through a twin-disc clutch and four-speed transmission in unit with the engine. The gearbox demanded active use, said Roy Salvadori: 'Because of its narrow power band, with absolutely nothing below 5,000rpm, I had to work very hard to keep the A6GCS engine in its restricted power band.' Added the British driver, 'On the credit side the A6GCS was very well balanced and it had excellent brakes.' Although not a lightweight at 1,540lb dry, the Maserati was quick, with 0-to-60 acceleration in 6.8 seconds and a top speed in excess of 130mph.

The A6GCS/2000 did indeed have brakes to match its power, with new front drums measuring 328 x 60mm and rears of 290 x 50mm. As in the 1953 version of the Formula 2 Maserati, the front drums had an outer sheet-aluminium cover over radial fins that centrifuged warm air out of the drums. Forward-facing scoops in the backing plates brought in cool air. They were inside the 4½in rims of 16in Borrani wheels, of which one row of wires were attached to the rim's periphery for maximum strength. The whole ensemble prompted Britain's

As fitted to the works-entered A6GCS/2000 Maserati in 1953, the dual ignition was sparked by two magnetos. A manifold fed from the rear of the engine delivered coolant directly to the cylinder head above its exhaust-valve guides.

The Autocar to say that 'this Maserati sports car is a most desirable property, the sight – let alone sound – of which will make any enthusiast's mouth water.'

Photos of the new model first appeared in March 1953 as it was being completed. The Orsis cheerfully leaked the news that it had been tried, unpainted, at the Modena Aerautodromo by works tester Guerino Bertocchi, Juan Fangio and Biellese driver Emilio Giletti, who was contemplating a move up in class from the smaller-displacement Nardis he'd been racing. On his third lap, the press learned, Giletti broke the outright track record for sports cars, previously held by a 3.0-litre Ferrari. Bertocchi later matched his speed. Though no times were quoted for the Argentine, Fangio was said to be enthusiastic, praising the engine and the 'extraordinary roadholding'.

In fact this Maserati was so well-balanced and easy to handle that its drivers affectionately dubbed it 'Auntie'. 'You can louse up a curve like crazy,' said American owner Fred Proctor, 'and the Maser will make you look like Ascari or somebody.' The sole disadvantage of its layout was its left-hand drive, following on the tradition of the earlier A6GCS. 'It was fine on left-handers,' said Roy Salvadori, but on 'right-hand corners not only was the driver's weight in the wrong place, but it was not possible to "sight" the car properly for the corner.' This held true for America's many airport races as well, but of course was no disadvantage in Italy's classic over-the-road contests.

Just such a race – the 676-mile Giro di Sicilia – saw the new model's first appearance on 12 April. It wasn't a fairytale debut for the works car; Giletti was not among the top ten finishers. On the 20th and 21st of the month his car and two more were being readied at the works for the Mille Miglia; Luigi Musso was the first to take delivery of the new model on the 23rd. Handsome Roman Musso would become one of the Sport 2000's strongest exponents, even featuring a red Trident on his white helmet.

In the Mille Miglia on 26 April Musso retired past Rome, but Sergio Mantovani finished tenth, with R. Palazzi, while the moustachioed Giletti was sixth

Bottom end of the A6GCS/2000 six had seven main bearings with four studs retaining the bearing cap nearest the clutch. Top and bottom of the clutch housing were cast integral with the block and sump.

Accompanied by Guerino Bertocchi, Emilio Giletti awaited his 5:25am start in the Mille Miglia on 26 April 1953. Their A6GCS/2000 Maserati triumphed in the 2.0-litre class and finished sixth overall.

accompanied by Bertocchi. They were first and second in their class, with the nearest 2.0-litre Ferrari well back in 15th overall, fifth in class. At a stroke the new Maserati model was category king.

Three weeks later in Sicily's gruelling 358-mile Targa Florio the new car's class was confirmed. Giletti was second overall behind a 3.0-litre Lancia, and Fangio – in one of his few races in the Sport 2000 – was third, co-driving with Mantovani. 2.0-litre Ferraris were not in view. June brought more successes with outright wins in two contests for 2.0-litre cars, the 143-mile Circuito di Caserta on the 21st and the 242-mile Giro dell' Umbria on the 28th. The first fell to Mantovani ahead of Musso, who led Giulio Musitelli's Ferrari. In the second, Musso led two Lancias to win. Musso was outright winner again at Avellino on 12 July in a tortuous race over 117 miles that saw no Ferraris in the top three.

Class victories came the way of the A6GCS/2000 in 1953 in the 12 Hours of Pescara, where Mancini and Dalcin were second overall, the Tuscan Trophy and the Supercortemaggiore race at Merano. At the end of the year Swiss racer 'Toulo' de Graffenried took a car to Brazil, winning a hillclimb and a sports-car race at Interlagos outright. Britain's Gilby Engineering acquired a green-painted car for Roy Salvadori to race; team patron Sid Green drove the car to the circuits on the road. Against less potent but lighter Bristol-powered cars Salvadori scored class wins at Castle Combe and Snetterton in '53 and several outright wins at Castle Combe in '54, plus a hard-fought triumph over Stirling Moss in a Lister-Bristol at Goodwood.

Although Salvadori initially raced his car with the full windscreen, for the 1954 season it was rebuilt with a screen for the driver alone and an aluminium tonneau cover over the passenger's seat. This was standard wear for most cars in 1954, for which engine power was raised to 170bhp at 7,300rpm on the higher compression ratio of 8.75:1 to cope with renewed competition from Ferrari. The revised car was officially known as the A6GCS/54. American racers tabled $8,000 to take delivery of their Sport 2000s, among them Ted Boynton and Tom Friedman as well as Fred Procter.

In all Maserati made 52 cars of this type through 1955, a signal commercial success. Acquired by Guglielmo 'Mimo' Dei of the Modena-based Scuderia Centro-Sud, three chassis were bodied as coupés by Pininfarina. Although fabulous-looking, these cars never achieved racing success to match their insouciant style. One roadster was bodied by Frua while Vignale clothed another as a spectacular roadster for American entrant Tony Parravano.

The Maserati's successes and popularity did not go unnoticed at Ferrari. Flaunting Giletti's 1953 success in the Mille Miglia, his car's maker boasted of 'The return of the glorious Maserati to racing …' in advertising. This was as a red flag to a bull for the Magus of Maranello. When in 1953 he began developing a new family of sports-racers powered by four-cylinder engines, he didn't overlook the need to create a rival to this annoying Maserati.

This recidivism of Ferrari in his power-unit philosophy was one of the most remarkable of the many striking steps he took during his career. As

In Britain Roy Salvadori enjoyed success with Gilby Engineering's Sport 2000 Maserati, seen at Castle Combe in late 1953 en route to a class victory. On clockwise circuits, visibility from the left-hand seat wasn't ideal, as Salvadori was demonstrating.

previously related he recanted from his advanced V12, an exceptional engine in its time, to four-cylinder engines, a type that had been all but extinct in top-line racing since the First World War.

One reason for this surprising change, wrote Gianni Rogliatti, was that Ferrari was 'extremely open to all the proposals put forward by those who worked with him and was willing to test anything that could reasonably be tested. This enabled the company to accumulate enough experimental and statistical data to make any of the large car manufacturers green with envy.' Enzo Ferrari subjected his early engines to a ruthless Darwinian selection process: many were created so that only the most worthy survived.

The first target of Ferrari and his chief engineer Aurelio Lampredi had been Formula 2 racing, where the new 2.0-litre Type 500 F2 four demonstrated its decisive superiority over the previous twelves. If the light, efficient and torque-rich four-cylinder engine worked so well in a Formula 2 car, reasoned Ferrari and Lampredi, why

Pininfarina gave three A6GCS/2000 chassis this heartbreakingly gorgeous coupé bodywork, commissioned by 'Mimo' Dei. Though not successful in racing, the Maserati coupés are icons of Italy's styling excellence in the 1950s.

Driving Ferrari's new Type 500 Mondial to scrutineering for the 1954 Mille Miglia was Vittorio, eldest of the racing-mad Marzotto brothers. New for Ferrari, its shape was the work of Sergio Scaglietti from an idea by Dino Ferrari.

not try it in larger sizes? By the end of 1953 Aurelio Lampredi had crystallised his ideas for sports-racing cars using his four-cylinder engines.

The chief engineer would build a new chassis that was capable of taking a family of larger four-cylinder engines, up to 3.0-litres, as well as a variant of the 500 F2's four to compete against the resurgent Maseratis in the 2.0-litre category. In fact, the concept cannot be overlooked that with the end of Formula 2 Ferrari found himself with a storehouse full of Type 500 F2 engines and transaxles for which he had no immediate requirement. Recycling them into 2.0-litre sports-racers was both cost-effective and potentially successful in racing, especially as the cars were largely intended for private owners.

Chassis of the 2.0- and 3.0-litre sports-racing Ferraris were so similar that it was easy to convert a smaller one to a bigger one, as often occurred. To distinguish it from its single-seater sister the 2.0-litre Type 500 sports car was given the 'Mondial' name in honour of the two World Championships won by Ascari using its power train. The larger-engined car would earn the 'Monza' appellation.

As usual, the new type was given its debut by a factory team to secure its reputation. No less a pairing than Ascari with Gigi Villoresi drove a Mondial to second overall behind a big Ferrari V12 in a 12-hour race at Casablanca on 20 December 1953. To their credit they defeated a 4½-litre Talbot and two private DB3S Aston Martins.

Some time elapsed before Mondial and Maserati met head-on. Giletti and Musso teamed up on 24 January 1954 to take an A6GCS/2000 to sixth place overall in the Buenos Aires 1,000 Kilometre race with no other 2.0-litre cars in sight. Soon

afterwards the Ferrari raced again in Africa, François Picard winning his class at Agadir on 27 February and Maurice Trintignant doing likewise at Dakar on 7 March, placing second overall. A similar result fell to Picard at Marrakech on 19 April.

Not until the Mille Miglia of 1954, on 2 May, did the two rivals clash in earnest. Among those driving A6GCS/2000s were Maserati ace Luigi Musso and Bruno Venezian, both carrying passengers. In the new Ferraris were Franco Cortese, Enrico Sterzi and the oldest of the racing Marzotto brothers, Vittorio. He was the only one of this group to tackle the 992-mile race solo.

The outcome could not have been closer. At Rome, the nominal halfway point, Musso had taken 6:09:01, a scant 16 seconds longer than his timing the previous year. Marzotto was a fraction of a minute faster in his Ferrari at 6:08:49. Save for Venezian, whose Maserati was nine minutes behind at this stage, no other 2.0-litre car was close to menacing these two. On the run back north to Brescia the pairing of Musso with Augusto Zocca clearly ran into trouble, because their finishing time was 12:00:10, more than 20 minutes longer than the previous year's time of Giletti, who had been much slower than Musso to Rome. Vittorio Marzotto also had his problems, including an unwanted change of spark plugs – 'It's going fine!' he protested. His time at the finish was 12:00:01, a negligible nine seconds faster than Musso after half a day's racing. He was second overall, Musso third, Venezian's Maserati fifth and the Mondials of Cortese and Sterzi 14th and 15th and fourth and fifth in class.

Here was a real rival at last for the A6GCS/2000 in its second season. Like the Maserati, the Ferrari

The Trident mustered its 2.0-litre-class-champion A6GCS/2000 for the 1954 Mille Miglia on 2 May to face the Prancing Horse's challenge. Luigi Musso sat on his late-model example while awaiting pre-race verification.

had an engine proven in Formula 2. Unlike the Maserati it avoided cylinder-head gasket problems by unifying the head and block in an aluminium alloy casting that extended downward three-quarters of the length of the cylinder. Screwed into this head/block unit, reaching right up to its combustion chambers, were four cast-iron wet cylinders. Bore and stroke of 90 x 78mm gave 1,985cc in an engine that Ferrari designated as the Type 110 internally. Stems of the two valves per cylinder were symmetrically inclined at an included angle of 58°. Almost flat-topped to give a compression ratio of 8.5:1, the aluminium pistons were full-skirted and carried two compression rings and one for oil control.

Grooves at the bottom of the cylinders carried O-rings that sealed the bores into the top of the crankcase. Cast of aluminium, the latter extended down to the bottom of the engine and was enclosed at its base by a shallow aluminium sump. Internal ribs supported the five main bearings, made 63mm in diameter instead of the Formula 2 engine's 60mm in the interests of endurance-race reliability. Carrying a forged-steel crankshaft with integral counterbalancing masses, the Vandervell Thinwall bearings were of equal width save for a broader centre main. I-section connecting rods were forged of steel. The dry-sump lubrication system had two gear-type pumps: one for pressure and the other a triple-gear pump to give an excess of capacity for scavenging, picking up at two locations.

Gear trains at the front of the Mondial's engine ran upward to the twin camshafts and downward to the oil and water pumps. Above the latter was a major addition to the Formula 2 engine: a transverse case of magnesium carrying a shaft and

bevel gears to drive three vertical Marelli instruments: a central dynamo and two magnetos or distributors to supply the dual ignition. Carburetion was by two Weber 40 DCOA3 dual-throat instruments on the right, with efficient blended-pipe exhaust manifolding on the left.

Carried over to the Mondial was the Type 500 F2's elaborate valve gear, housed in individual magnesium camboxes bolted to the cylinder block. The valves themselves were closed by hairpin-type valve springs, while the mushroom-shaped tappets had their own coil springs to hold them against the cam lobes. The latter were very narrow, as they had only to contact large-diameter rollers set into the

The works 500 Mondial's fluid Scaglietti/Dino lines brought a new look to the sports-racing Ferrari. With his beret and cane, Luigi Bazzi stood guard while Marzotto – driving solo – took care of the Mille Miglia formalities.

Below: The Formula 2 pedigree of the 500 Mondial Ferrari's four-cylinder engine was evident, although its twin magnetos flanked a generator atop a new front-end gear case created for the sports-car engines.

top faces of the tappets. Created by Lampredi expressly to eliminate valve-gear problems, this belt-and-braces mechanism was largely successful.

Ferrari initially rated the Mondial's engine at 160bhp at 7,000rpm. Powering the first 20 Mondials, this Type 110 engine was uprated through 1954 with bigger 42mm carburettors and compression ratio raised to 9.2:1 to bring its output to 170bhp at 7,200rpm. Encased in a bell housing at the engine was a twin-disc clutch, from which

the drive was taken through an engine-speed propeller shaft to a rear-mounted transaxle like the Type 500 F2's. Initially this contained four forward speeds; a fifth ratio was added later. The transaxle had its own pressure oil pump and a ZF limited-slip differential for the final drive. The latter was driven by a set of step-up gears from the longitudinal transmission shafts, thus allowing the gearbox to be placed as low as possible.

Aurelio Lampredi carried over the single-seater's de Dion rear suspension to the Mondial. This used a curved 2½in steel tube to join the rear-wheel hubs together in a solid axle that was relieved of the weight and torque effects of a live axle. It was controlled laterally by a bronze block sliding in a groove in the back of the differential housing, while the hubs were guided by parallel radius rods at each side.

Springing was by transverse leafs and adjustable Houdaille dampers at both front and rear. Placed low at the front, the transverse leaf was linked to the parallel suspension wishbones. Unequal in length, the wishbones were made up of pairs of forged-steel arms. The longer lower wishbones compressed soft rubber buffers that gave the springing a rising rate. No anti-roll bars were fitted. Forward-facing steering arms were connected by a three-piece track-rod linkage to a worm-and-wheel steering box on the right-hand side. Ferrari elected from the start to seat the Mondial's driver on the right to suit sports-car racing's predominantly clockwise circuits.

Shared as they were with the bigger-engined Monza, the Mondial's brakes were much larger in

diameter than the Maserati's at 350mm, although no wider at 48mm. Mechanisms were Lampredi's centre-pivoted shoes at both front and rear, applied by twin master cylinders. Sixteen-inch Borrani wire wheels carried tyre sections of 5.50 in front and 6.00 at the rear, the latter being the same size that the Maserati used at all four corners.

On a wheelbase of 88.6in, the Ferrari was shorter than the Maserati's 90.9in. The A6GCS/2000 had a much wider front track, at 52.6in versus 50.3in, while the rear tracks were in an inverse relationship with 48.0in for the Maserati and 50.6in for the Ferrari. For its Mondial Ferrari quoted a dry weight of 1,560lb, close enough to that of its hometown rival.

The Mondial came into being at a time of rapid evolution in Ferrari body designs. A fresh impulse came from Enzo Ferrari's son Alfredo 'Dino', to whom his father gave a spare 166 MM chassis. To clothe it, Dino came up with some ideas of his own

Pininfarina bodied some of the first-series Ferrari Mondial 500s with this appealing style, similar to its bodies for bigger-engined Maranello machines. Headlamps were recessed behind Plexiglas covers.

Above left: In the 1954 Mille Miglia Luigi Musso crossed the line with a time just nine seconds slower than class winner Vittorio Marzotto's Mondial Ferrari. The Ferrari was second overall behind Ascari's winning Lancia and the Maserati third.

This Pininfarina-bodied 500 Mondial Ferrari was driven by Franco Cortese in the 1954 Mille Miglia. Running without a navigator he was fourth in the 2.0-litre class and 14th overall.

to be executed by local coachbuilder Sergio Scaglietti. Born in 1920, Scaglietti had crafted bodywork for the Scuderia Ferrari before the war and set up his own *carrozzeria* in 1952. Together they conceived an aggressive and fluid line for Dino's 166 MM. Based on this design, with its unusually small fishlike cooling-air intake, Scaglietti bodied the car that scored the early-1954 successes for the Mondial.

Initially, however, Ferrari turned to the proven source of Pininfarina for bodies for its customer Mondials. Scaled-down versions of the bodies that the Turin coachbuilder was making in 1954 for Ferrari's big V12-engined racers, Pininfarina's Mondial bodies had a personality of their own with forward-thrusting snouts and speedlines along their flanks from the front-wheel openings. In addition Pininfarina made two clean-lined

Berlinettas on the Mondial chassis. Toward the end of Ferrari's production of the first series Mondial in 1954, body manufacture was taken over by Scaglietti, who had refined and sharpened the lines originated by Dino Ferrari. In all, six of the first 20 Mondials were Scaglietti-bodied.

The 1954 season saw battle well and truly joined between these outstanding 2.0-litre sports-racers. There was some adept selection of courses for horses, as the early Ferrari entries showed. In the Giro di Sicilia on 4 April, an event that should have suited the Mondials, Musso's Maserati was fourth overall and first in class with no 2.0-litre Ferraris in the top ten. On 15 May a six-hour race at Bari for 2.0-litre cars saw Maserati the winner with Cesare Perdisa ahead of the Ferrari of Mario Della Favera, while on the next day Musso won outright over 153 miles at Naples, beating Giulio Musitelli's 3.0-litre Ferrari. In Sicily again on 30 May for the Targa Florio, Luigi Musso was second overall and class winner, with Luigi Bellucci's similar Maserati fourth; the top six finishers showed no Mondials.

Save for its narrow win in the Mille Miglia, the Mondial wasn't having much fun yet in the European contests. Its luck turned on 20 June at Imola in the 156-mile inaugural race for the city's new circuit. Robert Manzon set the fastest lap in a Mondial in a race won in a similar car by Umberto Maglioli, with Musitelli second in another Mondial. Trident advocate Luigi Musso could only manage third place. At Collemaggio on 4 July, however, the positions were reversed, Bellucci winning with his Sport 2000 after Musso set fastest lap and retired. Cortese's Mondial was second and Giorgio Scarlatti's Maserati was third. In the Dolomites on 11 July Sergio Mantovani was the outright winner with an A6GCS/2000, defeating bigger-engined Ferraris.

On Northern Ireland's demanding Dundrod road circuit both marques competed for the Tourist Trophy on 11 September. Of the four Maseratis that came to the start of the 697-mile race, three retired or were disqualified. The fourth, driven by Musso and Mantovani, finished an outstanding third, beaten only by a Lancia D24 and a Ferrari Monza. Four laps behind in ninth place was a Mondial driven by Americans Bob Said and Masten Gregory. Theirs was the last of the Series 1 Mondials, with a refined interpretation of the Scaglietti bodywork.

Complex and pedigreed though it was, through 1954 Ferrari's Mondial hadn't succeeded in establishing the same dominance over the A6GCS/2000 that its Formula 2 car had enjoyed over the comparable Maserati. Indeed, the Trident was still in the ascendant. For the second year in succession Luigi Musso and his Sport 2000 were Italy's 2.0-litre sports-car champions. This would satisfy neither Ferrari nor its loyal customers for long. Maranello would produce a Series 2 version of its Mondial in 1955 to compete against Maserati's upgrade of its stalwart six. The battle for 2.0-litre sports-car supremacy was not over, not by a long shot.

Alfons de Portago (pictured) and Carlo Tomasi shared an 'Aseigiciesse' at Le Mans in 1954. At the 10th hour of 24 the Maserati was 14th amongst the special Bristols that won the 2.0-litre class – one following here – when it lost oil pressure and retired.

CHAPTER SEVEN

625 and 553/555 vs 250 F

Though overshadowed by the successful return of Mercedes-Benz to Grand Prix racing in 1954 and '55, Ferrari and Maserati had their hometown credentials to defend. The rivalry was as intense as ever, with accusations of espionage and open poaching of drivers and engineers.

During the two years when the World Championship was fought with Formula 2 cars, 1952 and '53, Ferrari and Maserati dominated. Modena ruled the world. Ferrari had the measure of Maserati and both swept aside such

On the fifth lap at Syracuse in 1954 Mike Hawthorn's Ferrari 625, at right, hit the wall and burst into flames. Mike escaped but Froilan González, thinking his team-mate was still in the car, stopped to help only to have his brand-new Squalo, left, roll into the blaze and itself be destroyed. A Maserati passed the hecatomb.

rivals as Gordini, OSCA, Connaught, HWM and Cooper-Bristol. Though Ferrari had two World Championships in its pocket with Alberto Ascari, Maserati won the last race of 1953 and was on a roll. Thus when a new Grand Prix Formula 1 was announced for 1954, both Modena companies had every reason to think they'd continue to rule the roost. They couldn't have been more wrong.

The new Formula 1, known to the racing world since October 1951, restricted supercharged engines to only 750cc – a successful attempt to handicap them heavily – and held unblown engines to 2½-litres. This was only 25 per cent more displacement than the Formula 2 engines that raced for championship points in 1952–53, so Ferrari and Maserati saw merit in scaling up their existing engines to compete under the 1954 rules.

They could have been more ambitious. For decades Grand Prix racing had been dominated by engines of eight, 12 and even 16 cylinders. Indeed, Ferrari had reaped the benefits of the V12 in his early years. The last four to have enjoyed success in proper Formula 1 racing was Maserati's 4CLT/48 in the 1940s, while sixes hadn't been prominent since the early 1920s. Yet Ferrari and Maserati had

done well in Formula 2 with fours and sixes respectively and decided to carry on in the same vein in 1954.

Against these strategies, it was no secret that new opposition was coming and that it planned to be well-armed. Lancia was building a V8, Mercedes-Benz a straight-eight and Coventry Climax a V8 that companies like Kieft and Connaught were planning to use. Alfa Romeo was planning a comeback with its Type 160, a flat-twelve with four-wheel drive. In France straight-eights were brewing at Gordini and Bugatti. Though the Alfa and Climax engines didn't make it to the track, it seemed likely that Modena's racers would be undergunned with only fours and sixes.

Truth be told, that was probably all they could muster. Neither company was in the best of shape. Enzo Ferrari was in one of his periodic pouts. At the end of August 1953, said one of his drivers, Mike Hawthorn, 'the newspapers carried startling stories to the effect that Ferrari had decided to give up motor racing. He pleaded that he was tired and needed a rest; he was known to be worried about his son, who suffered from chronic ill-health, and he even alleged that one of his draughtsmen had

been smuggling drawings out of the factory for use by his rivals.'

At that year's Italian Grand Prix Ferrari unveiled a new model, his Type 553, which was seen as a harbinger of his 1954 Formula 1 car. It didn't perform well, however. Nor was it liked by his star driver, Alberto Ascari. Not until 12 December, when Ferrari held his season-ending dinner, was the uncertainty about his plans dispelled. He would compete in the major events, Enzo said, while bemoaning the lack of support he was receiving from the infrastructure of the nation whose prestige he felt he was upholding internationally.

Enzo Ferrari's prolonged sulk meant that his engineers were less advanced than they might have been in their preparations. 'They wouldn't tell us what we would be doing in 1954,' Ferrari driver Luigi Villoresi said. 'They produced no programmes and said not a word, causing us to waste a lot of time.' On 29 December Ferrari handed Ascari an ultimatum. He would extend the driver's contract that expired at the end of April, but only if he signed on the dotted line there and then.

The gentlemanly Ascari was deeply offended by this *diktat* from a man he'd looked up to, almost as a father, since he raced Ferrari's first self-built car, the Type 815, in the 1940 Mille Miglia. 'I returned to Milan the same evening with a sad heart,' said Ascari. 'I'd made too many sacrifices for the house of Maranello and the collaboration had given me too much satisfaction to be able to close a chapter as passionate and as attractive in my life without having some regrets, some nostalgia.'

At 5:15pm on 30 December 1953 the Ferrari press office released a communiqué stating: 'Effective 31 December the existing collaborative relationship with the racing driver Alberto Ascari will cease.' It went on to claim – falsely – that the 'sole reason' for this was Ascari's desire to orient his activities more commercially for the sake of his family. It attributed the schism to Ferrari's inability to offer his driver the rewards that other motor companies could provide. In this case the other motor company was Lancia, which was quick to seize the talents of both Ascari and his friend and mentor Villoresi for its new Grand Prix team.

This was a catastrophe for Grand Prix racing. Delays in the Lancia's gestation meant that the reigning World Champion sat out most of the 1954 season. In 1954 Ascari, the only driver Juan Fangio feared, would be loaned briefly to both Ferrari and Maserati but would fail to finish any races in their cars. By mid-1955 he was dead, killed in an impromptu test of a Ferrari sports-racer.

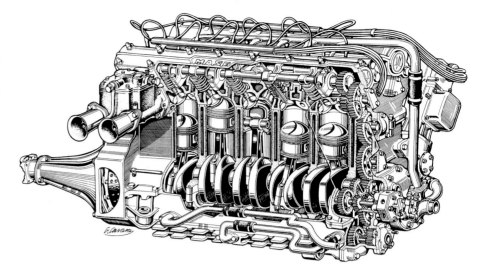

This perturbation at Maranello was matched by turbulence in Modena at Maserati. The good news that the Korean War was settled by an armistice in mid-1953 was bad news for the interests of the Orsi family. One of its businesses was machine tools, which had been in great demand during the conflict. Orders collapsed when the war ended, leaving redundant stocks of tools that were calibrated in inches instead of the millimetres that would have made them saleable in Europe.

The thoughts of Adolfo Orsi and his son Omer turned to South America, where their long-time co-operation with Juan Manuel Fangio opened opportunities in Juan Perón's Argentina. Their best chance to flaunt their engineering capabilities and cement business contacts would be the Argentine Grand Prix on 17 January 1954, first World Championship race of the new Formula 1. This meant immense pressure on the Viale Ciro Menotti staff and workshops to complete a mini-armada of new Grand Prix cars in time for this crucial event.

The patrimony of the A6 was still evident in the 2,494cc six of the 250 F Maserati, with its seven main bearings and finger-type cam followers. Skew gears drove the two magnetos vee-inclined at the front of the engine.

As introduced in 1954, Maserati's 250 F six had dual ignition and triple twin-throat Weber carburettors. Its water pump delivered coolant both to its block and to its cylinder head through the manifold visible on the right.

Seen from the right side, with the cover removed from its reverse gearing, the four-speed transaxle of the 250 F Maserati was pictured during its assembly. On the right was the vertical groove that gave lateral guidance to the de Dion axle tube.

Removing the fuel tank showed the transaxle and rear suspension of the 250 F Maserati, including the two pairs of rollers carrying its transverse leaf spring. Brakes had vented back plates and centrifugal cooling for the drums.

Design of the new car was initiated by Gioachino Colombo, who joined Maserati from Alfa Romeo late in 1952 and greatly improved the company's racers for 1953. In the summer of 1953 Colombo recruited a young engineer, Valerio Colotti, who'd been with Ferrari since 1948. Colotti's task was the chassis and suspension of the new car, which in the company's tradition was provisionally named the 6C2500. Later it was called the 250/F1 and finally simply the 250 F. Colombo

left in October 1953 after sharp disagreements with the engineer in charge of the workshops, Vittorio Bellentani, about the engine's configuration.

From the start of the project Bellentani had been overseeing the new engine's design, with guidance from Colombo and detail assistance from Domenico Nicola. Bellentani's choice for its cylinder dimensions was 84 x 75mm for a capacity of 2,494cc. An aluminium-alloy cylinder block extended down to the centreline of its crankshaft while its upper one-third served as a coolant tank surrounding nitrided-iron wet cylinder liners.

A deep casting bolted to the front of the engine housed scavenge and pressure oil pumps for the dry-sump system, the water and fuel pumps – plus their helical and spur-gear drives – and all fluid inlets and outlets. The crank nose carried two helical gears, one to drive this unit and the other to rotate the gear train to the camshafts and two short longitudinal shafts with bevels that turned twin Marelli magnetos.

Scavenge pumps drew from two screened pickups in a very deep magnesium-alloy sump and pumped oil through a cooler to a 4.4-gallon reservoir. All bottom-end bearing shells were Vandervell lead-indium, with mains 60mm in diameter and big-end journals 51mm. Polished connecting rods were forged steel with heavy I-section shanks. With steep peaks providing compression ratios of up to 12.5:1, the pistons were made by Borgo.

Valves were inclined at 36° for the inlets and 41° for the exhausts, giving an included angle of 77°. Initial valve diameters were 42 and 38mm respectively. Cam side thrust was absorbed by pivoted fingers between the lobes and the valve stems. The combustion chamber was a hemisphere, with twin spark plugs flanking the valve seats. Induction was through three twin-throat Weber 42 DCO3 carburettors, later enlarged to 45mm Webers.

Running on methanol fuel the 250 F six initially produced 245bhp at 7,600rpm, just short of 100bhp per litre. From a clutch in unit with the engine it transmitted its torque to a rear-mounted transaxle, which was placed transversely in the manner of the pre-war Grand Prix Mercedes. Providing four forward speeds, all indirect, its shafts were on the right side of the chassis in Colotti's design. Drive to the wheels was through a ZF limited-slip differential to Hooke-type inner universal joints and pot-type joints at the hubs that allowed length variations in the half-shafts to accommodate suspension movement.

De Dion-type suspension, using a solid axle to guide the wheels while the differential was chassis-

mounted, appeared for the first time in a Maserati. This was the work of Valerio Colotti. It was his defection to which Enzo Ferrari had referred, suggesting that he'd pinched from Maranello the idea of curving the de Dion tube forward of the transaxle instead of the usual rearward position. The axle tube was guided laterally by a square block which slid in a vertical slot in the front of the transaxle case. The hubs were positioned by parallel radius rods at each side.

Ferrari inspiration was also evident in Colotti's mounting of the transverse rear leaf spring in two widely separated rollers so that it was flexible in jounce but stiff in roll. Shock absorbers front and rear were adjustable rotary Houdaille units. An anti-roll bar was used at the front, where springing was by coils acting on the bottom arm of an unequal-length wishbone suspension. At the recommendation of Bellentani this was carried over from the Formula 2 cars. In the Maserati tradition the worm-and-sector steering box was mounted on the clutch housing. A drag link connected it to a three-part steering linkage, mounted forward of the front suspension.

Each drum brake contained two leading shoes, for maximum braking power, with automatic adjustment. The shoes were elegant filigreed castings of light alloy, a tribute to the skills of Maserati's in-house foundry. Radial finning on the exterior of each aluminium drum was covered by an aluminium shroud that centrifuged hot air out and away from the drum's interior. Cooling was helped by Borrani's light but rugged wire wheels, carrying 16in Pirelli tyres. Depending on circuits, 17in rear tyres were sometimes used. Wheelbase was 89.8in.

Sales appeal of Maserati's new 250 F was enhanced by an exceptionally handsome body. Initially outlined by Valerio Colotti – 'the shape of jet aeroplanes inspired me in designing the car's form' – the body was formed by Medardo Fantuzzi, swathed in cooling louvres. Initially flanking the engine, the engine-oil reservoir was later repositioned in the tail, behind the 44-gallon fuel tank. Tanks, aluminium body and other components were attached to a tubular-steel frame from the pen of Gioachino Colombo.

Both engineers and mechanics at the Viale Ciro Menotti worked in shifts to complete the designing and building of the first 250 F in time to compete in the vital Argentine race. On the day after Christmas 1953 the first car was ready for tests at Modena's Aerautodromo. Typically for the season it

Stripped of its Fantuzzi bodywork the Maserati 250 F revealed its truss-type tubular-steel space frame and heavy-duty oil cooler, ahead of the radiator, to cope with the heat of the summer for its first race in Argentina.

Pictured in the pits of Modena's Aerautodromo, the 250 F Maserati was a great-looking racing car with a grille design carried over from 1953. This December 1953 image was taken before its rear-view mirrors were fitted.

Omer Orsi regarded his company's new Maserati Type 250 F with a mixture of pride and apprehension. It represented a major investment that would have to be earned back with the sale of cars and parts.

was a damp and misty day. Adjudicator of the work of the technicians would be Guerino Bertocchi, who functioned as both chief racing mechanic and test driver. Associated with Maserati as a mechanic since the birth of the marque in 1926, on a track that he knew Bertocchi was as fast as anyone.

Under the anxious eyes of the Orsis and their senior designers, Bertocchi took the 250 F out on the Modena track. When he returned after its baptismal laps, the burly veteran prolonged the

suspense. Climbing out, he pulled off his skullcap and goggles and tucked them neatly away with his gloves. Finally Adolfo Orsi broke the pregnant silence: 'Guerino, what?'

'Gentlemen,' Bertocchi replied, 'at last we have an automobile deserving of the name.'

The talents of Bertocchi and his fellow tester Umberto Stradi contributed to sales of the 250 F with demonstrations that were unfailingly convincing. Orders rolled in, requiring the production of ten cars in 1953–54. For sound commercial reasons Maserati's principal thrust was the sale and servicing of these cars, which took priority over the running of a factory team – a luxury it couldn't really afford.

Commissions arrived faster than Maserati could build cars, so it powered five of the existing 1953 Formula 2 chassis with the new 250 F engine, creating the A6GCM/250. Although the car was light, its live rear axle was heavily taxed by the more powerful six. Such cars were sold to Emmanuel de Graffenried, Prince Bira, Harry Schell and Argentines Roberto Mieres and Jorge Daponte. Bira and Mieres would trade theirs in for true 250 Fs. Encouraged by good performances of the A6GCS/2000 sports-racer driven by Roy Salvadori in 1953, Britain embraced the 250 F. Orders came from Stirling Moss, the Owen Organisation as a BRM test horse, and Gilby Engineering for Salvadori.

At Maranello, in contrast, emphasis was entirely on new cars for use by the factory team. The three racers it sent to Argentina for the season-opening

Grand Prix were 1953 Formula 2 cars re-engined. Fitting a 2.5-litre engine was child's play for Ferrari chief engineer Aurelio Lampredi; indeed, the Type 500 2.0-litre chassis first raced at Bari in 1951 with a 2.5-litre four. Its overhead valves were at a 58° included angle and its dimensions of 94 x 90mm gave 2,498cc, good for 230bhp at 7,000rpm. For best torque it kept the 50mm Weber carburettors of the developed 2.0-litre engine. In recognition of the capacity of one of its cylinders the new model was named the Type 625.

Although Froilan González had partnered his compatriot Juan Fangio in the Maserati team in 1952 and '53, the two men went different ways in 1954, Fangio signing for Mercedes-Benz to drive its new car when it was ready. Enzo Ferrari was quick to sign González, the burly and mercurial racer who'd been the first to drive his car to victory over all-conquering Alfa Romeo in 1951. Veteran Nino Farina was still aboard, as was 1953 newcomer to the team Mike Hawthorn. In Buenos Aires they faced Fangio in a new 250 F and his young Argentine protégé, Onofre 'Pinocho' Marimon, in a sister car.

After its 110-day gestation Maserati's 250 F was ready – just barely. Negotiating cables flew between the Orsis and the Argentine Auto Club to bring two of the new cars to Buenos Aires. Agreement was reached that Maserati's cars would come as works entries but with a heavy financial commitment from the Auto Club. Maserati's mechanics worked through Christmas to get the cars ready for the last possible boat to Argentina.

Although two new 250 Fs went to Argentina only one was raceworthy, such was the engine attrition owing to oiling problems in the 105° heat of the Argentine summer. Six fresh engines were airlifted to Buenos Aires to ensure that customer entries could be fulfilled. In desperation Bertocchi bought up local supplies of olive oil and mixed it with engine oil to suppress frothing that was ruining engine bearings. Cooling was a problem too; slots were cut in the noses to admit more air.

At first the Ferraris had the upper hand; both Farina and González qualified faster than Fangio and Froilan led, setting the fastest lap. When the thunderstorms came, however, Fangio took command, opposite-locking his way around the circuit. He made a quick stop for rain-slitted tyres in a 250 F for which cooling was no longer a problem.

Thinking wishfully that the Argentine would be disqualified for too many mechanics working on his car at that pit stop, Ferrari team manager Nello Ugolini didn't press his drivers to attack. Fangio came home more than a minute ahead of Farina as the winner of the first Grand Prix of the new Formula 1. He also gave the Maserati 250 F a victory in its first race, a rare distinction in the world of racing cars. González was third and Maurice Trintignant fourth in a private Type 500 Ferrari re-engined as a 625.

With first blood to Maserati, Aurelio Lampredi buckled down to the job of completing the 2.5-litre version of his Type 553. He hoped that its new engine would be able to run reliably at high revs – the immediate goal was 7,500 – and that its

Ferrari and his chief engineer Aurelio Lampredi initially tackled the 1954 season by fitting enlarged engines to their successful Formula 2 cars to create the 2.5-litre 625 F1. Piero Taruffi drove this one to sixth in the German GP on 1 August.

In the first race of the new 2.5-litre Formula 1, in Argentina on 17 January 1954, the stage was set for the rivalry with the Trident victory of Fangio, here leading, and Hawthorn's combative attack on behalf of the Prancing Horse.

top end could breathe well enough to be useful at this speed. Both objectives led to oversquare dimensions of 100 x 79.5mm for a displacement of 2,498cc.

As in Lampredi's V12 engines the cylinder head and water jacketing of the 553 were cast in one piece of silicon-aluminium alloy, including the entire cam-drive gear casing at the front. Cast-iron cylinder liners, screwed up into the combustion chambers, hung down below the bottom edge of the water jacketing. When the head/jacket unit was bolted to the deep crankcase, these liners were made watertight by a close fit plus rubber O-rings. The head assembly was retained by four studs at the corners of the crankcase and by eight long studs emerging between the cam boxes in the centre of the engine.

About half the height of the entire engine, the light-alloy crankcase was notable for its smooth sides and considerable width, planned by Lampredi to reduce power losses from oil churning. It carried the crankshaft in five 60mm Vandervell main bearings. Finished all over, the connecting rods were conventional in layout, with 50mm big ends, while the pistons had full skirts carrying one of their four rings below the wrist pin.

The Type 553 housed many of its accessories in a cover plate bolted to the front of the crankcase. Scavenge and pressure pumps for the dry-sump system were at the lower right and left of the cover. Between them and a bit higher, just below the crank centreline, was the Fimac mechanical fuel pump. At

the upper left and right of the cover, at both sides of the crank nose, were two Marelli magnetos which rested horizontally pointing forward.

Driven from a bevel gear above and between the magnetos was the water pump with double outlets. These delivered cool water to the engine through the centre of the side of the crankcase, thus near the heavily loaded centre main bearing. From there water flowed upward to emerge from risers cast above the centre of each combustion chamber and returned to the radiator through a manifold.

A train of narrow gears rose from the crankshaft nose to drive the twin camshafts. Carried in five bearings in detachable tappet boxes, the large-diameter cams were hollow. The 553's valve gear was a development of that used with satisfaction in the Formula 2 engines. The narrow cam lobe lifted a roller, which was mounted in the upper face of a wide aluminium mushroom tappet. In the hollow stem of the mushroom tappet was a shouldered steel plug. Clearance was set by grinding this tip. The short, sturdy valve was closed by a massive pair of hairpin springs.

Intake valves of 50mm diameter were inclined at 40° to the vertical, 5° less than the 46mm exhausts for an included angle of 85°. Double-bodied Weber carburettors, eventually of 58mm bore size, were mounted on small steel frames which in turn were bolted to the chassis to reduce float-bowl frothing caused by vibration of the engine, which was connected to the carburettors by lengths of flanged rubber piping.

Lampredi's high-rev goal was indicated by the very large diameter of the high-mounted scavenging exhaust system. Weighing 352lb, the 1954 Type 553 four was rated at between 265 and 270bhp at 7,600rpm, a speed which was found to be above the limit of safe continuous operation. Power was transmitted by a multiple clutch in unit with the engine and a central propeller shaft to the rear-mounted transmission, which had a layout new to Ferrari.

For the new gearbox the four-speed-and-reverse gearing of the usual rear-mounted gearbox was carried over, with its indirect drive on all forward speeds and selection of ratios by dog clutches on the secondary or output shaft. Instead of being placed well in front of the final-drive gearing, however, the box was moved back and under the differential, getting it out of the driver's way and allowing a much lower seating position.

The gearbox transmitted torque to the final-drive bevels through a set of coarse-toothed spur gears which were easily reached by removing the rear cover plate of the assembly. The overall drive ratio could be changed in about 20 minutes, a convenient feature that may have been inspired by the quick-change axles that Lampredi saw during his trip to Indianapolis with Ascari's 4½-litre car in 1952.

Mounted in the removable cover was a small gear-type oil pump driven by a square connection from the primary shaft. This scavenged the box and fed oil to the centre of the secondary shaft and to the gears and carrier bearings of the final drive. A ZF limited-slip differential took the drive through beautifully machined half-shafts to the wheels on which both splines and outer pot-joints were tried, the latter finally being chosen.

Though it was later supplied with integrally cast brackets, the gearbox was initially mounted on a tubular subframe which was fixed by Silentbloc bushes to one of the most revolutionary parts of this Ferrari: its frame. For the first time a Ferrari was built with a genuine small-tube space frame. Its design accounted for much of the weight reduction that was accomplished. It scaled 1,310lb dry, higher than the 1,200lb 1953 prototype but less than the 1,430lb of the 1954 Type 625. The 250 F Maserati started 1954 at a hefty 1,475lb but by the end of the year was slimmed to 1,390lb.

At the rear, de Dion suspension was newly conceived to suit the arrangement of components in the 553. Its axle tube passed ahead of the final-drive unit instead of behind it, affording ready access to the quick-change cover plate. This was the very feature that Enzo Ferrari thought Maserati had obtained by espionage. The layout also

Lampredi's new four-cylinder engine for his Type 553 of 1954 had valves at an 85-degree included angle and magnetos placed low at the front. The water pump had twin outlets to both side of the cylinder block.

resembled the 250 F's in that the axle was laterally guided by a block sliding in a vertical slot in the front of the transaxle casing. Parallel radius rods of light-alloy tubing guided the hubs. The flexible transaxle mountings of the early 1954 cars gave reason to doubt the precision of the axle's lateral location. This could have accounted for some of the 'wandering' tendency criticised in early trials.

Springing was by a slim transverse leaf placed above the gearbox and mounted from a pivot at its

As installed in the Type 625 F1 chassis, the new wide-valve-angle engine for 1954 stood its magnetos upright at the front, making use of the accessory-drive case developed in parallel for use in sports-racing Ferraris.

In its intended home, the Type 553 Squalo of 1954, the new four-cylinder Ferrari engine nestled between the tubes of the car's true space frame, a first for Maranello. This contributed to the impressive lightness of the new model.

much shorter than the lower wishbone. Mounted in a pair of double rollers to increase its roll resistance, the transverse leaf spring passed below the lower wishbones and was linked to them. Tubular rubber buffers between the lower wishbones and frame extensions gave a spring-rate increase with wheel jounce.

Steering was also new. The column ran between the cam boxes to a steering gearbox in the centre of the chassis. The box was linked to trailing steering arms by two equal-length track rods, a much simpler – but less geometrically correct – system than the traditional three-part-track-rod Ferrari linkage.

Radical for Ferrari was the placement of the main fuel tanks along the sides of the car, the filler cap being on the right-hand tank. The small rear tank and the oil tank behind it were moved up atop the gearbox to facilitate ratio changes. The fuel location, allied with the rearward engine placement and compact transaxle, gave the 553 a low polar moment of inertia and a correspondingly sensitive control response. It also gave it an unusual adipose appearance that prompted the car's popular nickname of '*Squalo*' or 'Shark'.

The first entry of a Squalo in 1954 was in April, in a non-championship race at Syracuse in Sicily. It saw González equal-fastest qualifier with Marimon's Maserati and quick in the race. But when Froilan stopped to help team-mate Hawthorn, whose Type 625 was on fire, his Squalo rolled into the flames. Both cars were burned out. González did better at Silverstone's International Trophy in May, where he was fastest qualifier and first-heat winner in the surviving Squalo. Before starting the final, however, he found his engine locked solid. Allowed to switch to a 625, he won the final.

These were but skirmishes before the main World Championship battle resumed in earnest at the daunting Spa-Francorchamps circuit in Belgium on 20 June. Pros and cons applied to the attacking forces of both Modenese teams. In Ferrari's favour was its compact factory-team effort directed by the experienced Nello Ugolini. Aurelio Lampredi was in complete control of the engineering and not afraid to chop and change to achieve results. Among Ferrari's drivers Froilan González was at the peak of his considerable powers while Nino Farina still had something to offer. On the negative side was Ferrari's inability to decide between his evolved Type 625 and his radical new Type 553.

Counting in favour of Maserati's effort was the sparkling new design of its 250 F and the added power potential of a six against a four. In addition, apart from the interim models all its cars were the same, easing servicing. Business at the Viale Ciro

Tom Fornander's drawing of the Squalo Ferrari's exposed tail revealed the narrow quick-change gears taking the drive from its transmission to its final drive. Also shown was the de Dion tube curving forward of the transaxle assembly.

centre to lower the rear roll resistance, tending the chassis toward understeer. This was a change from the 1953 car, which had high rear roll resistance. Houdaille hydraulic dampers were actuated through wishbone-type arms.

Lampredi added several more innovations at the front end. Ball joints at the outer wishbone ends replaced trunnions and king pins, the ball supports and king post being entirely between the wishbones for the lightest possible weight. The top wishbone was very short and narrow,

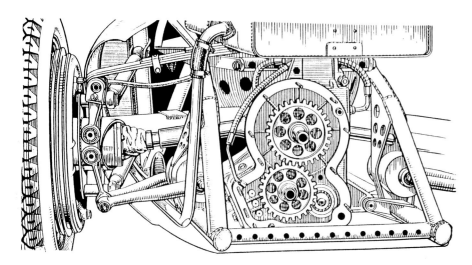

Menotti was looking up, thanks to the company's bold Argentine adventure. Juan Perón expressed his gratitude to Adolfo Orsi for providing a car for his national champion, Fangio, by releasing rare import permits for Maserati machine tools. Setting up an Argentine branch, Maserati also began importing tools from other Italian makers. The company was again secure – for the time being.

Another asset continued to be Maserati's anchor as chief mechanic and tester, Guerino Bertocchi. 'Bertocchi is shrewd and deliberate,' fellow mechanic Alf Francis told Peter Lewis. 'There must be some point in everything he does and no time is wasted with a smile and small talk unless it is strictly necessary. He is completely wrapped up in his work and I do not think he has ever done anything else other than look after racing cars.'

Working against Maserati's thrust was its commercial approach, which landed it with a disparate group of 250 F owners. It took time for early problems, such as breaking de Dion tubes and fragile bevel-gear inputs to the transaxle, to filter through to all the cars. The customer-car servicing burden meant that the works was often late in getting cars to the circuits. Nor did its multiplicity of cars and drivers lend itself to rigorous racing-team control, even if it had been in more experienced hands than those of 30-year-old

engineer Giulio Alfieri, who joined Maserati in August 1953 and was immediately thrown into front-line racing management.

No Maserati asset was greater than the skill of Juan Fangio, which was still available to it at Spa because Mercedes hadn't yet called him to duty. Both man and car were ready for the Belgian Grand Prix. Given a new higher rev limit after improvements to the engine, Fangio began duelling for pole with the Ferrari Squalo of González. On this daunting road course he triumphed by 1½ seconds with a staggering 120.5mph lap that equalled the qualifying record he'd set there in 1951 with the far more powerful Alfa Romeo Type 159.

It had been no small effort. Anthony Pritchard wrote that 'back at the pits the 250 F was leaking oil from just about every joint, the brakes were red hot and the car shimmered in a haze of heat.' When a 250 F was revved to more than 8,000rpm, said Denis Jenkinson, it was 'pumping oil out of every possible place. It was normal procedure with the Maserati mechanics that as soon as one of the new cars came in from a very fast lap they fell on it with bundles of rag and started mopping-up operations.'

In the race – filmed to feature in *The Racers* on the big screen – Fangio was slow away but soon battled for the lead with his old rival, Squalo-

The Type 553 Ferrari's 'Shark' nickname was owed to the adipose appearance caused by the placement of the main fuel tanks along its flanks. Lampredi aimed for compactness and light weight in its design.

Silverstone in May 1954 provided a comparison between the 625 F1 Ferrari (left) and the 553 F1. The new car had ball-joint front suspension, with steering arms behind its front-wheel centres, and exhaust pipes of much greater diameter.

His Mercedes-Benz not yet ready, Juan Manuel Fangio drove a 250 F in the Belgian GP on 20 June 1954. He prevailed for the Trident in a dramatic battle with the Ferrari Squalos of González and Farina, both of which retired.

mounted Nino Farina, after the sister car of González retired. Farina's default for the same reason, a broken piston, placed Fangio under less pressure, which was just as well as his Maserati was visibly sagging, having broken bits of its suspension and at the victorious finish steaming from a holed radiator. Trintignant brought a 625 home second and Stirling Moss was third in his private 250 F.

For the French Grand Prix at Reims on 4 July the Italian squads made a reasonable fist of joining forces to defend their honour against the onslaught of the new streamlined W196 racers from Mercedes-Benz. Gianni Lancia released Ascari and Villoresi to drive Maseratis in support of works driver Onofre Marimon. Both Hawthorn and González had Squalos, the Englishman finding that his 'did not steer well and felt very peculiar in the corners.' Nevertheless González qualified at 2:30.6 against Fangio's 2:29.4 in the Mercedes and Ascari's 250 F was on the front row with 2:30.5.

On this extremely fast track the Italian challenge soon shot its bolt. Ascari was out early with piston trouble. The two Squalos were the only cars to stay within sight of the flying Mercedes-Benz team until both retired. With all factory Ferraris breaking the

day was saved for Maranello by Robert Manzon's Rosier-entered Type 625 in third. Maserati-mounted Bira was fourth and Villoresi fifth in another 250 F.

During mid-season Nino Farina was missing from Ferrari's team, convalescing after a sports-car injury. Thus for the British GP at Silverstone on 17 July the Ferrari strength was González, Hawthorn and Trintignant, all in 625s. Ascari and Villoresi were again on loan to Maserati, whose organisational chaos completely vitiated this generous Lancia gesture. Already late in leaving the factory, the misinformed mechanics drove to the wrong cross-channel port. The upshot was that the cars arrived too late for official practice and had to start from the back of the grid. Sharing the front row with Fangio's Mercedes were Hawthorn and González in Ferrari 625s and Moss's private 250 F.

With the Mercedes all at sea on a damp Silverstone the Italians had a chance for revenge and it was Ferrari that took advantage. González won with Hawthorn second after Moss relinquished that spot with a driveline failure only ten laps from the finish. Marimon was third for Maserati. Ascari thrust forward but retired early. Taking over Villoresi's car he found that 250 F

Nino Farina's forceful style was vivid in this image of his attack at the 1954 Belgian Grand Prix. He led the first two laps and then overtook eventual winner Fangio, leading laps 11 to 13 before retiring with engine problems on lap 14 of 36. He'd shown that the Squalo didn't lack for pace on this fast circuit.

failing as well. Pit-row reporters swore that the genial Ascari uttered the Italian equivalent of 'Any more Maseratis?' Amazingly the race's fastest lap was shared by Fangio, González, Ascari, Hawthorn, Marimon and Jean Behra's French Gordini.

Two weeks later at the Nürburgring, a track on which the agile Italians should have enjoyed an advantage over Mercedes, their assault was blunted by Marimon's death in a crash during practice. Maserati withdrew Villoresi's works 250 F in sympathy but let its privateers compete. Ferrari brought 625s, one of which Hawthorn qualified at 9:53.3 against Fangio's pole of 9:50.1. Moss completed the front row at 10:00.7 but knew that his hard-worked six wouldn't last long. Hawthorn took over the Ferrari of a dispirited González to place second behind Fangio with Trintignant's 625 third. The best Maserati was the steady Sergio Mantovani in fifth.

After Maserati's early-season success, Ferrari had reversed the tables on its hometown rivals. For the Swiss Grand Prix at Bern on 22 August it had a new high-tailed version of the 625 for González, who put it on pole a fifth of a second faster than Fangio's Mercedes. Moss was third fastest 1.9 seconds back. Both he and Maserati-team newcomer Harry Schell retired in the race with oil-pump trouble, eviscerating Maserati's attack.

González placed second, on the same lap as Fangio, with Mieres and Mantovani fourth and fifth in 250 Fs.

Each of the first three rows of the grid for the Italian GP at Monza on 5 September had one car apiece from the major protagonists. Fangio's aerodynamic Mercedes-Benz was on pole with 1:59.0. Next to him at 1:59.2 in a 553-engined 625 was Alberto Ascari, loaned to Ferrari by Lancia to fight the Germans on Italian soil. Only a tick behind was Moss's 250 F at 1:59.3. In the next row were Kling (Mercedes), Villoresi (Maserati) and González at 2:00.0 in a Squalo with a new front end. Lampredi gave up on the Squalo's ball-jointed suspension, substituting a standard Ferrari kingpin and triple-track-rod layout to gain its better steering geometry. The third row held Herrmann (Mercedes), Hawthorn (Ferrari 625) and Mantovani (Maserati).

In the race Froilan González set fastest lap on his second – showing that Lampredi's central tank placement was a boon with a full load of fuel aboard. By far the staunchest defender of the Squalo throughout the season, González held second and then third place before oil-system failure forced him to take over Maglioli's 625, which he drove to third behind Hawthorn's similar Ferrari. Both had been lapped by winner Fangio. The bold

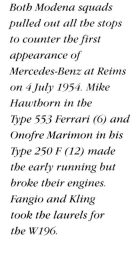

Both Modena squads pulled out all the stops to counter the first appearance of Mercedes-Benz at Reims on 4 July 1954. Mike Hawthorn in the Type 553 Ferrari (6) and Onofre Marimon in his Type 250 F (12) made the early running but broke their engines. Fangio and Kling took the laurels for the W196.

At the Nürburgring in 1957 this Type 500 TR showed the crackle-finished red camshaft covers that marked the birth of the 'Testarossa' era at Ferrari. This entry by Gotfrid Köchert, for himself and Erwin Bauer, placed 13th in the 1,000-kilometre race on 26 May 1957.

A glimpse inside the Modena garage of Guglielmo 'Mimo' Dei's Scuderia Centro-Sud (right) showed his array of 'Aseigiciesse' Maseratis used for driver training. The evolution of the twin-cam A6GCS is shown (below, from back): the 1952 transition model, the 1953 version and the late-1955 edition.

Revised for 1957 as the Type 500 TRC, Ferrari's four-cylinder Testarossa (left) was a handsome beast with twin bulges over its cam covers. Maserati's counterpart for the 1957 season was its Type 200 SI (below). Producing 190bhp at 7,500rpm against the Ferrari's 180bhp at 7,000rpm, the Maserati maintained its winning form into 1959.

Developed as a sibling of the 450 S V8 in a concept introduced by Vittorio Bellentani, Maserati's Type 200 S four shared cylinder-head and valve-gear technologies with the eight. It first raced in 1955, appeared in greater numbers in 1956 and came into its own as the Type 200 SI in 1957.

Maserati's Type 250 F was popular with private entrants like Bristol's Horace Gould (left), seen warming up his car in the paddock. His was a 1954 chassis rebodied to the cleaner 1955 design, like the glossily restored example below. This was the main mount of Stirling Moss in his 1956 battles with Fangio in a Ferrari.

Early Type 250 F Maseratis were rebodied along later lines, like the Scuderia Centro-Sud's 1954-chassis car (right), non-qualifying for Monaco in 1958 in the hands of Gerino Gerini. Chassis number 2529 was raced by Juan Fangio in his 1957 World Championship year and driven to second place at Lime Rock (below) by Chuck Daigh in 1959.

For the 2.5-litre Formula 1, which started in 1954, Maserati's 250 F six proved a sound compromise between Ferrari's fours and the eights of Lancia and Mercedes-Benz. Not until 1957, however, did it win a World Championship with the help of Juan Fangio and the shrewd addition of nitromethane to its methanol fuel.

In 1955 Ferrari used this Type 555 engine both in its Supersqualo and in its classic Type 625 chassis. In Grand Prix racing this was the final gasp of the four-cylinder concept that Aurelio Lampredi introduced in 1951.

Ascari led the race until retirement on lap 48 of 80. It then seemed that Moss would win for Maserati, but his 250 F failed ten laps from the finish.

After Monza Aurelio Lampredi took the Type 553 in hand again and installed coil springs in its front suspension, for the first time in a Ferrari, in conjunction with an anti-roll bar. This and other improvements added up to Monza laps at 1:58 during tests which led Mike Hawthorn to write that the Squalo 'was improved out of all recognition and had become a very nice little car.' The Englishman proved it by throwing the revised Ferrari around the Barcelona circuit with his usual abandon to win Spain's final championship Grand Prix of the 1954 season on 24 October.

A Maserati led the first two laps in Spain, but it was Harry Schell on a half-full fuel tank acting as a 'rabbit' to exhaust his rivals. Villoresi had now joined Ascari in the new Lancia D50 at last, since after the Italian GP Maserati had promoted Luigi Musso to Formula 1, following his excellent drives in A6GCS/2000 sports cars. After Moss's retirement it was Musso who led the Maserati attack, ultimately finishing a commendable second on the same lap as winner Hawthorn.

Maserati could look back at two early-season wins in championship GPs, helping Fangio to a second World Champion trophy. Ferrari had two wins as well, but many more podium finishes than

its Modena rivals. In what he considered his best-ever season Froilan González finished 1954 with 25 championship points, second to Fangio's 42. Applying the later points criteria for makes saw Ferrari a close second to Mercedes with 36 points against 39 and Maserati third with 30. Neither of the Italians had done badly against the vaunted might of Daimler-Benz.

With Mercedes committed to another season in 1955 and the new Lancia D50 showing electrifying pace in the hands of Ascari, the two Modena firms were relegated to their intramural battles, which they took very seriously indeed. Developments over the winter saw Vittorio Bellentani leave Maserati to join Ferrari and – an even greater blow for Viale Ciro Menotti – Stirling Moss signing to drive for Mercedes-Benz. While Moss was replaced by Frenchman Jean Behra, Bellentani's departure brought a promotion for Giulio Alfieri, who was named chief engineer in May. He continued to supervise team activities during practice but left the conduct of races to others, principally Bertocchi.

Maranello also had its defections. Froilan González would race for Ferrari at home in Argentina but would no longer drive red cars in Europe. During the season Enzo Ferrari would sign up-and-coming Eugenio Castellotti and lure Hawthorn back from an intermezzo with Vanwall to restock his team. Nevertheless Aurelio Lampredi

Though the silver Mercedes were to the fore at the start of the German GP on 1 August 1954, the Ferrari 625 F1 of González (1) and private Maserati of Moss (16) were in the hunt. Hawthorn (3) placed second in the car of González after rear axle problems in his own 625.

Froilan González drove a new high-tailed version of the Type 625 F1 Ferrari at Bern on 22 August 1954, powered by the latest Type 553 four. He placed second, one minute behind Fangio's Mercedes-Benz. The best 250 F was fourth, driven by Roberto Mières.

The atmosphere of the magnificent 3.6-mile road course through the Bremgarten at Bern, Switzerland, is evoked by this 1954 Mailander image of Moss's Maserati chasing the Ferrari of González. This was the last year the circuit was used for racing.

later reflected that 'we lacked men rather than cars, at that time.'

Neither company made major changes to its Grand Prix engines. With a new cylinder head giving larger inlet valves and passages, Maserati raised 250 F power to 260bhp and, during the season, introduced a five-speed gearbox. Ferrari claimed 270bhp at 7,200rpm for an uprated four during the year. Both were stressed to the very

limit in their internecine battles, said Maserati historians Luigi Orsini and Franco Zagari: 'The fierce rivalry between the Italian marques tended to carry the engines toward an acute exasperation.'

As usual the first championship race of the new season on 16 January at Buenos Aires was fought by cars that were largely carryovers from the previous year. This promised intense competition, with the grid's front row occupied by González

(Ferrari 625), Fangio (Mercedes), Ascari (Lancia) and Behra (Maserati), all within seven-tenths of a second. In tropical heat Fangio won, followed by two Ferraris, each of which needed three drivers in succession. Like Fangio, Roberto Mieres drove through on his own, finishing fifth in his works 250 F, while Schell and Behra shared the sixth-place Maserati.

Thereafter the Modena teams settled down to the design of their definitive 1955 contenders. Maserati cleaned up the skins of its 250 Fs, of which two new chassis were built for 1955. Replacing their many rows of louvres, Medardo Fantuzzi fashioned new bodies that were much smoother with large individual vents. Ferrari did much the same with its 625, which to the surprise of many was still a major weapon in its 1955 armoury. It had the new coil-spring front suspension that had worked so well at Barcelona.

At Maranello hopes were highest for a new version of the Squalo, the Type 555, inevitably known as the 'Supersqualo'. Technically it was a shadow of its former self. It was essentially the late-1954 Type 625 fitted with the special Squalo transaxle, side and tail tanks, a reinforced frame and a rakish new Scaglietti body with a long, spatulate snout and – unusually for a racing car – a styling touch of bright metal down the centre of its hood. The side-tank bulges were now vented to exhaust warm air and continued back to shroud a portion of the rear tyres.

The 555's engine and quick-change transaxle were mounted in a new frame based on two large-diameter tubes tapered at the rear. Above this frame was a lattice of smaller tubes which also supported the body. The 1953 prototype had a wheelbase of 82.5in, which was reduced to only 78.7in in 1954. For 1955 it was expanded again to 84.1in – still half a foot shorter than the 250 F with its longer six-cylinder engine.

The Supersqualo gained repute as a car with strong understeer, a grievous fault in a season when most of the races were run on relatively tight courses. A fully recovered Nino Farina was the first to try one in anger on Turin's Valentino circuit in March but it broke, so he didn't race it. Both cars (Farina and Trintignant) retired in a race at Bordeaux in April in which they'd shown clear inferiority to the best 250 Fs.

Serious business began at Monaco on 22 May with the year's second race for championship points. With Behra and Musso leading its campaign Maserati was better-equipped than Ferrari, whose drivers were all of the second and third rank. This was reflected by the grid, which had Behra in the second row and Musso and Mieres in the third, all pedalling Maseratis. Driving 625s, Trintignant and Farina were in the fourth row while the new Supersqualos, with Schell and Piero Taruffi, were relegated to the sixth and seventh rows.

While the agile Maseratis were in their element at Monaco, the Type 555s were in trouble with gear

Lap four of the Italian Grand Prix on 5 September 1954 saw three red cars contesting second place behind leader Fangio on Monza's stone setts. The 553 Ferrari of González led Ascari's 625 ahead of the Maserati of Moss.

ratios, their quick-change gear sets not going low enough. With their understeer their front ends drifted out so much that they could barely squeak around the tightest hairpins. While the latest Ferraris were insignificant in the race, Roberto Mieres kept his 250 F well in the hunt, and with the retirements of the Mercedes and Ascari's Lancia he might well have stolen a win, but his drive shaft broke. Stealing the win instead was Maurice Trintignant in his Type 625 Ferrari.

At the fast Spa-Francorchamps circuit on 5 June the Type 555 was much more in its element, its understeer ideal for drifting the Ardennes track's fast bends. For the first time three Supersqualos started, Nino Farina qualifying in the second row with fourth-fastest time. Next to him was Jean Behra in the quickest Maserati. Another Modena pairing was in the third row with Luigi Musso and Belgian journalist-racer Paul Frère, right at home in the Belgian Grand Prix.

Frère it was who at Monaco had begged the mechanics to decouple the front anti-roll bar to reduce the 555's crippling understeer, only to be told that because it 'was part of the car' it couldn't be touched. The Belgian placed fourth and Nino Farina finished third, both on the same eight-mile lap, as the two leading Mercedes. Trintignant came home sixth.

The only Maserati remaining to be beaten into fifth place was the car of Mieres, taken over by Behra after the latter crashed. Spa had been a fiasco for Maserati, whose cars didn't arrive until the second day of practice. It was also a turning

point for Grand Prix veteran Nino Farina, who, in spite of his honourable podium position, gained on a demanding circuit by a fantastic drive that lived up to his personal standards, was frustrated by the Supersqualo's lack of sheer power. Dismayed by the inadequacy of the equipment at his disposal, the imperious Farina stepped down from the cockpit and didn't race in Formula 1 again.

The weekend after Spa was the 24 Hours of Le Mans, a race that transformed the season's character. With a driver and more than 80 spectators killed on the pit straight, racing authorities throughout the world recoiled in shock. Championship Grands Prix in France, Switzerland, Germany and Spain were cancelled, leaving only three more points-scoring races in which Ferrari and Maserati could settle their domestic rivalry.

Contemporaneously financial problems at Lancia and the death of its lead driver Alberto Ascari caused that company to withdraw its team of advanced D50 models. Enzo Ferrari was quick to take advantage, hiring the talented Eugenio Castellotti. The Roman and Mike Hawthorn were on deck for Maranello at the Dutch Grand Prix at Zandvoort on 19 June. 'It was the first time I had driven the Supersqualo which had been developed from the car I drove at Barcelona and I could not do much with it on this circuit,' wrote Hawthorn. 'It suffered from extreme understeer and even with the steering on full lock it seemed to keep on going straight ahead for an awfully long time on corners.'

In contrast, Maserati under Giulio Alfieri was getting its act together. A compact works team of

For the 1955 season Ferrari updated its 625 F1 with sleeker bodywork and downward-curving exhaust pipes. This was the high-tailed version with greater fuel capacity.

Behra, Musso and Mieres came to Zandvoort, Musso qualifying fastest behind the three Mercedes. With Behra not on form it was up to Musso to beat the Ferraris, which he did with an excellent third place on the same lap as the leaders. Mieres was fourth, after setting fastest lap, and Castellotti fifth, an ignominious three laps behind the leading trio.

Run for the first time at Aintree, the British Grand Prix was held on 19 July. Intramurally it was another triumph for Maserati. Back on form, Jean Behra shared the front row of the grid with the Mercedes of Moss and Fangio. He held them in the race as well but was out early with a burst oil pipe – an all-too-frequent 250 F failing. Mercedes grabbed the first four places but next behind them was the persistent Luigi Musso's Maserati.

Relegated to sixth place was a Ferrari 625 taken over from an unwell Hawthorn by Castellotti. All three of Ferrari's Aintree entries had been Type 625s, the fastest of which had been no higher than the fourth row of the grid. Chopping and changing

In this low-tailed Type 625 F1 Ferrari, Maurice Trintignant won the 1955 Monaco Grand Prix when all the Mercedes-Benzes retired. Castellotti's Lancia was second and the Maserati shared by Behra and Perdisa finished third.

In the Red-Hot Rivalry at Monte Carlo in 1955, Maserati-mounted Argentinean Roberto Mieres chased the Ferrari of eventual winner Trintignant. Mieres was in with a chance of a win until his final drive failed on lap 64 of 100.

between Ferrari's two types of cars saw the team going resolutely backward during much of 1955. 'As so often happens in time of difficulty,' wrote Laurence Pomeroy Jr, 'controversy arose as to who was really responsible for this state of affairs, and stemming from this Lampredi left the company after some five years of service and joined Fiat.'

'1955 was an awful year at Maranello,' recalled team manager Nello Ugolini. 'Ferrari was hyper-agitated, as usual seeking to squeeze the maximum out of his people, but refused to accept

the idea that the recurrent defeats were due to the inferiority of his cars versus their rivals. Lampredi, the technical director, walked out and so did I. We quarrelled one evening – I don't remember over what issue – and that was the end.' The next day found Ugolini sitting down with Adolfo and Omer Orsi: 'A handshake and I went over to the "enemy".'

The departure of Lampredi and Ugolini coincided with the arrival of the complete Lancia D50 racing team and equipment, a gift from the

Behind a Supersqualo in its 1955 guise were key members of the Ferrari strength. At left Luigi Bazzi explained a point to Nino Farina. Burly mechanic Luigi Parenti leaned against the pit counter while engineer Mino Amorotti (in shirtsleeves), responsible for car preparation, surveyed the scene.

Turin firm. Also stepping in was veteran freelance engineer Alberto Massimino, who had contributed much to earlier Maseratis. He took the Supersqualo in hand. Massimino modified the rear of its chassis to take the standard Ferrari five-speed racing transaxle. The de Dion tube now ran behind the differential, guided laterally by a vertical channel that was mounted to the frame instead of the gearbox. A compromise was struck with the 555's fuel tanks, the rear one being much enlarged but its side tanks remaining.

All four 1955 Supersqualos came to the start of the Italian GP at Monza on 11 September. Their best qualifying time was 2:49.6 on the power-hungry combined road and banked circuit against the pole of Fangio's Mercedes-Benz at 2:46.5, putting Castellotti in the second row. Maserati's best was 2:50.1 for Behra in the third row. The Frenchman's 250 F had a new aerodynamic body based on scale-model tests Alfieri had conducted in Milan University's wind tunnel. Unlike the Mercedes all-enveloping bodies it kept the tops of its wheels exposed for better tyre cooling.

Although Maserati prepared assiduously for the race, adding Peter Collins to its official strength, it had to give best to the well-driven Supersqualo of Castellotti. The Ferrari was third at the finish, only 45 seconds behind the winner. Just over three minutes in arrears was Behra's aerodynamic 250 F, which clattered over the line in fourth with a broken piston. Carlos Menditeguy's works Maserati was fifth, and sixth was Umberto Maglioli in a Supersqualo.

Last gasps for the Squalo were the Argentine races in January 1956, which Ferrari used as a test session for new concepts. A normal end-1955 Supersqualo was driven there by Peter Collins. Olivier Gendebien was entrusted with a combination of 555 chassis and Lancia D50 V8 engine. Ferrari also brought along a Supersqualo on which all the fuel tankage was behind the driver, but this wasn't judged worth running. None of these 555s showed as much merit as the inherited Lancia D50s, which became the basis for Ferrari's GP cars of 1956 and '57.

Statistically Ferrari got the best of Maserati in 1955. Its drivers Castellotti and Trintignant were third and fourth respectively in championship points, although Castellotti benefited from his second place for Lancia at Monaco, where the Frenchman had what can only be described as a fluke win for Ferrari. Seventh, eighth and ninth in the points were 250 F pilots Mieres, Musso and Behra.

Allocating championship points on the later manufacturers' basis also showed an advantage for Ferrari, with 24 to Maserati's 16. The eight-point margin was entirely attributable to Trintignant's Monaco victory. That excepted, the Modena rivals can be seen as level-pegging through the season, both beset by confusion but both having their moments of glory. Of the two, Maserati seemed most on the rise.

In 1956 the story would be different. In the absence of Mercedes-Benz and Lancia, Grand Prix racing would revert to the status of 1952 and '53: a straight fight between Ferrari and Maserati. Each would have one of the world's best drivers. The Red-Hot Rivalry would be back to centre stage.

Last gasp for the Supersqualo was its entry in two races in Argentina in early 1956. In the Argentine GP on 22 January Peter Collins chased a Maserati before shunting a different one and retiring. This 250 F placed fourth in the hands of local hero Chico Landi and Roman Gerino Gerini (shown).

CHAPTER EIGHT

750 Monza vs 300 S

Inspired by their latest Grand Prix cars, Ferrari and Maserati squared off in 1955 and '56 with great 3.0-litre sports-racers that had stunning good looks as well as customer-friendliness. Each had its moment in the sun.

Hot on the heels of its creation of the World Drivers' Championship in 1950, the FIA turned its attention to sports-car racing. Endurance races like Le Mans and the Mille Miglia were acknowledged as great classics, but no championship linked them in a manner that might excite both racing fans and participants. That changed in 1953 with the FIA's establishment of the World Sports-Car Championship. Rightly enough it was for car makers, not drivers.

Here was fresh inspiration for the world's builders of sports-racing cars. Jaguar, Aston Martin, Cunningham and Mercedes-Benz took notice. In the new trophy's first season, 1953, points would

Stirling Moss enjoyed a productive personal affinity with the Maserati 300 S. He was flagged home the winner of the 75-mile sports-car race that accompanied the British Grand Prix on 14 July 1956. He set fastest lap as well.

be awarded for finishes in the Sebring 12 Hours, Mille Miglia, Le Mans 24 Hours, Spa 24 Hours, Nürburgring 1,000 Kilometres, Tourist Trophy and Carrera Panamericana. While the races in Florida and Mexico were newcomers, the others were great international events. Success in the new championship would bring major kudos and act as a spur to sales. How would the Italians respond to this new challenge and opportunity?

One Italian maker would make a brief appearance in the new series. From Turin a resurgent Lancia under Gianni Lancia's leadership fielded V6-powered sports-racers that tied with Cunningham for fourth in the 1953 results and placed second in 1954, when Lancia turned all its attention to its D50 Grand Prix car. Exploiting its big V12 engines to the full, Ferrari won the championship in both 1953 and '54, collecting a Le Mans victory as well in the latter year. Maserati was an also-ran, with nothing bigger than its 2.0-litre A6GCS/2000 to challenge for outright victory.

The sports-racing activities of the hometown rivals began to converge during 1954. With Ferrari and Maserati working from existing bases of technology, by the end of that year both were

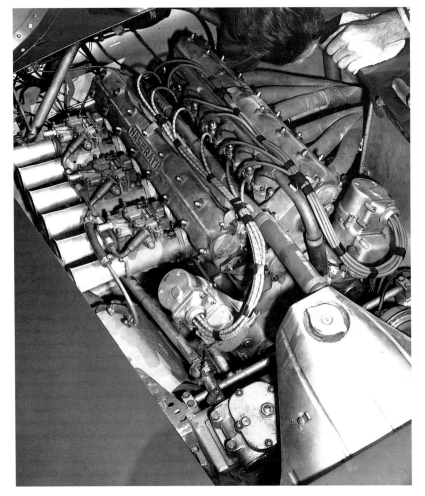

The straight six of a Maserati 300 S at Elkhart Lake in 1956 illustrated the pure-bred quality that Modena invested in their 3.0-litre sports-racers. Both it and the 750 Monza Ferrari were category champions and frequent contenders for outright victory.

fielding 3.0-litre sports-racing cars that put them in head-on competition every bit as ruthless as their epic clashes in the 2.0-litre class.

An important catalyst in this respect was the new 1954 Grand Prix Formula 1. Favouring as it did engines of 2.5-litres, the formula produced power units with the potential to be enlarged to 3.0-litres. The latter size suited the international Sports 3000 category and was big enough as well to contest for outright victories. This was the philosophy of Mercedes-Benz, which planned from 1954 to have engines of those sizes in its Grand Prix and sports-racing cars respectively.

Having benefited under chief engineer Aurelio Lampredi from punchy four-cylinder engines in his racing cars, Enzo Ferrari approved Lampredi's plan to extend the technology to larger dimensions for a new 3.0-litre sports-racer in parallel with work on its virtually identical sibling, the 2.0-litre Type 500 Mondial that made its debut at the end of 1953.

A lengthy evolution in four-cylinder capacity began in 1952 with a 2.5-litre four for the Type 500 F2 chassis in preparation for the new GP Formula of 1954. In 1953 similar engines, tuned for petrol fuel, were installed in two Vignale-bodied cars, a coupé and a spyder. Known as the 625 TF (for 'Targa Florio'), the open car made its first appearance in the two-heat Autodromo Grand Prix at Monza on 29 June 1953. Driven by Mike Hawthorn, it placed fourth.

In some of his first team drives for Ferrari, Umberto Maglioli placed third in the Dolomite Cup with the ex-Hawthorn 625 TF spyder on 12 July and second in the Susa-Montcenisio hillclimb a week later. They also competed in an 87-mile race at Senigallia on the Adriatic on 9 August but the Ferrari retired there.

The two-heat Monza sports-car race at the end of June 1953 also saw the debut of an even bigger version of the four. With 102 x 90mm dimensions for 2,942cc it produced 225bhp at 6,800rpm. It was installed in an open sports-racer that was bodied at Maranello to a design by Aurelio Lampredi.[1] This 735 S showed great pace when driven in the first heat of the Autodromo GP by Alberto Ascari but crashed when the reigning World Champion had to avoid another car.

In January of 1954 the two 625 TF Ferraris were exported to Argentina with Type 735 S 2.9-litre

---

1 The name 'Autodromo', that of a Modena coachbuilder that specialised in commercial vehicles, has often been associated with the bodywork of this car. Ferrari expert Antoine Prunet suggests that this may have been related to the race in which the car made its debut, not to its coachbuilder. He also surmises that Scaglietti may have helped create its body, which he calls an 'ugly duckling'.

engines. They competed in the 1,000 Kilometres of Buenos Aires, where one had the measure of the Ferrari twelves until the four's torque shattered its final drive after a pit stop. Its sister was driven to a conservative fifth place. Both cars remained in South America.

During 1954 the definitive new sports-racing model was developed in parallel with Ferrari's struggles with Mercedes-Benz on the Formula 1 circuit. A key event in its evolution was the 1,000km Supercortemaggiore sports-car race at Monza on 27 June 1954. Mike Hawthorn and Umberto Maglioli took first place in a proto-Monza based on a Mondial chassis, with Gonzales/Trintignant second in a sister car. After this triumph the new model was further developed in preparation for a tranche of production in the winter of 1954–5. The first entry for a singleton 750 S Monza (named after its 1954 success there), with its definitive Scaglietti body, was at Buenos Aires in January 1955.

The main line of development toward the Monza was via its engine, which was designated Type 105 by the Ferrari drawing office. In classic Lampredi style its head and cylinders were integrated in an aluminium casting which included the ports, combustion chambers and water jackets but not the cylinders themselves, which were separately cast of iron and screwed up into the chambers. Dimensions were 103 x 90mm, daringly close to the Class D limit at 2,999.6cc.

By any standards this was a remarkable engine. Here was a four-cylinder unit with as much cylinder capacity as many of Ferrari's twelves. A twelve-cylinder engine of similar cylinder size would displace nine litres! Not since the years

before the First World War had a serious European racing car been powered by such a colossal four-cylinder engine. As a big four in the racing world its only rival in the 1950s was America's Meyer-Drake Offy. The latter's bore size of 4.375in (111.1mm) was only slightly larger than that of this astonishing Ferrari.

While the Offy had the advantage of four valves per cylinder, unfashionable in the Europe of the 1950s, the Monza made do with two huge valves. Inlets of 50mm were inclined at 45° from the vertical and 46mm exhausts at 40°, the latter having sodium-filled stems. The combustion chamber was a modified hemisphere with special contouring around its two spark-plug holes. The twin plugs were closest to the exhaust valve, a position which, with a bore of over 4in, was vital to proper ignition of a thinly spread mixture.

Lampredi's proven techniques were incorporated in the Monza's elaborate valve gear. Twin hairpin springs, in a fore-and-aft plane, closed the valves through a collar retained by split keepers. Above this the tappets and camshaft were

As purposeful as any Ferrari ever made, this was the Type 735 S driven by Alberto Ascari in the first heat of the Autodromo Grand Prix at Monza on 28 June 1953. The unique 2.9-litre prototype was a forerunner of the Type 750 Monza.

Aurelio Lampredi created a unique tappet design for his in-line Ferrari engines, including the 750 Monza. Each light-alloy tappet had its own coil spring to close it, carrying a roller follower on an anti-friction bearing.

Seen from the exhaust side, the 750 Monza four was Ferrari's Type 105 engine. Its elaborate valve gear required bulky cam boxes. At the front an accessory case drove the vertical dynamo and, on this customer car, twin ignition distributors.

carried in separate cast light-alloy boxes. Light-alloy tappets, guided by their stems, carried narrow rollers which protruded only slightly from their wide tops.

To keep this tappet assembly in contact with the cam, a pair of concentric coil springs acted against its upper surface, leaving the hairpin springs to cope solely with the valves. The separate tappet box, which accounted for the Monza's unusually high and wide cam boxes, allowed thorough lubrication of cams and followers without forcing leakage down the valve stems.

Exhaust porting was generous, the outer opening being flared considerably from its size at the valve. Tuned manifolding paired the pipes from cylinders 1-4 and 2-3, with these two later joined at a single expansion chamber. Induction was by two 58 DCOA3 Weber twin-throat carburettors, fitted with 44mm venturis. Angled alloy pipes connected the carburettors to the ports and stubby ram pipes were fitted.

The short head-cum-cylinder unit bolted directly to the very deep Silumin crankcase, with rubber O-rings forming water seals at the bottoms of the individual cylinders. Solid webbing supported each of the five main bearings, which were 60mm in diameter. The webbing continued down an inch and a half beyond the crank centreline to give the deep, I-sectioned bearing caps some lateral support. Two studs retained each cap. The centre main was 14mm wider than its 28mm brethren so it could carry the oil supply to the crank and the big ends.

Devoid of elaborate balance weighting, the Monza's forged-steel crankshaft carried 50mm big-end journals. Vandervell thin-wall bearings were fitted, as at the mains. Connecting rods were short and simple, the sides of the I-section shank being perfect tangents to the outer diameter of the wrist-pin end. Two bolts retained the big-end cap, while the fully floating pin received lubrication from splash alone. Full-skirted pistons carried two compression and two oil rings, one of the latter being below the pin.

In the transition from the 735 S to the 750 S the peak-power speed was cut back from 6,800 to

In one of its first racing appearances, the 12-Hour race at Reims in 1954, this works Ferrari 750 Monza was equipped with twin magnetos. One of the Houdaille hydraulic dampers of its front suspension was visible.

6,000rpm, at the latter giving 250–260bhp for the Monza. Nevertheless the four big pistons continued to impose a high level of stress on the rest of the engine and drive train. As a result the standard Monza's racing capability deteriorated after the first seven hours. Beyond that its tune lapsed and clearances became excessive, requiring a rebuild and renewal of stressed components. Nevertheless, with knowledgeable care the Monza's endurance could be stretched to 12 hours, as its racing record attests.

An alloy cover at the front of the engine concealed the accessory and camshaft drive train of 10mm-wide spur gears. The upper gears drove the cams while the water and oil pumps were placed low at the front. Dry-sump lubrication was used. Two screened pickups scavenged the front and rear of the intricately finned cast light-alloy sump. The scavenge oil pump had two idlers, to augment its capacity, and supplied a riveted tank on the right-hand side of the engine bay. Reluctant to complicate his crankcases with too many cast or drilled-in oil passages, Lampredi relied heavily on external and internal piping to carry the oil around.

Simplicity marked the Monza's cooling system, which circulated water with a twin-outlet pump adjacent to the scavenged oil supply. Drawing from the bottom of the gilled-tube radiator, the pump sent the coolest water to both sides of the crankcase, where it could absorb some of the heat generated by the main bearings. From there it rose past the cylinders to outlets directly above each combustion chamber. Thus the water was at its warmest when it reached the exhaust valves.

A bevel-gear extension from the camshaft gear train drove a cross-shaft within a magnesium-alloy box at the engine's front. Further bevels rotated the central 12v generator and the twin Marelli distributors that replaced the magnetos used on the 735 S and the early 750. A Fimac mechanical pump driven from the rear of the exhaust camshaft supplied fuel to the back end of the carburettor pipework, while the front end was fed by a rear-mounted Autolex electric pump.

The starter motor protruded rearward from the top of a shallow housing that enclosed a 10in dry double-plate clutch with flexible disc centres. A short extension supported the Hooke-type universal joint at the forward end of the drive shaft to the rear transaxle. Four heavy crankcase brackets mounted the engine package to the chassis on rubber inserts.

Placed just ahead of the final-drive gears, the transmission was split vertically in line with the mainshaft and carried the countershaft on the right and the selector mechanism on the left. Dog

clutches engaged constant-mesh gears in the top four of the five speeds, while a jointed shaft transmitted the driver's desires from the centrally placed shift tower. A compact conventional gate was used, with a simple reverse latch-out. While the proto-Monzas had four-speed boxes, the five-speed version was ready in time for early 1955 use on both the Monza and the Type 625 Grand Prix car.

Ferrari's early angled-tube chassis experiments were refined into a smoothly contoured structural base for the Monza. Two oval-section tubes were the main members, cross-linked and integrated into the body by many smaller steel tubes. Rear suspension was de Dion, its 2.5in steel axle tube curving behind the differential and connecting the fabricated hubs. At the tube centre a ball carried a square bronze block vertically between steel plates in the back of the differential casing to locate the tube laterally. Two parallel radius arms on each side guided the tube and absorbed braking torque.

Frame-mounted above the axle casing, a transverse-leaf spring was connected to the hubs by long drop shackles. Jounce was limited by rubber buffers acting against the de Dion tube while dampers were Houdaille vane-type. The early Monza front suspensions also used transverse leaf springs, as was then current on the GP cars. After Barcelona in 1954 proved the superiority of a coil layout on the Squalo Ferrari a switch to coils was made on the parallel-wishbone suspension of all Maranello models.

The front-suspension geometry gave a roll centre very near ground level. Thanks to a strong anti-roll bar more of the overturning couple was resisted by the front wheels, producing heavy understeer and leaving the rear wheels free to put power on the road. This, plus the limited-slip differential, frame-mounted final-drive gears and

Similar to the unit used in Grand Prix Ferraris, the 750 Monza's transaxle carried its transmission low and ahead of the final-drive gears. At the left of the differential was the vertical channel that gave lateral guidance to the de Dion tube.

At the end of 1954, Rudy Mailander photographed this factory-fresh 750 Monza at Maranello. As with its 500 Mondial sisters, the lines of the Scaglietti coachwork were inspired by the ideas of Enzo's son Alfredo 'Dino'.

The first version of Scaglietti's bodywork for the 750 Monza had a relatively small radiator-air inlet. Headlamps were fully faired.

low rear unsprung weight gave the Monza excellent traction, albeit at the cost of heavy understeer.

Brakes were of Lampredi's distinctive design with a central guide for each shoe to balance out the servo effect and wear. Two double-acting cylinders per wheel applied force equally to all four shoe ends. Air circulation inside the deeply finned drums was induced by radial ducts in the drum faces that acted as a centrifugal extractor. Borrani wire wheels were set well out from the brakes, leaving the finning of the latter exposed to best advantage.

Early Monzas had bodies by Vignale and Farina, but the final shape was based on the concept first tried on a Mondial by Enzo's son Alfredo 'Dino' Ferrari. Executed by Sergio Scaglietti's coachworks, the 750 S had splendidly aggressive lines that were penetrative but susceptible to lift, especially at the rear. In combination with the Monza's understeer this created treacherous handling at the limit that caught out some of the world's best drivers. Versatile Briton Ken Wharton was killed in a Monza crash in New Zealand early in 1957. In Sweden in 1955 the experienced Paul Frère found his Monza 'like driving without suspension, there was considerable friction in the steering, the brakes

were very hard and not very efficient and the understeer was monstrous.' When qualifying Frère understeered off the road, luckily escaping with a broken leg. In 1960 the Belgian drove a Monza as a practice car for the Targa Florio and found that 'its behaviour was completely unpredictable'. He went off the road twice and 'was not the only one to find himself in difficulty' with the 750.

Less fortunate was Italian star Alberto Ascari, who was killed at Monza in a Ferrari 750 S at the fast left-hand bend that now bears his name. At the time of Alberto's death no one dared suggest that the great master had made a mistake. Rather it was hypothesised either that his tie had flown in his face – he was testing in street clothes – that a strong crosswind had hit, that he swerved to miss a workman crossing the road, that he suffered a blackout following his accident the weekend before, that a wheel rim dug into the asphalt, or that he was simply fated to die then and there. It's most likely, however, that the Monza's deep understeer ended in a snap oversteer that not even Ascari could control.

When driven within its limits the 750 Monza proved a lively competitor, its engine's rich torque range a help to its drivers. There was no denying its

Rivals in different classes. In the Tourist Trophy held on 11 September 1954 the Musso/Mantovani Maserati A6GCS/2000 (57) was third on handicap and 2.0-litre class winner, while the 750 Monza of Hawthorn – driving here – and Trintignant (15) was second on handicap and leader on distance to clinch the World Championship for Ferrari.

lack of cylinders, however. 'In third gear there is a permanent vibration at all revs which makes you feel as if you have spent the day sitting on a steam hammer,' wrote Hans Tanner, who also found 'that at about 3,500rpm it sounds like a boiler factory working overtime.' 'Although it is not smooth,' reported John Bolster, 'the engine has an effortless feeling about it that has always been a feature of big four-cylinder units.'

After the Ferrari's successful debut at Monza, 1954 saw wins for González on Portugal's Monsanto circuit on 25 July, and on 8 August at Senigallia on the Adriatic in the hands of Maglioli. Further successes came in minor events at Agadir and Dakar in February and March of 1955. An entry by Texas oilman Allen Guiberson at Sebring in March for Phil Hill and Carroll Shelby found both his Ferrari and a Cunningham Jaguar D-Type credited with 182 laps in 12 hours; the final verdict in a contested result saw the honours go to the English car. Only two laps behind these leaders at the Florida finish on 13 March 1955 was the Maserati of Bill Spear and Sherwood Johnston. Two laps behind that was another Maserati, a lap ahead of a Chinetti-entered Ferrari Monza.

Having built its biggest-engined sports-racer since the war, Maserati was immediately on the pace with its new 300 S. The six-cylinder model made its debut at Sebring by finishing both Spear's private car, which set the race's fastest lap in Johnston's hands, and a works entry for Gino Valenzano and Cesare Perdisa.

Unlike Ferrari, which was racing 4.9-litre cars in 1954, Maserati had based its post-war product range on cars no larger than 2.0-litres. This was the maximum capacity of both its road and racing cars until the launch of the 2.5-litre 250 F in 1954. Self-evident as it was that the new car's components would lend themselves to a sports-racer, work began on prototypes early in 1954 under Vittorio Bellentani, Giulio Alfieri and chassis specialist Valerio Colotti.

Based on a chassis not unlike that of the concurrent 200 S, a new car was powered by a 2.5-litre six tuned to run on petrol. Called the 250 S, it produced a promising 240bhp at 7,200rpm. After careful study of the D-Type Jaguar and the Le Mans Bristols it was fitted with a low-drag body given slight finning at the rear.

This prototype made its debut at the 1954 Supercortemaggiore race in the hands of Fangio and his countryman Onofre Marimon. They kept it in second behind Hawthorn's winning Ferrari Monza until shortly before the end, when it was retired by the oil-feed and foaming problems that were also plaguing the Grand Prix version. Musso and Mantovani were wheeling a second 2.5 Maserati, which had a similar engine in a much-modified A6GCS/2000 chassis. The only visible change was the addition of a headrest. With the added power overwhelming its live rear axle, the latter car performed poorly and didn't finish.

The next step was a 2.8-litre version contrived by increasing the bore from 84 to 89mm while

In the Dundrod Tourist Trophy of 1955 the Monza of Jacques Swaters and Johnny Claes (7) chased the 300 S driven by Jean Behra (14). While the Maserati retired – a sister car was fifth – this Monza finished 13th overall.

holding the stroke at 75mm. This, however, was unsuccessful in tests so work on the 280 B, as it was called, was abandoned. A new 2.8 was then built with a bore and stroke of 81 x 90mm. Known as the 280 S, this was more in line with the long-stroke approach favoured by Bellentani over the shorter-stroke advocacy of the now-departed Gioachino Colombo.

Built to run on alcohol fuel, the 280 S gave 280 horses at 7,500rpm. In a hydroplane driven by Liborio Guidotti this engine scored a number of wins. One of the alcohol versions was installed in the Supercortemaggiore car for testing at Monza. Villoresi caused an uproar by lapping at 1:59, a timing not even reached by Grand Prix cars since the days of the Type 159 Alfa Romeo. At the time it was popularly believed that the Maserati was of 3.0-litre capacity and running on petrol, while in fact the 3.0-litre engine hadn't yet been bench-tested. This 'stunt' was one in the eye for Ferrari

The grid at Hagerstown, Maryland, in 1955 typified the battles between the Monza – here Phil Hill in George Tilp's car – and the 300 S, in this case Bill Lloyd's successful racer. Hill was the SCCA's Class D Modified champion that season.

This was one of the late-1954 prototypes of the future Maserati 300 S, powered by an increased-capacity version of the 250 F six, using much running gear from the A6GCS/2000. It was still left-hand-drive.

and fair notice to potential customers that Maserati might have something exciting to offer them.

The first full 3.0-litre built was the 300 S Ex, a final test of the oversquare approach favoured by Colombo. With dimensions of 92 x 75mm (2,991cc) this delivered 225bhp at 6,000rpm, its performance suffering from overheating of its more-crowded wet liners. The bore was therefore returned to the GP engine's 84mm diameter, which with a 90mm stroke gave 2,993cc. The resulting 300 S engine

produced an initial 245bhp at 6,200rpm. Subsequent development and experimentation with compression ratios produced alternative ratings of 250 at 6,700 and 260 at 6,500, depending on the type of racing for which a specific car was intended. Thus the Monza and 300 S were on power parity, though the Trident engine needed more revs to deliver it.

Few changes were made from the successful structure of the 250 F engine in creating the 300 S.

The seven-main-bearing crankshaft of Maserati's 300 S was fully machined with substantial counterweighting. Drillings on the counterweights showed the results of balancing.

The block extended from the centreline of the crankshaft up to the top of the cylinders, which were capped by a conventional detachable head. At the bottom of the block – the upper half of the crankcase – was heavy webbing to support the seven main bearings. Fourteen long studs ran upward from this webbing to clamp the head down and downward to retain the main bearing caps. All bottom-end bearing shells were Vandervell lead-indium type and all mains were 60mm in diameter.

Machined with full counterweighting from a steel forging, and balanced fully, the crankshaft had big-end journals 50mm in diameter. The connecting rods were also forged steel, with robust H-section shanks and two bolts per cap. These were polished with bronze wrist-pin bushings. Both circlips and aluminium plugs kept the pins in place in the pistons, which was rather like Maserati racing manager Nello Ugolini's habit of wearing a belt and braces at the same time. With different crown shapes for compression ratios of 8.6:1 or 9.5:1, the full-skirted pistons were made by Borgo.

Below was the cast-alloy two-part sump, deep and baffled to catch oil being flung from the whirling crankshaft. Its bottom cover plate was heavily finned for cooling and stiffness except at two circular areas into which were recessed wide, screened oil-scavenging pickups. Crankcase breather pipes were ducted from these points to the left-hand side of the engine to remove air from the system at this critical stage and thus eliminate the early oil-foaming problem. External oil pipes, broken by sections of hose to give some flexibility, drew from the twin pickups and fed the siamesed scavenge pump at the lower right front corner.

A deep casting at the front carried the scavenge and pressure oil pumps, the water and Fimac mechanical fuel pumps, plus the helical and spur gear drives to these units and all the fluid inlets and outlets. The crank nose drove two helical gears, one to motivate this unit and the other to rotate the gear train. This latter consisted of two big drilled gears vertically disposed to drive the four camshaft gears in the head, plus two short longitudinal shafts with bevels which turned the twin Marelli magnetos.

Roughly double the capacity of the pressure pump, the scavenge unit sent the SAE 60 oil back to the rear-mounted 5.5-gallon tank by way of an oil cooler in front of the radiator. Basic shape of this cooler was a 'U'-bent gilled tube placed horizontally with connections on the right-hand side of the car. Early cars had a single tube, while the later versions for both factory and customers had two parallel gilled tubes joined by a welded 'Y'

at each end. This gave better cooling while avoiding the weight, complication and possible failure of a conventional radiator core.

The pressure pump took oil from the reservoir and sent it to a full-flow filter mounted along the left-hand side of the crankcase. From there it crossed through the block to an external gallery for the mains along the right side. All the major oil-system joints were by two-bolt flanges sealed by rubber O-rings.

The 300 S engine used Maserati's advanced cooling-water circulation system which split the output of the centrifugal pump, sending a small amount directly to the block while directing most of the water to the exhaust-valve guides and seats by means of a special manifold down the centre of the head. A similar manifold above the inlet valves returned hot water to the radiator. Three attachments held the radiator: two Silentbloc bushings at the bottom and the radiator hose itself at the top. This was flexible enough to ward off twisting which might rupture the core's welding. Copper cores were used, experiments with aluminium having indicated an additional cost of around $1,000 which was judged too pricey by the Orsis.

Helical timing gears were used all the way to the last idler, which shared a shaft with the spur gear that drove the spur on the end of each cam. These cams rotated in seven white-metal bearings each with wide thrust surfaces at the centre journal.

Best Italian practice of the 1950s was shown in the pistons and connecting rods of the Maserati 300 S. Rod shanks were substantial and pistons full-skirted to carry a lower oil ring.

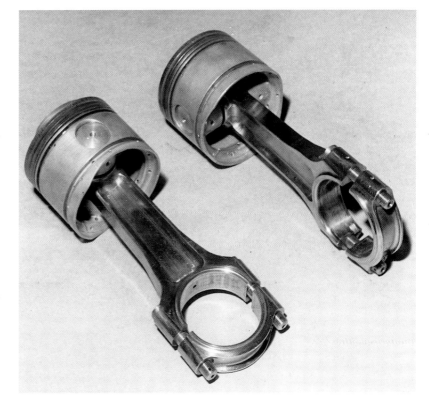

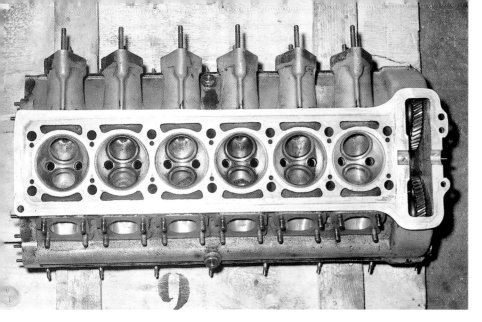

Spark-plug apertures for dual ignition were visible in the hemispherical combustion chambers of the 300 S six. Long integral inlet-port extensions allowed direct attachment of the Weber carburettors.

Light finger-type followers accepted side force from the cam lobes of the Maserati 300 S. Triple coil springs closed its valves.

Parallel to each cam in the head was a shaft which carried six finger-type cam followers. The finger-pivot shaft was hollow to deliver oil to each finger and, through a hole drilled in the base of the finger, to spray oil on the critical sliding surfaces.

Each valve was closed by three nested coil springs with a total compressed pressure of 385lb. This was over 100lb more than needed by the similar Grand Prix engine, but the latter had only 8.0mm lift while the inlet lobe on the 300 S lifted 12.5mm to supply the additional air needed by the bigger engine. With steep acceleration ramps, such a scheme was conducive to the mid-range torque that was useful in sports-car racing.

In its porting the 300 S head was identical to the Grand Prix unit with 46mm inlets at 36° from the vertical and 40mm exhausts at 41°. Valves were polished all over and well shaped, with triple notches in the stem to insure locking. The inlet-valve guide extended out into the port, a ridge

being gradually built up from the outer port opening to the guide to split the incoming charge and direct it around the stem. All ports were smooth with round inlet and oval exhaust openings.

Combustion chambers were hemispheric with their curvature shallower at the outside edges than in the central section bordered by the valves and the two plug holes. Combined with the shape of the piston crown, this gave a compact chamber with squish areas at the sides for good turbulence. Feeding 44mm inlet ports were Weber type 45 DCO3 twin-throat carburettors. Exhaust layout was a model of smooth, wide-radiused bends combined in the standard six-cylinder pattern of two groups of three leading into two pipes down the left-hand side.

Top and bottom of the clutch housing were extensions of the block and sump, the bottom half having vents for cooling. A multiplicity of studs bound the crank to the steel flywheel, a deep pot-type with internal splining for the multiple-disc clutch. Two steel driving discs, plus the pressure plate, engaged three interspersed aluminium driven discs. The latter were splined to a fabricated hub, which in turn was splined to the clutch shaft. Eight bolts held the clutch cover plate, with its three withdrawal levers, against the nine coil springs and the flywheel face. Complete with clutch the flywheel weighed 15lb. Covering the clutch assembly was a cast plate with four circular vents and double bearing support for the clutch shaft.

Drive to the rear transaxle was by a tubular shaft with Hooke-type joints at each end and a sliding spline at the front. Common to the 250 F Grand

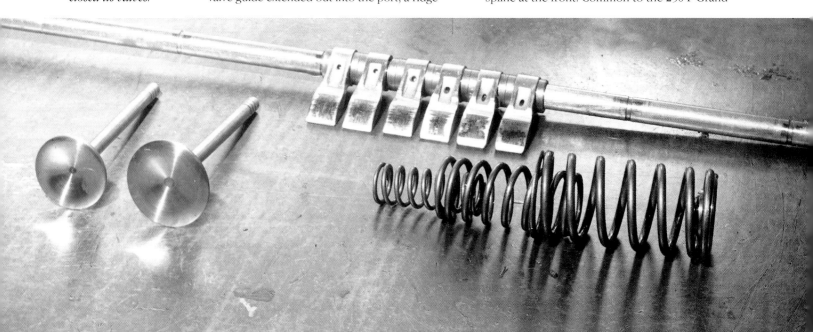

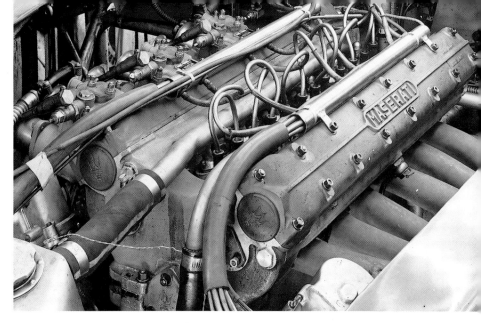

Prix car and the 300 S, the Maserati's transmission was akin to the rest of the car in being advanced in design but not so complex that it was hard to service and rebuild. Its two shafts were placed transversely, the lower or input shaft being driven by a pair of straight-cut bevels. Four pairs of constant-mesh spur gears gave the forward ratios. The desired pair was selected by a rugged dog clutch that gave clean, quick shifts with maximum reliability. The 300 S had a rudimentary reverse gear overhung inside the right-hand case cover where the GP car fitted a low starting gear.

Just above the input bevels at the left-hand end of the case was the spur drive up from the mainshaft to the eight-cam ZF differential. For both the incoming bevels and the outgoing spur gears there was a choice of five combinations each, giving a wide and precise choice of overall ratios.

Output from the differential went to a Hooke-type joint on each side, one yoke of each being blended and polished into the tubular axle shaft. The transaxle was bolted to the chassis through six Silentbloc bushings. The de Dion tube, much heftier on the 300 S than on the GP car, swept forward of the gearbox assembly and joined the two hub assemblies, which were large in diameter to house the pot-type outer universal joints.

The axle tube's hubs were guided by two parallel radius rods at each side, the ends of which were rubber-bushed. Lateral location of the axle was by a square bronze block, pivoted at the centre of the tube, which rode up and down between two steel guides bolted to the front face of the differential housing. Because the geometry of the trailing arms was such that the axle moved forward as it went up or down from its static position, the steel guide plates had a slight curvature to accommodate this.

A transverse leaf spring high above the hubs was connected to them by forged shackles. Mounting the spring between two wide-spaced pairs of rollers had a beneficial effect on its roll stiffness. In straight running and acceleration out of corners the Maserati's tail was supple, squatting down under power. In a corner, however, the action of the spring between the rollers increased the roll stiffness considerably, allowing the tail to be easily broken loose for the drifting, sliding driving that got the best from the 300 S.

Identical to that used in the production 250 F, front suspension was akin to that in Maseratis dating back to 1953. It was a beautifully finished coil-and-wishbone assembly, the top forged wishbone being shorter than that at the bottom. The small-diameter coil was actuated by a pivoted pad on the bottom wishbone, enclosed the rubber

bump stops and was anchored at the top against the fabricated box member from which all the arms were pivoted. Crossing the frame above the top wishbone, the anti-roll bar was connected to the bottom suspension arms by two long rubber-bushed links. Shocks were rotary-type Houdaille.

At the outer wishbone ends were conventional bushings and a short, angled kingpin. Forged steering arms extended forward and were connected by a three-piece track rod system with the steering box on the right and an idler arm on the left. Mounting these components was a frame of which the basic network was a low platform welded of oval tubing. Two of these ran wide at each side and tapered inward to the respective suspensions, while two more ran closer down the middle for engine support and added stiffness. Big round cross-tubes were just behind and forward of the seats and at the front, connecting the suspension boxes.

Twin magnetos supplied the dual ignition of the Maserati 300 S. This car, one of the 1955 Sebring entries, had a built-in engine-room lamp to ease pit work in the night-time of the 12-hour race.

Seen from the rear, the transaxle of the Maserati 300 S revealed its bevel input gears. Final drive from the all-indirect transmission was through a ZF differential in the tower with its pressure-oil nozzles.

Akin to those in the 250 F, the 300 S brakes were heavier for more arduous long-distance racing. In Maserati tradition the drums were large in diameter but narrow, with a centrifugal-air-pump system cast into their outer faces and covered by an alloy plate. Drum construction was predominantly light alloy with steel liners pressed into place and then riveted for retention. Separate master cylinders were used for the front and rear systems with braking effort proportioned 60/40 front/rear. Each brake had two leading shoes to generate a high self-servo effect.

In proportion to its added cylinders the Maserati had the longer wheelbase of 90.9in against 88.6 for the Monza. Both dimensions were identical to those of the rivals' respective 2.0-litre sports-racers. Their tracks were similar as were their weights, 750–760kg, some 1,650lb.

Unlike Ferrari, Maserati built its own competition bodies with the help of the redoubtable Medardo Fantuzzi. In all its guises the 300 S was everybody's idea of what a sports-racing car should look like. Early cars had a neat but short snout, with brake ducts hidden inside the

grille, while later versions had longer noses for better penetration and radiator airflow. Brake-air inlets were moved between headlamps and radiator scoop.

Official announcement of this handsome new Maserati was made at New Year 1955. Entry for Sebring in March specified 2.0-litre cars to avoid embarrassment if the new cars weren't ready. As already mentioned two did appear, taking third and fourth places. Bill Spear, Bill Lloyd and Briggs Cunningham acquired these plus a third, marking the beginning of an important relationship between the redoubtable Cunningham team and Maserati.

With the 300 S just gaining traction, the 1955 SCCA season saw Ferrari's Monza in the ascendant. In George Tilp's white car Phil Hill was the Club's Class D Modified champion with 9,500 points ahead of the Maseratis of Lloyd and Spear with 5,500 and 3,500 points respectively. Hill's season included an epic battle against Sherwood Johnston in a Cunningham D-Type in the inaugural 148-mile main event at Wisconsin's Road America. Easily lapping the field, the two fought a furious duel that saw Hill the winner by two cars' lengths after

Like its Grand Prix sister the 250 F, Maserati's 300 S had superb lines in this, its original 1955 body style. The wheel was now on the right side to suit road racing's predominantly clockwise circuits.

setting the virgin track's new lap record on his final round. Maseratis were fourth and fifth, those of John Gordon Bennet (in Cunningham's car) and Bill Spear respectively.

SCCA category honours in America were reversed in 1956, when Bill Lloyd won Class D Modified for Maserati, ahead of Ferrari Monzas driven by Carroll Shelby, Gene Greenspun and John von Neumann. Phil Stewart, in sixth, was the only other 300 S driver to score Class D points. Outright wins were less easy to come by for 3.0-litre cars when bigger-engined machinery was arriving, but Phil Stewart won for Maserati in Wisconsin and Carroll Shelby for Ferrari at Fort Worth. Major Monza exponents were Masten Gregory, Dabney Collins, Jack Hinkle, Sterling Edwards and Loyal Katskee, Ferrari having seized a numerical advantage.

Monza and Maserati fought it out in Europe on terms that were satisfyingly even. The first victory for the 300 S came to combative Frenchman Jean Behra at Bari on 15 May after a duel with Taruffi's 3.75-litre Ferrari six. Musso was second in another Maserati. Behra and Musso were to do well through the rest of the 1955 season in these cars.

The major 1955 showdown, the *mano a mano* between Maserati and Ferrari, came as it so often did in the Supercortemaggiore Grand Prix for sports cars over 626 miles at Monza on 29 May. Entries were limited to 3.0-litres, so the Red-Hot Rivals were on even terms. They mustered top teams, Ferrari pairing Hawthorn with Maglioli and Maserati marrying Musso with Behra, each company entering three works cars.

Two Maseratis flanked Hawthorn's Monza at the start of a race in which the Ferrari led early but was finally outpaced by the Behra/Musso 300 S, which took a fuel splash-and-dash two laps from the end to win by 17 seconds. Another 300 S was third, three laps back, followed at some distance by the other two works Monzas. His other individual placings, including third in the Giro di Sicilia, made Musso – with the Trident on his helmet – 1955's Italian champion.

In the premier league, the World Sports-Car Championship, 1955's results found Ferrari second behind Mercedes-Benz with 22 points to 24. Jaguar was third with 16 points and Maserati fourth with 13. A final non-championship confrontation in 1955 was the Grand Prix of Venezuela on 6 November at Caracas, to which Maserati sent a team led by Juan Fangio, now free of his Mercedes-Benz commitments. The Argentine won handsomely ahead of the Ferraris of Alfons de Portago, Emmanuel de Graffenried and Piero Carini.

With Fangio opting to race for Ferrari in 1956, the Orsis snapped up his Mercedes team-mate, Stirling Moss, thus setting the stage for a great rivalry on the tracks. 'From 1956 to 1958 I started thirteen races in 300 S Maseratis,' wrote Moss with Doug Nye, 'and I took them over after having started in a different type of Maserati on three more occasions. From that total of sixteen events the 300 S gave me nine wins, three second places, a

Both Ferrari and Maserati called on top Grand Prix drivers for their sports-racers. Guerino Bertocchi explained the facts of life to (from left) Jean Behra, Cesare Perdisa and Trident chief Omer Orsi.

At Le Mans in 1955 the 300 S of Gino Valenzano and Luigi Musso, driving here, ran second for a long time to the Jaguar D-type of Mike Hawthorn, only to retire with transmission trouble in the 20th hour.

third and a fifth and only two retirements. With a record like that, can you see why I have fond memories of these beautiful cars? There really was something about the 300 S and me. We seemed to be made for each other.'

Moss began 1956 in the best possible way by winning the 1,000 Kilometres of Buenos Aires in partnership with local ace Carlos Menditeguy. This was Maserati's first success in a World Sports-Car Championship race. 'Fangio chased us so furiously in a Ferrari [410 Sport] that it blew up,' Moss recalled, 'which was one in the eye for Maranello; our mechanics' jubilation was lovely to share.'

Ferrari's response to the exigencies of 1956 was to create an even bigger Monza. It kept the 102mm bore and lengthened the stroke to 105mm for 3,432cc, making it the largest four-cylinder engine ever produced by Ferrari and indeed the biggest four used seriously in road racing since the First World War. Only three works 860 Monzas to this new specification were made and they proved useful in 1956, starting by winning the Sebring 12-Hours. But they were the final gasp of the four-cylinder line initiated so daringly by Ferrari and Lampredi in 1951.

A useful twist for 750 Monza owners was that the FIA accepted Ferrari's assertion that at least 50 such cars had been built and that they thus qualified to compete as International Production Sports Cars, making them eligible for successes outside the unlimited Sport category. In fact Keith Bluemel's

authoritative tabulation shows that only 37 were produced, among which some were originally 2.0-litre Mondials. The two models were so similar that their engines were often interchanged to suit racing requirements. The total of Monza and Mondial production well exceeded 50 cars, so this would have provided a basis for Ferrari's claim.

Although the fine balance and versatility of the 300 S promised much in the championship for 1956, Ferrari prevailed with its wins at Sebring, the Mille Miglia and in Sweden, the latter two with the V12-engined 290 MM. Though seemingly an ideal mount for the Mille Miglia, the 300 S never tasted success there. Maserati's major 1956 triumph after Buenos Aires was at the Nürburgring, where Moss and Behra took over the Taruffi/Schell 300 S after their own had broken and defeated the 860 Monza of Fangio/Castellotti by less than half a minute after almost eight hours of racing. The final world points tally was 24 for Ferrari and 18 for Maserati.

Helped by the installation of a five-speed transaxle, other international victories fell to the 300 S in 1956 at Chimay, Paris, Silverstone, Bari, Caracas and in Australia. His excellent placings, including second in the Targa Florio, made 300 S-mounted Piero Taruffi Italy's champion driver for 1956.

A flying start to the 1957 season saw Fangio win in Cuba and a second-place performance at Sebring for the Moss/Schell partnership which indicated that the 300 S would have won outright if the new 450 S had failed – which it didn't. As late as 1958,

when it was withdrawing from racing, Maserati provided 300 Ss to Stirling Moss for races in Portugal, Sweden and Denmark, all of which he won. Unsurprisingly he remembered it as 'one of the nicest of all Maseratis'.

The book can be closed on these great Red-Hot Rivals with a sense that neither decisively prevailed. Given an early start, the 750 S Monza took advantage by placing more than three dozen cars with enthusiastic owners around the world. Driving within its limits they enjoyed many successes in a car that could be treacherous at the periphery of its footprint. Coming later, the 300 S benefited from a balanced design that blessed it with longevity. When the chips were down at Monza in 1955, it was the Maserati that triumphed. Perhaps the 300 S came out of this epic contest with the slightest of advantages.

In Portugal's Vila Real sports-car race on 13 July 1958, the 300 S Maseratis filled all three podium places, led home by Stirling Moss in the model he called 'one of the nicest of all Maseratis'.

Ferrari's ultimate version of the Monza, the Type 860 of 1956, had these huge pistons and valves, the latter still closed by hairpin springs. It was the last of Maranello's four-cylinder sports-car line.

CHAPTER NINE

500 Mondial, TR and TRC vs A6GCS /2000 and 200 SI

That Maserati's A6GCS/2000 so dominated its 2.0-litre category in 1954 was as a red flag to Ferrari's bull. Maranello responded with a 'Red Head' that triumphed in the showdown race at Monza in 1956. But Maserati had the last word.

The pride and passion that enlivened the Red-Hot Rivalry were brilliantly portrayed in the reception given to Mike Hawthorn (left) and Peter Collins after they won for Ferrari against Maserati opposition in the 1956 Supercortemaggiore Trophy at Monza.

Apart from a narrow class victory in the Mille Miglia and a win in the 2.0-litre race at Imola, Ferrari failed to enjoy a profitable return for fielding its all-new Type 500 Mondial in 1954. Although ambitious and pedigreed, the four-cylinder Mondial hadn't displaced from the high ground the Maserati A6GCS/2000, which although a year older was still the star of the 2.0-litre class, especially in Italy where the category was hard-fought. Maserati's six still had what it took to attract the wins – and the customers – from its cross-Modena rival.

Neither Ferrari nor the private racers and teams that were the lifeblood of its commercial activity could long tolerate this situation. Late in 1954 Enzo Ferrari and his prolific chief engineer Aurelio Lampredi decided to update their Mondial for the 1955 season. They did this in concert with improvements to their Type 750 Monza, the 3.0-litre sports-racer that shared its chassis with the Mondial.

Although commercially sound, their use of the same chassis for sports-racers in two categories – what today we would call 'platform sharing' – inevitably worked to the disadvantage of the smaller-engined version. All elements of the car

from frame to brakes and driveline had to be sized and stressed to suit the bigger and faster Monza model with half-again as much horsepower. With minor exceptions the chassis were identical, so much so that more than a few Mondials raced as Monzas with a simple engine swap and vice versa. Though this was not unsatisfactory for long-distance races, where durability was all-important, it disadvantaged the Mondial in shorter sprints and hillclimbs.

The chassis gained useful improvements for 1955, when production of Series II Mondials began in January. Although the frame continued as a twin-tube structure with central X-bracing, its oval main tubes were reshaped to improve stiffness, especially through the cockpit and at the rear. Rear suspension continued as de Dion, located by parallel trailing arms at the hubs and a block sliding in a groove for lateral guidance, with springing by transverse leaf. Five speeds in the rear-mounted transaxle were confirmed for the Series II.

Lampredi made major changes at the front of his chassis. For the Spanish Grand Prix the previous October he'd equipped his Type 553 Squalo racing car with a new coil-spring front suspension. Still

During practice for Le Mans on 11–12 June 1955 Luigi Musso tried the works-entered Sport 2000 Maserati of Francesco Giardini and Carlo Tomasi. In the race it retired in the ninth hour with ignition maladies.

In April 1955 Maserati sent an A6GCS/2000 and Jean Behra to a racing-driver school at Campione, Italy, to show the students how it was done. In spite of Ferrari's efforts the Trident was still king of its category.

The A6GCS/2000's superb lines were shown to advantage in Rodolfo Mailander's overhead shot at Campione in April 1955. Free of vents and louvres, the Maserati worked well in spite of its live rear axle – leaking here.

using parallel wishbones, the coils plus an anti-roll bar replaced the previous transverse-leaf spring, which had been mounted to give an increase in stiffness with roll. A big success on the Squalo, which won in Spain, the new suspension was used across the board on Ferrari's 1955 racers.

Nestling between the front frame rails was a heavily overhauled engine that also reflected Lampredi's latest thinking on Grand Prix design. Internally designated the Type 111, it kept his classic integration of head and cylinders in an aluminium casting which included the ports, combustion chambers and water jackets, but not the cylinders themselves, which were separately cast of iron and screwed into the chambers. Dimensions were unchanged from the Series I's Type 110 four at 90 x 78mm for 1,985cc.

Instead of the narrower 58° valve angle of the Series I, the Series II had an 85° angle with inlet valves at 45° from the vertical and exhausts at 40°, the latter having sodium-filled stems. The deeper combustion chamber that resulted constrained the new engine's compression ratio, which was 8.5:1 instead of the previous 9.2:1. The new Mondial shared the Monza's elaborate valve gear. Twin hairpin springs, placed in a fore-and-aft plane,

closed the valves through a collar retained by split keepers. Above this the roller-faced tappets, with their own coil springs, and tubular camshafts were carried in separate cast light-alloy boxes.

The four breathed through 40mm Weber twin-throat side-draft carburettors with 36mm venturis; one car had larger 42mm Webers. Inlet ports measured 34mm in diameter while the exhaust ports flared out to 48mm. A nine-disc clutch with alternating steel and aluminium plates accepted the Type 111's output, which was 170bhp at 6,800rpm. Maximum torque of 150lb-ft was delivered at 5,000rpm. This was similar horsepower to its predecessor, the Series I, albeit at a speed 400rpm lower and with better-placed peak torque. It promised, however, only parity with the 1954 version of Maserati's A6GCS/2000, not superiority.

Influenced as it was by the thinking of Dino Ferrari, with its long tail and downsloping snout the body shape of the late-1954 Mondials and Monzas was carried over to the 1955 models. The new car's rear was more voluminous to accommodate a fuel tank enlarged to a generous 33.0 gallons from the Series I's 26.4 gallons. Scaglietti made the bodies for the ten Series II

As late as 1957 Maserati's A6GCS/2000 was still proving its usefulness. This headrest-equipped example was driven to fifth in that year's European Mountain Championship, the best placing by a private entry.

Mondials that Ferrari produced between January and August of 1955. Apart from one chassis, number 0560, which was used initially as a works car before being sold, all were delivered to private owners.

Meanwhile in Modena the Officine Alfieri Maserati, flush with the continued success of its six-cylinder Sport 2000, produced 18 more in 1955, of which – as with Ferrari – the last left the factory in August. Though few basic changes in its architecture were needed for the new season, several of the final cars were given the new body shape being developed in parallel for the 3.0-litre 300 S. This had faired-in headlamps and a fuller centre section that smoothed the aerodynamics and gave the driver more protection.

Luigi Musso, who'd been Maserati's 2.0-litre star for two seasons, moved up to the 3.0-litre class in 1955. Segueing smoothly into his former role was Luigi Bellucci, who drove Sport 2000s to the Italian Championship for 2.0-litre cars. Bellucci used both his own car and one of the rebodied works cars to achieve his success. Others who did well in Italy with their *Aseigiciesse* Maseratis were Cesare Perdisa and Franco Bordoni. In the contests counting for the championship Ferrari scored only one win in the 2.0-litre class, that of Joao Dos Santos and Oscar Caballen in the 10 Hours of Messina on 23–24 July. Their Series II Mondial covered just seven more miles than the Maserati of Giulio Musitelli and Maria Teresa de Filippis.

1955's international season started with an unopposed Maserati success, class victory and third overall in the 1,000 Kilometres of Buenos Aires on 23 January. A future owner of Maserati, Alejandro de Tomaso, co-drove to seventh overall in a similar car. Not until 27 February did the first of the Series II Mondials make its bow at Morocco's Agadir, where Mario Della Favera won his class. In another African race uncontested by major Maseratis, Dakar in Senegal, Belgian Jacques Swaters was class winner in an older Mondial.

Neither Modena rival achieved much at Sebring. Their first serious showdown of 1955 was in the Giro di Sicilia on 3 April. There Mario Della Favera in his Mondial Series II prototype faced Sport 2000 Maseratis driven by Gino Valenzano and the 'Rampant Baron' Antonio Pucci. Theirs was a close battle, with Valenzano leading in the 676-mile hegira around the coast of Sicily. After Gino retired the Maserati of Pucci seized the class lead, but the Baron wasn't given signals to that effect. Near the finish he relaxed and let Della Favera's Mondial through to take fourth place and the category laurels. The margin between them was a scant

Close kin to half a cylinder bank of the 450 S V8, Maserati's 200 S four was the work of Vittorio Bellentani. Its Weber carburettors had 45mm bores and its flywheel carried a multiple-disc clutch.

Carved from the solid, the 200 S Maserati's crankshaft had five main bearings and thick cheeks, thanks to generous cylinder-bore spacings inherited from the 450 S V8. Counterweighting was at the centre and ends.

Twin plugs fired the hemispherical chambers – one damaged here – of Maserati's 200 S four. Carburettor mountings had rubber-damped inserts to keep engine vibration from aerating the fuel/air mixture.

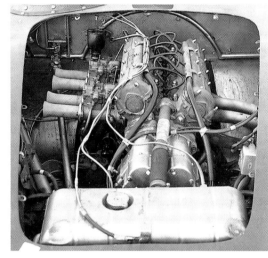

As installed in the 200 S Maserati, the 2.0-litre four was inclined slightly to the left to make room for its carburettors and the long ram pipes used in this car. Dual ignition was still by magnetos.

Squared-off camshaft covers and red paint gave a fresh look to the engine of Ferrari's 500 TR for 1956 and provided its 'Testa Rossa' sobriquet. Ferrari and Maserati now faced each other with rival 2.0-litre fours.

minute and 22 seconds after 11 hours of racing. Other 2.0-litre Maseratis were seventh, eighth and tenth overall.

Maserati riposted in the Mille Miglia on 30 April, making up for its narrow loss in 1954 by placing fourth overall, Francesco Giardini running solo and winning his class. Bellucci was ninth and second in class while – in a calamity for Ferrari – all four new Series II Mondials retired, Della Favera's while leading the class. This marked the beginning of a reputation of unreliability for the new model, whose connecting rods in particular were suspect.

Battle was rejoined in the heel of Italy's boot at Bari on 15 May, where Perdisa's Maserati triumphed over Della Favera's Ferrari. Modena's two champions regrouped for a battle royal at Monza on 29 May in the Supercortemaggiore Grand Prix for sports cars over 1,000km. Italy mourned her great hero, twice World Champion Alberto Ascari, who was killed while practising for the race in a friend's Ferrari Monza. The Mondial's more powerful big sister was earning a reputation for deceptively tricky handling.

Reflecting the disparity in numbers, the 2.0-litre class at Monza was contested by ten Maseratis and seven Ferraris, four of the latter the new Series II Mondials. Two of the new model retired, while two others placed eighth and tenth overall and third and fourth in class. Luigi Bellucci teamed up with motorcyclist Bruno Ruffo to place their Maserati sixth behind the 3.0-litre cars and first in class, ahead of Valenzano and Pagliai in seventh in a similar car. This was a signal triumph for the Trident, which also claimed the overall win at Monza.

Neither marque was a serious contender at Le Mans on the 11–12 June 1955 weekend which, however, saw a serious setback for Ferrari. On the Sunday its flagbearer for the Series II, Mario Della Favera, was killed while contesting a hillclimb in Parma. His Mondial, first of the new breed, was written off. Luigi Bellucci and Enrico Sterzi placed their Maseratis second and third behind a 3.0-litre Ferrari.

In the inaugural race for 2.0-litre sports-racers at Imola a year earlier the Series I Mondial scored one of its few wins over the *Aseigiciesse* that season. The Shell-sponsored event in 1955 on 19 June was over 156 miles of flat-out racing for Italy's 2.0-litre bragging rights. This time it was a triumph for the Trident. Rising star Cesare Perdisa set fastest lap at 90.07mph and won at an average of 87.86mph, useful improvement on Umberto Maglioli's 1954 speed of 87.06mph. Maglioli was second in a brand new works Series II Mondial, 21.5 seconds back, with Harry Schell third in an

older Mondial. A week later Sport 2000s rubbed it in with a one-two-three finish in the 143-mile Circuito di Caserta, led by Luigi Bellucci. New Mondials were fourth and fifth.

In July Eugenio Castellotti took over the factory Mondial. On the 3rd he won the 15.2-mile Bolzano-Mendola hillclimb, demoting the Maseratis of the brothers Valenzano Piero and Gino into second and third respectively. A week later he was second overall in the Dolomite Cup, with the Maseratis nowhere. After 3½ hours the winner by 21 seconds in a Mercedes-Benz 300 SL was Olivier Gendebien. This so impressed Enzo Ferrari that one week later the Belgian rally ace found himself behind the wheel of the works Series II and competing in the Aosta-Gran San Bernardo hillclimb. Gendebien

justified his first-ever Ferrari ride with second overall, splitting two 3.0-litre cars.

On 31 July Luigi Bellucci took his *Aseigiciesse* to Catanzaro to compete in the 450-mile Giro Della Calabria. He brushed Pietro Carini's Mondial into second place by a quarter-hour. Four weeks later Maserati-driving Franco Bordoni and Maria Teresa De Filippis were first and second in the 164-mile Pergusa Grand Prix.

Some big events still remained in 1955 to test the hometown combatants. Two were World Championship races, Britain's Tourist Trophy and Italy's Targa Florio. In the first of these on 17 September André Loens entered his A6GCS/2000 and chose as co-driver a promising Swede named Jo Bonnier. Although as high as

The bland appearance of the 500 TR Ferrari's brake drums was deceptive. Behind their aluminium covers were radial passages that centrifuged warm air away from the shoes and their linings.

In search of lightness Ferrari adopted a live rear axle for its 1956 500 TR, locating it laterally with a robust tubular A-arm giving a low rear roll centre. Coil springs acted on rearward extensions from the axle's ends.

Although built by
Scaglietti, the 1956
Ferrari Testarossa's
shape was the work of
Pininfarina. Their
artistry shows in its
voluptuous lines and
the fine detailing of its
bonnet, cockpit and
headrest.

For a sports-racer
designed to be sold to
private entrants it never
hurts to make the car
gorgeous, as was the
1956 500 TR Ferrari
with its tapering tail, a
legacy of its predecessor,
the Scaglietti-bodied
Mondial.

fifth at one point in the 623-mile race, various problems dropped them back to 18th at the finish, but still first in the 2.0-litre class. Engine trouble stopped Luigi Bellucci, who'd chosen Irishman Cecil Vard as his partner.

In the Targa Florio on 16 October, over 581 miles of Sicily's worst roads, only one Mondial accepted the challenge. A Series I in the hands of Franco Cortese and Antonio Pucci, it retired. In their class the six-cylinder Maseratis filled places one through six, led by the entry of Franceso Giardini and Carlo Manzini in fifth place overall. This completed a season in which the doughty and biddable Maserati, pairing power with reliability, shrugged off Ferrari's latest challenge. Complementing these successes were those of Swiss racer Benoit Musy with his *Aseigiciesse* at Spa and Montlhéry.

Musy, the son of a former president of Switzerland, had done well enough in his private Maserati to be drafted in to co-drive a new model in the 1955 Targa Florio with Fernando Mancini. Paired in a second example of the new racer were veterans Giovanni Bracco and Franco Bordoni. The volatile Bracco threw his off the road early while its sister retired after four of the 13 laps.

This was the muted Targa debut of a new sports-racer, the 200 S, that Maserati had developed during 1955 to replace its A6GCS/2000. It traced its origins to a new four-cylinder engine designed by engineer Vittorio Bellentani. Since 1953 he'd been working on an eight-valve four that could have the potential to be built in both 1.5- and 2.0-litre sizes. Its block and detachable head were aluminium castings with five main bearings, each retained by a deep aluminium cap. Wet-steel cylinder liners were fitted in the dry-sump engine.

At the four's top end the Viale Ciro Menotti designers incorporated several novelties. Valves were symmetrically deployed at an angle of 80°, with their heads in a hemispherical combustion chamber fired by dual ignition. To cope with anticipated high engine speeds, valve closing was by hairpin-type springs for the first time in a Maserati engine. As used by Ferrari, these contributed to shorter valves of lower mass, had less reciprocating mass themselves and were thought less susceptible to resonance that could keep the valves from following their cams.

Bellentani also contributed a new type of valve gear. Pivoted finger-type followers were interposed between cam lobe and valve, with the important difference that each carried a roller on a needle bearing. A narrow cam lobe contacted this roller, which smoothly translated rotary motion into the valve's reciprocation. Each finger had its own rat-

trap spring to help hold it against its cam lobe. Unusually for a racing engine, the layout provided for an adjusting screw in the tip of the finger follower to set valve clearance. This proved to be a durable and versatile valve gear.

The 200 S's dimensions were 92 x 75mm for 1,994cc, making it slightly more oversquare than the Ferrari's 90 x 78mm. A compact unit weighing 330lb, it was fed by twin Weber 45 DCO3 carburettors. Its power was delivered through a multi-disc clutch and a five-speed transmission in unit with the engine.

Over the winter of 1954–5 Valerio Colotti had been working on a new chassis design under chief engineer Giulio Alfieri's direction. Retaining coil springing, Colotti produced a new and lighter parallel-wishbone front suspension using I-section steel wishbone legs. A three-piece track rod gave more precise guidance from the steering gearbox, mounted on the right for the first time in a post-war sports-racing Maserati. Ventilated drum brakes inside 16in Borrani wheels were close kin to those of the Grand Prix 250 F. Large thin-walled steel tubes formed a robust and light platform frame.

Colotti's concept for 200 S rear suspension was a de Dion design with its axle tube crossing the chassis behind the frame-mounted differential.

American owners preferred the right-hand accelerator pedal of the 1956 500 TR Ferrari, the bulk of which had right-hand steering. This owner took the precaution of fitting a Sun electric tachometer.

Springing was by a transverse leaf positioned under the axle tube and attached to it by links. He tried several methods for locating the axle tube, including a high-placed A-arm, but his solution proved to be a frame-mounted vertical slot in which the axle was guided laterally by a projecting boss. With the hubs guided by parallel trailing arms, this was close kin geometrically to the Mondial's suspension.

Unlike Ferrari, which shared its 2.0-litre car's chassis with a larger model, Maserati twinned its 2.0-litre with a 1.5-litre sister, its 150 S. This meant that if anything the disadvantage of greater strength and weight than necessary fell to the smaller car. With a wheelbase 4in longer than the 150 S's at 88.6in, the same as the Mondial, 200 S dry weight was commendably light at 1,390lb.

Before the Targa a 200 S prototype made a subdued debut at June's Imola Grand Prix. This car, the one driven by Bracco in Sicily, delayed the de Dion suspension by using instead a variation of the live rear axle of the A6GCS/2000. This in fact was the design of the first three 200 S models, including two made early in 1956. Thereafter they were given the de Dion axle. From the chunky forms used in '55, new body shapes for the 1956 season had a lower and more angular profile, carried out by Medardo Fantuzzi according to the results of wind-tunnel testing in the Milan Polytechnic.

Ironically, while Maserati was abandoning its live axle to adopt de Dion suspension for 1956, Ferrari was doing just the opposite. It gave up its complex and heavy transaxle-cum-de Dion arrangement to adopt a live axle for its 2.0-litre sports cars. Contributing to this was none other than ex-Maserati man Vittorio Bellentani. In 1955 Enzo Ferrari found himself short of engineers when Aurelio Lampredi left to join Fiat. He persuaded Bellentani to shift employment from Modena to Maranello to help fill the gap. Bellentani was in place for the 1955–56 winter, as was talented journeyman Alberto Massimino, whose ties with Ferrari dated from the straight-eight 815 of 1940.

Massimino addressed the updating of the new car's engine. He rejected the wide-valve-angle version used in the Series II Mondial in favour of the earlier Type 500 engine with its 68° valve angle. This gave a more efficient combustion chamber with the 2.0-litre engine's 90mm bore and allowed a 9.0:1 compression ratio. The four's susceptible bottom end was reinforced with better main-bearing support, improved counterbalancing and a lighter flywheel. This allowed the Type 131, as it was designated, to cope with output increased to 180bhp at 7,000rpm. To distinguish the new four from that of the Series I Mondial its camshaft covers were restyled with a squared-off look.

For its works 500 TRs in 1956 Ferrari commissioned special bodies from Carrozzeria Touring. This car, here with Hawthorn, was the winner of the 621-mile shootout with Maserati at Monza in June 1956.

Bellentani's work on the chassis left the new-for-1955 coil-spring front suspension largely unchanged. While still based on two tubes, the frame gained added stiffness from tubular truss structures through the cockpit area. Simplification of the frame at the rear was the by-product of the change to a live rear axle. The axle itself was made as light as possible without a sacrifice of rigidity. Split laterally, its two-piece aluminium centre section was held together by 12 studs. At each side 12 more studs attached the inner end of a fabricated steel axle housing and, at its outer end, a low-placed abutment, behind the axle, for a coil spring.

Location of the axle was simple yet robust. A joint below the axle's centre section linked it to an A-frame fabricated of steel tubes. Very wide in plan, it pivoted from the frame just ahead of each rear wheel. This A-frame located the axle laterally and established the rear roll centre. It also resisted the torques affecting the axle, in concert with a trailing radius arm at each side above the hub. Adjustable rotary Houdaille dampers continued to be used, while anti-roll bars were fitted at both front and rear.

Traction shortcomings with a live axle were addressed by making a ZF limited-slip differential standard equipment in the new Ferrari. It took the drive from a Porsche-synchronised gearbox, now in unit with the engine, and a twin-plate clutch. Although initially four speeds were seen as adequate, later versions had five. For the drum brakes Bellentani brought a technique from Maserati: a drum face with vents and radial ribs over which a sheet-aluminium cover was fitted to generate centrifugal warm-air-pumping action.

Although Modena's Scaglietti built the new Ferrari's bodywork, Turin's Pininfarina penned its design.[1] It featured a wide, low, egg-crated air inlet, squared-off wheelhouses, subtle bumps to clear the cam covers and large single engine-room vents at each side. A headrest-cum-fuel filler behind the driver was a racy feature. Though they were predominantly right-hand-drive, at least one left-hand-drive car was produced.

With its approximately 500cc per cylinder the new Ferrari was still a Type 500, but with creative flair its cylinder head was crackle-painted red and the new model was dubbed 'Testa Rossa' for 'Red Head'. Thus 500 TR became its designation. It wasn't ready to compete in the early-1956 races,

Wind-tunnel testing resulted in this sensational shape for one of the 200 S Maseratis fielded at Monza in June 1956. Used by Stirling Moss to set fastest practice lap, it was wrecked beyond repair in a practice crash by Nino Farina.

---

1 Although the company was then known as Pinin Farina, the more familiar joined-up name is used here.

which saw American Jim Pauley partnering swarthy Dominican diplomat Porfirio Rubirosa in the latter's Series II Mondial to win their class at Sebring in March, finishing tenth overall. In April Giorgio Scarlatti's A6GCS/2000 was 2.0-litre class winner in the Mille Miglia in 13th place overall.

One 500 TR started in the Mille Miglia, but retired. When the New York Show opened on the same weekend, 28–29 April, a sister car was on display. Meanwhile Ferrari was readying a trio of factory-team cars with bodies by Carrozzeria Touring. These had no hood bulges, sharper nose

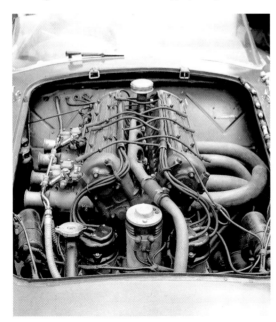

The under-bonnet view of a Ferrari 500 TRC during a spark-plug change showed its twin coils and distributors with central dynamo. The scavenging exhaust pipes were generously dimensioned.

contours and wheelhouses that opened out, toward the rear, like those of an Aston Martin DB3S.

Over the winter of 1955–56 Maserati concentrated on producing and fielding the smaller version of its new four-cylinder model, the 150 S, while the Orsis, father and son, and Giulio Alfieri restructured their engineering office in the wake of Vittorio Bellentani's defection to Maranello. His place as works director was taken by Carlo Galetto. Guerino Bertocchi continued as the vital development tester while his son, Aurelio, won promotion from quality control to an engineering post. Wary of nepotism, Bellentani had previously blocked his advancement.

Two of the new 200 Ss were nominated for the 1956 Mille Miglia, but Maserati, swamped with the preparation of 32 cars, failed to ready them for the starting ramp in Brescia. In fact in 1956 it would complete only seven such racers, including one upgraded from a 150 S. In contrast, Ferrari built 17 of its new Testa Rossas in 1956. The balance of 2.0-litre power was threatening to swing toward the Prancing Horse.

The rivals now set as their targets the fourth edition of the Supercortemaggiore Trophy race. On 24 June this would be run for the first time over the full circuit at Monza, including the newly completed high-banked oval. Covering 100 laps or 621 miles, the contest was limited to 2.0-litre sports cars and offered a total of 20 million lire – some $32,000 or £11,400 – in prizes, making it Europe's richest race. This was destined to be a

titanic battle, a decisive showdown between Ferrari and Maserati in the 2.0-litre category.

Both teams brought the full force of their Grand-Prix-driving talent to Monza for this all-important confrontation. A sense of the atmosphere at Monza was reported by Rodney Walkerley in *The Motor*: 'The full temperament and brio of Italian opera and the backstage of international ballet had been reproduced in the pits, with mechanics in tears, drivers offering physical violence, team managers having near-hysterics, Fangio playing patience outside his pit in complete indifference to what was going on inside and no one completely certain as to who was supposed to be driving with whom in what car.'

Against the three new Touring-bodied Ferrari Testa Rossas, Maserati mustered a trio of its latest 200 Ss with sleek, low, wind-tunnel-shaped Celestino Fiandri bodies. One was a solid-axle chassis from 1955 while two had the latest de Dion rear suspensions. Among the Modena pilots were Stirling Moss, Piero Taruffi, Nino Farina and Cesare Perdisa, while Ferrari fielded Juan Fangio, Peter Collins, Eugenio Castellotti and former works driver Mike Hawthorn, who rather opportunistically joined the team when his Lotus ride broke – to the disappointment of Phil Hill, whom Hawthorn displaced.

Jean Behra, also on the Maserati strength, was hospitalised for a knee operation, so the Trident drafted in spirited veteran Nino Farina, then 49. In the team's lead car, its most advanced de Dion-suspended version, Stirling Moss was fastest qualifier, the only driver to break the three-minute barrier and by six-tenths of a second. He then saw his car wrecked beyond repair during practice by Farina, who broke a collarbone in the crash.

Ferrari had its own problems, with Fangio breaking two cars in practice and requiring the rushing of a replacement from Maranello. Fangio, Castellotti and Collins lapped within half a second of three minutes in practice in their Ferraris, while Hawthorn and Perdisa were only two seconds off their pace. The final line-up saw 11 Maseratis pitted against 15 Ferraris and a lone Gordini in the 2.0-litre category.

After the Le Mans-type start the glowing prospects for an epic confrontation faded when Moss's 200 S, the Taruffi de Dion car to which he'd moved, broke its propeller shaft during its first lap. An Italian reporter suggested that this was caused by the Englishman's 'too hasty' start, though it's hard to imagine how a racing start could be 'too hasty'. Team manager Nello Ugolini then asked Moss to share the remaining live-axle 200 S with Cesare Perdisa, who boldly kept his Maserati among the leading Ferraris in the early laps.

Sharing with Mike Hawthorn, Peter Collins moved his 500 TR into the early lead with the Fangio/Castellotti pairing third in another Ferrari. Fangio had lost half a minute when his Testa Rossa was reluctant to fire up at the start. Under the control of team manager Eraldo Sculati, the Ferraris held a pace that Italian observers considered

At Le Mans in 1957 a class win fell to the Type 500 TRC Ferrari of Lucien Bianchi and Georges Harris. An entry by Belgian Ferrari dealer Jacques Swaters, it averaged a commendable 100.172mph for 24 hours.

Maserati's 2.0-litre upgrade for 1957 produced its 200 SI, with a body shape influenced by the 1956 Monza prototypes. The dry-sump oil system's reservoir was alongside the passenger seat on the left of the cockpit.

Crew chief Warren Olson contemplated Lance Reventlow's 200 SI Maserati at Sebring in 1957. It had lightened parallel-wishbone front suspension and de Dion rear suspension, the work of Valerio Colotti.

'English' in its regularity. Meanwhile Moss and Perdisa set out to chase the leader, holding the gap to a minute. A late 'splash and dash' for fuel by Hawthorn dropped the gap to 20 seconds but Collins, taking over, increased it again to 27 seconds at the finish after more than five hours of racing. Fangio and Castellotti were third and Gendebien/De Portago fourth in the third works Testa Rossa. Peter Collins and Ferrari turned the fastest lap.

This Ferrari victory symbolised the rivals' status in the 1956 season. With its 200 S not yet fully fit and its *Aseigiciesse* long in the tooth, Maserati was caught on the hop by Ferrari's purposeful and serviceable 500 TR. Franco Cortese took Italian 2.0-litre Championship honours in his Testa Rossa. Among Cortese's successes were the Giro delle Calabrie and the Circuito di Caserta. In the latter he won outright, with another 500 TR second in the hands of Gaetano Starabba, another proponent of the new model. In August's Five Hours of Messina the outright winner against 3.0-litre machinery was a Testa Rossa driven by Phil Hill, who also set fastest lap.

The veteran Maserati six wasn't quite ready to give up. Its ease and forgiveness of handling was still praised, especially in contrast to the 200 S. When he tested the latter's first prototype Luigi Bellucci was critical of its cornering unpredictability and queasy braking. In fact the new model would never be thought as biddable as the six. While fast through corners it demanded more skill at the limit, skill that not all its semi-amateur owner-drivers would possess. It would, however, have power. A Maserati dynamometer curve of 7 August 1956 showed peak output of 186bhp at 7,200rpm and torque of 148lb-ft at 5,500rpm.

While the four's development continued Maserati's six carried on, winning the Italian Hillclimb Championship in 1956 for Attilio Buffa. In July in the Dolomites Francesco Giardini's A6GCS/2000 bested a new 500 TR in the hands of Pietro Carini. In both 1956 and '57 a Maserati six was the fastest 2.0-litre car in the Giro di Sicilia, in the latter year defeating Gino Munaron's Testa Rossa by 42 seconds after almost 11 hours of racing. Even as late as 1959 the A6GCS/2000 was still able to place fifth in the Targa Florio, so versatile, rugged, serviceable and competent did it prove to be.

1956 brought several international successes to Ferrari's Testa Rossa. The feminine pairing of Anna-Maria Peduzzi with Gilberte Thirion won their class in the 1,000 Kilometres of Paris at Montlhéry, while Picard/Manzon were fifth behind four D-Type Jaguars in the 12 Hours of Reims. In January 1957 a 500 TR was class winner and seventh overall at Buenos Aires.

Bill Pollack, cornering here, partnered Lance Reventlow in the latter's Type 200 SI Maserati at Sebring on 23 March 1957. They retired with engine trouble after completing 88 laps.

During 1957 Maserati evolved this lower and sleeker form for its Type 200 SI, still with the full-width windscreen required by the authorities. It was fast but less forgiving at the limit than the well-loved 'Aseigiciesse'.

For 1957 new international Appendix C rules required full-width windshields and convertible tops for sports-racers, which resulted in some odd-looking arrangements. While the 2.0-litre category was falling out of favour internationally it was still interesting at the national level for private owners, so it was for these that Ferrari laid down a tranche of 19 chassis for what it called the 500 TRC in recognition of its observance of the new rules. Still bodied by Scaglietti, the reshaped 1957 Testa Rossa combined the best of the two styles used in '56. Its low nose was bulge-free and its front wheelhouses were cut away at the rear, while rear wheelhouses were circular. Large side vents from the under-hood area were horizontal rather than vertical. The proven chassis and power train were left substantially unchanged.

Gino Munaron had an excellent 1957 with his 500 TRC. He was eighth in the Mille Miglia, winning his class, and Italy's 2.0-litre road-racing champion. The Le Mans entry of Belgian Ferrari distributor Jacques Swaters placed seventh and won its class, while another class win from ninth place overall resulted from a local entry of a 500 TRC in the Swedish Grand Prix. By the latter part of 1957, however, Ferrari was applying its 'Testa Rossa'

sobriquet to a new V12-powered 3.0-litre sports-racer. The 500 TRC was at the end of its development. One such, however, would take Swiss-born Gaston Andrey to the SCCA's Class E Modified national title in 1958 and '59.

Hinting at things to come was success in the 1957 Italian Hillclimb Championship for Adolfo Tedeschi, driving a Maserati 200 S. For its international clientele Maserati had begun producing an updated version in February of 1957, designated the 200 SI in recognition of its conformity with the new international regulations. Their frames were produced by a Milan specialist, Gilberto Colombo's Gilco, and their bodies by Medardo Fantuzzi.

With the 200 SI Maserati moved its sports-car frame design a step forward. Large steel tubes were still used from the front suspension back along the propeller-shaft tunnel to the rear of the chassis. At the frame's perimeter, however, smaller tubes formed a stiff yet light truss-type structure. A single box-section crossmember carried the steering box and front suspension. Valerio Colotti's new independent suspension had short upper and longer lower wishbones assembled from I-section steel forgings. Coil springs were controlled by Houdaille rotary dampers.

Parallel trailing radius rods at each side positioned a de Dion axle tube at the rear, while a boss travelling in a frame-mounted vertical channel continued to provide lateral guidance. Originally located below the axle, the transverse multi-leaf rear spring was later raised to a position above the axle. Mounting it in two wide-spaced rollers gave it an inherent anti-roll effect. The frame-mounted final-drive unit was equipped with a ZF limited-slip differential. Brakes had ventilated light-alloy backing plates, two-leading-shoe mechanisms and – in the style aped by Ferrari – turbo-cooled aluminium drums.

The 200 SI's output at the peak of its development was 190bhp at 7,500rpm on a compression ratio of 9.8:1, lively motivation for a car weighing 1,480lb. Initially slim-flanked and angular, with air-exit grilles in its sides, the body shape of the 200 SI became progressively smoother and more rounded. Its nose was made longer and more penetrative, with an oval air opening that shrouded a Trident emblem. Its good looks contributed to an excellent production run of 24 cars in 1957.

Indubitably fast, the 200 SI nevertheless demanded skill to be driven at its limit. That was the verdict of the experienced Giorgio Scarlatti, who won his class and placed third overall in April 1957's 671-mile Giro di Sicilia. Nevertheless, the beautiful 200 SI enjoyed European successes in the hands of such drivers as Jo Bonnier, Franco Bordoni, Odoardo Govoni and Mennato Boffa and were raced well in America by Charlie Kolb, Jim Hall, Jack Hinkle, John Fitch and Lance Reventlow.

Happiest hunting ground for the 200 SI in 1957 proved to be the inaugural European Mountain Championship, based on results in six major hillclimbs. Maserati provided a works 200 SI to a Swiss driver, Willy Peter Daetwyler, who made excellent use of it to dominate the championship by winning three of the six events against strong competition from Porsche and Borgward. At the end of the season Giorgio Scarlatti was loaned the 200 SI to compete in the Pontedecimo-Giovi hillclimb, which he won. The date was 29 September 1957. With Maserati in financial trouble, it was significant as the final entry of a works Maserati in an Italian competition during the Orsi era.

In the Italian Hillclimb Championship the 200 SI ruled its roost. Maserati-mounted Odoardo Govoni took the laurels in both 1958 and '59. Italy's road-racing trophy was also Maserati's thanks to Adolfo Tedeschi in 1958 and Mennato Boffa in 1959. In 1958 Ferrari made a return to the 2.0-litre fray with its V6-powered Dino 206 and in 1959 its 196 S, but without great conviction. In 1960, with its Type 60 'Birdcage', Maserati created a 2.0-litre sports-racer that was unbeatable in its day.

Clashes between the Red-Hot Rivals in the 2.0-litre category would never again soar to the intensity that they reached in the 1950s. This was an extraordinary era that produced some wonderful cars. It began with a great classic sports-racing Maserati, the *Aseigiciesse*, continued with a bold Ferrari four-cylinder experiment that attained success as a 'Red Head' and ended with Maserati again triumphant. The benefits of competition were never better demonstrated.

Jean Thepenier entered a Maserati 200 SI at Le Mans in 1958, exposing its 190-horsepower four before the start. However after only 20 laps Eugene Martin retired it with gearbox problems.

CHAPTER TEN

D50 and 801 F1 vs 250 F 1956–57

After Mercedes-Benz and before Vanwall, Ferrari and Maserati had the Formula 1 field virtually to themselves in 1956 and '57. They made the most of the opportunity in the last years before new rules in 1958 spelled the beginning of the end of the great era of front-engined racers.

The main issue for the 1956 Formula 1 season was clear enough: where would Fangio and Moss go? In 1955 Mercedes-Benz cornered the market in master drivers, one a proven maestro and the other an obvious talent for

With Britain's Vanwalls and BRMs not yet in race-winning form, the red cars from Modena dominated Formula 1 racing in 1957. In their Lancia-derived Ferraris Mike Hawthorn and Peter Collins led the Maseratis of Juan Fangio and Jean Behra at the start of that season's German Grand Prix.

the future. With the Stuttgart team's sudden withdrawal at the end of '55, both were now free agents. Moss had ties with Maserati, for whom he'd competed as a works driver toward the end of 1954, but the picture was different for Fangio. He was planning to retire.

Juan Fangio had already carried on for five more Grand Prix seasons after his first in 1949, the single year he'd planned to race in Europe before returning to his businesses in Argentina. In 1956 he'd be 45; eager drivers half his age were nipping at his heels. Moss had already shown in 1955 that he'd be a deadly future rival. 'I was going to get out of racing,' Fangio said. 'When Daimler-Benz announced that it was pulling out, I thought the time had come for me as well. I wanted to return to Argentina for good.'

But Argentina had other plans for the driver who'd represented it so successfully abroad. Fangio's first World Championship in 1951 had coincided with the apogee of the career of another Juan, a man who strongly encouraged his activities abroad, Juan Domingo Perón. That was the year of his re-election as Argentina's leader, on the arm of the much-adored Evita. But by the end of 1951 Argentina had exhausted her gold reserves. Although Juan Perón had done much to democratise Argentina, his nationalistic approach to its economic problems failed to arrest its decline.

The Catholic church, which strongly supported Perón at first, excommunicated him in 1954. In September 1955 Perón's fellow military officers presented him with an ultimatum: either resign or face civil war. Perón chose the former. He left Argentina, ultimately to exile in Spain.

As a post-Christmas present in 1955 to 172 companies and 586 individuals, Argentina's provisional government froze their assets until they could prove that they had legally acquired them during the Perón years. Among the individuals were industrialists, diplomats, sports stars, film and theatre actors and racing drivers – including Fangio. They had 150 days to prove the legality of their rights to their property; if they failed their assets could be confiscated. Fangio would be cleared by his government, but it would take agonising years, not mere months. Under these circumstances, said the three-time World Champion, 'I decided to postpone retirement for another year. I returned to Europe to race in 1956, but I wasn't very happy about it.'

Fangio had even stronger links with Maserati than Moss. He'd led their team in 1952 and '53 and competed in the 250 F early in 1954. And then in his first race after leaving Mercedes he won the Caracas sports-car contest with a 300 S Maserati in November 1955. Afterwards, however, there was a kerfuffle over the winner's trophy between himself and Maserati's management. That there might have been to-ing and fro-ing over the trophy wasn't surprising. It was a solid gold cup weighing 5kg, 11lb, which was later valued at some $500,000. Fangio was not best pleased that Maserati kept it.

Equipment was a factor too, admitted Maserati's Giulio Alfieri: 'Fangio probably thought that Maserati wasn't up to his level in that period.' If not

Such was Juan Perón's passion for motorsport that Maserati took its brand-new 250 F to his Casa Rosada *in January 1954. Perón tried its cockpit with Fangio beside him. To the right were Adolfo Orsi and, in white suit, Onofre Marimon.*

Maserati, then who? The only realistic alternative was Ferrari. The two Modena companies that had enjoyed spirited intramural competition behind the Silver Arrows in 1954 and '55 were now the main rivals in Formula 1. France's Gordini was a spent force while Britain's Connaught, BRM and Vanwall were yet to show their best. 1956 was shaping up as an all-red season in which Fangio's only option was Ferrari.

Coincidentally, Ferrari needed Fangio. It wasn't easy for him to admit this. He was a builder of great racing cars; ergo the best drivers queued for them. But Ferrari had to be seen to do well in 1956 with the complete stable of D50 V8 single-seaters that Lancia had given him in 1955 after its withdrawal from racing. They were the only cars that had been able to rival the Mercedes on sheer speed. In addition, Ferrari was heavily bankrolled by Italian business interests including Fiat, which had underwritten an annual subsidy of £30,000, some $84,000, to carry on racing.

But drivers were a problem. The consummate artist who had mastered the tricky Lancia, Alberto Ascari, had been killed in a test at Monza. 'I will take the drivers that no one else wants,' Ferrari boasted in 1956. 'I don't have the money to throw away on people. I will certainly have Castellotti and Musso.' He also engaged Britain's Peter Collins. None of these, however, was a proven team leader. So late in 1955, in fact before Fangio had decided to carry on, Ferrari contacted Juan Manuel, who was on holiday at Italy's coastal resort of Pescara: 'He phoned me and asked me to come and have a chat with him at Maranello. "Fangio, I know you cost a lot, but I need you." I remember those words of his very well.'

Fangio did indeed cost a lot. 'Mr. Ferrari liked Fangio the driver but not Fangio the man,' said Ferrari's then-assistant Romolo Tavoni, 'saying, "I provide the cars, you provide the driving skills, so I think a 50–50 sharing of prize money is correct." When Fangio insisted on a salary also, Ferrari felt that he was breaking with tradition.' Fangio was less interested in tradition than he was in stability and security; with a salary he knew where and when his next lira was arriving. Grudgingly, yet in a way proudly as well, Enzo Ferrari agreed to Fangio's terms.

Another factor was clearly at work in Fangio's choice, said Maserati's Ermanno Cozza: 'It's possible that Fangio chose Ferrari because at the time they had the Lancia cars, which were more innovative and promising, and he was always looking for the best car.'

The Lancia D50 was the creation of Vittorio Jano, whose résumé included work at Fiat in the

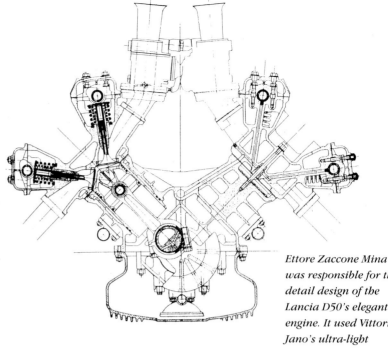

Ettore Zaccone Mina was responsible for the detail design of the Lancia D50's elegant V8 engine. It used Vittorio Jano's ultra-light mushroom tappets and had rugged four-stud main-bearing caps.

Unusual for a Grand Prix engine of the 1950s was Jano's use of roller chains instead of gears to drive the D50's overhead camshafts. The technique was carried over from Lancia's four-cam sports-racing vee-sixes.

decade before 1921 and development of the P2 with which Alfa won the 1924 French Grand Prix. Jano streaked on to design the classic yet radical Type B 'P3' Alfa Romeo of 1932 and the other Alfas of that time with which Nuvolari worked some of his greatest wonders. Joining Lancia in 1938, after the war he presented the company with the first successful V6-engined car, the Aurelia.

Hiding below broad brims and behind dark glasses, nearly 60 and thin to the point of gauntness, Jano fairly vanished next to the burly Giovanni 'Gianni' Lancia. Taking over Lancia's leadership from his founder father, Gianni was keen to flaunt its credentials through racing. He

Under Ferrari's aegis the Lancia V8 still breathed through four twin-throat Solex carburettors. Twin Marelli magnetos for dual ignition were on the driver's side of the firewall, driven by the inlet camshafts.

When first raced by Ferrari the D50 retained its novel de Dion rear suspension with rocker arms operating inboard shock absorbers. Springing was by a low-placed transverse semi-elliptic leaf.

and Jano warmed up with several seasons of sports-car racing and then put their team to work on a Grand Prix car for the new 2½-litre Formula 1 of 1954.

Working to Jano's concepts, the design team included Francesco Faleo as chassis designer and overall co-ordinator, Ettore Zaccone Mina as engine designer, and Luigi Bosco for the drivetrain. Other contributing engineers were Gariglio, Cibraro and Mattei. Together they conceived a light and compact Grand Prix car with many advanced features.

The D50's 2,490cc V8 engine was a logical progression from the four-cam V6 engines of the sports-racing Lancias of 1952–53. Like those it used chains to drive its overhead cams, a solution that was then rare among Grand Prix cars, most of which used gears. A one-piece high-silicon-aluminium block and crankcase was the heart of the V8. Inserted ferrous wet liners formed the cylinders.

The bottom of the block was machined off on the centreline of the crank with deep, thick webs

supporting the five main bearings. Attached to them by two big studs close in and two smaller ones farther out were massive webbed aluminium main-bearing caps. Carried in them was an alloy-steel crankshaft whose mass was kept as low as possible to aid responsiveness and acceleration. An oil reservoir was in the tail of the car and an oil cooler was mounted inside the front of the left-hand pontoon, between the wheels, with a scoop on the outboard side.

Unusually for a racing engine, the big ends of the Lancia's I-section connecting rods were split diagonally so they could be pulled up through the cylinders for rebuilding. At first the pistons were high-domed with full skirts which carried five rings each – one below the big wrist pin. Heavy ribs under the crown curved down to carry loads to the pin bosses.

After experiments with finger-type cam followers Jano reverted to the compact type of tappet that he first developed for Alfa Romeo. This was a mushroom tappet screwed directly to the valve stem, in some versions with a surrounding collar for extra security. Valve clearance was easily set by rotating the tappet in relation to the valve and locked by a series of notches under the pressure of the coil valve springs. Valves were large, 46.0mm inlets and 44.5mm for the exhausts, and symmetrically inclined at an 80° included angle.

The V8 was fed by four twin-throat Type 40 PII Solexes. Twin Marelli magnetos were driven off the back ends of the inlet cams and protruded through the firewall into the cockpit. At the rear of the V8 was naught but a small cover for oil sealing and a direct connection to the driveshaft which, like the engine, was angled from right front to left rear of the chassis to bypass the driver, allowing a low profile.

The engine sat in a deeply trussed tubular frame to which it made a major structural contribution. Attaching the cowl and firewall to the structure carrying the front suspension was the V8 itself. Lugs cast into the front and back of each cylinder head were bolted into the frame. In addition, two lugs at the lower surface of each head mated with mounts welded to the bottom frame members, adding substantially to frame and beam stiffness. The cylinders and crankcase hung suspended between the cylinder heads in this unique and pioneering installation.

Early power figures quoted for the V8 ranged between 230 and 260bhp, a typical figure being 250bhp at 7,700rpm. They tried two bore x stroke combinations: 76 x 68.5mm and 73.6 x 73.1mm, finally settling on the latter. First set at 8,100, the rev limit crept up to 8,400. After the cars had been given to Ferrari, Mike Hawthorn took one engine to 8,900 at the end of 1955.

Assisted by creator Jano, Ferrari experimented with the V8 after he was given the cars in 1955. Retuning the Solexes, allied with the use of a separate tuned pipe from each exhaust port, brought power in at 5,000rpm instead of 6,500 and raised peak output to 265bhp at 8,000rpm. The cars were geared for 8,200–8,600 on the fastest straight of a given course and drivers were asked to stay under 8,100 in the gears. The V8 would stay together at 9,000rpm but would blow sky-high at 9,100. Fangio proved the point in Belgium, where he left a broken car with 9,200 showing on the tell-tale.

By mid-1956 the structure of the engine was heavily reworked. Ferrari elected to use the more oversquare dimensions that had previously been rejected. To raise compression new pistons were made and gaskets between the heads and block were eliminated. A heavier oil pan contributed more stiffness to the bottom end. Chiefly for ease of installation, Ferrari gave up the use of the engine as an element of the car's chassis frame and inserted tubes instead.

The angled propeller shaft extended back to a pair of bevel gears driving a dry multiplate clutch, hydraulically actuated, which turned the lower input shaft of a transverse transaxle. Its lateral placement was an echo of the design solution adopted, at the same time, by Maserati for its 250 F. A rearward extension from the propeller shaft was provided to engage with the probe from a separate electric starter. The gearbox had five forward speeds with first mainly for starting.

With major members of steel tubing about an inch and a half in diameter, the D50's chassis was a truss-type design with extremely high – about shoulder-height – upper tubes. Two boxed towers just ahead of the engine served as mounts for the front suspension's parallel wishbones, welded of tubing with forged connections. The outer ends were ball-jointed into the forged spindle and upright. At the outer tips of the bottom arms were enclosed rollers, which were sprung by the main leaf of a single transverse spring.

A transverse leaf also sprung the D50 at the rear. A de Dion tube curved behind the differential, with its hubs located by parallel trailing arms on each side. Lateral guidance was by a block bolted to the frame sliding in a guide that hung below the de Dion tube, to gain a low rear roll centre. Tubular dampers at the rear were isolated from actuation in roll by mounting them vertically about a foot apart in the centre of the car. Links and rocker arms actuated them from the top and a third rocker joined them at the bottom. When the car rolled the whole shock absorber assembly rolled with it. The dampers only worked when both wheels jolted up and down in unison.

Finned-iron drum brakes were outboard-mounted, with four wide leading shoes per wheel, filling the insides of the 16in wire wheels. A handsome drilled-spoke steering wheel was attached to a short shaft to a steering box just behind the dash. The Pitman arm worked a long drag link down the centre of the engine vee which rotated a bell crank pivoted to the upper front crossmember. The bottom arm of the bell crank turned the wheels through a split track rod and drilled I-section steering arms.

Visually the D50's most radical feature was its fuel tankage. Instead of the usual tail location, fuel was carried in two sponsons that extended

Though running on Englebert tyres instead of the Pirellis on which it had been developed, the Scuderia Ferrari D50 Lancia of Mike Hawthorn seized pole position for the 161-mile Oulton Park Gold Cup race on 24 September 1955.

between the front and rear wheels on both sides. Recalling the design of some land-speed-record cars, the concept was seen as having multiple benefits. It was useful aerodynamically, smoothing the turbulent flow between the wheels to reduce drag. It also reduced the car's change in weight distribution between full and empty tanks.

In practice, however, the tankage solution was found wanting by Ferrari. A disadvantage was that the amount of weight on the rear wheels was insufficient for maximum drive traction. Another was that the D50 was visibly tricky to drive at the limit. Ferrari's team tackled the latter problem at the end of 1955 by fitting an anti-roll bar above the front suspension with links connecting the ends to the bottom wishbones. The objective was to make the D50 understeer mildly up to breakaway and then gradually slide away more controllably at the rear.

The rear suspension was changed as well. The tubular dampers and their linkage were ash-canned in favour of tried and true rotary Houdaille dampers. New frame members at the rear carried a high-mounted leaf spring, mounted in rollers to increase roll stiffness and attached to the de Dion tube by links. In the course of these revisions the wheelbase was lengthened about 4in.

Also changed was the fuel tankage, to shift more weight to the rear. A new rear-mounted fuel tank was riveted up and only the very front portions of the sponsons used for fuel. Several cars to this specification were built for the first race of 1956 in Argentina, where the individual exhaust pipes protruded through the rears of the sponsons. That race saw a win for Fangio's modified D50 with

Behra second in a Maserati. The final 1956 Ferrari-Lancia D50 appeared at the first major European Grand Prix, at Syracuse on 15 April. Its side sponsons were now faired into the body for aerodynamics only. The main fuel supply was in the tail with small saddle tanks next to the cockpit.

The Syracuse race was indecisive in our Red-Hot Rivalry, with a lone 250 F for Jean Behra against four of the new-look Ferrari-Lancias. Behra broke an oil pipe on his first lap while three D50s, led by Fangio, swept the podium places. Not until the GP of Monaco on 13 May did the Modenese opponents encounter each other in full strength in Europe in 1956. Leading the Maserati team was Briton Stirling Moss, whose attachment to the Italian squad had been by no means taken for granted.

With several British teams showing promising form, the loyal Moss wanted to drive a green car if he felt one was suitable. In November of 1955, at Oulton Park and Silverstone, he organised tests of the budding British contenders to see if any of them were likely to measure up. Friend and house guest Bob Rolofson summed up the findings: 'The Vanwall was by far the easiest car to handle, especially in the wet, but seemed to be heavy, and lacked power. The BRM had power to burn – and in a very wide range – but handled badly, lifting in the front at high speed, and snaking dangerously coming out of the turns. The Connaught handled better than the BRM, but not as well as the Vanwall, and retired due to engine trouble.'

Stirling was impressed by the Vanwall operation. With its fuel-injected four-cylinder engine and Cooper-designed chassis using Ferrari

The all-red front row of the Oulton Park grid in September 1955 featured Hawthorn driving a Ferrari-entered Lancia, then Moss and Musso in Maseratis and Castellotti in another Lancia. Moss was the winner, ahead of Hawthorn.

components, the Vanwall was quickest at Silverstone. Moss told its patron, Tony Vandervell, that he'd be happy to drive his Vanwalls where there was no conflict with the commitment he felt obliged to make to the Trident for 1956 in order to keep his career moving forward.

Thus the stage was set for the Ferrari-Maserati rivalry to resume centre stage in 1956 with Moss and Fangio as direct rivals. The prospect was mouth-watering. I assessed their chances in an article in *Speed Age* titled 'Duel of the Decade: Moss vs. Fangio'. 'Fangio has been actively engaged in Grand Prix racing for all of his seven years on the European circuits,' I typed on my Olivetti, 'while Moss has been in the top bracket for only four years. Each of Fangio's three championships was won with a team that was technically equal if not superior to its contemporaries, and this year will find him on the line with a Ferrari of questionable background but considerable promise.

'Moss, on the other hand,' I continued, 'has enjoyed only one full year under the wing of one of the great racing factories. His 1956 Maserati is the result of two full years of experience, and its basic design is probably reaching the end of its effective racing life. Appropriately paired,' my article concluded, 'Moss-Maserati and Fangio-Ferrari should be scrapping wheel to wheel at the head of every drive for the 1956 Championship. Nineteen

fifty-six will see them meet directly for the first time, with neither possessing any marked advantage. Luck willing, this year may tell us which is the better man.'

There was in fact an advantage, and it was Fangio's. In those days a driver could still take over a team-mate's car during a race and salvage valuable championship points. Fangio had strong backup in Collins, Castellotti and Musso, who could keep cars in contention that Juan could drive to the finish. Maserati typically fielded three cars for Moss plus Behra, who had his own ideas about winning, and the promising but inexperienced Cesare Perdisa. The balance of backup favoured the Argentinean in a manner that was to prove decisive.

Potentially advantageous for Moss were the skills and drive of Maserati's chief engineer, Giulio Alfieri. Born in 1924, Alfieri received his engineering degree from the Milan Polytechnic in 1948. After a year working on naval steam turbines in Genoa, Alfieri moved to Innocenti where he designed engines for Lambretta scooters. He arrived at Modena and Maserati on 1 August 1953 when work on the original 250 F was in full swing. It was a happy coincidence that the surname of this engineer, who would contribute so much to Maserati in the coming decades, was the given name of the Maserati brother who had led the formation of the company in the 1920s.

Jean Behra's 250 F, seen at the German Grand Prix on 5 August 1956, typified the cleaner trim in which the works Maseratis appeared that season. The feisty Frenchman was third behind team-mate Moss and winner Fangio on Ferrari.

Early in 1956 Giulio Alfieri was developing this version of Maserati's 250 F six with direct fuel injection into its cylinders. It produced more power but with a peaky curve that made the car more difficult to drive at the limit.

In 1954–55 Mercedes-Benz exploited three relatively new design techniques with success: fuel injection, 'desmodromic' or positively-closed valves, and aerodynamics. Alfieri tried all three in his determinedly autodidactic style. A 250 F with port-type injection was used by Moss to win at Goodwood on Easter Monday and raced by Jean Behra at Syracuse in April, but proved ineffectual when tried in practice for the Monaco Grand Prix. Attention turned instead to injection directly into the cylinders, using a modified diesel-type pump running at one-quarter engine speed.

In Alfieri's injection, a simple disc-cam system controlled fuel supply in relation to the opening of the six separate throttles. 'We worked day and night' on this system, he said, 'terribly hard, and found more power with injection.' A fuel-injected car was entered at the fast Spa circuit for the Belgian GP. It was quick in practice but too heavy in fuel consumption to finish the race without refuelling, so it wasn't used. His injection's main failing, said Alfieri, was that 'the power curve was too sharp. The power came in too hard and made the car difficult to control as the cornering power of the tyres of the time was really very small.'

At the Belgian Grand Prix on 3 June 1956 Stirling Moss seized the lead in the latest 250 F with low-drag bodywork and more enclosed cockpit. Ferrari-mounted Fangio, second here, passed him before the end of the lap.

For 1955 Alfieri had given his 250 Fs much cleaner bodywork with large vents and ducts replacing the original acres of louvres. Alfieri had more time to prepare for 1956, a season in which he conducted numerous experiments on all aspects of his 250 F. 'All my designs were my own,' he said. 'I never copied from anyone, so I alone was responsible for my mistakes.' It did not help Stirling Moss's challenge that not all Alfieri's experiments in 1956 proved fruitful.

Desmodromics also proved to be a costly dead end. With the help of consultant Alberto Massimino a special cylinder head was designed and tested that used two cams for each valve – one to open it through a conventional finger follower and the

other to close it through a roller-tipped rocker arm. Conventional valve springs were eliminated. 'Desmodromic was very difficult, very expensive,' Alfieri said. 'We never found higher revolutions through desmodromic; it was really wasted time.' The special engine was never raced.

Advanced aerodynamics were considered from the 250 F's gestation. An enclosure for the cockpit was designed and built, with Plexiglas windows like a fighter plane, but never used in racing. For 1956 Giulio Alfieri tried two approaches. One was a new body distinguished by much higher cockpit sides and improved radiator ducting, with a smaller air inlet and release of the warm air upward ahead of the engine. This car practised at Spa in 1956 and was raced by Moss at Reims and the Nürburgring.

The first big clash of the rivals at Monaco found Fangio stamping his authority on an elite field of cars with a storming pole-position performance. The race was another story. 'Fangio was a crazy mixed-up racing driver that day,' said *Autosport*. Damaged in an early spin while chasing Maserati-mounted Moss, in the lead, his Ferrari was damaged even more when its driver began using all the roadway and more in his furious chase. He brought the car in and at two-thirds distance was given that of Peter Collins, who was then in a strong second place. Collins, said *Autosport*, 'was so vexed that he went straight to his hotel and turned his back on the race passing its doors.'

Fangio couldn't catch Moss but his second-place Monaco finish, after his Buenos Aires win, saw him leading the championship. Nevertheless it was a messy performance by his standards. 'Many people have said it was not Fangio in the car that day,' he told Nigel Roebuck, 'but they don't know what was going on in the car! For me it was the fastest way around that track in that car. It may not have been pretty to watch, but it *was* the quickest way.' Though Fangio set the race's fastest lap, Moss was the flag-to-flag winner. Helping him was Alfieri's high-torque camshaft and head combination and a special four-speed gearbox with ratios tailored to the circuit.

The tables were turned at the Grand Prix of Belgium three weeks later. In qualifying over the 8¾ miles of high-speed swerves at Spa Fangio was a staggering *five seconds* quicker than the next-fastest man, Stirling Moss. Although Stirling was first away at the start, he wrote that 'Fangio was all out to rehabilitate himself and win the World Championship and passed me at the end of the Masta Straight.' The Argentinean gained a commanding lead but suffered a transaxle failure at two-thirds distance, letting his team-mate Peter Collins through to his first win in a championship Grand Prix.

The next championship Grand Prix at Reims on 1 July trailed by a week the battle royal between the 2.0-litre sports cars of Ferrari and Maserati at

Losing a wheel from his original mount at Spa, Moss took over the 250 F of Cesare Perdisa to be a lap behind the eventual winner, leading here, Peter Collins in a Ferrari-modified Lancia. Moss finished third.

The Red-Hot Rivalry was in full flow at Silverstone on 14 July 1956 with Eugenio Castellotti's Lancia-Ferrari mixing it with the Maseratis of Francesco Godia-Sales (10) and Luigi Villoresi (11). Of this group the last had the best finish in the British GP, sixth.

Monza that we described earlier. Hot from its stimulating atmosphere the teams arrived for the French GP at Reims, with its daunting high-speed bend at Gueux. Fangio's car was the first built on a new Maranello-made frame, having a stiffer front section and other refinements.

In Reims qualifying Denis Jenkinson lent an ear to the sound of Fangio's Ferrari-Lancia: 'As he went past the pits at nearly 160mph everyone listened for him to lift his foot off the accelerator as he approached the long right-hand curve; the scream of the eight megaphones remained constant until it died away in the distance and everyone, drivers included, paid tribute to the World Champion.' Eyebrows went sky-high afterwards when Juan explained that he was having to hold the shift lever in fifth halfway around the curve because it was jumping out of gear!

Maserati drafted in Piero Taruffi and Francesco Godia-Sales to make up a five-car works team for the race in France's Champagne district. In sheer speed on this fast track, however, they were outpowered by the Ferrari-Lancias. As at Spa, Reims resulted in mechanical problems for Fangio while leading, this time a fuel line that sprung a leak. Peter Collins took another win ahead of Castellotti with Behra the first 250 F in third.

With his frequent retirements beginning to niggle, Fangio thought he had a solution. 'I had always had a mechanic exclusively on my car,' he said, 'but Ferrari had a different system. Halfway

through the season I was able to arrange it, and then everything was much better.' Pasquale Cassani was delegated to look after his cars. It seemed to work. Reliability was in Fangio's favour at Silverstone, where four works Maseratis faced five Ferrari-Lancias.

Enjoying superior handling on a circuit where medium-fast corners prevailed, like Silverstone, Moss took pole position and moved his Maserati into the lead. Fangio was in contortions trying to keep up. He spun once and the World Champion's face wore an expression of terrific strain while Moss circulated in his habitual 'Sunday drive' style. However, Fangio scored his sole victory on British soil when the leading 250 F retired. Moss's car lost power with an ignition fault but continued in second place before stopping with transmission trouble seven laps from the finish. Best-placed Maserati was again Behra in third, behind a Ferrari shared by de Portago and Collins.

The teams went to the Nürburgring with Fangio and Collins virtually tied in the championship and Moss only three points in arrears. The German race showed that Ferrari had the ex-Lancias well in hand. Special preparation for the bumpy 'Ring included added bracing for the damper mounts and the fuel tank. Fangio, Collins and Castellotti all qualified in less than the magic ten minutes, while Moss was 3.4 seconds short in the fastest Maserati. Fangio's Ferrari-Lancia had the legs of Moss's Maserati in both practice and the race, which Juan led from flag to flag. Of the five works Ferraris that

started, his was the only one to finish. Trident-mounted Moss and Behra were second and third.

Though Fangio had increased his points margin, Moss still had a crack at the championship in the final race at Monza. Ferrari-mounted Collins had only an outside chance if he won and set fastest lap and Fangio failed. To help his star driver Giulio Alfieri produced the first radical transformation of the 250 F. Instead of being placed on the centreline, the engines in two new chassis were angled toward the left, like the D50, so that the driveline could pass under the driver's left knee to a leftward extension from the input to the rear transaxle. With the cockpit offset to the right, this allowed the driver's seat – and the car's lines – to be lowered by almost 8in.

Two of these new chassis were built; Moss received one and Behra the other. The frame had lower and longer side sections than the 'standard' 250 F, particularly from the cowl forward. Although geometrically akin to the older 250 F, with coil springs and markedly unequal-length wishbones, the arms themselves were I-section instead of round, granting a slight weight reduction.

At the rear the de Dion suspension remained substantially unaltered, as did the transversely mounted five-speed gearbox which sat to the right of the car's centreline. A new input casing carried the extension shaft and bevel that shifted the driveshaft from the centre far to the left. All four wheels carried two-leading-shoe brakes, with an

additional central guidance point giving automatic adjustment of each shoe. The cast light-alloy shoes were backed by an almost lacy truss structure and a multitude of tiny fins.

Airflow both inside and outside the offset Maserati's nose was improved by its elongated form. While Alfieri's earlier attempts at cleaner body shapes ducted the warm air upward, the

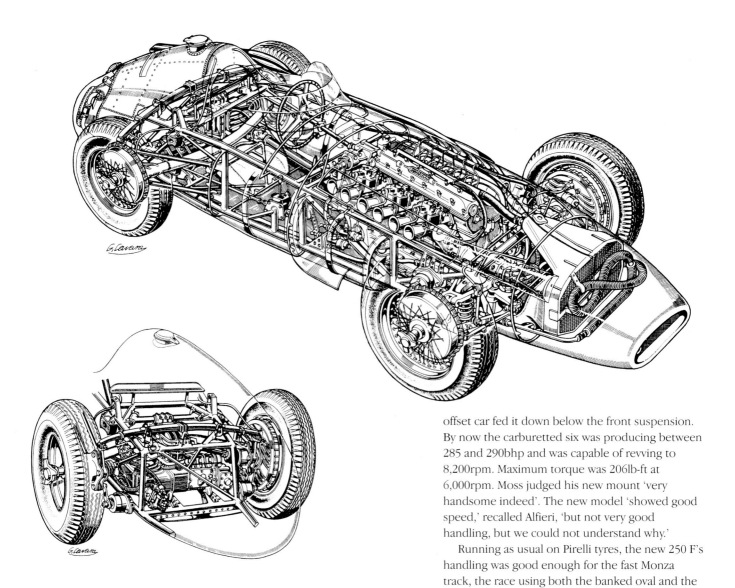

offset car fed it down below the front suspension. By now the carburetted six was producing between 285 and 290bhp and was capable of revving to 8,200rpm. Maximum torque was 206lb-ft at 6,000rpm. Moss judged his new mount 'very handsome indeed'. The new model 'showed good speed,' recalled Alfieri, 'but not very good handling, but we could not understand why.'

Running as usual on Pirelli tyres, the new 250 F's handling was good enough for the fast Monza track, the race using both the banked oval and the

Giovanni Cavara revealed the secrets of the low-chassis 250 F, two of which Maserati prepared for the Italian GP on 2 September 1956. He showed how its drive line was strongly angled to the left to permit a much lower seating position.

Behra, in white short-sleeved shirt, and Moss, in dark shirt, drove the two super-sleek Maseratis at Monza. The Briton won to give the Trident the winter's bragging rights, though the championship was Fangio's for Ferrari.

road circuit in 1956. This threw up severe problems for the Ferrari-Lancias, which were contracted to Englebert for tyres. These threw treads both in practice and early in the race, blunting the Maranello attack that had seen its cars dominating the front row of the grid. While the V8s of Musso, Castellotti, Portago and Fangio retired one by one with broken steering arms or blown tyres, Moss toured around in the lead in idyllic calm.

Moss's reverie was interrupted on the 47th of 50 laps when his engine started sputtering through the Lesmo bends. He was running out of fuel. He waved to Luigi Piotti in another Maserati. Piotti grasped the situation and swung in behind Moss, gently nudging him around the circuit to the straight in front of the pits, where Moss coasted in for a frantic splash and dash. Then he was off to recapture the lead and win.

Meanwhile Fangio had been standing carless in the pit lane. A stony-faced Musso, hoping to do well on his home ground, snubbed him during a tyre change. Juan's only hope of taking the championship well out of the reach of the leading Moss was Peter Collins, circulating in third place. Stopping for tyres on lap 34 of 50 Collins made it clear that he expected Fangio to take over his D50. 'I was astonished when he handed over his car,' said Juan, 'but I didn't stop to argue. I don't know whether in his place I would have done the same. Collins was the gentleman driver.'

In Collins's Ferrari-Lancia Juan Fangio finished second in the Italian Grand Prix, only six seconds behind a Moss who was doubly fortunate with the retirement of Musso, who broke a steering arm three laps from the finish. Fangio was World Champion for the fourth time. With their best five scores counting, Fangio had 31.5 points against 27 for Moss, 25 for Collins and 22 for Behra. Had there been a championship for makes the standings would have been 43 for Ferrari and 34 for Maserati.

As had happened in 1953, however – and with a similar last-minute drama – Maserati had winter bragging rights. The Italian result was, said Moss, 'a victory which delighted everybody at Maserati and perhaps compensated for our disappointment in this race in 1954. Winning at Monza means the world to them, for the Autodrome really was the spiritual home of Italian racing. Much like Indy to American enthusiasts.'

To the disappointment of Alfieri and the Orsi family that owned Maserati, Moss would not be driving for them in 1957. The Vanwall had shown good pace in 1956, so much so that the patriotic Stirling signed with the British team to drive its cars. With Vanwall not ready for the Argentine race in mid-January, however, it freed Moss to drive there for Maserati.

This South American race reunited the 'dream team' of Fangio and Moss. Fangio had returned to Maserati after his single season with Ferrari. Enzo Ferrari had been resigned about his prospects of keeping the Argentinean. In 1957, he said, 'we won't have the World Champion. We won't have him because we don't have enough money.' One

The three Maserati 250 F team cars built for 1957 had stiffer space frames and more rearward weight distribution. They ran on a stock of Pirelli tyres specially produced in advance by the Milan company.

season with Enzo Ferrari had been enough for both men. Besides, as Maserati's Cozza said of the modified D50, 'those cars were not as good as Fangio expected.'

Visiting the Maserati works at the end of his 1956 season, Juan Fangio found that the Orsis and Giulio Alfieri had not been idle. A formidable new V12 engine would come on stream during the season. The main engine for '57 was still the straight six, now with an improved cylinder head with inlet and exhaust valves of 46 and 40mm. A

hood-top duct fed fresh ram air to the triple 45mm Weber carburettors.

Maserati was brewing up another speed secret: a judicious addition of oxygen-bearing nitromethane to the fuel blend. 'We tested 43–44 different mixtures,' said Alfieri, and 'found widely different power outputs and characteristics.' According to circuits the mixtures used were M14 and M16, blending butyl and methyl alcohol with benzene and nitromethane. Weighing 434lb, the sixes now produced 270bhp at 7,500rpm and torque of

As developed for the 1957 season, the Lancia-Ferrari V8 had a more inward inclination for the Solex carburettors to improve flow into its ports. Upper tubes had replaced the engine as part of the car's frame.

209lb-ft at 6,000rpm. Starting 1957 with a redline of 7,800rpm, works 250 F engines were running reliably to 8,400rpm at the end of the season.

Alfieri incorporated lessons learned with the special offset 250 Fs built for the Italian Grand Prix in a completely new 250 F for 1957 that would only be raced by the factory; three were made. 'We did a completely new-design tubular frame to improve the problem of low chassis stiffness,' said the engineer, 'using more tubes and smaller tubes.' Suspension remained the same in principle – parallel wishbones and coils in front and de Dion with transverse leaf in the rear – but was refined in detail. Placed behind the engine, the steering box was now mounted on the frame instead of the clutch housing, a change that had proved beneficial in the 'offset' cars. The five-speed transaxle was driven from a triple-disc clutch at the engine.

With the new frame and an increased use of magnesium castings – a Maserati tradition – weight was reduced from the 1,390lb of the end of 1956 to the range of 1,320–1,340lb. Nevertheless the frame's torsional stiffness was increased by 40 per cent. Weight was distributed more rearward with 52 per cent on the rear wheels dry and, of course, much more on the rear when the oil and fuel tanks were filled. This allowed the front and rear two-leading-shoe brakes to be close in size, with drums 350mm in diameter and 45mm wide in front with corresponding dimensions of 340mm and 50mm in the rear.

Borrani wire wheels were normally 16in, though 17in rear wheels were used for high-speed tracks where tyre durability was at risk. Pirelli ceased its official racing participation at the end of 1956, seemingly halting supplies of the Stelvio tyres on which the 250 F performed so well. However, thanks to Giulio Alfieri's close relationship with the Milan firm's racing engineers, Pirelli 'made many, many tyres for us to use in 1957 so as not to hurt Maserati,' Alfieri recalled.

Juan Fangio and Adolfo Orsi shook hands on a co-operation for 1957, a traditional 50–50 sharing of starting and prize money. Their relationship was one of friendship and mutual respect, 'a very frank relationship,' said Giulio Alfieri, 'without being ashamed of saying no. Sometimes Fangio would come back a year later and race on the same car he had refused' – as he was doing now. 'Maserati never had a formal agreement with Fangio, partly because of his very good relationship with Commendatore Orsi. They thought that their word was good enough.'

Most importantly, the four-times World Champion liked the car. 'They had changed their 250 F model considerably since I first drove them in 1954,' Fangio said. 'The car was lighter, had a bit more power and had ended up very well balanced. You could do what you liked in that sort of car. It was nicely poised, responsive, fast and suited my driving style.' He showed how well it suited him by winning at Buenos Aires in January with Jean Behra second in a sister Maserati. Moss started from pole

Seen on test at the Aerautodromo in the spring of 1957, Peter Collins at the ready, the Lancia-Ferrari still resembled the model raced in 1956. Deceptively simple but treacherous, the Modena track had taken the life of one of Enzo Ferrari's driving talents, Eugenio Castellotti.

New for 1957 was coil springing for the front end of the modified Lancias, now known as the Ferrari Type 801 F1. An anti-roll bar was low-mounted while gilled tubes provided oil cooling.

Shorn of side sponsons, the Type 810 F1 Ferraris showed their new look as Hawthorn and Collins led from the start of the German GP on 4 August 1957. Fangio feinted to the outside in his Maserati 250 F.

and set fastest lap but lost many laps with a pit stop to fix his throttle linkage.

While Maserati had its new trio of cars tested and ready, Ferrari relied on its 1956 models in Argentina, three of them having new Ferrari-designed space frames. Three of the Maranello drivers were 1956 models too: Peter Collins, Eugenio Castellotti and Luigi Musso. Collins's colleague Mike Hawthorn rejoined the Maranello strength after two years away, during which he

tried both Vanwall and BRM but enjoyed little luck with either.

Enzo Ferrari told Mike Hawthorn that he wouldn't designate a team leader – a man entitled to commandeer other cars in the team if he needed to in order to score points. After the first three of 1957's seven Grands Prix were run, however, the driver who was in the lead in the points would get the team's support, said *Le Patron*. The season started with 1956's Eraldo

Sculati as Ferrari team manager, but by March he was replaced by Romolo Tavoni, Ferrari's personal assistant. Mino Amorotti remained in change of car preparation. A serious blow to the team's hopes was the loss in March of Eugenio Castellotti, killed in a testing crash at the Modena Aerautodromo.

Early in 1957 the Ferrari technical team under Vittorio Bellentani completed work on the new season's former Lancia racers. A major rework of the V8 brought new 80 x 62mm dimensions and a reduction in compression ratio from 11.9:1 to 11.5:1 that improved the combustion-chamber shape. New Solex carburettors were fitted, angled to give a straighter air path to the valves. Output was now claimed to be 285bhp at 8,500rpm with 8,800rpm allowed. An improved torque curve added 18bhp from 4,500 to 7,000rpm. Like Maserati, in this last season of unlimited fuel Ferrari experimented with exotic brews, using 6 per cent nitromethane in some early-season races with inconsistent results.

As he had in 1956, so too in 1957 Enzo Ferrari showed the final shape of his new season's car in his entry for Peter Collins at Syracuse in April's non-championship race. His engineers completed the Lancia's transformation by stripping off the side sponsons, exposing the exhaust pipes and their mildly megaphoned outlets, and putting all the fuel in the tail. An adapter clamped to reshaped bottom wishbones allowed the use of coil springs instead of the previous transverse leaf. In recognition of the extensive changes Ferrari's racer was now

known as the Type 801 F1. The 801 F1 won its first race at Syracuse and another at Naples at the end of the month, both times driven by Collins without works Maserati opposition.

As in 1956 the first European encounter between the hometown rivals was at the Grand Prix of Monaco, held in 1957 on 19 May. Fangio stamped his authority on the proceedings with a pole-winning practice time in his usual 250 F after a valiant struggle with the V12 on a circuit which its peaky power curve didn't suit. On the fourth lap the brakes on Stirling Moss's Vanwall played up and he went straight at the artificial harbour-side chicane, followed by Ferrari-mounted Collins.

'At that moment I arrived on the scene,' said Fangio. 'I saw posts, torn up by the two cars, rolling in a haphazard way towards the centre of the track. I managed to brake just enough to arrive in the middle of that confusion at no more than walking pace. My right wheels went over a post, jolting the Maserati but nothing more, and went straight off, taking advantage of the clear road. Behind me the posts continued rolling, almost entirely barring the road.' They caught Hawthorn's 801 F1 as well. Fangio got through scot-free and went on to win.

The 7th of July found Modena's finest at Rouen-les-Essarts to dispute the French GP over the smooth, sinuous curves of this picture-book circuit. On his way to an unchallenged victory from pole Juan Manuel put on a memorable demonstration of controlled power-sliding. Suffering from too much understeer, the Ferraris lacked the speed to rival

A jewel in the golden crown of Juan Fangio's career was his drive to victory in the 311-mile German Grand Prix in August of 1957. After the finish the front suspension on his Maserati was found to be seized solid.

During 1957 Maserati was developing its 2.5-litre V12, with inlet ports between the cams of each head because there was no room for them in the central vee. It had distinctive short mushroom tappets and hairpin-type valve springs.

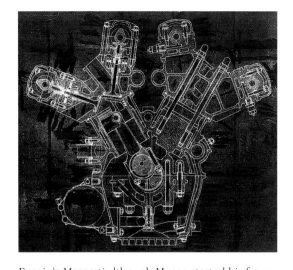

For 1957's Italian GP on 8 September, Maserati prepared a low-chassis 250 F powered by a high-revving V12. Driven by Jean Behra, its strongest supporter, the twelve retired after 50 of the race's 87 laps when the engine overheated.

Fangio's Maserati although Musso started his from the front row. A week later in a non-championship race at Reims Musso qualified only fourth fastest but there he and his Ferrari were in their element, seizing victory ahead of Jean Behra's 250 F.

With Rouen the third 1957 race for points, Ferrari's commitment to his drivers should have been coming into force, but results so far were inconclusive. Musso was in the van with seven, Collins next with four and Hawthorn trailing with three. Fangio, on the other hand, was storming ahead with 25 while his principal team-mate Behra had eight. Franco-American Harry Schell was also on the Maserati strength but making little headway.

In the 20 July British Grand Prix at the flat and unrewarding Aintree track Musso proved equal to

his standing, progressing through the field to place second behind the winning Vanwall successively crewed by Brooks and Moss – the first championship victory for the British marque. That in turn was a gift from Behra, whose Maserati had led from lap 23 of the 90-lap race, only to grenade its clutch on lap 69. Fangio had an indifferent race for a change and retired.

The reigning champion retained his lead in the World Championship, which he hoped to put on ice at the next race on the Nürburgring. He accepted the strategy proposed by team manager Nello Ugolini and chief mechanic Guerino Bertocchi, which was to run as light as possible in the German Grand Prix and refuel, fitting fresh tyres, at the mid-race point. This, they thought, would be easier on the car on the bumpy and hilly 'Ring. Ferrari elected to fill its tanks and run non-stop.

In practice Fangio set the pace by carving *26 seconds* from his record pole time of the year before. He had three seconds in hand over his closest rival, Mike Hawthorn. In the race he let the Ferraris of Hawthorn and Collins lead at first; Fangio was always careful to bed in his Pirellis before demanding more of them. Then he passed the Ferraris and set about building up the 30-second margin Bertocchi told him he'd need for his pit stop. His third lap was a new record, and so were his fifth, sixth, eighth and tenth. He broke records, wrote Rodney Walkerley in *The Motor*, 'with a machine-like regularity that left us gasping, but his car was never straight, nose pointing off the

road, wheels clipping the verges in the most breath-taking exhibition of driving since Nuvolari.'

Collins took the lead, followed by Hawthorn, on the 12th of 22 laps, when Fangio made his stop with a 28-second lead. He got out of the car and selected a new pair of goggles while the mechanics made a total muddle of the refuelling and rear-tyre change, taking four seconds short of a minute instead of the promised half that. Back in the race, Fangio's first laps were deceptively calm. Again, he was settling in his new tyres. But on the long 'Ring, with pit signals only every nine and a half minutes for the leaders, he was also misleading the inexperienced Romolo Tavoni in the Ferrari pit. Collins and Hawthorn, blithely confident, were signalling each other that the latter should win. Hawthorn duly took the lead on the 15th lap.

Then the new lap records started coming for Fangio: the 17th, 18th and 19th. 'I started using third where I'd been using second and fourth where I'd been using third,' he said. Walkerley: 'Lap 20 and uproar in the grandstands, hysteria in the Ferrari pit; they gesticulated and tore the air, they fell on their knees to their drivers, and in the Maserati box Ugolini smiled at his watch. Fangio was on their tail – three seconds behind' the two British chums. On the next lap he passed them, first Collins and then Hawthorn, who held on grimly to finish 3.6 seconds behind, with Musso fourth. Juan Fangio, renowned for his poker face in the cockpit, flew by the chequered flag with a huge grin.

After one of the greatest GP victories in history, the rest of the 1957 season was anticlimactic. Two points races, those in Belgium and Holland, had been cancelled, so the 15.9-mile road course at Pescara on Italy's Adriatic Coast was drafted in for a 286-mile championship contest. Upset by the way the Italian authorities were persecuting him after one of his cars crashed with loss of spectator life in the Mille Miglia, Enzo Ferrari declared a sabbatical from racing, but he could hardly refuse Musso a car for a contest on his home territory. He entered a singleton 801 F1 for the Roman racer – much to the irritation of Collins and Hawthorn.

Musso found himself facing not only three Vanwalls but also ten 250 Fs, four of which were works entries. Fangio took pole by ten seconds from Moss's Vanwall on a lap of almost ten minutes while Musso joined them in the front row. The works Maseratis of Behra and Schell were in the second rank. The brave Musso led the first lap and then was second behind Moss until loss of oil from his Ferrari's tank retired him at half-distance. Changing wheels after spinning on Musso's oil, Fangio was second behind winner Moss with Schell third.

No stops were left unpulled by either team for the season finale at Monza on 8 September, run on the road course without the banked oval. Maserati made a serious entry of its V12 for the first time. The 'dodici', as it was known, was developed during 1957 to produce 310bhp at 10,000rpm. 'We destroyed many in early tests,' Giulio Alfieri

Though the epitome of Italian elegance at the wheel, Luigi Musso soared no higher than fifth in the 1957 Italian GP and finally placed eighth in his slim-line Type 801 F1 Ferrari.

recalled, 'running late at night and keeping all Modena awake!' At Syracuse in April it practised in a standard 250 F chassis but didn't compete. In July this car was entered in the Grand Prix at Reims, where it burned a piston. A similar 250 F T2 practised at Monaco and Rouen but wasn't raced.

The definitive 250 F T2 was based on one of the low-profile 'offset' chassis built for the 1956 Italian Grand Prix. Here was an awesomely impressive car, with its long nose, deep-set cockpit and NACA ducts set into its bonnet to deliver air under pressure to its six twin-throat Weber carburettors. A refinement was a set of step-down gears behind the clutch with ratio choices of 1.39, 1.35 or 1.26:1 to adapt the engine's high revs to the existing transaxle.

After practising but not racing at Reims and Pescara, this magnificent Maserati was entered in 1957's Italian GP for Jean Behra, who'd strongly encouraged its development. He qualified it in the second row for the race only 0.3 of a second slower than Fangio in the fastest Maserati. The 'dodici', its shrill exhausts screaming in anger, led several early laps of the hard-fought Grand Prix but succumbed to overheating that led to engine damage.

Though the Ferraris looked the absolute goods, knocking bystanders sideways by the force of their side exhausts, they were well off the pace at Monza. 'The Ferrari technicians tried all types of modifications to improve the speed of the cars,' wrote Denis Jenkinson, 'using deflectors on the

exhaust megaphones to help extraction, heat baffles between the engine and carburettor intakes, long air intakes on the bonnet running right forward to the radiator cowling, and numerous gear ratios and tyre sizes, but it all made very little difference, the cars were just outclassed and that was all there was to it.'

Collins qualified seventh, new man Wolfgang von Trips eighth, Musso ninth and Hawthorn tenth. Maserati was much better placed, with Fangio fourth, Behra fifth and Schell sixth, though all the red cars had to give best to the hated green Vanwalls that were the three fastest qualifiers. Fangio upheld Italian and Maserati honour with a second-place finish behind winner Moss, with von Trips third for Ferrari. Collins retired with a broken valve when third but not before being lapped by the leading Vanwall at one-third distance.

The end of 1957 found Ferrari in a right old state. 'The whole team had become terribly disordered,' wrote Denis Jenkinson, 'the drivers were no longer consistent in their efforts, the designers were inconsistent with their modifications and, in fact, there seemed to be no master-plan of development, everyone just muddling along in a rather incoherent manner. Enzo Ferrari's indecision on policy did little to help, and it would have been reasonable to expect the whole team to stamp off in disgust after the Monza debacle.'

In the Monza paddock Guerino Bertocchi warmed up Juan Fangio's 250 F Maserati under the eyes of Omer Orsi, jacket over his shoulders. Fangio shared the front row of the 1957 Italian race with three Vanwalls, into their stride at last.

Instead, Ferrari decided to develop its successful Dino V6 Formula 2 car into a full Formula 1 entry for 1958, discarding much of its Lancia patrimony. This proved a brilliant strategy that took Mike Hawthorn to the World Championship – the first of the post-Fangio era. But in '58 it faced no challenge from Maserati, represented chiefly by private owners who scored only seven makers' points against Ferrari's 45 in the first official year of that championship. The unofficial tally in 1957 had been 41 for Maserati and 25 for Ferrari.

Overextended financially, the Orsis let it be known during 1958 that Maserati was withdrawing from all factory racing activity. They did so to help get their financial house in order; in fact their works was under the protection of receivers while it continued to service the cars of its customer racers. For the French GP at Reims it provided a shorter, lighter 'Piccolo' 250 F for a one-off drive by Juan Fangio which turned out to be his valedictory Grand Prix appearance. He placed fourth.

While Ferrari's 801 F1 has passed unloved into history – none of the 1957 design survive – Maserati's 250 F has passed into legend. 'On no particular count was the car superior to its rivals,' wrote Denis Jenkinson of the gorgeous six, 'but it had no particularly weak point in its basic design, so that the combination of all the variables resulted in a very race-worthy car.' New rules in 1958 mandated shorter races and the use of aviation petrol. A tip of the nitro can was no longer allowed. The 250 F had reached its coruscating apotheosis just in time.

CHAPTER ELEVEN

335 S vs 450 S

The rivalry between the two Modena-based companies reached a dramatic peak of intensity in 1957, a hard-fought season that turned out to be the last for unlimited sports-racers and that witnessed the final running of the classic Mille Miglia.

All efforts to rein in the big sports-racing prototypes seemed fruitless. The very name 'prototype' – technically a model of which fewer than 50 were made – was taken to mean that such cars were the precursors of road cars from their makers. Only a few companies such as Cunningham and Jaguar gave more than lip service to this idea. Most built exotic sports-racers for the World Sports-Car Championship, launched in 1953, that they had no intention of producing in series for use on the road. The apogee of such efforts was the 300 SLR Mercedes-Benz of 1955, incredibly costly and complex.

Though he found the Type 450 S Maserati 'really a handful', Stirling Moss piloted it with his usual skill, as here in practice at Sebring in 1957. Paired with Behra, Moss won with the car in Sweden over 589 miles on 11 August of that year.

Vittorio Bellentani was the quintessential back-room boy of Modenese engineering. He kept Maserati ticking over during the difficult first half of 1949 and later defected to Ferrari in time for the 1955 season.

As built for racing in 1956, the Type 130 Ferrari V12 had Lampredi-like features in its crankcase and new cylinder heads with rat-trap springs helping to close its rocker arms. The drawing showed both wet and dry sumps.

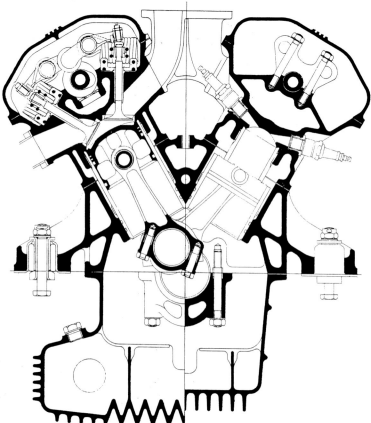

From the early 1950s Enzo Ferrari was urging that such cars be restricted in displacement to place prototypes on a level playing field. He suggested a limitation to 2.5-litres, the same size as the concurrent Grand Prix Formula 1, and saw this adopted in 1956 by the Le Mans organisers. Le Mans also brought in tougher rules on windscreens, cockpits and doors to oblige prototypes to bear a closer resemblance to their road counterparts.

Though its independent line in 1956 meant its exclusion from the World Championship, the Le Mans 24 Hours was supported by both Ferrari and Maserati. The former fielded three of its 625 LM model, a 500 TRC with a 2.5-litre four-cylinder engine. One placed third. The latter supplied 2.5-litre sixes to France's Talbot for two entries. Both retired, the best after reaching seventh place.

Meanwhile in the World Sports-Car Championship Ferrari resumed normal service by taking the trophy in 1956. Its role as the season points winner since 1953 was interrupted only by Mercedes-Benz in 1955. With its 300 S Maserati put up a good fight in 1956, winning two rounds, but a new 350 S, using the basic six-cylinder engine destined for the touring 3500 GT, was insufficiently ripe for racing.

At Maranello, fully expecting Mercedes to carry on for another year, Ferrari had armed itself with two 3.5-litre weapons for the 1956 season. One was the 860 Monza, a further evolution of Aurelio Lampredi's four-cylinder 750 Monza. The other was a completely new V12, the Type 130, displacing 3,491cc (73 x 69.5mm). With Lampredi leaving to join Fiat in 1955, the new twelve was designed under his successor, the youthful Andrea Fraschetti.

Assisting Fraschetti were two engineers of great experience. One was Vittorio Bellentani, whom we recall as the works manager at Maserati and one of the architects of its successful 250 F and 300 S. At the end of 1954 Bellentani told Maserati's owners, Adolfo and Omer Orsi, that he was leaving to take up a teaching post. In one of the more overt examples of top-level personnel transfer between Modena's rivals, he turned up at Ferrari instead. The other engineer at Fraschetti's shoulder was none other than Vittorio Jano. Although 65 in 1956, the gaunt, bespectacled Jano was still a fount of creative ideas.

The new twelve that these engineers created drew on the Lampredi heritage but in a novel manner. Cut off at the crankshaft centreline, the Type 130's crankcase had new vertical exterior walls that enhanced its overall stiffness. Its upper surfaces were low because its heads enclosed the

upper one-third of the cylinders in the manner established by Lampredi, with steel wet liners screwed into the combustion chambers. Connecting-rod big ends were split diagonally to ease engine assembly.

The Type 130's top end was akin to that of the Lampredi twelves, with a single chain-driven overhead camshaft operating hairpin-sprung valves through rocker arms with rollers contacting the cam lobes. Instead of being slightly offset the vee-inclined valves now faced each other directly, requiring the rocker arms to be offset instead. Long flues from the sides of the combustion chamber carried mixture to the twin spark plugs, one in the central vee and the other outboard. Its wide rocker covers and nine hold-down studs along their outer surfaces (versus six for Colombo's engines and seven for Lampredi's) identified the Type 130.

Producing 320bhp at 7,300rpm from its triple twin-throat 40 DCF Webers, the dry-sump 3.5-litre twelve had a 9.0:1 compression ratio. It was installed in a Type 520 chassis not unlike that of the latest Monza. Sharing a more rounded and purposeful-looking Scaglietti body with the 860 Monza, it was dubbed the 290 MM in the time-honoured Ferrari system of using the size of one

cylinder as a designation. It won the Mille Miglia, justifying its initials, and the Swedish Grand Prix to contribute to Ferrari's 1956 World Championship.

In the Swedish race on 12 August, on the Rabelov circuit near Kristianstad in the south, Ferrari had sight of a serious new rival. It wasn't a surprise – few secrets failed to travel the ten miles between Modena and Maranello – but seeing Maserati's new V8 was a shock nevertheless. A car 'of formidable appearance and sound,' said *The Autocar*, it looked like a 300 S on steroids with a tall hood bulge and quadruple exhaust pipes behind the front wheels on both sides. Several team drivers practised with it; Stirling Moss said that 'its brakes were totally inadequate'. No attempt was made to race this immature prototype of the 450 S.

Accounting for its internal Type 54 designation, this mega-Maserati traced its origins to 1954. In that year the Orsis first contemplated building a big-engined sports-racer to challenge for ultimate honours at a time when the all-conquering 375 Plus Ferrari disposed of almost five litres. In fact as early as 1953 Maserati's Gioachino Colombo thought of developing a new racing-car range in which smaller fours would share cylinder heads with a V8.

The Type 130 V12 powered Ferrari's 290 MM, which won the first race of 1957 at Buenos Aires. This one was being driven at Sebring by Wolfgang von Trips, at the wheel here, and Phil Hill. Electrical troubles stopped its run.

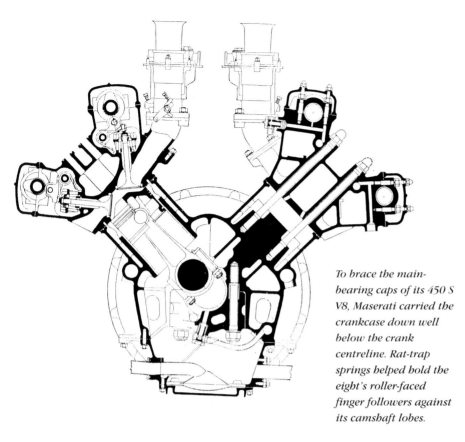

To brace the main-bearing caps of its 450 S V8, Maserati carried the crankcase down well below the crank centreline. Rat-trap springs helped hold the eight's roller-faced finger followers against its camshaft lobes.

High peaks on its pistons showed that this was the 4.2-litre version of Maserati's V8, built to race at Indianapolis. Tony Parravano's order for such engines helped kick-start the 450 S project at the Viale Ciro Menotti.

In 1954, after Colombo's departure, Vittorio Bellentani picked up the project. He saw the merit of planning a V8 whose two banks could exploit the design features he was using in the new family of four-cylinder engines that powered the 150 S, 200 SI and ultimately the 250 S. In 1954–5 the idea of such a V8 was taken forward to an initial design by Guido Taddeucci under the direction of Giulio Alfieri, new engineering chief for the marque of the Trident.

Thus Maserati built the second V8 engine in its history. The first was the Grand Prix V8RI of 1935–36 which produced 320bhp from 4,788 supercharged cc. The new one was slightly smaller at 4,478cc from dimensions of 93.8 x 81mm but destined to be much more powerful. It had the advantage over its predecessor of twin overhead cams per bank instead of the V8RI's single cams. This feature alone put it in a rare category; fewer than a dozen four-cam automotive V8 designs had hitherto been realised. Its cams were driven by a train of gears from the nose of the crankshaft.

The big V8 shared its valve gear with the new Maserati fours, having hairpin-type springs to close its valves and finger-type followers to open them. Each follower was held against its cam lobe by a rat-trap spring and had a small needle-bearinged roller contacting the cam. Valve sizes were 49mm for the inlets and 43mm for the exhausts, angled from the vertical at 39° and 41° respectively. The inlets were fed by downdraft 45mm Weber carburettors. These were vertical on the first engines (hence the huge hood bulge in Sweden) but sloped toward the central vee on later eights to straighten the inlet path.

The left cylinder bank was offset forward of the right bank to accommodate the side-by-side connecting rods of the 90° V8. With its throws at 90°, the massive crankshaft had lead masses inserted in its counterweights to add to their effectiveness. Borgo pistons gave a compression ratio of 9.3:1. The front-end gear train turned the pressure and scavenge pumps for the dry-sump system and the twin water pumps, one for each cylinder bank. Water was delivered both to the bases of the galleries around the wet-linered cylinders and directly to the head above the exhaust valves and their guides. In sports-car installations the front-end gears turned one magneto and one distributor for the dual ignition. The hope was that faults might affect one or the other but rarely both.

Appealing though these features were they remained on paper in 1955. The tragic crash at Le Mans that left 82 dead brought the threat of reduced displacement for sports-racers and, indeed, the limitation to 2.5-litres for prototypes in the 24-Hour race of 1956. Early in the latter year, however, such concerns receded. At the same time wealthy American racing patron Tony Parravano was becoming a Maserati customer. In 4.2-litre form, he said, such a V8 would be great for Indianapolis.

Parravano's order for two such engines as well as a 4.5-litre sports car spurred the Viale Ciro Menotti foundry and machine shop into action. His

Indy eights of 4,190cc (93.8 x 75.8mm) were destined never to make history at the Speedway, though they produced 420bhp on alcohol-based fuel. Weighing 525lb, the petrol-fuelled 4.5-litre sports-car version first ran in June 1956.

'It is known affectionately by all at Maserati and most of Modena as the "*quattro mezzo*",' wrote Denis Jenkinson, 'and the sound of its thunderous exhaust note as it is run on the test bed causes most of Modena to give knowing smiles for it is many years since 400bhp have been absorbed by the German-built water dynamometer used at Maserati. Watching one of these engines undergoing a test-bed run is a most impressive happening, for the whole building and concrete floor vibrate while the noise is such that that it is physically impossible to stand within six feet of the engine without wearing ear-plugs.'

Producing some 360bhp at this early stage, the 'four and a half' was installed in the new chassis that was designed for it. Ready earlier, this had competed with a six-cylinder engine as a 350 S in the '56 Mille Miglia. Then after a brief test at Monza it made its public debut with V8 power in the explosive Swedish manifestation in August that put the wind up Ferrari.

Premature though it was, that first dramatic appearance by Maserati's eight encouraged Enzo Ferrari and his team to carry out a further upgrade of their Type 130 engine for the 1957 season. On the same basic crankcase and bottom end they created the Type 136 V12. It had the signal distinction of being the first-ever four-cam Ferrari twelve for use in a sports car.

Ferrari had previously fielded vee-twelves with twin cams on each bank, but only in single-seaters. The first was the G.P.49 of 1949–50, a two-stage-supercharged 1.5-litre twelve that was the work of Gioachino Colombo. Not a success, it was ousted from Ferrari's Grand Prix arsenal by Aurelio Lampredi's unblown 4.5-litre. Then in 1951 Ferrari

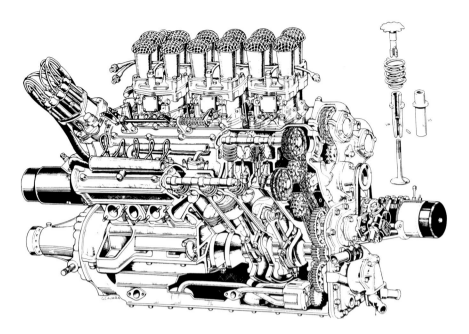

Jano were in plain view. For the first time a Maranello engine used valve gear in which a circular tappet was screwed directly onto the top of the valve stem. The latter was keyed to the guide to keep it from rotating, while the outer of the two coil valve springs had a tang that engaged with notches around the periphery of the tappet to keep it from turning once its running clearance had been set. Valve sizes were 35mm for the inlets, 29mm for the exhausts.

This simple, light and rugged valve gear was a Vittorio Jano hallmark of long standing, notable for introducing the first use of coil valve springs in a Ferrari engine.[1] Another new feature was the way in which the camshaft box and carrier surfaces were machined. On each head both cambox-cover surfaces were on the same plane and parallel to the head/block joint face. This technique made head machining faster and easier while in no way compromising the valve gear. Twin spark plugs now screwed right to the surface of the hemispherical chamber, giving much-improved ignition.

---

1 Ferrari had experimented with coils previously, for example in the Type 116 two-cylinder engine of 2.5-litres built and tested in 1955 but never raced. In the D50 V8 Ferrari had inherited coil springs from Lancia. This was his first use of coils in an engine of his own design that was used in competition.

Building on the Type 130 foundation, Ferrari readied the four-cam Type 136 V12 for its 1957 season. Cavara's cutaway showed its roller-chain camshaft drive and, in a detail, its Jano-type screwed-in tappets.

prepared two 2.0-litre engines for Formula 2 racing. While one was the in-line four that went on to fame and fortune, the other was a four-cam V12 of 1,995cc (63.5 x 52.5mm). Built Lampredi-style with steel liners screwed into its heads, this produced 160bhp at 7,200rpm early in its development. With the four performing so well this first unblown four-cam Ferrari was never raced.

On the new twin-cam cylinder heads of the 1957 sports-racing Ferrari the fingerprints of Vittorio

A spark-plug change was no minor operation with the dual-ignition V12 of Ferrari's 1957 3.8-litre Type 315 S. Inlets of its six twin-throat carburettors were screened to discourage entry by foreign objects.

Driven from the nose of the crankshaft were two half-speed gears. Each of these drove a double-roller chain to its respective cylinder bank and camshafts. The chains ran over three idler sprockets, the one on the slack side of each chain being a hydraulic tensioner. Gear trains downward drove the pumps for the dry-sump system and a single water pump low at the front of the V12. Other accessories at the front of the Type 136 were the fuel pump and belt-driven dynamo. Connecting-rod big ends now had conventional instead of diagonal splits.

Scaling 450lb, this impressive engine was initially unveiled as the power unit of the 290 S Ferrari for 1957 with the same 73.0 x 69.5mm dimensions as the 290 MM. Although six twin-throat Solex carburettors were used on early versions of the twelve, a reflection of the Jano/Lancia influence, Weber of Bologna finally prevailed. Breathing through three four-throat Webers, giving a separate inlet for each cylinder, the Type 136's output was 350bhp at 7,200rpm, a 9.4 per cent increase over the previous two-cam engine on the same crankcase. Maximum torque was 231lb-ft at 5,200rpm. The rev limit was 7,500; the V12's architecture offered the potential for still higher revs and a much-diminished risk of valve damage through over-revving.

With the starter motor directly above it, a multiple-disc clutch took the twelve's torque via an engine-speed shaft to the rear-mounted transaxle of the 290 S. This was of now-traditional Ferrari design with its four speeds on two shafts placed flat, geared to a ZF limited-slip differential. A slot in the back of the transaxle gave lateral guidance to the de Dion tube running behind the unit. A high-mounted transverse leaf spring, joined to the hubs by links, was carried by two rollers to give additional stiffness in roll. Positioned to carry its mass as far forward as possible and deeply notched in its underside to clear the leaf spring, the riveted-aluminium fuel tank contained 40 gallons.

Adjustable rotary Houdaille dampers were used at both front and rear. Front suspension of the 290 S was by coil and parallel wishbones supplemented by an anti-roll bar. With the steering gear on the right, a three-piece track rod was forward of the front hubs. Braking used the centrally located shoes pioneered by Lampredi in drums that measured 360mm in front and 330mm at the rear, all positioned outboard. Inside 16in Borrani wire wheels, the brake drums evolved during 1957 to considerably increased width, using fine-finned cast-iron components like those that Jano had employed at Lancia.

Holding the whole together was a steel tubular frame, the main lower members of which were stiffened by lighter tubular latticework along each side. A substantial reservoir for the dry-sump

Appearing initially as the 290 S in Argentina in January 1957, Ferrari's four-cam sports-racer for 1957 was impressively light for such a complex machine. It was sprung by coils in the front and a transverse leaf in the rear.

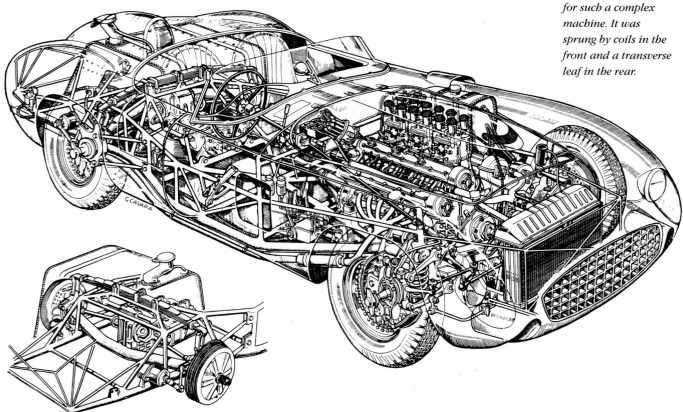

Visible through the vent in its front wing was the 315 S Ferrari's dry-sump oil reservoir. In both Grand Prix and sports-car events in 1957 Ferrari raced on Belgian Englebert tyres while Maserati still had stocks of Pirellis.

system was strapped to the frame's left side, forward of the door, and piped to a front-mounted oil cooler. The impression given by the completed 290 S was of a massive machine, but in fact its weight was kept under close control. While claimed dry weight was 1,940lb, the four-cam Ferraris at Le Mans scaled an average of 2,230lb. This was not excessive for such powerful cars.

With its team still managed by the 1956 season's Eraldo Sculati, Ferrari had every reason to arrive with confidence at Buenos Aires for the 1,000 Kilometre race on 20 January 1957. It fielded three of its new 290 S racers – two of them actually re-engined 1956 cars – plus one proven 290 MM. Driving the only brand-new 290 S, Mike Hawthorn considered that the new model was 'very fast and cornered well, but I found steering and braking required a lot of effort. I was acutely uncomfortable because the car was built as usual to the dimensions of the smaller type of Italian. My knees were up alongside the steering wheel in such an awkward position that after a few laps my leg began quivering whenever I pressed the brake pedal.'

Held on an anodyne freeway circuit not unlike Berlin's Avus with a chicane in the middle, the Argentine race simmered under the summer sun. At flag-fall Stirling Moss rocketed away so rapidly in

his 450 S Maserati, leaving everyone else behind, that he thought he must have jumped the start and backed off momentarily. In fact – as Fangio had shown in practice – his new V8 was able to slash five seconds a lap from the times of its nearest pursuers.

Nicknamed the 'Bazooka' for its noise and devastating performance, the 450 S rocketed away from all its rivals. 'Even so,' wrote Moss, 'I was handling the car with great discretion because it really was a handful. There's little doubt I *could* have gone quicker still if I'd been pressed, but I was happy not to be.' Maserati engineer-tester Guerino Bertocchi had been certain that the new model would be a non-finisher, anticipating both engine and brake problems. The end came from another source altogether.

Not long after lap 33 of 98, when Fangio took over from Moss in the race-leading Maserati, its clutch linkage failed and he had to shift without it. Such was Fangio's adeptness at clutchless racing that this was unlikely to have been the reason for the failure of the transaxle's ring and pinion that retired the 450 S after 57 laps. Engine problems knocked out two of the three new Ferraris while their sister finished third. The race was won by the 1956 Ferrari 290 MM while a 300 S Maserati was second, thanks to the efforts of Stirling Moss.

Here was a spectacular transformation from the ungainly beast that had ornamented practice at Kristianstad the previous August. After that premature trial, said Moss, 'Maserati scrapped that chassis and went back to the drawing board.' The final 450 S chassis resembled a scaled-up 300 S with a platform of big steel tubes, two down the centre and two at the periphery, the latter having a superstructure of smaller tubes.

Like the Ferrari but unlike the 300 S, the 450 S's de Dion tube curved behind the transaxle. It was laterally located by a bronze block sliding in a vertical slot that was part of the frame, not the gearbox. Just like the Ferrari the hubs were guided by parallel radius rods and a transverse-leaf spring was roller-mounted. Tanks at the rear of the chassis could carry 4.4 gallons of oil and 30.8 gallons of fuel.

Parallel-wishbone front suspension was akin to that of the 300 S with its right-hand steering box actuating a three-piece track rod forward of the hubs. The drum brakes of the developed 450 S were the largest yet, 400mm in diameter in front and 350mm in the rear, with cast-in radial venting for cooling. Their mechanisms were of powerful two-leading-shoe design with cast-aluminium shoes that had their own cooling fins. Far too big to fit inside the 16in Borrani wire wheels, the front drums had to be offset inboard where they were in the oncoming airflow.

The brakes were needed to stop a Maserati that could accelerate from rest to 100mph in some 11 seconds. As fully developed the thundering

'quatro mezzo' V8 produced 400bhp at 6,800rpm and could be revved safely to 7,200. Its torque of 325lb-ft – fully 40 per cent more than the 3.5-litre Ferrari – peaked at 5,500rpm. From a five-disc clutch at the engine a solid steel propeller shaft

A lever in a central gate controlled the rear-mounted transaxle of Ferrari's Type 315 S for 1957. To suit an international driver cadre the Maranello cars had right-hand accelerator pedals instead of the central pedals that were favoured in Italy.

As completed late in 1956, this was the initial configuration of the 450 S Maserati, with its nose sloped low and quadruple exhaust stacks on both flanks. This car was liveried for delivery to Tony Parravano in America.

with two Fabbri universal joints, designed to flex in torsion, took the engine's output to a rear-mounted transaxle.

Like much of the chassis the 450 S transaxle was the work of former Ferrari engineer Valerio Colotti. Instead of the 250 F/300 S transverse layout he placed its five forward gears longitudinally in front of the final-drive gears. The drive entered on its lower shaft with all-indirect gear pairs to the upper shaft and thence to the ring and pinion and ZF differential.

The low-placed propeller shaft was facilitated by a pair of drop-down gears in a special housing behind the clutch. These could easily be changed to alter the overall drive ratio. For the Mille Miglia Colotti transformed this step-down gear pair into a two-speed transmission to give the option of a higher set of gear ratios, the idea being that when stopping at a race control the suitable ratio could be selected to suit the roads ahead, either straights or mountains. In fact it proved to be easy to shift the two-speed box on the move so that it gave a high sixth gear on which the 450 S could reach just over 180mph.

With his usual artistry Medardo Fantuzzi bodied the 450 S in aluminium. The prettiest car was the first one sold, a slope-nosed beauty which went to Tony Parravano. Subsequent bodies were more robustly rounded, with large nostrils for brake-cooling air. The 450 S was no lightweight at 2,465lb

With its massive transaxle protruding forward of the differential, the 450 S Maserati of 1957 curved its de Dion tube to the rear. Small-diameter tubes added stiffness to its frame, which was based on a large-diameter tubular platform.

on the Le Mans scales. It was as brutal as it looked, 'a very powerful, big, hairy machine that wasn't very delicate to handle' according to Stirling Moss.

The required response from Maranello wasn't long in coming. One action was the firing of Sculati as team manager after some peculiar incidents in the allocation of drivers at Buenos Aires. Taking his place were two men. Technical preparation was headed by Mino Amorotti, an experienced engineer and long-time Ferrari ally, while team management was assigned to Romolo Tavoni. They faced off against Maserati's respected Nello Ugolini, who had piloted Ferrari's racing efforts from 1952 to 1955. Here was another transfer of talent between the two Red-Hot Rivals.

Implemented in time for Sebring on 23 March was a further stage in the development of the four-cam Ferrari. Increasing its bore from 73.0 to 76.0mm brought capacity to 3,783cc with the stroke remaining at 69.5mm. Designated the Type 140, this enlarged V12 was rated at 360bhp at the higher speed of 7,800rpm. Two such cars, both with new 1957 chassis, were mustered as the Type 315 S for the 12-hour race in Florida.

Facing the Ferraris at Sebring was a lone 450 S piloted by Juan Fangio and Jean Behra. They set fastest laps in both practice and the race. The big Maserati 'cantered home the winner,' wrote Denis

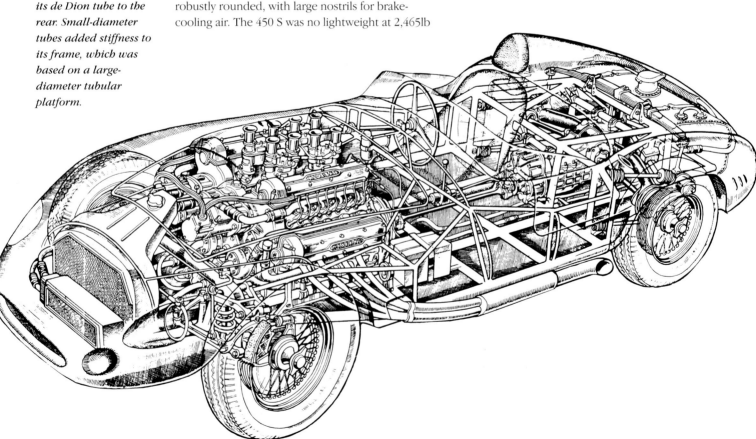

Jenkinson, leaving 'everyone aghast at the leisurely way it dealt with the opposition.' With Sebring notoriously hard on brakes, this was testimony to the good work being done by Maserati under Giulio Alfieri. He had tested disc brakes – which Moss had urged that Alfieri consider after Buenos Aires – but concluded that in Italy the technical backup to support their use was still lacking.

In contrast the Ferraris suffered from poor brake durability at Sebring, to add to the excessive pedal pressures that Mike Hawthorn reported. Peter Collins was sent out as the Ferrari hare at Sebring and indeed led the race for the first hour, only to hand over a virtually brakeless 315 S to Maurice Trintignant at the end of his first stint. Their car finished sixth, completing one more lap than its sister in seventh, driven by Luigi Musso and Alfonso de Portago. The latter had been running near the front until a clogged fuel line delayed them almost half an hour for carburettor repairs. After the first two races Maserati led the championship with 14 points to Ferrari's 11. There seemed no chance of stopping the powerful 450 S.

During the almost two months between Sebring and the Mille Miglia on 12 May both teams made important sports-racing progress in spite of the exigencies of their parallel Grand Prix programmes. At Maranello Jano, Fraschetti and Bellentani further enlarged their four-cam V12. Adding 1.0mm to the bore and 2.5mm to the stroke gave new dimensions of 4,023cc for an engine now designated the Type 141. Though clearly closer to 4.0-litres it was generally known as the '4.1', with its 9.2:1 compression ratio producing 390bhp at 7,800rpm. Installed in the same Type 520 chassis this became Ferrari's 335 S, thanks to its lightness a potential power/weight rival to the 450 S.

At Maserati the aim was durability rather than power, which the 'Bazooka' had aplenty. Preparing for the Mille Miglia, Jean Behra drove a 450 S over the mountains to Siena and back without managing to break anything. At Eastertide he took it to Monza to cover 300 hard miles and then for further tests to the Nürburgring, where it lapped 'at speeds that would have done credit to a Grand Prix car' according to Denis Jenkinson. Though the test V8 failed a rear-spring retainer after another 400 hard miles on the Mille Miglia circuit, it looked to have the toughness needed to take on the Italian 992-mile race.

The Mille Miglia turned out to be a race of vivid light and shadow for Enzo Ferrari's team. He entered a formidable phalanx of four-cam machinery: two of the 315 S and two of the potent new 335 S. Luigi Musso should have been among his strength but was unwell, so instead 51-year-old

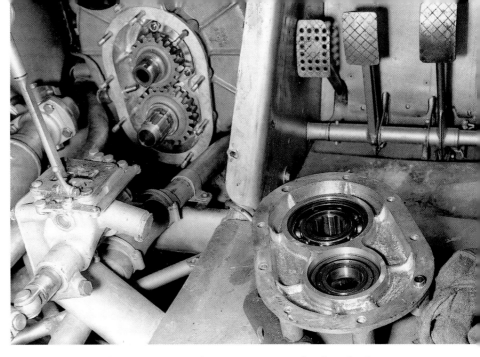

veteran Piero Taruffi drove his 315 S, the same 3.8-litre type handled by Wolfgang von Trips. Fon de Portago and Peter Collins were given the two 4.1-litre cars, the Englishman's a brand-new chassis.

These were the most potent sports-racing Ferraris yet. 'The speeds were so different from anything I had experienced before,' found Collins's navigator Louis Klementaski. 'The impression of leaping upwards urged on by the power in second and third gears was unforgettable. The pressure in the back as we accelerated in the gears, the lateral

Behind its clutch, a pair of step-down gears lowered the Maserati 450 S's drive line and facilitated changes of overall ratio. For the Mille Miglia this evolved into a two-speed transmission to suit both fast plains and twisty mountains.

Needing a lot of stopping, from Sebring in March of 1957 the 450 S Maserati had front brake drums that were offset inboard from its wheels to permit an internal diameter of 400mm, 15.7 inches. Centrifugal vents were cast into the drums.

Deceptively simple instrumentation faced the driver of 1957's most powerful sports-racer, the Type 450 S Maserati. Electrical connections were exposed on the dash panel for quick access in case of problems.

In a belt-and-braces approach to reliability the 450 S Maserati raced with one magneto and one distributor to spark its 16 plugs. The quadruple twin-throat Weber carburettors had 45mm bores.

force against which I had to brace myself when we took tight corners … soon became quite exhausting, to say nothing of the general tossing about from the hard suspension.'

Piero Taruffi calculated that the top speed of his 315 S was 175mph and 'wherever there was 200 or 300 yards of clear road the speed went straight over 125mph. In second it could spin its wheels even at 90–95mph and one's body was pressed back into the seat with a force not far short of its own weight.' On a wet road, he found, 'if I tried to use full throttle in fourth at 125mph severe wheelspin set in.' On two successive days Taruffi completed a full practice lap of the course in his race car, with a mechanic his passenger the first day and his wife Isabella the next.

Spanish nobleman de Portago took it easiest of the four, having been assured by Enzo Ferrari that he'd have a drive in the Monaco Grand Prix as long as he placed no worse than fourth in the Mille Miglia. That's where he and passenger Ed Nelson lay when a tyre was damaged by a road marker and, failing, threw the 335 S into a ditch only 30 miles from the finish. It killed its occupants and nine spectators, leaving 20 more injured. The tragedy unleashed a storm of protest against Ferrari and the race organisers that spelled the end of the Mille Miglia.

The Maserati menace melted away. During a last practice two days before the race Behra couldn't avoid a high-speed crash with a truck that wrote off the front of his 450 S and injured his wrist. Moss and Jenkinson had no chance to exploit their two-speed auxiliary gearbox, retiring when the brake pedal broke off at its root only seven miles from the start at Brescia. The lead was seized by Peter Collins – who'd been promised a 250 GT by Ferrari if he won – and held until the 4.1's final drive failed 125 miles from the final flag.

That left Piero Taruffi, leading, and Wolfgang von Trips duelling for the win in their 3.8-litre Ferraris. According to Taruffi he pre-planned a cornering manoeuvre that convinced von Trips he was in the ascendancy, although his transmission was making ominous noises. According to Enzo Ferrari he tipped gentleman von Trips that this was Taruffi's race to win after 17 attempts. Either way it was the silver-haired Roman who prevailed, keeping his promise to Isabella to retire from racing after his victory. Ferrari was back in the championship lead with 19 points, a two-point margin over Maserati.

After de Portago's crash the Italian authorities impounded two of the Ferraris, so Enzo could send only two of his four-cam machines to the 1,000 Kilometres of the Nürburgring a fortnight later on 26 May. Collins was back in his repaired Mille Miglia

335 S with Olivier Gendebien while Hawthorn and Trintignant took Taruffi's 315 S. They placed a commendable second and third in the order of their displacement. Victory went to an interloper in the Red-Hot Rivalry, a well-driven Aston Martin DBR1 that ideally suited the demanding 'Ring.

Armed with two 'Bazookas' at the start, Maserati ended the German race with none. Moss seized the lead with his but retired when the left rear wheel's hub broke between its two ball-bearing rows. Escaping injury in the resulting spin, Stirling returned to the pits to try the other 450 S after an attempt was made to repair its oil tank, but this didn't last and both V8s were out of the fray. The margin was now 25 points to Ferrari and 19 to Maserati, in spite of the latter fielding the car that was widely forecast to sweep the season.

With power to spare the rivals from Modena and Maranello were expected to set the pace at Le Mans on 22–23 June – and they did. 'Rarely in the whole history of the race has the circuit record been beaten by so handsome a margin as was the case during the Wednesday and Thursday evening practising periods this year,' reported *The Motor*. Two cars, Juan Fangio's 450 S and Luigi Musso's

335 S, were the first to break four minutes for the 8.36-mile lap, Musso being the first to lap Le Mans at better than the magic 200kph in the car he shared with Mike Hawthorn.

Although braking was again a weak point of the Maranello entries – their drivers being warned that they couldn't use them too harshly – the two big-engined cars suffered from a technical change. 'Our Ferraris had been fitted with a new type of piston for the race,' Mike Hawthorn recalled, 'and this proved our undoing. Peter [Collins]'s car began smoking in practice and it was found that the piston rings had seized up on one bank of cylinders, so six of the old-type pistons were installed on that side of the engine.

'At the start,' added Hawthorn, 'Peter made a magnificent getaway and put up a new record for the standing lap, but his engine soon began laying a smoke screen and he was out of the race within a few minutes.' After setting a new lap record – while still nursing his brakes – Hawthorn with Musso too retired with piston failure. The lone remaining four-cam was the 315 S of Maranello test-driver Martino Severi and Englishman Stuart Lewis-Evans. After two changes of front brake drums and shoes

Partnering Peter Collins, Frenchman Maurice Trintignant, seen here, drove his Type 315 S Ferrari to sixth place at Sebring on 23 March 1957. As usual at Sebring, stopping was a bugbear for the drum-braked cars.

they soldiered on to place fifth behind four D-Type Jaguars, the British cars expressly designed to suit this race.

While the 315 S was timed on the straight at 165.38mph the best 335 S timing was 170.38mph. This was exactly the same as the best speed measured for a 450 S, the lone open car from the Viale Ciro Menotti. At the suggestion of Stirling Moss its sister was given a Zagato-built coupé body from the pen of British aerodynamicist Frank Costin. Though expected to be much faster on the crucial Mulsanne Straight its poorly executed body made it 5mph slower. Nevertheless, both Trident entries were among the leaders during the early stages but by the fifth hour both were out with breakage of a drive half-shaft caused by failure of lubrication to its inboard universal joint.

Ferrari now stood at 27 points and Maserati at 19. The season's final race, the Tourist Trophy at Dundrod, having been cancelled meant that the 1957 championship now hinged on the six-hour Swedish Grand Prix on the 4.05-mile Rabelov circuit outside Kristianstad in that country's south-east. Maserati could only take the lead if it won with a Ferrari placing no higher than fifth.

With the aim of forestalling victory for the Trident the Prancing Horse sent two 335 S twelves to Sweden for Hawthorn/Musso and Collins/Phil Hill. 'Everyone was under a strain,' Hawthorn recalled, 'as up to now the Ferrari team had not won a single Grand Prix race during 1957 and nerves were on edge as we moved into the last phase of the season.'

Two 450 S Maseratis were assigned the task of winning. To enhance their chances of surviving for six hours they were detuned to 365bhp. As a result, said Mike Hawthorn, when Moss passed him in a 450 S 'to my surprise I found that I could pass the Maserati again fairly easily on acceleration and we had a ding-dong battle until I calculated that my brakes could not possibly last the race at this pace and I slowed down.' With brakes alternately fading and grabbing both Hawthorn and Musso made embarrassing excursions into trackside wheat fields on their way to a fourth-place finish.

While one of its V8s retired with the same axle failure as at Le Mans – not to Maserati's credit – the other was driven 116 laps by Behra and 29 by Moss to the fastest lap and victory. Second, only a lap in arrears, was the 335 S of Phil Hill/Peter Collins. 'At the chequer,' Hill recalled, 'the brakes were non-

Red-helmeted
Argentinean Carlos
Menditeguy, winner
with Stirling Moss of the
1956 Buenos Aires
1,000 Kilometres in a
300 S Maserati, was on
standby at the
Nürburgring in 1957 if
the works drivers
needed relief. With a
watchful Guerino
Bertocchi (left) he
discussed the prospects
with Juan Fangio over a
450 S Maserati.

Arriving at a British venue in 1955 (right) was the Ferrari Type 750 Monza of Briton Michel Poberejsky, who raced under the name 'Mike Sparken'. The versatile Monza found favour with private entrants, as did Maserati's Type 300 S (below), a 1955 edition of which was competing at Connecticut's Lime Rock Park in 1957.

The immaculate engine room of a Type 300 S displays the Viale Ciro Menotti's 1950s technology at its best. Comparison with page 127 shows the sports-racer's derivation from the 250 F, both having twin magnetos in vee formation at the front of the in-line six. A shield protects the left-hand magneto from exhaust heat.

In the dramas of the 1957 season a prime protagonist was Maserati's Type 450 S, powered by a four-cam V8 engine (right). From 4.5-litres and its four Weber twin-throat downdraft carburettors it produced 400bhp at 6,800rpm. Juan Fangio (below) won at Sebring with this car, in partnership with France's Jean Behra.

Initially outgunned in 1957 by the 450 S Maserati with 'only' 360bhp at 7,800rpm from 3.8-litres (left), the 315 S Ferrari was later enlarged to 4.0-litres, capable of 390bhp at the same revs to propel the Type 335 S. Among the Grand Prix stars on Maranello's driving strength were Mike Hawthorn, Luigi Musso and (below) Peter Collins.

After their final 1957 appearance at Caracas, winning both the race and the Makes Championship, the 335 S Ferraris were sold. This one, seen at Elkhart Lake, was Alan Connell's car.

With international sports-racers capped at 3.0-litres in 1958, 450 S Maseratis also gravitated to the New World. Carroll Shelby won at Lime Rock with this John Edgar entry.

This 450 S, bodied by Zagato to the designs of Frank Costin, was rescued from the junk heap at Maserati to have its wheelbase lengthened, creating a road car as spectacular as it was unique.

With new six-port cylinder heads on his V12, Enzo Ferrari was well prepared for the 3.0-litre limit on prototypes from 1958. In that year Olivier Gendebien (left) and Phil Hill won Le Mans in a works Testarossa. Gendebien won again in 1960 with fellow Belgian Paul Frère (below) in Ferrari's updated Type 250 TR/59.

For its Eldorado-sponsored entry in the 1958 500 Miles of Monza, Maserati raided its 450 S parts bins to create this magnificent Fantuzzi-bodied 420 M/58. At the centre of the group its driver, Stirling Moss, pondered his chances. Carroll Shelby (in white overalls) was the potential relief driver, while Dan Gurney (right) was looking for a ride.

existent. I'd driven for nearly five of the full six hours, and I felt that this was one of my most satisfactory efforts to date.' Their placing meant that Ferrari had the championship locked up – or did it?

Three weeks later the authorities said that 1957's final points-scoring round, replacing the Tourist Trophy, would be the 1,000km Grand Prix of Venezuela on 3 November. The third such race on the roads of Caracas, its 6.17-mile circuit used parts of an expressway and overpass plus chicanes to slow the cars on the long straights. 'The whole circuit was ridiculous,' said Phil Hill, 'like some kind of surrealist nightmare. The road was unmarked, except for people standing at the side and pointing in various directions.'

With only the four best performances of each marque counting, Ferrari now had a three-point lead over Maserati, 28 to 25. As in Sweden, Maserati was challenged to win and keep Ferraris out of high places. For the first time it fielded three of the booming V8s. One was a customer car for American Temple Buell, fitted with a 4.7-litre engine, while the others were works 4.5s for Behra with Harry Schell plus Moss with fellow Englishman

Tony Brooks, in his first and last factory drive for the Trident.

Against them at the sharp end of the Ferrari attack were two 335 S twelves. Both were rebodied in the style of a 3.0-litre V12 Ferrari that had first appeared at Le Mans, with a distinct separation between the wings and the nose to allow air to flow over the front brakes. Dubbed a 'pontoon' design, on the 3.0-litre car this was complemented by cutaways behind the front wheels that let warm air escape. With their dry-sump oil tanks in the way, the latter feature wasn't implemented on the two four-cam racers.

World-class pairings of Hawthorn/Musso and Collins/Hill were assigned to the Ferraris. Indications of relative pace at the end of the season were the qualifying laps of 3:41.1 and 3:42.6 for the two factory Maseratis versus 3:45.8 and 3:49.6 for the Ferraris. The cars from the Viale Ciro Menotti held an edge in sheer speed over the latest effort from Maranello, whose braking shortcomings still counselled forbearance by its drivers.

Forbearance was also recommended to the Maserati drivers, who were informed by Nello Ugolini that word had come from the factory that

A rare race outing for Maranello tester Martino Severi, driving, resulted in a fifth place at Le Mans on 22–23 June 1957, behind four D-type Jaguars. His co-driver was Britain's Stuart Lewis-Evans.

their cars had all been sold and were to be
delivered to their new owners in good condition
after the race. Through no fault of their pilots, this
admonition wasn't obeyed. Moss couldn't avoid
hitting a driver who swerved in front of him and
crashed heavily, putting his car out of commission.

Harry Schell, in the sister 450 S, was passing a
works 300 S Maserati when the latter's chafed rear
tyre blew, swerving it into the V8 and putting both
cars out of the race, the Schell machine burning
out completely. The private Buell car was out on
the first lap, crashing on the overpass. No Trident
remained to puncture the Ferrari onslaught that
found the Collins/Hill car victorious, flanked at the
finish by its four-cam sister a lap behind. In the
next two spots were 3.0-litre Testa Rossas that
foreshadowed the 1958 season.

Luckily all the Maserati drivers had no more
than light injuries but the hecatomb of machinery
was a body blow to the economics of the Officine
Alfieri Maserati. It also suffered a default on the sale
of a large shipment of machine tools to Argentina
that tipped the company into losses of 453 million
lire – some $750,000 – on its books for 1957. Early
in December came the announcement from the
Viale Ciro Menotti that the Trident wouldn't be

seen among works entries in 1958 in either Grands
Prix or sports-car races. It would relent slightly,
giving cars to Fangio for the Argentine and French
GP races, and only gradually make a return to
factory-backed racing.

Ferrari suffered a critical loss of its own during
1957. In addition to his precocious engineering
talents, its Andrea Fraschetti was a capable test driver.
In that role the Tuscan was proving a Formula 2 Dino
156 single-seater at the Modena Aerautodromo on
Thursday, 29 August, when he lost control and
crashed, suffering fatal injuries. The decisive success
of his four-cam sports-racers remained on the record
as a tribute to Fraschetti's skills.

With the FIA imposing a 3.0-litre limit on
prototypes from 1958, the big cars from both
companies were ineligible to compete. The picture
was different in America, where the SCCA's
modified category imposed no constraints. Carroll
Shelby enjoyed success with John Edgar's 450 S
while others racing the big Maseratis were Jim Hall,
Walt Cline, Masten Gregory, Bill Krause and Ebb
Rose. Four-cam Ferraris raced in the New World in
the hands of E.D. Martin, Gaston Andrey, Gene
Greenspun and numerous top drivers for entrant
George Tilp.

Thus did Ferrari score a decisive victory over its hometown rival. For 1957 the final score in the World Sports-Car Championship was a net 30 to 25 from respective gross points of 41 and 28. This success for the Prancing Horse paled, however, in comparison to the reversal suffered by Maserati.

With its magnificent 450 S it soared to a glorious apogee in 1957 – also winning the World Drivers' Championship with Juan Fangio – only to tumble out of contention under harsh financial constraints. For the time being, at least, Ferrari had scored a knockout blow.

The second and only other victory in 1957 for the 450 S Maserati, seen at scrutineering, came in Sweden's Grand Prix on 11 August. Behra and Moss defeated the 335 S Ferrari of Hill and Collins by a single lap.

Carroll Shelby was a blur at Lime Rock, Connecticut, as he raced to a 1957 win in John Edgar's Maserati 450 S. He won at Virginia International, Palm Springs and Riverside as well.

335 S vs 450 S   **219**

CHAPTER TWELVE

412 MI vs 420M/58

Goaded by a challenge from invading Americans, lured by millions of lire in prizes, Ferrari and Maserati built spectacular and unique cars for high-speed challenges at Monza in 1957 and '58. This was a dramatic apogee of their fierce rivalry.

The 1958 season saw the most bizarre and spectacular confrontation between the Red-Hot Rivals in their long history. It took place in spite of the legal guardianship into which Maserati had collapsed and although Ferrari was in the hands of a new chief engineer after Andrea Fraschetti's death in a testing accident. The new man was Carlo Chiti, then 34, who in mid-1957 was installed in the same Modena flat that Aurelio Lampredi and his family had occupied until 1955.

Having been schooled at Milan's Alfa Romeo, a well-equipped automobile producer, Chiti 'was

In the first heat at Monza in 1958 Stirling Moss in the Eldorado Maserati finished fourth behind the second-fastest qualifier, Bob Veith in the Bowes Seal-Fast Kurtis-Offy. In the final classification Moss was seventh to Veith's eighth.

While Luigi Musso (left) and Mike Hawthorn discussed their prospects at the back of the Ferrari garage at Monza, Carlo Chiti made a point about the 412 MI to Phil Hill. Phil performed yeoman service in the potent Ferrari in the 1958 race.

astonished at the limited nature of the inheritance left behind by Lampredi,' said his biographer Oscar Orefici, 'Fraschetti of course not having had time to make his mark. The Tuscan engineer was amazed at the inability of the technical department to make large-scale calculations, at the irrational character of the use of resources and the lack of the "engineering spirit" which was essential to such a highly specialised working body.'

That Maranello's 'engineering spirit' was not what it had been in the Lampredi years was owed

in part to Ferrari's reliance for two seasons on the Lancia D50 chassis and engine concept that he'd inherited in 1955. Advanced though the Lancia was at its creation, by 1957 it was ageing. Also as he prepared for 1958 Chiti found a team that was deeply demoralised by 1957's triumphal progress by Maserati's 250 F and Juan Fangio. Though the Trident had previously threatened, as in 1954, this was its first defeat of the Prancing Horse in the Drivers' World Championship.

Balding, bespectacled and amply upholstered, the energetic Carlo Chiti found Ferrari's sports-racers as well as F1 and F2 cars awaiting his attentions. But that wasn't all. Enzo Ferrari informed him that cars would have to be prepared for the second running of the 500-mile race that was Europe's leg of the *Trofeo dei due Mondi*, the Trophy of Two Worlds, held in co-operation with the 500-miles of Indianapolis.

The European race was held on the 2.64-mile oval track in Monza's *Parco Reale* north of Milan. Always an adjunct of the fabled Monza road course, the oval was updated in 1955 to help Monza compete with Spa and Reims as one of Europe's fastest circuits. Recessed 10ft below ground level so a medium line would give a level transition to the straights, the new track's bankings were 45ft wide with a maximum slope at the top of 40°.

At a cost in excess of $300,000 or £110,000, the new bankings were cast of reinforced concrete in the manner beloved of Italian architects. Through mid-1955, however, this was done so hastily that sections of the banking were uneven from the outset. Nevertheless, 1955's Italian Grand Prix was run over the entire circuit, including the oval and its bankings. In that year 25 per cent of the entries retired from frame and/or suspension breakage, a quotient that rose to 37 per cent in the 1956 Italian GP. In spite of its faults the oval was popular for long-distance record breaking.

Monza's racing director, the resourceful Giuseppe Bacciagaluppi, had the genial idea of linking the track's oval with Indianapolis in a way that would encourage Indy's regulars to come to Europe to compete. He dreamed up the Trophy of Two Worlds to be awarded on a points system to the driver who did best in two successive 500-mile races at Indy and Monza. Expenses for ten American cars, their drivers and two mechanics apiece were covered and 50 million lire – $80,000 or £29,000 – in prizes was posted for the first race at Monza on 29 June 1957, a month after Indy.

The rules were tailored to suit the Americans. Allowable engine sizes were 4.2-litres unblown and 2.8-litres supercharged, just as Indy required for the first time in 1957. Fuel was free, allowing the use of racy alcohol-based blends. Run counter-clockwise, like the fabled Indiana Speedway, the distance was broken into three 63-lap heats to add spectacle with successive rolling starts and to provide one-hour intervals in which the cars could be repaired. There wouldn't be racing if it rained. Winner and runners-up were determined by adding up the total time taken to cover the total of 803.3km, or 499.1 miles.

The appearance of the Americans with their Offy- and Novi-powered Kurtis, Watson and Kuzma chassis was guaranteed in 1957 by USAC, which chose the representatives of the stars and stripes. But Bacciagaluppi's talents were tested to the utmost in recruiting a European field. He wasn't helped by a negative view on the part of Europe's drivers, who thought it a risky race too far. He attracted three D-Type Jaguars from the resourceful Ecurie Ecosse of Scotland. But what of our Red-Hot Rivals, who were invited to defend the honour of Italy at a circuit only 117 miles from Modena?

Both Ferrari and Maserati timed their 2.5-litre Grand Prix cars over laps of the oval. Peter Collins reached 160mph in the Lancia-Ferrari V8 while Juan Fangio was judged the fastest with 162.5mph in a Maserati 250 F. When Pat O'Connor arrived in April of 1957 to test suitable Firestones with a Pontiac-powered Kurtis his best lap was 170.8mph and his average over 226 miles a handsome 163.4mph.

The first race held over the updated Monza circuit, including the new banked oval, was the 1955 Italian Grand Prix on 11 September. The 2.5-litre Formula 1 cars lapped the 2.6-mile oval at speeds around 160mph.

Irrepressible competitor Jean Behra encouraged Maserati to prepare two cars for the 1957 running of Monza's 500-mile race. One was the 250 F T2 equipped with a 3.5-litre V12. Although qualified it was withdrawn before the race.

As prospects were explored for the 1958 running of Monza's 500-mile race, cartoonist Patrignani took an amusing view of the likely clash between Europe's entries and the specialised American track-racing cars.

Under the bonnet of Maserati's 1958 contender was the Indy-sized 4.2-litre version of the 450 S vee-eight. Twin magnetos sparked the engine, which was fed by carburettors after fuel-injection trials were aborted.

Although the Pontiac V8 was oversize, this was an impressive performance that gave the Italians something to think about.

The pre-race forecast indicated entries from both Modena-based rivals. 'Ferrari is preparing two special cars of 4.2-litres,' reported *The Motor*, 'one a V12, the other with cylinders in line.' The latter would use a version of the 4.4-litre in-line six that Ferrari raced at Le Mans in 1955. The report added that 'Maseratis are reducing their V8 4.5-litre to the required 4.2-litres.' This was easy enough because in fact American-Italian Tony Parravano's order for two engines of this size had been an important impetus for the 450 S sports-racing project of 1957. Forecasts further linked Italian driver Nino Farina not only with the Bardahl Kurtis he tried to qualify at Indy in 1956, powered by an in-line Ferrari six, but also with a conventional Kurtis-Offy.

In the event Ferrari, fully occupied with his GP and sports-car programmes, fielded no cars at Monza. Reports from Maranello were on the lines of 'it's too expensive to build a car just for one race,' conveniently overlooking the Trophy's concept which was to encourage entries at Indy as well. Neither did Farina compete. More in hope than expectation Mario Borniggia entered a 4.1-litre sports Ferrari for himself and Jean Lucas of France. It proved too slow to reach the minimum lap speed that permitted qualification.

'Maserati hasn't prepared any cars for the race,' stated its team manager Nello Ugolini. Thus there was surprise all round when a transporter decanted two Maseratis in the Monza paddock for the first day of practice. They were there because Frenchman Jean Behra, a fervid racing enthusiast who was not uninterested in the prize money on offer, persuaded the Orsis and their engineer Giulio Alfieri to make the effort at the very last minute, indeed on the Wednesday before the race weekend.

One Trident entry was a 450 S sports car with its alcohol-fuelled engine destroked to 4.2-litres. It was stripped of all road equipment and given a tight wraparound windscreen for the driver alone. This should have had a decent profile on the oval because its top speed in Mille Miglia form that year was just on 180mph. However, before it had a chance to improve on its best lap of one minute, just short of 160mph, the sports car lost its final-drive lubricant as a result of a failed half-shaft retaining boot. This was a known fault that retired the big Maseratis at Le Mans only a fortnight earlier.

The other car from the Viale Ciro Menotti was a single-seater. A 250 F Grand Prix chassis, it was powered by a 3,491cc (73.8 x 68mm) version of the 2.5-litre V12 that Maserati introduced that season for Grand Prix racing. Built for use in the 300 S sports-racing chassis, the enlarged twelve had raced briefly in the Mille Miglia and practised for the Nürburgring 1000 Kilometres. Now it was

powering a monoposto chassis and drinking alcohol instead of petrol. Like the sports car it was fitted with Halibrand magnesium wheels and the Firestone tyres specially prepared for the race.

Though it screamed impressively around the oval the Maserati V12's best timing was just short of 150mph, well off the pace of the same chassis with its smaller six. Credited with a three-lap qualifying time of 149.750mph, the vee-twelve was allotted a starting place just ahead of the slowest Jaguar at the back of the field. Explaining the lack of pace, Jean Behra said it wasn't handling at all well with its unfamiliar American rubber. With this car withdrawn as well, the Maseratis were loaded up for the trip back to Modena.

'We got the impression that Maserati were not really serious in their effort,' Jesse Alexander reported. 'Chief mechanic Bertocchi was all smiles as the sports car was pushed off the track, and it was obvious that they didn't want to have a real go with the American equipment at Monza, and if it hadn't been for Behra talking them into it, they would never have come.' But come they did, so in the first round of the Red-Hot Rivalry at Monza it was victory to Maserati over Ferrari, which hadn't shown at all.

It was eminently appropriate that Maserati made the effort, abortive though it was. The Trident had a tradition to uphold. An eight-cylinder supercharged Maserati had won the Indianapolis 500-mile race in 1939 and 1940 and was leading easily in 1941 when a wire wheel failed. It was a justifiable point of pride for Maserati that it had been the first foreign winner of the great American classic since Peugeot in 1919. Nor had any interlopers from abroad enjoyed subsequent success. Ferrari's semi-official entry in 1952 ended early with a broken rear-wheel hub.

Thus when a second edition of the Monza race was announced for 1958 Maserati took notice. Its chief engineer Giulio Alfieri laid down the design of a special car which had the potential to compete both at Monza and at Indianapolis. The heart of the 420 M/58 was the short-stroke version of the V8 from the 450 S, giving 4,190cc from dimensions of 93.8 x 75.8mm, the latter reduced from the sports car's 81.0mm. With the high compression ratio of 12.0:1 to run on alcohol fuel it produced 410bhp at the elevated speed of 8,000rpm. Although fuel injection was tried, at Monza the V8 was fed by four Weber 46 IDM carburettors.

To suit counter-clockwise racing the engine and drive line were offset 90mm, 3.5in, to the left, a feature that would have special benefits at Indianapolis. The engine-speed propeller shaft entered a rear-mounted transaxle designed by Valerio Colotti. Its two forward speeds were indirect, the drive entering on its left side with driven gears on the right powering the final-drive gears. No differential was fitted. High on the left side of his cockpit, atop the reservoir for the V8's dry-sump oiling system, the driver found a gear-selection gate, its lever protruding almost horizontally.

Suspensions were adapted from those of concurrent Maseratis. Rear hubs were those of the 450 S on a more rugged de Dion tube that reduced rear track from 51.2 to 49.2in. Springing was by

Viewed from its left side, this was the housing of the special two-speed transaxle designed for the 420 M/58 Maserati. Its leftward-offset transmission suited the displacement in that direction of the engine and drive line by 3.5 inches.

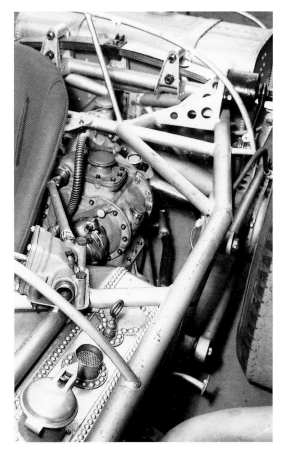

A rugged multi-tube frame formed the structure of Maserati's 420 M/58. Rear-suspension components were adapted from the 450 S, including hubs and transverse leaf. The oil reservoir was at the driver's left.

transverse leaf. Front track was also narrowed from that of the sports car, 51.2 instead of 53.1in, using the coil-sprung parallel wishbones of the Grand Prix 250 F. Steering was by the latter's three-piece track rod system from a right-hand steering box, while drum brakes – unimportant in this race – were from the 150 S sports car.

Uniting the componentry of the 420 M/58 was a steel tubular frame with truss-type side members of which the upper tubes were smaller than the lower longitudinals. On the left side its upper members dipped low to accommodate the engine's leftward offset. Forming a substantial foundation for the front suspension were robust upper and lower crossmembers. Inside the driver's headrest, offset to the right, was an unconvincing-looking rollover bar.

To be wrapped around his creation Giulio Alfieri designed a sleek shape with scoop for engine air and side vents for warm air. Its aluminium body would be fashioned by Medardo Fantuzzi, whose flair for the dramatic would cause a tail fin to sprout from an extension of the headrest.

Such a realisation of the 420 M/58 could only be a dream, however, for a bankrupt Maserati was struggling financially, so much so that its bank put the company into controlled administration on 1 April 1958. This put severe constraints on its financial flexibility. Ample though Monza's prize money might be, it would be too much of a gamble for Maserati to build the car in hopes of winning enough to offset its cost.

Fortunately Maserati found a gambler. Suave, silver-haired Gino Zanetti was a successful producer of ice cream in Milan and Naples under the Eldorado brand, its trademark a cowboy-hatted comic figure. With the 500-mile race offering a spectacular marketing opportunity, Zanetti stumped up the necessary funds, said to be $21,000 or £7,500, patriotically dubbing his white machine the 'Eldorado Italia Special'.

Unlike the rushed 1957 effort the 1958 Maserati was ready in time for testing at Monza by Guerino Bertocchi. After the first trials its wire wheels were changed to more rugged magnesium Halibrands carrying Firestone's special tyres for Monza. Though some frame members were drilled for

lightness, at 1,670lb the single-seater was only 70lb lighter than its sister sports-racing V8, Alfieri seemed to have taken no chances with the beating delivered by the bumpy bankings.

Who would drive this juggernaut from the Viale Ciro Menotti? The obvious choice was Juan Manuel Fangio. Reigning World Champion on Maserati, he was racing on and off for the Trident in 1958. He'd also tried driving at Indianapolis that May but waved off before trying to qualify, so he was up to speed on fast ovals. But Fangio had been offered the Kuzma-built Dean Van Lines Special that had won Monza's 1957 edition. He accepted this attractive ride for 1958.

Into the breach stepped Stirling Moss, former Maserati team driver who was still enjoying the occasional sports-car race for the Trident. His personal contract with fuel supplier BP was compatible with Maserati's backers. Arriving in Milan on Tuesday 24 June before the race on Sunday the 29th, Moss stepped into the Maserati to lap at a promising 164mph, although 'it skipped and bounded over the bumpy bankings and I cannot say I liked it very much.'

What of Enzo Ferrari in 1958? Surely the Maserati entry was provocation enough for the Merlin of Maranello. According to his team driver Mike Hawthorn, however, Ferrari only entered after some shrewd political provocation: 'He did not wish to run, but his arm was twisted by the Automobile Club of Italy. Every year there is a large sum of money given to the manufacturer of the most successful Italian racing car. This year the rules had been modified and a clause inserted that to qualify for this annual award the manufacturer must enter for the Monza race.' This was a clever tweak by the Auto Club's Luigi Bertett, one of the event's prime movers.

In fact Ferrari made two entries. Taking no chances with the Automobile Club's stipulation, one was a close relation to the V6 Dino Grand Prix cars with which Enzo was contesting the 1958 Formula 1 season. His chief engineer Carlo Chiti based it on a 1957 Formula 2 chassis with which he was experimenting with coil suspension at the rear as well as the front. Instead of its usual location at the extreme rear the engine-oil reservoir was carried under the left side of the cowl, its filler easily accessible for pit stops.

Meaningful looks? Giulio Alfieri and Stirling Moss contemplated their mission at the 1958 500 Miles of Monza. Sponsor Zanetti got his money's worth with the bold livery of Medardo Fantuzzi's handsome coachwork on the low-slung Maserati.

Engine designer Franco Rocchi produced the largest possible version of the Dino V6 that had started life in 1957 at 1,489cc. Expanded to 87 x 90mm it displaced 3,210cc, an amazing increase of 115 per cent. This was the 326 MI, which produced 330bhp at 7,500rpm, its unique 54 DCN Webers vaporising petrol instead of the free fuel that was permissible at Monza. As backup the team also had the 296 S V6 of 2,962cc, delivering 300bhp at 8,000rpm, which had raced in a sports-car chassis at Silverstone in May.[1] The engine was aligned with the driveline that angled across the chassis to the left side of the rear-mounted clutch and transaxle.

Unlike the GP cars, whose exhausts went all the way to the rear, the 296 MI, as the car was known, had short pipes ending in megaphones below the cockpit. Smoother than the Grand Prix Dinos, its bodywork faired into a much larger fuel tank that included a high headrest. Wheels were Borrani wires while drum brakes had circumferential fins instead of the helical finning used on the GP cars. Not having run before its arrival at Monza, the 296 MI was given its first laps there by tester Martino Severi.

While this gussied-up Formula 2 car seemed undergunned for Monza, there was method in Ferrari's madness. 'I was supposed to try to outlast the Indy boys,' explained its assigned driver Phil Hill, 'and aim for a placement based on overall distance.' Expected to be easy on its tyres and chassis so that it could cruise through to a good finish, the 296 MI was calculated by Enzo to be a car that the Americans might buy if it put up a good show. Only six years earlier he'd enjoyed a good sale of V12 Grand Prix cars to Indy entrants and a repeat couldn't be ruled out.

Unveiled as the principal weapon for Ferrari's 1958 Monza challenge was a formidable racing car, the most powerful single-seater that Maranello had yet produced. Dubbed the 412 MI, it rolled on a new chassis that was patterned after that of the 4.5-litre Grand Prix Ferrari of 1952 – the type of car that Alberto Ascari raced at Indy that year. Sprung

---

1 All contemporary reports refer to the 3.0-litre version of the engine as being the powerplant for the '296 MI'. Nevertheless, Ferrari's records also show the 326 MI, clearly intended for the 1958 Monza 500. We can't be certain which engine was used in the race.

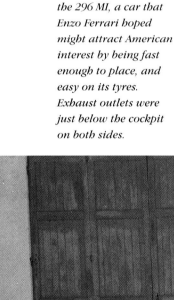

A 1958 Formula 2 Dino chassis was the basis for the 296 MI, a car that Enzo Ferrari hoped might attract American interest by being fast enough to place, and easy on its tyres. Exhaust outlets were just below the cockpit on both sides.

by transverse leaf, its de Dion rear suspension was snubbed by pairs of Houdaille rotary shock absorbers at each side.

The 412 MI fitted rugged production-car coil-spring suspension at its front wheels. Drum brakes with radial air exhausters were also from production Ferraris, albeit with new-design Al-Fin drums for the front brakes. Wheels were Borrani wires. Contracted as Ferrari was to Belgium's Englebert for its tyres, track versions of these were tried on the 412 MI at Monza by works tester Martino Severi but were judged unsuitable. Firestones were worn instead.

That the tyres were pressed to their limits was assured by the power unit of this big Ferrari. It was derived directly from the four-cam engine of the 335 S sports-racer of the previous season. In fact the engine used in the 412 MI was salvaged from the wreck of the car that Alfonso de Portago crashed with tragic results near the finish of the 1957 Mille Miglia.

Although not quite up to the allowable 4.2-litre limit, the 4,023cc of the V12 used in the 412 MI was a potent package with its six twin-throated 42 DCN Weber carburettors. For this car as well Ferrari eschewed exotic fuels to gain greater mileage from petrol. The twelve was revved to a heady 8,500rpm to deliver 415 horsepower on a compression ratio of 9.4:1. Power was transmitted through a shaft under the driver to a transaxle beneath his seat. Its design followed Ferrari tradition of 1950–55, albeit with forward speeds reduced to three, judged adequate for the Monza oval.

Coachwork for the 412 MI was sleek, marked by a small nose inlet for cooling air and recesses into the body's oval section for the wheels. As in its smaller sister the dry-sump system's reservoir was on the left side, in the engine bay in this instance. On both sides twin exhaust pipes curled out from the body's underbelly to terminate below the cowl. Pre-race tests showed the desirability of an aircraft-style harness to keep the driver in his seat on the bankings. Wearing the eminently appropriate number 12, this looked an awesome racing car.

The rest of the European opposition to the Americans numbered D-Type Jaguars again and a disappointing open-wheeled Lister-Jaguar from Ecurie Ecosse, plus an outdated 375 F1 Ferrari whose engine was reduced in size to meet the rules. Although the organisers had hinted at

Views of the Firestone racing tyres and front and rear suspensions of the 296 MI Ferrari showed its coil springs, which were rubber-coated to give a progressive effect that was hoped to be compatible with the track's bankings.

The Ferrari Type 296 MI's fuel tank contained petrol, instead of the allowable racing fuels, to improve its mileage at Monza in 1958. In place of the usual tail mounting, the oil reservoir was along the left side of the engine bay.

Under the hot sun of the Monza pits Enzo Ferrari explained his ultimate weapon for the 1958 Monza 500, his 412 MI. Although based on 1952 Formula 1 technology it was powered by his most potent 1957 sports-racing V12.

running the 500 miles non-stop to place the Indy cars at more of a disadvantage, needing repairs between heats as they did, in fact the intervals were increased to an hour and a half. The result was victory for Jim Rathmann in a Zink-entered Watson-Offy and second place for '57 winner Jimmy Bryan in George Salih's Belond Special.

Mixing appropriately among the Indy cars with its gaudy livery, the Eldorado Maserati was tried in practice both by Moss and by Carroll Shelby, engaged as a possible relief driver. Its deep booming exhaust thundered across the huge oval while observers on the bankings abandoned their posts, fearing their perches would collapse under the hammering administered by the big Maserati. When it rained on Thursday Moss alarmed the Americans by taking his white car out to lap at 145mph, embellishing his gamesmanship by slewing the Eldorado as he passed the pits.

In qualifying on Friday Stirling's speed was a moderate 164.385mph for three laps while the Indy machines were running around 170. It was overgeared, he found, reaching only 6,700rpm when entering the bankings, which scrubbed that off to 6,200 at the exits. Fitted with a lower ratio the 420 M/58 proved faster but Moss let his sixth-row qualifying speed stand.

In Ferrari's 412 MI its nominated driver, Mike Hawthorn, was little faster on the Friday. He qualified at an average of 160.06mph with a fastest lap at 164.49. 'I was being flung around like a pea in a kettle,' he recalled. 'The car went everywhere, up, down and around. The only thing to do was to hang grimly onto the steering wheel and hope for the best.' On Saturday Luigi Musso, the slender Roman who was Ferrari's only Italian driver, buckled on the vee-twelve's harness. Though he had qualified the smaller car he wanted to try the big one.

Musso's performance electrified the Monza crowd. Jesse Alexander reported that 'it was obvious that the car was a tremendous handful at speeds over 165mph. Musso worked very hard to hold the car on his chosen line and put it into full-lock slides all the way round.' Luigi turned three qualifying laps at an average of 174.653mph, putting the Ferrari decisively on pole with a time no one could match. His best lap was turned at 175.73mph.[1]

Hawthorn immediately ceded the big machine to Musso, agreeing to stand by as relief driver, while Phil Hill stepped into the 296 MI. In this, his first-ever race appearance in a single-seater Ferrari, Phil qualified at 161.226mph to start from the seventh of the ten two-car rows.

In Sunday's rolling start under a blazing sun Musso exploited the second of his three speeds to seize a long lead. He then battled the Indy regulars, who pulled ahead after the Italian's last lap in the lead, the tenth. After 26 of the first heat's 63 laps Musso steered into his pit from second place, woozy from heat and fumes from the exhausts athwart his cockpit.[2] The Ferrari needed new Borranis, some spokes having broken, and new tyres as well. Hawthorn took over in seventh place and brought the 412 MI up to sixth by the heat's finish.

In this Red-Hot Rivalry the first heat was a win for Maserati. Stirling Moss piled up places through the heat, rising from ninth to third and finally finishing fourth behind three Indy cars. Though priding himself on his fitness, Moss lay prostrate

---

1 Fast though this was it did not beat the pole-sitting qualifying time of Tony Bettenhausen in preparation for the 1957 event. His supercharged Novi recorded 175.878mph for three laps and a best lap of 176.9mph.

2 At the time much was made of the debilitating effects of 'methanol fumes' on Musso. Yet Ferrari's records of its engines, consistent in all other respects, show that both its cars at Monza in 1958 were burning petrol, not alcohol. Hawthorn testified that the screen that wrapped around the poorly ventilated cockpit did trap gases. It is the author's conclusion that some of these may have come from the car's unusually short exhaust pipes.

A rear view of Ferrari's 1958 Type 412 MI showed its high build with Musso, here, sitting atop its transmission. Unlike Maserati, which used Halibrand wheels, Ferrari remained loyal to Borrani wires for its Monza cars.

At the front end of the 1958 Type 412 MI Ferrari eschewed racing suspension, adopting rugged production-car components instead. The brakes were also from Maranello's production cars, albeit with special drums.

An anxious look under the bonnet of the Type 421 MI Ferrari showed that its 4.0-litre V12 was sparked by coil ignition, its twin distributors being driven from the rear of the exhaust camshafts.

Nominated to drive the big 412 MI Ferrari in 1958, Mike Hawthorn checked its restraint harness before qualifying. He relinquished the honour of taking the first rolling start to Musso but relieved him in the first heat and started the third one.

between heats on a cot in a corner of the paddock under an umbrella. Back in the Maserati, he wrote, 'in heat two I was beginning to get the hang of this type of racing … battling for third place, but with five laps to go my tyres started to lose grip so I had to ease down and finished fifth.'

This was another success for the Trident. In the first heat the Prancing Horse's smaller entry, running as high as sixth, retired after ten laps with what was called 'magneto trouble', but enough oil was in evidence to suggest that it was actually more serious. This left Phil Hill at leisure, which was fortunate because Luigi Musso only lasted 19 laps in the second heat. The American took over while wheels were changed. On the 40th lap, while seventh, he had to make another stop for fresh rubber, finally placing ninth.

For the third and final heat the cars lined up in their second-heat finishing order. Having lost clutch control, Moss lagged at the rolling start but pushed the Maserati back up to fourth and at the 40th of 63 laps was challenging an American newcomer,

A.J. Foyt, for third. Running high on the bankings he was having to apply steering force to hold the Eldorado away from the guard rails, when suddenly his arms twisted freely – the steering had broken. Slamming into the rails and their supports, bursting tyres and losing a wheel, the Maserati with its helpless and frightened driver spiralled down the banking into the dusty ditch at its bottom. Moss ranked ninth in the heat and was classified seventh overall.

Luigi Musso withdrew altogether from Ferrari's strength in the third heat, which Mike Hawthorn started. When he pitted after 24 laps to hand over to Phil Hill, Hawthorn was still in mid-field. 'Phil proceeded to wind it up very much better than I had,' said the Briton, 'and started picking up places right and left.' The heartening sight of the big red number 12 passing the Indy machinery was just what the crowd had come for. At the finish only two of the interlopers were still in front of the Ferrari, which had covered 60 laps to their 63. Maranello was awarded third in both the heat and the overall tally.

Thus, victory for Ferrari but an artistic success for Maserati. The latter's low-built car, running on Halibrands, had needed no stops for fresh tyres and wheels during the heats, unlike the taller Ferrari. Giulio Alfieri's decision to use Grand Prix front suspension and steering hadn't reckoned on the heavy control forces imposed by high speeds on the bankings that led to Moss's sudden retirement.

Its trio of drivers won the final podium position for Ferrari. 'Driving that monster around the Monza banking was the hardest job I ever tackled,' said Phil Hill. His gutsy performance sent his stock soaring at Maranello, which first offered Hill a Formula 1 seat for the Italian Grand Prix that year. He was on the road to his World Championship three years later.

As for Musso, hero of qualifying and the first heat, he was dead a week later, crashing his Ferrari during the French Grand Prix at Reims. The noble 412 MI, the most exciting racing car that Ferrari had yet produced, Monza pole-sitter and podium-

Phil Hill took over the 412 MI Ferrari from Musso in the second heat and from Hawthorn in the third. His dogged bravery contributed materially to its third-place ranking in the final standings of 1958's 500 Miles of Monza.

Lowered and lightened, the Eldorado Maserati became the Type 420 M/59 for its attack on the Indianapolis 500-mile race in 1959. When the car arrived at the Speedway, aficionados of the exotic were eager to inspect its technology.

The 1959 Indianapolis 500 witnessed an attempt to qualify a Kurtis powered by a Hilborn-fuel-injected Maserati V8. Engine failures prevented it from reaching lap speeds that were fast enough to qualify.

mounter in 1958, never raced again. Although a date was set for the 1959 500 Miles of Monza, in February of that year it was called off.

The option was available for Ferrari to run his car at Indianapolis, but the tyre problems that constrained it at Monza were sure to be more severe at the Indiana track with its shallow banking on tighter turns. This did not apply to the Eldorado, however, inherently lower with a leftward engine offset. Always on the cards for this Maserati, an entry for the 1959 running of the Indianapolis 500-mile race was filed by Eldorado's Gino Zanetti.

In preparation the V8-powered projectile was given a course of lightening. Omer Orsi having expressed severe reservations about an Indy venture, the work was farmed out to Modena craftsmen Gentilini and Allegretti. Shorn of its headrest and fin, the Maserati's lines were lowered, its tail turned under and its oil reservoir exposed on the left to shift more weight toward the inside of the track. This left space for a more conventional position for its shift gate and lever. Instead of a scoop, a submerged NACA duct now supplied air to the Webers. Painted red with 'Eldorado' in white, the slimmer and trimmer 420 M/59 was shaken down at Modena's Aerautodromo by Guerino Bertocchi before being shipped to Indiana.

On 8 May, a week after the famed Speedway opened for business, the Maserati arrived. On the

10th the car made its first track appearance in the hands of Bertocchi. Among the available drivers the man chosen on the 11th was Ralph Ligouri, an Indy newcomer who had to pass his novice test in the red machine. Completing this on the 15th, the day before the first qualifying weekend, Ligouri began looking for speed to match the timings in excess of 140mph needed to make the 33-car field. On the Sunday of the second weekend, with many race spots still open, he qualified at 136.395mph in a car called 'hopelessly outclassed'. Later that afternoon he was bumped from the starting field.

Reporter Bob Laycock remarked on 'the multitude of good friends made by the crew of the Eldorado Maserati with their sincere effort to put their car in the race and their obvious desire to learn so they could come back better prepared next year.' Such preparation would have to include the recruitment of a fast and knowledgeable driver, for Ligouri wasn't an asset to the team. In spite of several years of trying he never qualified for the Indianapolis 500-mile race. However, there would be no 1960 or later effort with a car from the Viale Ciro Menotti.

Sound though its engineering was, the four-cam V8 engine also had to bear its share of the blame. At Monza, Moss had observed that 'those Indy cars had lots of power' from their torque-rich Meyer-Drake Offys. Another Modena V8 had been at the Speedway in a Kurtis chassis, entered by California home-builder Frank Arciero. One of the engines originally ordered by Tony Parravano, it had Hilborn fuel injection, the better to burn alcohol fuels.

Driven by the capable Shorty Templeman, the Kurtis-Maserati broke its original engine and a spare on the successive days of the last qualifying weekend without ever showing convincing speed, albeit in a chassis that was clearly suited to the track. This was more than a hint that the venerable Offy hadn't yet met its match in the Maserati eight. Italian-car enthusiast Arciero didn't give up on his Maseratis. As late as 1965 Al Unser was trying to qualify one in a mid-engined chassis – without success.

Although Maserati never threatened to return to Indy-style racing, it was unfinished business for Enzo Ferrari. In 1987 he demonstrated a complete car with a 690-horsepower V8 engine built to the American CART rules. Though it served him well as a stalking horse during a period when he was having disagreements with the Formula 1 authorities, the Gustav Brunner design never raced at Indy or elsewhere. Ferrari died in 1988 without again seeing his Prancing Horses strut on the fabled oval.

CHAPTER THIRTEEN

250 TR vs Type 61

In the 3.0-litre class of 1958 and '59 its 250 Testa Rossa gave Ferrari a head start over Maserati, mired in its financial problems. With their astonishing 'Birdcage', however, the Trident's advocates fashioned a sharp new weapon for the 1960 season.

By the middle of 1957 it was clear that the cars competing for the World Sports-Car Championship would no longer be allowed unlimited engine size. Maserati had upped the ante with its 4.5-litre V8 while Chevrolet's SS, which shocked the Europeans with its speed in practice at Sebring, boasted 4.6-litres and was clearly capable of more. With their memories still intense of the chaotic crash at Le Mans in 1955 and its many fatalities, the FIA's panjandrums decided to curtail car speed by setting a limit on engine size.

During the 1957 season the most likely limit was thought to be 3.5-litres. This was the natural

Dan Gurney, driving, and Tony Brooks placed third with their 250 TR/59 Ferrari in Goodwood's Tourist Trophy on 5 September 1959. Ferrari, running similar cars early in the 1960 season, would be shocked by Maserati's new Type 61.

size of Jaguar's twin-cam six, although larger versions were being fielded. A 3.5-litre version of Maserati's V12 had made a few sports-car appearances. Ferrari had bored out a version of its Colombo V12 to 3.1-litres for experiments during 1957, while of course that season's four-cam twelve could easily be sized to 3.5-litres. Aston Martin had just introduced a bigger 3.7-litre six to complement its existing 2.9-litre engine; it could handily be trimmed to 3.5-litres.

Early in September of 1957 the edict came from the FIA's offices on Paris's Place de la Concorde. The limit for 1958 to 1960 would be 3.0-litres, not 3.5. This was soon academic for Maserati, whose financial woes saw it under legal guardianship in 1958. It would not be competing. Aston Martin could rely on its 2.9-litre engine, while Jaguar would destroke its six with lamentable results. At Maranello Enzo Ferrari and Carlo Chiti had to decide on a way forward.

Using the classic dimensions of 73 x 58.8mm, a 3.0-litre version of the Jano/Fraschetti four-cam V12 had been built and tested. The 312 S, it produced a healthy 320bhp at 8,200rpm on a 9.5:1 compression ratio. In this scaled-down form, however, its large ports and valves contributed to a shortage of the mid-range torque that an endurance-racing sports car needs.

In parallel, under the Andrea Fraschetti regime in 1957 Ferrari had been experimenting with higher-power versions of its veteran Colombo V12. An extensively revised engine was ready in time for Le Mans in 1957. Its principal feature was the use of individual inlet ports instead of the siamesed ports that had served the engine hitherto. For the first time each cylinder could be given its own carburettor throat and ram pipe for optimum tuning. Six twin-throat carburettors now handled induction.

With the new heads came a revised pattern of studs that featured four instead of three surrounding each cylinder to cope with higher combustion pressures. Improving access to the studs was the use of twin coil springs for each valve for the first time on a single-cam V12, replacing the hairpin springs that had been a feature of it from the outset. Crowded out of the central vee, spark plugs were moved to the exhaust-valve side of the heads.

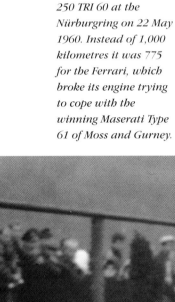

Julius Weitmann looked about to be mown down by Phil Hill's 250 TRI 60 at the Nürburgring on 22 May 1960. Instead of 1,000 kilometres it was 775 for the Ferrari, which broke its engine trying to cope with the winning Maserati Type 61 of Moss and Gurney.

Displacing 3,117cc (75.0 x 58.8mm) as it first appeared at Le Mans in 1957, for the 24-hour race this engine was mounted in a chassis like that of the concurrent 2.0-litre 500 TRC. It was the work of Vittorio Bellentani, who had laid down the original 500 TR chassis in 1956. Coil springs were used at all four corners with parallel wishbones in front and at the rear a live axle. The latter was guided by radius rods and a wide, low-placed A-arm that took lateral forces. To accept the longer V12 engine the TRC wheelbase of 88.6in was extended to 92.5in. Front track of 51.5in was unchanged while rear track increased 2in to 51.2.

This marriage of a gingered-up Colombo V12 with the light 500 TRC chassis was an ingenious expedient that recalled Ferrari's creation of a Formula 2 car by dropping its 2.0-litre twelve into its Grand Prix chassis. On the scales at Le Mans the car weighed only 1,885lb, some 350lb less than the average of the four-cam Ferraris. It was only 17lb heavier than the 3.0-litre car entered by France's Gordini, which rightly prided itself on building ultra-light racers.

Just as significant, and the focus of all cameras at Le Mans, was the Ferrari's unusual bodywork. The work of Sergio Scaglietti, it had gaps between the front wings and the main body. In addition the wheelhouse was cut away behind the front wheels, both measures being taken to help cool the drum brakes that were still a Ferrari feature. This was the first Ferrari to have the so-called 'pontoon' wing style that was also adopted on the four-cam cars for the last race of the 1957 season in Venezuela.

Although the hybrid racer failed to finish at Le Mans it showed excellent speed, holding second behind the winning Jaguar in the early hours in spite of being driven conservatively. Its lightness also contributed to improved fuel economy that brought benefits in long-distance races. Enzo Ferrari and new chief engineer Carlo Chiti concurred that this was the right formula for future sports-racing Ferraris.

On 22 November 1957 Maranello showed the press its 250 TR, carrying over the Testa Rossa name and crackle-finished red camshaft covers from the 2.0-litre model that supplied its chassis. It kept the Maserati-style centrifugal evacuation of

As first seen at Le Mans the previous year, this was the 1958 version of the novel 'pontoon' bodywork created by Sergio Scaglietti for Ferrari's 250 TR. This car, the entry of Belgian Jacques Swaters, crashed out of a wet 24-hour race.

warm air from its brake drums that Bellentani had introduced in 1956, but introduced Chiti's preferred helical finning for the drum periphery. While rear brakes kept Lampredi's centre-pivoted shoes, those at the front had two leading shoes for greater stopping power.

The V12's displacement was the 250's classical 2,953cc, fed by six two-throat 38 DCN downdraft Webers. With the high compression ratio of 9.8:1 its output was 290bhp at 7,500rpm. Unusually for a racing Ferrari the engine had an integral wet sump. This feature was kept through 1958 with dry sumps being adopted for 1959. Another unusual feature for a racing car was a transmission with synchromesh, using Porsche's patented system, for its four speeds. A ZF limited-slip differential gave good traction with the live axle.

Wearing Scaglietti's spectacular bodywork, this was the 250 TR Ferrari for the 1958 season. While these customer cars had left-hand drive, the works entries had steering on right or left. Several factory cars also had de Dion rear suspension. Starting with a single car that won the Targa Florio in 1958 the works Ferraris had more conventional front ends with slots for brake cooling. Responding to driver complaints of high-speed wandering, Chiti had concluded that the 'pontoon' design was a source of lift at the nose.

With four victories in the six qualifying events Ferrari comfortably swept the 1958 championship. It had a net 32 points ahead of Aston Martin and Porsche, placed equally with a net 18 points. Aston Martin won two races while Porsche was beginning to annoy the big boys with its consistent high places.

Responding to the Aston challenge in particular Carlo Chiti overhauled his works sports-racer, creating the 250 TR/59 for the next season. With right-hand steering confirmed to suit the majority of circuits, he offset its engine and driveline slightly to the left to achieve ideal balance. Important changes were the adoption of disc brakes by Dunlop and adjustable telescopic dampers by Holland's Koni, which was making a major effort to penetrate the racing market. During the season five-speed gearboxes at the engine were introduced.

Pininfarina advised on the shape of the 250 TR/59, whose body was constructed by Medardo Fantuzzi. With Maserati in a legal poorhouse, the skilled coachbuilder's defection to Maranello was no great loss to the Viale Ciro Menotti. He was drafted in to assist when Scaglietti found himself amply busy with bodies for competition GT cars. Among the prettiest of the front-engined competition Ferrari sports cars, the 1959 models had the Plexiglas air scoops over their carburettors that were hallmarks of the Chiti regime.

Seen from the side, the 1958 Ferrari 250 TR showed the manner in which its wings were cut away to permit air to flow through from the nose channels to cool the front brakes. This Le Mans entry of Fernand Tavano failed to finish.

Though 1959 started well with a win at Sebring, it was destined to be Ferrari's only success that year. Aston Martin closed out the season with three wins in a row to take the championship with 24 net points while Ferrari had to share second place with Porsche, both at 18 net points. The British team had its act together and prevailed, wrote Cyril Posthumus, 'thanks also to Ferrari's contrastingly bad pitwork and general disorganisation that year.' Poor reliability often let down its drivers, among whom were team newcomers Jean Behra and Dan Gurney.

A minor meeting was held during that season, on 12 July 1959, on the delightful road circuit at Rouen in France. It offered two events, both of 143 miles: a Formula 2 race and a contest for 2.0-litre sports cars. Stirling Moss won them both. In the sports-car race he scored a decisive victory, lapping the Type 15 Lotuses of Alan Stacey and Innes Ireland to win the Delamarre de Bouteville Cup. Moss was driving a brand-new Maserati.

This new car, the Type 60, was the results of ruminations during 1958 by Maserati chief engineer Giulio Alfieri. In October he began considering the creation of a new sports-racing car for which he had some radical ideas. In November he started making the first chassis frame to see how well it would perform. Its tests proving satisfactory, Alfieri and his colleagues completed the design of the new car.

Crackle-finish red paint for its camshaft covers made good the 1958 Ferrari 250 TR's moniker of 'Testarossa'. Six-port cylinder heads accommodated six twin-throat Webers to produce 290bhp at 7,500rpm.

Early in December the new design and its potential were presented to Maserati's chief, Omer Orsi, as a car that Maserati could build and sell to private owners to compete in the international 2.0-litre class, still an important category and one in which Maserati, from its A6GCS onward, had always been competitive. Orsi gave Alfieri the go-ahead to build a prototype.

Meanwhile the Orsis were pulling out all the stops to restore their company to health. Adolfo,

Americans Rod Carveth and Gil Geitner brought their splendid-looking 250 TR Ferrari to the 'Ring for the 1959 1,000-kilometre race on 7 June. An accident kept them from finishing in their unusual right-hand-drive Testarossa.

At Le Mans on 20–21 June 1959 the 250 TR Ferrari of E.D. Martin and Bill Kimberly flaunted its superb lines and rules-mandated full windscreen. Gearbox problems stopped their run in the 9th hour when they were in the top ten.

said his grandson of the same name, 'sold some personal properties and the milling-machine division and with my father reorganised the company so that within a year he had paid off all the debts and the company returned to profit. The main reason for this was the success of the 3500 range of GT cars, which sold in many markets around the world.' Maserati's legal shackles were thrown off on 4 May 1959.

By that May the first unpainted 2.0-litre Type 60 Maserati was ready for testing in the hands of Guerino Bertocchi. On the public road from Modena towards Verona he found the new car very satisfactory. Its next test was at the Modena Aerautodromo on 19 May with Stirling Moss at the wheel. Moss then tested it at the Nürburgring from 4 to 6 June. He broke the lap record there for 2.0-litre sports cars and had useful suggestions for the car's improvement.

Although Maserati didn't intend to race the Type 60 itself, it felt a need to demonstrate the capabilities of its new creation in order to attract customers. Moss suggested that they enter the car in the Rouen meeting, where he was driving a Formula 2 Cooper-Borgward. Odd-looking though it was, with its bulging wings and trelliswork dash panel, the new Maserati was blindingly fast.

The striking feature of the Type 60 was its frame of many small steel tubes welded together to form an elegant and idealised space frame. This concept was originated by Alfieri. His fresh point of view was responsible for the complete novelty of the new car's structure. It was said at that time that a proper space frame should be built up around a parakeet: if the bird could fly away when the job was completed, it hadn't been done properly. This was the principle followed by Alfieri in his design of the aptly nicknamed 'Birdcage' Maserati's frame, a construction that was a *tour de force* by the car's stress-conscious designer.

Although obviously complicated, the frame was in fact based on a completely logical premise. This was that the more frame tubes you use, the smaller they can be and, if they're properly placed, the lighter the structure will be for the same stiffness – or the stiffer it will be for the same weight, if that's what the designer is trying to accomplish. The ultimate would be a near-infinite number of tubes of near-infinite thinness: a smooth, complete skin. In other words, a pure monocoque structure. The 'Birdcage' represented the closest approach to a monocoque achieved through the use of steel tubing.

Lacking experience in monocoque construction but having craftsmen superhumanly skilled in the

use of welding torches, Giulio Alfieri decided to get the same effect with a myriad of chrome-molybdenum-alloy steel tubes. The main framework was formed of 20mm tubes, which were diagonally braced by smaller tubes some 12mm in diameter. The frame was strengthened by steel-sheet weldments, for example along its front-wheel houses and under the front end. Stressed sheet was also added along the floor pan and over the door sills and propeller-shaft tunnel, where there were fewer frame tubes. The original Type 60 frame was impressively light at only 66lb.

Because the tubes went almost everywhere there was little need for extra body supports. In fact Maserati simply omitted body panels where they served no useful purpose. Typical was the gap between the exiguous dash panel and the base of the windscreen. Aluminium was simply draped over the rest of the car where needed. At first the Type 60 had no cover for its carburettors but they were enclosed for Rouen.

In his selection of the Type 60's key dimensions Alfieri, like Ferrari two years earlier, chose those that had been successful in a previous 2.0-litre model. With an 86.6in wheelbase, 49.2in front track and 47.2in rear track its parameters were identical to those of the 200 SI. All were significantly smaller than the 250 TR's measurements.

To lower both its hood line and its centre of gravity the new Maserati's four-cylinder in-line engine was canted 45° to the right. At the same time the crankshaft centreline was offset to the left side of the chassis to keep the engine's weight centred. This required the propeller shaft to angle back to the right again as it ran rearward – but only slightly, because the input shaft to the rear-mounted gearbox was also offset to the left. This opened proportionally more room for the driver on the right-hand side of the prop shaft.

The Type 60's engine was derived from that of the 200 SI, which in turn had been developed from the 150 S. Most closely related to its forebears was the aluminium-alloy cylinder block, which housed wet nitrided-iron cylinder liners and carried the crankshaft in five main bearings. Massive main-bearing caps, each held on by four studs, restored the lateral strength that was lost by ending the bottom of the block at the crank centreline. In the design of the crankshaft, connecting rods, pistons – the whole bottom end – use was made of the experience gathered with the similarly proportioned 450 S V8.

A new, deep aluminium sump was cast, liberally finned on its left side and shaped to conform to the engine's 45° slope. Pressure and scavenge pumps for dry-sump lubrication were

Ferrari bodied its 250 TR works entries less radically in 1958. Nose and wings were conventional, while a bonnet bulge collected high-pressure air from the base of the windscreen. This was Olivier Gendebien in the 1958 Le Mans winner, shared with Phil Hill.

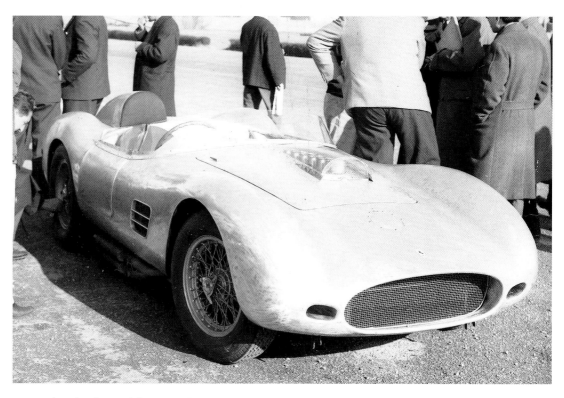

On test at Modena's Aerautodromo in January 1959, the Type 250 TR/59 Ferrari was lighter and more compact, as well as disc-braked and coil-sprung. Defecting from struggling Maserati, Fantuzzi shaped the body to Pininfarina's design.

As revised for 1959 under Carlo Chiti's direction, the Ferrari Testarossa's V12 had an improved torque curve and peak power of 306bhp at 7,400rpm. Ignition was by coils and twin distributors.

exposed at the front of the sump, below the nose of the crank. Nearest to the engine, the single pressure pump drew oil from the reservoir on the left side of the engine bay and pumped it to the engine by way of a large filter, frame-mounted next to the reservoir. Oil was drawn from the pan by two pickups and two scavenge pumps and returned to the tank by an oil cooler at the left of the water radiator.

When the Maserati 200 SI's cylinder-head design had formed the basis for the head of the 450 S V8, a major change had been made to the layout of its water passages. The four-cylinder 200 SI engine simply let hot water out through a pipe at the front, between the cam-drive gears. For the V8 the water piping of the 250 F and 300 S sixes was adopted: hot water exited though separate manifolding above the inlet-valve seats (on the 'high side' of this angled engine) while cool water was pumped direct to the exhaust-valve seats and guides by another manifold on the other side of the head vee. With its single cylinder head placed at the precise angle of the right-hand bank of the 450 S V8, the new engine could well afford to keep this new form of water manifolding.

An additional major change from the V8 was the abandonment of the elaborate roller-finger cam follower that had come in with the 150 S and spread to the 200 SI and 450 S. For his new engine Alfieri reverted to the simple, light, space-saving finger follower that had been proven on the Maserati twin-cam sixes. In the latter engines it was combined with coil springs, while in the new engine it was allied with hairpin-type springs for the first time.

The twin valves for each cylinder were inclined at a 76° included angle: 37° from the vertical for the inlets and 39° for the exhausts. While the dimensions of the 200 SI had been 92 x 75mm, the Type 60 engine was more oversquare at 93.8 x 72mm. Its 200bhp at 7,800rpm were transmitted through a

multi-plate clutch in unit with the engine and an engine-speed propeller shaft to the rear-mounted transaxle that had been a Maserati feature since it was introduced on the 1954 Grand Prix car. It provided five speeds and the right-hand shift location that was familiar to American customers.

Using this transaxle meant that Alfieri could also keep the de Dion rear suspension that was introduced on the 250 F, with its axle tube running forward of the gearbox where it was laterally located by a steel-sided slide in the front of the transaxle casing. Parallel trailing arms guided the wheel hubs individually. High above the axle shafts was the rear transverse leaf spring.

An utter novelty for Maserati was rack-and-pinion steering, mounted ahead of the front-wheel centres. It actuated forward-facing steering arms through short tie rods of remarkable thinness which preserved traditional Maserati steering geometry. The front suspension drew directly from the Viale Ciro Menotti parts bins with its components from recent Maserati Grand Prix cars.

The Type 60's brakes marked a major step forward. Maserati took up an experimental Girling design, which was tried by Ferrari on his Formula 1 car at Morocco at the end of 1958 but dropped in favour of Dunlop discs. The Girling units had a deeply dished disc which kept its rubbing surfaces out in the airflow and a unique three-cylinder caliper. The easily changed, fully machined caliper used on the Type 60, made by Maserati to Girling's design, was virtually identical to that first tried by

Ferrari. Front discs were 355mm in diameter and those in the rear 315mm.

At an early stage of the testing and racing of the Type 60, that most thoughtful and creative of drivers Stirling Moss suggested to Giulio Alfieri that he had in this 2.0-litre car the basis of a machine that could compete in bigger leagues. Taking his recommendation, they enlarged its four-cylinder engine. The bore was increased to 100mm, as much as the block and liners would allow, while a stroke extended to 92mm gave 2,890cc. This required the casting of a new cylinder block 10mm taller. An attempt to lengthen the stroke to 95.5mm to bring displacement to 2,985cc failed when the test engine destroyed itself on the Maserati dynamometer.

With a compression ratio of 9.8:1 the engine of the Type 61, as it was designated, produced 255bhp at 6,500rpm. Torque reached a maximum of 229lb-ft at the 5,000rpm peak of a very strong curve that gave great flexibility. The driveline was beefed up to match, including constant-mesh engagement for all five speeds.

The Type 60/61's low and compact build was an asset to its speed. Alfieri verified the efficiency of its shape with clay models tested in Maserati's wind tunnel. Claimed top-speed capabilities for the small and large 'Birdcage' versions were 168 and 177mph respectively, figures which were closely approximated in testing using high final-drive ratios.

Not surprisingly, early races revealed some durability faults in this advanced car. Two cars

Tony Brooks, at the pit wall, and Jean Behra, refuelling, drove this 250 TR/59 to third place in the 'Ring 1,000-kilometre race on 7 June 1959. Mino Amorotti measured the fuel level while Vic Barlow, in tie, checked his Dunlops.

The Ferrari 250 TR/59 of Gendebien and Hill (14) took the lead at Le Mans in 1959 in the 11th hour and held it, with a four-lap lead, until retirement in the 20th hour with overheating and loss of coolant. The NART-entered 1958 250 TR (17) bowed out in the third hour with gearbox trouble.

broke their de Dion tubes at Nassau in the Bahamas at the end of 1959; a new stronger design was produced and retrofitted to existing cars. Stirling Moss was at the wheel for the Type 61's first victory in Havana, Cuba, in February 1960.

The Type 61 Trident's arrival on the scene was a severe shock for the Prancing Horse stable. In 1960 its international race entries were made by an American team, Camoradi USA, founded by Miami car dealer Lloyd 'Lucky' Casner. Goodyear-backed Camoradi bought three of the cars, engaged the drivers and made the race entries, while Maserati took care of preparing the Type 61s. With such first-rank drivers as Stirling Moss, Dan Gurney, Carroll Shelby and Masten Gregory, Camoradi seemed to be well equipped for the 1960 season.

For its part Ferrari prepared for 1960 with revisions to its 250 TR that included independent rear suspension by parallel wishbones and coil springs concentric with tubular dampers, pivoted from an improved multi-tube frame. The two 1960 cars equipped thus in place of de Dion axles were called the 250 TRI/60. Another change was a wheelbase shortened from 92.5 to 89.8in. Extracting 2.7in just behind the front wheels helped reduce the car's turning circle, a qualifying criterion at Le Mans. Like its Modenese rivals Ferrari had to fit higher windscreens to meet new FIA demands.

Carlo Chiti shifted his V12 engines rearward. He sought further dispersion of weight to the rear by using transaxles in both four- and five-speed

versions. However, the engine-mounted five-speed was the staple equipment in 1960. Ingeniously it was an all-indirect unit that allowed the engine to be set even lower in the chassis. A V12 equipped with Bosch fuel injection was tested, but although it delivered 300bhp at 7,500rpm this 250 I engine was not raced. In fact the carburetted version was credited with more punch than that at 315bhp at the same revs.

Carryover Ferraris from 1959 had their first encounter with a lone Type 61 in the Argentine 1,000 Kilometre race on 31 January. With Dan Gurney at the wheel the Maserati led easily, setting the race's fastest lap, but a broken rear damper mounting kept team-mate Masten Gregory from being able to hold off the best Ferrari, which took the lead just after half-distance. Gearbox trouble soon retired the Type 61.

With fuel-contract problems keeping the factory Ferrari team away from Sebring, Camoradi's two 'Birdcages' (their third broke in practice) and Briggs Cunningham's similar car should have had a walkover. The powerful pairing of Gurney and Moss took one of them to a four-lap lead but retired after eight of the twelve hours with a broken ring and pinion. A 250 TR/59 Ferrari entered by Luigi Chinetti's North American Racing Team (NART) was keeping the 'Birdcage' honest until it succumbed to engine woes. Patient Porsche took the victory.

The finances of neither Camoradi nor Maserati could extend to thorough testing of their highly-

strung new cars, with the result that in these long-distance races they often suffered retirements for various technical reasons. After Sebring the Orsis and Giulio Alfieri responded to Camoradi's complaints by strengthening key components in the transaxle and reinforcing the Type 61's frame and rear hubs. The four's main bearings were increased in diameter from 60 to 65mm while its rod journals were enlarged from 50.7 to 57mm. 'Birdcage' Maserati maintenance required an eagle eye on the many small tubes for cracks that could impair the frame's normally exemplary rigidity.

A lone Camoradi entry – with support from the Orsis – in the Targa Florio saw local man Nino Vaccarella take the lead ahead of menacing Porsches and Ferraris that included one of the new all-independent-suspension 250 TRI/60 models.

At the urging of Stirling Moss, Maserati entered its first Type 60 in an event for 2.0-litre sports cars at Rouen on 12 July 1959. It handily defeated the cars that were hitherto considered best in class.

Pictured by Edward Eves in March 1959, Maserati's Type 60 took shape in the workshop at Viale Ciro Menotti. Low and light, it was the radical brainchild of chief engineer Giulio Alfieri.

A glimpse in the cockpit of the Type 60 Maserati as it looked in March 1959 showed the multi-tubular structure that Giulio Alfieri adopted in order to achieve maximum stiffness with minimum weight.

Expanded internally from the Type 60's 2.0-litre four, the 2,890cc engine of the Type 61 Maserati was inclined at 45 degrees to the right to lower the bonnet line and make room for its two twin-throat 48DCO3 Weber carburettors.

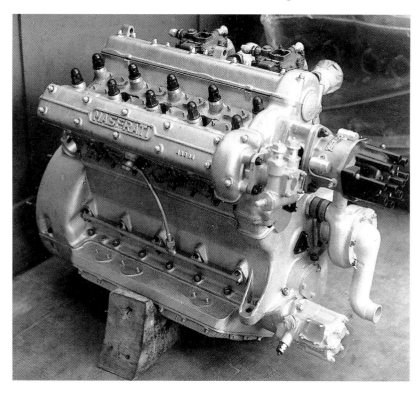

The Maserati retired, however, after a stone holed its fuel tank. The Testa Rossas faded as well and another win went to Porsche. So far the new 'Birdcage' had led every endurance race it had entered, only to falter before the finish.

A noteworthy and noble exception was the performance of the Type 61 at the Nürburgring. There in the 1,000 Kilometre race on 22 May 1960 the Camoradi 'Birdcage' was successful in the hands of the Moss/Gurney partnership that had been so effective at Sebring. Their race survived a

scare when an oil line came adrift with Dan Gurney at the wheel, but repaired quickly under the eyes of team manager Piero Taruffi the Type 61 went on to win.

Challenging the white car with its blue striping were two Testa Rossas, one with independent rear suspension. In rain and mist they found themselves battling not with the Type 61 but with the pesky Porsches that were so much at home on the 'Ring. After the 250 TRI/60 retired team manager Romolo Tavoni put Phil Hill in his surviving de Dion-axle car to close the gap. Though he preferred its handling the best Hill could do was third place behind a Porsche and the Maserati.

Heartened by this success, Maserati made a major effort with Camoradi's cars for Le Mans on 25 and 26 June. It fielded three Type 61s, one standard, one with a long tail and one with a similar tail plus an extended nose with a huge Plexiglas windscreen that sloped all the way forward to cover the engine completely. Faired to a bullet-like shape after wind-tunnel experiments, this car was Alfieri's response to the demands of the long Mulsanne straight. There Masten Gregory was timed at 169mph in early practice, an astonishing pace for a 2.9-litre car. The Kansan hinted he could go even faster; in fact he was timed at 170mph during the race against 149 for an ordinary 'Birdcage'.

The three Maseratis were astonishingly light. They weighed in at 1,558lb for the streamlined car and 1,518lb for the normal models. Against this the four factory Testa Rossas hit the scales at 1,745lb for the latest independent-rear model and 1,885lb for updated 1959 cars. In spite of their weight disadvantage the proven de Dion-rear Ferraris were clearly quickest on this high-speed circuit, more at home on the fast turns than their independent-rear stablemates in spite of much experimentation with the springs and dampers of the latter.

At between 155 and 162mph the maximum speeds of the four works Testa Rossas as timed at Le Mans ranged far below the speed of the new 'Birdcage'. Thus it was no surprise when the latter, driven by Masten Gregory, rocketed into a first-lap lead from 19th at the start. He easily outpaced the field but couldn't restart after his first pit stop. A faulty starter motor – also affecting another Type 61 – was the culprit. Though it was replaced the Maserati never recovered the lead and finally retired, as did its sisters.

Meanwhile Ferrari halved its chances of success by miscalculating the fuel needed to get two of its Testa Rossas to the first stop; both retired on the circuit. One independent-rear car failed its gearbox while the de Dion model piloted by the Belgian team of Olivier Gendebien and Paul Frère survived to win the 24-hour race. Second, four laps behind, was a 250 TR/59 entered by Chinetti's NART. By then the Maserati men had long gone, their 'Birdcages' and equipment packed up for the long drive back to Modena.

With the cancellation of races in Britain and Venezuela only five events qualified for the 1960 championship and of these only the best three finishes counted. Maserati had 11 points from its Nürburgring win and a non-'Birdcage' fourth place at Buenos Aires. Ferrari and Porsche were equal with a net 22 points, a tie that was broken in Maranello's favour by its greater number of third-place finishes. Although clearly the scintillating star of 1960's endurance races, Maserati had to give best to Ferrari.

Reflecting on the travails of the Trident's season, 'Birdcage' historian Joel Finn surmised that 'this could have been caused by the fact that some of Maserati's best racing mechanics departed from the firm when it quit running a factory effort in 1958. The new people had to learn how to prepare a car for competition and, like Camoradi, simply needed more experience. While the 1960 results were much less than promised [by Camoradi], they were still better than detractors thought would be achieved.'

Although the FIA extended its World Sports-Car Championship by a scant single year to 1961, approving only five events, both Ferrari and Maserati wheeled out new machinery to contest it. Some were rear-engined, as described in Chapter 15,

but the Testa Rossa and 'Birdcage' continued their rivalry from the year before.

Carlo Chiti, now well settled-in at Maranello, produced a completely new space frame for the 250 TR61, with a wheelbase that split the difference between preceding designs at 91.5in. He continued all-independent suspension by tubular wishbones and the all-indirect gearbox at the engine that facilitated its low positioning. The two cars built to this new design had long cut-off tails with spoilers and noses that had the twin-oval air inlets that Chiti had adopted for aerodynamic reasons.

One of the new Ferraris and a prototype of the new model confronted Camoradi's Maseratis in the first race of 1961 at Sebring. In a reversal of the previous year's form, neither Casner's Type 61 nor Briggs Cunningham's 'Birdcage' succeeded in grabbing the lead. Both retired with trivial and well-known faults. Instead the Ferraris dominated. The newest car won followed by its prototype and two more Testa Rossas. All Stirling Moss had to show for his spell in Camoradi's Type 61 was the fastest lap.

Built chiefly for fast circuits, the new Testa Rossa wasn't expected to do well in the Targa Florio and indeed retired after three of the ten laps. No Type 61s were entered, a pity as their chances would have been good. Nor was the V12 Ferrari thought ideal for the Nürburgring, but one was fielded in the 1,000 Kilometre race as a works-backed NART entry for the Mexican Rodriguez brothers, Ricardo and Pedro. They'd shown electrifying form at Sebring on their way to third place.

Ingeniously, Giulio Alfieri made use of existing transaxle and front and rear suspension components when he fashioned his 'Birdcage' Maseratis. Frame, disc brakes and rack-and-pinion steering were novelties for the Trident.

Belying its racing number, this Type 61 Maserati was campaigned by the Cunningham team in 1960. Walt Hansgen was at the wheel in a winning drive at Cumberland, Maryland.

Piloting the Type 61 'Birdcage' owned by Mike Garber, Swiss racer Gaston Andrey brought the SCCA's Class D Modified championship to the Trident in 1960. This was the car test-driven by the author in its (and his) prime.

Having lost Goodyear's backing, Lloyd Casner brought his sole remaining Type 61 to the 'Ring to make a promotional film. Offering the bare minimum of financing, the organisers persuaded him to stay and race. Lacking any spares, not even tyres, he and Masten Gregory knew they'd have to pace themselves. This they did so successfully that they swept to a surprise victory while others failed in wet and icy conditions. For once Casner's 'Lucky' nickname was entirely appropriate. At the finish he and Gregory had a full-lap margin over the Rodriguez Testa Rossa.

No Type 61s contested Le Mans, which was won by a brace of Testa Rossas. Easily capable of lapping in under four minutes, Phil Hill and Olivier Gendebien set a new record for the race in their 250 TR/61 with their victory at 115.901mph. Three laps behind them was the prototype of the new model driven by Mike Parkes and Willy Mairesse. The only race had been with the TR/61 of the Rodriguez brothers, who had led until slowed by a pit stop and finally wrecked their engine two hours from the finish.

With the championship in the bag after Le Mans, Enzo Ferrari loaned a Testa Rossa to the Scuderia Centro-Sud of Mimo Dei to compete in the four hours of Pescara in August. On the demanding 15.9-mile road course on the Adriatic the Type 61 Maserati of Lloyd Casner was right at home. Past the mid-point of the race he had a five-minute lead and looked uncatchable. However, when passing another competitor the American strayed onto the marbles, spun and flipped. He

suffered burns from which he recovered. The victory in this final race of the World Sports-Car Championship went to Lorenzo Bandini and Giorgio Scarlatti in the Testa Rossa.

Although sports-racing cars were allowed to continue competing in the classic events, thanks to some jiggery-pokery at the FIA and among race organisers, the great battle between the 'Birdcage' and the Red Head was over. The account was settled decisively in favour of the cars from Maranello, but the Viale Ciro Menotti had produced machinery that astonished and, occasionally, won.

Type 61s that raced in North America had many successes. They were used to win the SCCA's Class D Modified championship, for 3.0-litre sports-racing cars, by Gaston Andrey in 1960 and by Roger Penske in 1961. Drivers such as Jim Hall, Bob Drake, Walt Hansgen, Jim Jeffords, John Fitch and Carroll Shelby raced them with great success for private teams, their own and those of others.

The works Testa Rossas were sold off to private stables both European and American. In the US they added successes to those of the 1958 250 TRs, winning at Watkins Glen in 1961, for example, but they lacked the agility and lightness that the Trident's Type 61 exploited so insouciantly in American sprint-style racing. While the Testa Rossa has gone down in history as the finer collector of long-distance trophies, few will argue that the 'Birdcage' was not the quintessential expression of the front-engined sports-racer.

In 1961 the Trident's Type 61 was still so competitive in Class D Modified that it won the SCCA's championship the second year in a row, now driven by Roger Penske. He had sponsorship from du Pont's Telar for his red Maserati.

CHAPTER FOURTEEN

Dino 156 F1 vs Types 6 and 8

Though crippled financially, Maserati found ways to compete in Formula 1 and in fact helped encourage mid-engined racing cars while Ferrari struggled with this novelty. It was Maranello, however, that had a year of glory and tragedy in 1961.

I n the increasingly lengthy canon of Ferrari in competition few topics are more controversial than the hesitancy with which the founder approached the conversion from front-engined racers to the mid-engined style. Many observers feel that Enzo Ferrari took longer than he should have to react to the shock successes by the cheeky

On Portugal's Monsanto street circuit on 23 August 1959 Mario Cabral, in a Centro-Sud Cooper-Maserati, led the Ferrari Dino of Tony Brooks. Cabral, making his Grand Prix debut, finished 10th and last, a lap behind Brooks who was ninth.

Though it was in no position to field a racing car, Maserati didn't want to be left out of the new 1.5-litre Formula 1 starting in 1961. This was its Type 6 four-cylinder Grand Prix engine, being dynamometer-tested by Guerino Bertocchi.

At Sebring in 1957 Roy Salvadori, shown, and Carroll Shelby drove one of the rare Type 250 S Maseratis. Though suiting no sports-car class, its four was ideal for mid-mounted use in cars for the 2.5-litre Formula 1.

Coopers in the first races of 1958. Here, after all, was a man who had seen Alfa Romeos from his *Scuderia* humbled by mid-engined Auto Unions through much of the 1930s.

Ferrari was unmoved by the success of the Auto Unions. 'From time immemorial,' he was quoted as saying, 'the horse has always drawn the cart, not pushed it.' Though first Cooper and then Lotus demonstrated the virtues of the mid-engined racing car, though his drivers begged him to make

the conversion, and though his engineers stood ready – for his V6 engine was ideal for such a transformation – Ferrari remained the adamantine advocate of the front-engined Grand Prix car through 1958, 1959 and well into 1960.

Horses and their relationships to carts did not in fact account for Ferrari's reluctance to make the change. For a decade he'd been successful as a car maker by producing road cars that bore a relationship to his racing cars. Customers tooling along the Corniche or the Autostrada in his cars could imagine themselves Fangio, Ascari or Musso piloting one of Enzo's long-nosed racers. He valued this empathic synergy and was reluctant to endanger it. He was also encouraged in his affinity to front engines by some of his technical team, among them engineer Giotto Bizzarrini.

Thus Maserati, not Ferrari, became the first to power mid-engined Grand Prix cars. This came about in the most serendipitous manner possible. With full 2.5-litre Coventry Climax FPF fours in very short supply at the beginning of the 1959 season, British racing-car entrant C.T. 'Tommy' Atkins thought of another four-cylinder engine of that capacity that was available off the shelf: the motive power of Maserati's 250 S sports-racer.

One of the Trident's more obscure models of which only a half-dozen were made, the 250 S was an expanded version of the 200 SI. The latter's

engine dimensions of 92 x 75mm were increased to 96 x 86mm for 2,490cc, a conversion so straightforward that such American customers as Jim Hall added the useful half-litre to their 200 SIs. Engine weight was much the same at 330lb. With Formula 1 cars limited to 2.5-litres and running on petrol since 1958, the sports-car compression ratio of 9.7:1 was appropriate for GP use. Maserati claimed 235bhp at 7,000rpm breathing through 48 DCO3 Weber carburettors.

To carry his Maserati four Tommy Atkins acquired a mid-engined Cooper chassis, a Type 45 of the sort that had been shaking up the establishment in 1958. His mechanic Harry Pearce made the installation, marrying the engine to a gearbox made by former Trident engineer Valerio Colotti. Pearce fitted a larger radiator and bigger oil reservoir to match the Maserati's appetites.

Engaged to drive the Cooper-Maserati was a quick Briton with an Italian name, Roy Salvadori. He officiated at its debut in the Glover Trophy race at Goodwood on 30 March 1959. In wet conditions Salvadori qualified second fastest but struggled to finish seventh. The driver was scathing about his engine's output. 'Our Maserati was rather less powerful than the equivalent Coventry Climax with inferior torque characteristics,' he wrote. 'Maserati claimed 210/215bhp, but whenever you put an Italian engine on the brake its power never matched the claims made and this Maserati engine was developing less than 200bhp.'

At Aintree in April Salvadori was holding fifth behind the leading Ferraris of Tony Brooks and Jean Behra when his gearbox played up and he retired. He finished fifth in a Formula 1 race at Silverstone in May and on the following weekend, the 10th, entered the Monaco Grand Prix. There he not only qualified among the 16 select starters but also was eighth fastest on the grid's third row. In the race he'd just risen to third place, splitting the Ferraris of Tony Brooks and Phil Hill, when his gearbox failed. Salvadori pushed his racer over the line to be credited with sixth.

In July the fast Reims circuit was unkind to the Cooper-Maserati, which failed a piston. The engine failed again in the Italian GP with Jack Fairman at the wheel, while the transmission broke in the US Grand Prix at Sebring in December. The Atkins car's best 1959 finish was fourth in the Oulton Park Gold Cup in September, headed by three Climax-powered Coopers. In 1960 the car was taken over by Sid Greene to be driven by his son Keith, for whom it managed two double-digit finishes in British non-championship races.

By the time of the Italian Grand Prix on 13 September there'd been a 200 per cent increase in the Cooper-Maserati population. Backed by oil company BP, the Modena-based Scuderia Centro-

Roy Salvadori drove the Atkins Stable's Cooper-Maserati in its baptismal outing at Goodwood on 30 March 1959, giving the Trident a lead in mid-engined GP cars over the Prancing Horse. He qualified second-quickest in the Glover Trophy race.

Completed in the winter of 1956–57, Ferrari created its 1.5-litre Dino V6 to a concept originated by Vittorio Jano. It had no clutch housing, the clutch being mounted at the transaxle in the manner of Jano's Lancia D50.

refreshment of car and driver he finished fourth, a lap ahead of the Dino 246 F1 of Wolfgang von Trips and on the same lap as another Dino driven by Cliff Allison, who placed second.

Another excellent placing for a Centro-Sud Cooper-Maserati came in Silverstone's 146-mile International Trophy on 14 May. Although his sixth place doesn't sound impressive, thrusting Masten Gregory was a lap ahead of Cliff Allison's Dino 246 F1 and a lap behind the best-placed Ferrari of Phil Hill in fifth. Although this was more a sign of the Prancing Horse's travails than of the Trident's ascendancy, such results were heartening to Maserati chief Giulio Alfieri and his backers Adolfo and Omer Orsi. By 1960 their auto company had shrugged off legal administration and was accelerating its racing activities with the help of paying customers.

In the Monaco Grand Prix on 29 May 1960 Ferrari entered its first mid-engined prototype. It qualified in mid-field and placed sixth in the hands of American Richie Ginther. Though it raced no more as a 2.5-litre car, in the French Grand Prix in early July another mid-engined Ferrari-powered car appeared. This was the Cooper chassis that Ferrari had bought, now powered by a 1955-vintage Type 555 Supersqualo four. In those days 270bhp at 7,200rpm was claimed for it on the alcohol blends then allowed. It would have delivered less on the petrol now mandated.

Ultimately two such cars were at the disposal of the Scuderia Eugenio Castellotti, set up in tribute to the lost Ferrari driver. One had been present at Monaco but was too slow to qualify in the hands of Giorgio Scarlatti, who was a prime mover of the project and team. The solo French debut in Gino Munaron's hands ended in retirement after troubles with the Colotti gearbox. Two weeks later it finished 15th in the British GP, a lap behind Gregory's Cooper-Maserati.

Both Castellotti Coopers were at the Italian Grand Prix, which the English teams boycotted for its use of the bumpy banked track in addition to the road circuit. There the Cooper-Ferrari with 'Eugenio' on its crackle-blue cam covers had its finest hour with a fourth-place finish, driven by Giulio Cabianca, behind three works Ferraris. Its sister retired and no Maserati-powered cars finished.

It was all change for 1961, when Grand Prix cars adopted the 1.5-litre limit to which Formula 2 cars had been racing for four years. Although the twin-cam Coventry Climax FPF four was the series' staple engine, used by Cooper, Lotus and many others, Ferrari also intervened with his Dino V6. This 1,489cc engine was first constructed in 1956 around dimensions of

Sud run by Mimo Dei retired its hard-worked 250 F Maseratis and invested in three new Type 51 Cooper chassis. In two of these it installed 250 S fours from the Viale Ciro Menotti. Dei recoupéd some of his costs by selling the third chassis to Enzo Ferrari, who was beginning to take an interest in this mid-engined lark. Carlo Chiti subjected the Cooper to close examination.

The debut of a lone Centro-Sud Cooper-Maserati was on 2 August 1959 in the German GP on the fast Avus track. Impressively the Italian engine survived the high-speed caning to finish sixth, in an aggregate of two heats, in the hands of Englishman Ian Burgess. But his deficit to the winning Ferrari was four of the total of 60 laps. Nor was the hybrid a threat to the Ferraris in the Portuguese GP three weeks later. Local man Mario Araujo Cabral drove it to tenth and last in the first Grand Prix of his six-year career.

At Monza in September Mimo Dei fielded both his Trident-powered Coopers, which finished 11th and 14th. On 6 February 1960 one of these Cooper-Masers posed the first serious Maserati challenge to its Red-Hot Rival at Buenos Aires. There Carlos Menditeguy showed great form in the searing heat of his native Grand Prix. In spite of two pit stops for

70 x 64.5mm. Mike Hawthorn wrote of visiting the factory before Christmas: 'Ferrari claimed that the engine was producing nearly 190bhp [actually 186 at 9,300], or over 125bhp per litre, which was really phenomenal, and said that Vittorio Stanguellini, one of his neighbours in Modena who knows a great deal about extracting power from small engines, had maintained that it could not possibly produce more than 160 horsepower. He had furthermore bet Ferrari that for every horsepower he could produce over 160, Stanguellini would buy him a dinner for five people. When I saw him, Ferrari was looking forward to eating well and cheaply for some time to come.'

The new Dino six first competed in the Naples GP on 28 April 1957. It then appeared in Monaco practice and won an F2 race at Reims. After this Ferrari's staff concentrated on developing the 2.5-litre Type 246 F1 version (85 x 71mm) that won the World Drivers' Championship for Hawthorn in 1958. The 156 F2 Dino made assorted appearances in the next two years. In 1958 Peter Collins drove it at Reims and Phil Hill helmed it in the German GP. In 1959 Behra drove at Syracuse while Cliff Allison used it in two races at Monaco and Reims.

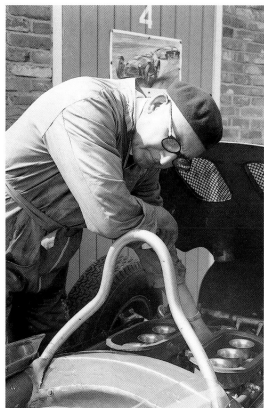

Driven by Luigi Musso in its first race at Naples on 28 April 1957, the 1.5-litre Dino, at left, qualified on the front row of a grid of 2.5-litre Grand Prix cars. Over 153 miles it finished third to the D50-based Ferraris of winner Collins (centre) and Hawthorn (right).

Like all new racing Ferraris hitherto the mid-engined Dino was developed under the critical gaze of Enzo's technical lieutenant Luigi Bazzi. At the 1961 Dutch Grand Prix he carefully warmed up the engine of one of the team cars.

Maserati introduced its 150 S sports car in the 1955 season, offering a challenge in the 1.5-litre class for the first time since the original A6G. Its four-cylinder engine suited Formula 2 from 1957 and Formula 1 from 1961.

Below: Maserati's 150 S engine was an obvious choice for Italy-based teams aiming to enter the new 1.5-litre Formula 1. Its top end used hairpin-type valve springs and, contacting its cam lobes, finger-borne rollers with anti-friction bearings.

Below right: Pictured in December 1954 as it was being prepared for dynamometer testing, the Type 150 S Maserati engine had twin front-mounted magnetos. They or distributors had to be moved to the engine's rear when the four was mid-mounted.

By late 1959 Ferrari was accelerating his 1.5-litre's development in preparation for the 1961 Formula 1. Carlo Chiti began by experimenting with the stroke/bore ratio, finally deciding on dimensions of 73 x 58.8mm which, in fact, were exactly those of the immortal Type 250 Ferrari V12. After inlet and exhaust tuning to improve the six's mid-range power it was used by Wolfgang von Trips to win at Syracuse in March 1960. However, Stirling Moss in the F2 Porsche had led easily until the German car broke down.

This was the trigger for Enzo Ferrari's decision to build a rear-engined racing car. As recently as January 1960 he had denied any such intention, saying, 'What have Coopers done? They have taken up the idea from Prof. Porsche and, after ten years of faith in the design, are now reaping their rewards. It is only fair that if one sets out along a road, follows it faithfully and sticks to it, one should reach one's destination one day.' After Syracuse Ferrari found it prudent to follow that road too, in spite of the decades of tradition that

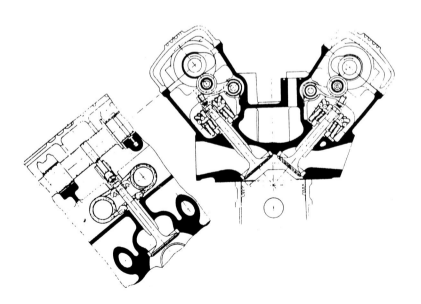

opposed the change, in spite of the divergence from his road-car designs, in spite of the derision the Italian public had heaped on the Coopers when they first raced in Italy. It was not an easy road for him to take.

By early April the frame of the rear-engined car had been welded up and by early May it had taken shape as an automobile. Medardo Fantuzzi finished hammering out its body and on Sunday 22 May it was tested for the first time at Modena's Aerautodromo. Only a week later it was racing at Monaco. It performed very well for an undeveloped prototype after its crew ironed out shift-linkage problems that caused Richie Ginther to over-rev its engine violently a couple of times. In the race on the 29th it broke a ring-gear tooth but clattered over the line to place sixth.

After a brief appearance in practice at Zandvoort the next weekend the rear-engined car was converted into a lower, sleeker 1.5-litre machine. In went the revitalised 156 F2 Dino engine with long exhaust pipes that ran forward, then curled around to exit at the back in gentle megaphones. Sparkling and naive in its newness, this car – the 156 F2/60 – was first tried at the Modena track on 20 July. By 22 July it was at Solitude for practice and on 24 July it won its first race.

As at Syracuse, von Trips's win at Solitude was not commanding; Jim Clark's Lotus had led at first. After experiments with a similar rear suspension to the Lotus the Ferrari's rear hub carriers were redesigned to provide a small amount of permanent toe-in. At the same time the front suspension was given the new geometry that had been developed in tests with the front-engined Ferraris to preserve negative camber at all times on the outside wheel in a corner.

Dino 156 F2/60 raced in this form in the Italian Grand Prix at Monza on 4 September, where von Trips took it to fifth place behind the 2.5-litre cars. It ran again at Modena in a Formula 2 race on

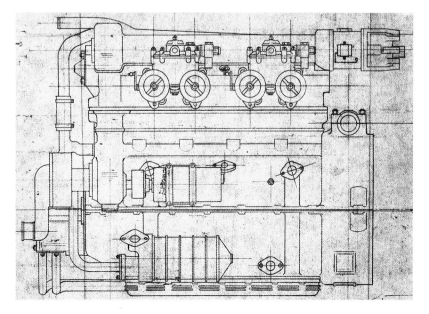

Carlo Chiti and Franco Rocchi collaborated on the creation of the superb 120-degree V6 that Ferrari introduced during the 1961 season. Skew gears drove its two distributors, each of which sparked a set of six plugs.

Cavara's cutaway showed the 120-degree Dino's Jano-type tappets and the half-speed gears that drove roller chains to the twin cams on each bank. Weber provided its special triple-throat downdraft carburettors.

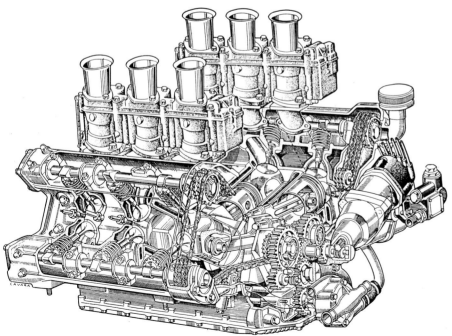

2 October, when Trips finished third with failing brakes behind a Porsche and Ginther's front-engined Dino. Having led the race, however, the unusual-looking mid-engined Ferrari was clearly a sound basis on which to plan the Maranello team's cars for Grand Prix racing in 1961.

Modena's spectators that October had two other hometown entries to cheer. The Scuderia Centro-Sud fielded a Cooper and Lotus, both Maserati-powered. With the 150 S sports-car engine a virtual twin of the 250 S engines the team had been running during 1960, installing it in the same hard-worked chassis to compete in Formula 2 was an obvious expedient to earn added starting money. That was all they did at Modena, where both cars retired.

Mimo Dei's Centro-Sud had been dipping its Cooper-Maseratis in and out of Formula 2 racing during the 1960 season. Masten Gregory was let down by his engine at Pau in April. In July he took part in the 142-mile race at Solitude, on Stuttgart's

outskirts, that saw von Trips win with the new mid-engined Ferrari. Though the Cooper-Maserati offered no contest to its Red-Hot Rival it placed ninth and was the last unlapped car on the 7.1-mile road course.

New at the October Modena race was Centro-Sud's installation of a 150 S engine in a Lotus 18 chassis. The 18 was the sensation of the 1960 season, the first mid-engined Grand Prix designed as such from first principles by Colin Chapman. Entrusted to Ian Burgess, it failed to make an impression before retiring at Modena.

Although its engine's 1960 Formula 2 performance had been far from breathtaking, Maserati had in its 150 S four an attractive power unit for the new Formula 1, especially to a Modena-based team like Centro-Sud. Cooper-Maseratis were also appetising to race organisers who were drowning in a sea of Cooper-Climaxes. Accordingly early in 1961 the Viale Ciro Menotti announced that it would be offering its Type 6

engine for use by Grand Prix competitors in the new season.

At 1,484cc the Type 6's dimensions of 81 x 72mm were unchanged from those of the 150 S. Having adopted magnesium for some peripheral castings Maserati quoted a weight of 287lb for its twin-ignition four, which was fed by two twin-throat 45 DCO3 Weber carburettors. On a compression ratio of 10.5:1 it was said to produce 165bhp at 8,500rpm. This was well up on the 150 S, which in its first incarnation in 1956 had delivered 140bhp at 7,500rpm. It was offered at 2,400,000 lire, about $3,850 or £1,370, with Maserati's multi-disc clutch optional.

This was by no means the limit of Giulio Alfieri's ambitions. After a visit to Modena in February of 1961 the man from *The Motor* gave this breathless account: 'No signs were to be seen in the racing department of the long-rumoured new Maserati Grand Prix car, but this now exists in the drawing office stage and will be seen before

Concentric coil/damper units sprung all four corners of the 1961 Dino 156 F1, which was notable for the negative camber of its drive wheels. The Ferrari's tail was elegantly enclosed.

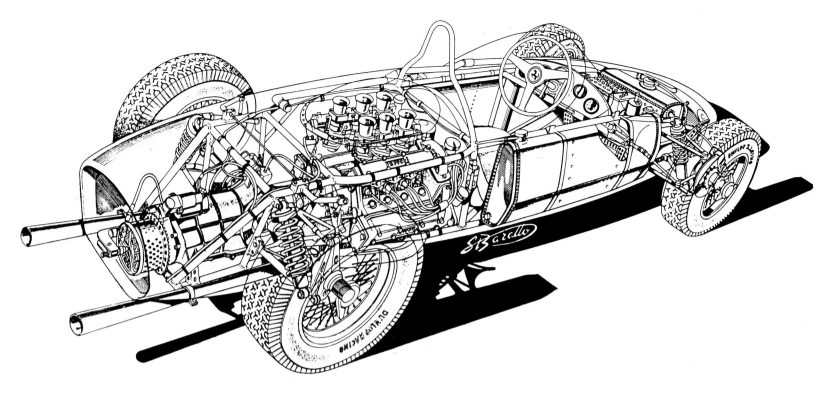

Sergio Baratto's drawing showed the Dino 156 F1's side fuel tanks, tubular frame and clutch exposed at the rear of the transaxle. Though late to the mid-engined brigade, Ferrari made a good fist of its first serious effort.

long in the metal, for construction of six cars will begin just as soon as the department has finished rushing through the rear-engined sports cars for Sebring, of which several are on order. Three of the Grand Prix cars have been ordered by the Camoradi International Racing team, and it is possible that this équipe will race Maseratis only in Formula 1 events in 1962 should their showing this season be sufficiently promising. The other three cars have been ordered by Juan Manuel

Fangio, with the intention of running an Argentinean team, thereby giving promising young drivers in that country a similar opportunity of racing in Europe as he himself received in the late 1940s.'

Any such hopes evaporated after Sebring, the disappointments of which ruptured relations between the American Camoradi team and its principal backer, Goodyear. It also triggered a break between Camoradi and Maserati, which

Cockpit space was not yet at such a premium as to demand a small steering wheel. Ferrari's 1961 Dino 156 F1 had an elegant wood-rimmed wheel, minimal instrumentation and a short gated shift lever on the right.

henceforth put deliveries to the team on a COD basis. Although Camoradi did struggle on in Formula 1 in 1961, entering Cooper-Climaxes for Ian Burgess and Masten Gregory, it was in no state to order Grand Prix Maseratis. Nor did Juan Fangio's attractive plans fructify.

Out of the blue, however, another team came knocking on the Trident's door. Jacques Swaters, enthusiastic Belgian racer and Ferrari importer to that prosperous country, was patron of the Equipe Nationale Belge (ENB). Impressed by the performance of a British Emeryson Formula Junior in 1960, Swaters commissioned a trio of Formula 1 cars from the company for 1961. With Ferrari not in the business of supplying current engines, the Belgian followed his Italian connections to arch-rivals Maserati for suitable power units and to Colotti for transaxles.

Paul Emery and his son Peter were resourceful designers and builders of special racing cars – hence 'Emeryson'. With the backing of racer Alan Brown they moved into the former Connaught premises in Surrey to build mid-engined racing cars to Paul's design. Frame construction was subcontracted to Lister in Cambridge. With its

power train installed in Modena, the resulting Emeryson-Maserati was a pretty car with unique light-alloy wheels to Emery's design.

The ENB's racing manager and driver Lucien Bianchi shook down the prototype at Modena only a few days before two of the cars made their racing debut on 3 April in the 171-mile Grand Prix at Pau in France. It couldn't have been worse; both crashed, although Bianchi was running as high as fourth before disaster struck. Finishing third and fourth behind two Lotus-Climaxes were Maserati-powered cars of the Scuderia Centro-Sud. Investing in newer Type 51 Coopers, the Modena team stayed loyal to its Maserati fours.

Mimo Dei's outfit also had a promising new driver, Lorenzo Bandini, whom it introduced to Formula 1. Their first encounter with Ferrari came at Syracuse in Sicily on 25 April. The 156 F1 Dino had its initial 1961 outing in this non-championship 195-mile race not as an official Maranello entry but in the hands of a private team and a virtually unknown driver, Giancarlo Baghetti. He proceeded to shrug off all opposition to win. The closest a Maserati-powered driver came was Bandini in seventh place, three laps in arrears.

Not content with its radical change to mid-mounted engines, for 1961 Ferrari adopted the twin-nostril inlet that prompted its 'Sharknose' nickname. Ferrari was unique in its continued reliance on Borrani wire wheels with knock-off hubs.

In the Dutch Grand Prix on 22 May 1961 Ferrari-mounted Richie Ginther (2) resumed the tussle with Stirling Moss's Lotus-Climax that had enlivened the Monaco GP. At the finish Moss just pipped Ginther for fourth place.

Judged by its rivals to be offensively ugly when first unveiled, the Type 61 Maserati (left) looked better when it started strutting its stuff. Designer Giulio Alfieri was responsible for the wind-tunnel-tested shape and the astonishing concept of its multi-tube space frame (below). The four-cylinder 2.9-litre engine sloped at 45 degrees to the right.

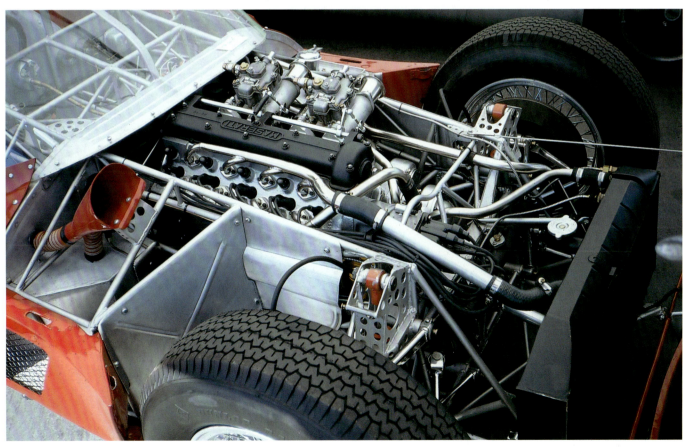

Far left: Raced at Sebring in 1965 by Bob Grossman and Skip Hudson, Ferrari's 4.0-litre 330 P showed how well Maranello had adapted to the mid-engined era. A similar car won at Montlhéry and in the Tourist Trophy in 1964.

Left: The requirements of mid-engined mounting in the Type 63 prepared Maserati's V12 for installation in Cooper's T81 chassis for Grand Prix racing in 1966. Ready for the assault on Maranello were Jochen Rindt (in the cockpit), team manager Roy Salvadori (left), and Cooper designer Derrick Walker.

That Ferrari's Type 312 F1 for 1966 looked impressive was beyond doubt, with quadruple exhausts from its four-cam V12. However John Surtees, here conferring with chief racing engineer Mauro Forghieri, knew it lacked the lightness and power it needed to be fully competitive. Surtees was denied the 'Tasman' V6 that he much preferred.

At Watkins Glen in 1966 Lorenzo Bandini (above) gave his new 36-valve Ferrari 312 F1 a superb run, holding the lead until its engine failed after 34 of 108 laps. Cooper-Maseratis finished second and third. At Monza in 1967 Ferrari introduced its 48-valve V12 (left). There the best Modena-motor finish was fourth for a Cooper-Maserati.

Swede Jo Bonnier, who favoured red for his private Cooper-Maserati (right), picked up points in both 1966 and 1967. At Monaco in 1967 Pedro Rodriguez (below) finished fifth in his T81 Cooper-Maserati. Ferrari had the advantage with a third for Chris Amon. His team-mate Lorenzo Bandini was running second before crashing with fatal consequences.

The shrewd intelligence of Austrian Jochen Rindt shone from this portrait, though his erratic demands were a trial to Cooper-Maserati team manager Roy Salvadori. This photograph, taken at Watkins Glen by Stanley Rosenthall in 1966, shows the new inward-sloping inlet throttles and ram pipes introduced at Monza to reduce aerodynamic drag.

By 1967 Ferrari's race preparation had moved into the former production workshops after new manufacturing halls were erected. Glimpsing the holy of holies where the 48-valve Formula 1 car was being prepared for Monza, Max Le Grand pictured wall-to-wall red racing cars. The Red-Hot Rivalry, however, was nearing its end.

Syracuse witnessed the retirement with engine trouble of a new Maserati-powered entrant. Count Volpi's Scuderia SSS Serenissima di Venezia acquired a Type 51 Cooper to be driven by reliable Frenchman Maurice Trintignant. Suffering many retirements during the season, he did well to qualify at Monaco and place seventh. Sicilian Nino Vaccarella took the car over for a two-heat race at Vallelunga near Rome in October and placed third on aggregate.

Such was the gap between Ferrari and Maserati in 1961 that Trintignant's seventh at Monaco (where he usually went well) was the closest the rivals would be all season. While Maserati advanced little in engine development, Ferrari took a great leap forward with a new 120° version of its Dino V6. Against the weight of the 65° 1.5-litre engine at 320lb, the new unit, designed strictly as a 1,500cc engine, scaled only 265lb. Its wide vee angle also placed more of that weight nearer the ground.

Weight was significantly reduced in the crankshaft, which needed only three big-end journals instead of the six the 65° engine required. Each cylinder head had eight hold-down studs instead of the 12 the narrow-angle Dino used. Each cylinder bank had its own double-roller chain system, driven by two half-speed gears at the nose of the crankshaft. Wide cam lobes attacked broad mushroom tappets of the Jano design, screwing directly to the valve stem for guidance and clearance adjustment, above coil valve springs.

Induction was through two special triple-throat downdraft Weber carburettors, type 4 IF3C. Improved balance of the new engine allowed it to rev as high as 10,000rpm, with peak power of 190bhp measured at 9,500. By late March the first wide-angle engine had completed 50 hours of dynamometer testing without a single snag. That it performed smoothly off the drawing board was a tribute to the work of Franco Rocchi.

The Dutch GP at Zandvoort witnessed this one-two finish for the Ferrari Dino 156 F1 with Wolfgang von Trips winning and Phil Hill second. Hill would go on to win at Spa and Monza, becoming Ferrari's first World Champion since Mike Hawthorn in 1958.

In a wet British Grand Prix at Aintree on 15 July 1961, Californian Richie Ginther piloted his Dino 156 F1 to third place. The best finish for a Maserati-engined Cooper was Lorenzo Bandini's Centro-Sud entry in 12th.

Working with Walter Salvarani, Vittorio Jano schemed the Ferrari's unique transaxle. Instead of being in unit with the engine, its multiple-disc clutch was carried at the back of the five-speed gearbox, driven by a pair of gears from a long shaft that extended from the engine underneath the transaxle. The layout kept the clutch out in the open where it was well cooled. The unique design also allowed the engine to be placed as low in the chassis as its shallow dry sump permitted. This was several inches lower than would be possible if the clutch and starter gear were conventionally mounted at the back of the crankshaft.

Visually the most striking feature of the new Ferrari was its extended double-nostril nose. The advantages of this design were brought to Carlo Chiti's attention by Fantuzzi, who had used it on 250 F Maseratis he had updated for the private Temple Buell team. Chiti's tests in the small wind tunnel he established at Maranello satisfied him that it provided better penetration than a conventional single air scoop. It also offered the advantage that rivals knew just what was overtaking them and – as it turned out – could move smartly out of the way.

Soon nicknamed 'Sharknose', the new Ferrari was denied victory on its first appearance by the Lotus 18-Climax and the artistry of Stirling Moss. His Monaco-winning margin over Richie Ginther in the sole 120°-engine car was a wafer-thin 3.6 seconds. The superiority that the wide-angle model demonstrated there over the 65° Dinos of Hill and von Trips was strong ammunition that Carlo Chiti used to overcome Enzo Ferrari's mistrust of the new engine.

Against his chief's explicit instructions Chiti used the wide-angle engine in all three cars for the Grand Prix a week later in Holland to sweep the first two places. Except for another demonstration of artistry at the Nürburgring by Stirling Moss the Ferraris won the rest of 1961's Grands Prix, with Phil Hill taking the World Championship.

The season's final championship contest at Monza on 10 September was sunlight and shadow for Ferrari. While Hill confirmed his ascendancy with victory, Wolfgang von Trips crashed fatally into the crowd. Fourteen spectators died of their injuries and more than 40 were injured.

Four Maserati-powered cars were in the Monza field from four different stables. Best-placed was Lorenzo Bandini in eighth in Mimo Dei's Cooper.

The previous weekend he'd been awarded the same position in a race at Modena although, as Paul Sheldon wrote, his 'hard-pressed Maserati engine exploded on the main straight in a spectacular fashion'. At Modena he'd been as high as sixth in a 147-mile race to which, surprisingly, Ferrari sent no cars, complaining that it needed the time to prepare for the Italian Grand Prix.

At Monza Maurice Trintignant finished ninth in Serenissima's Cooper-Maser while Renato Pirocchi was 12th and last in a similar Centro-Sud car entered by the Pescara Racing Club. A first appearance in a championship Grand Prix was made by the Lotus 18-Maserati of Prince Gaetano Starabba, former racer of a 500 TR Ferrari sports car. He'd blooded his racer the previous weekend at Modena, where its driver Giorgio Scarlatti was last on the grid and first to retire with engine trouble. The same malaise put Starabba himself out at Monza.

Astonishingly the progress of Ferrari's British rivals was such that the Sharknoses failed to be first across the line in any of the championship Grands Prix of 1962. Progress at Maranello wasn't helped by a major bust-up between Enzo Ferrari and key members of his team, including Carlo Chiti and

Giotto Bizzarrini, that prompted them to leave Ferrari by October 1961. Made public in November, their resignations deeply undermined preparations for the 1962 season. Not until 1964 would Ferrari recover championship-winning form.

Some four-cylinder Maseratis persevered beyond 1961. Without great success Lucien Bianchi briefly raced the prototype Emerson-Maserati with a nostril-type nose, renamed the ENB-Maserati. Prince Starabba persevered into 1963 in Italian races with his Lotus-Maserati, placing fifth at Vallelunga in May. Mimo Dei wheeled out his Cooper-Maseratis occasionally, as at Solitude in July where Mario Cabral was 10th and next to last. Vittorio Brambilla – a new name – couldn't qualify one for the 1963 Italian Grand Prix.

Early 1962 witnessed the arrival at Pau of a new car that's one of the trivia questions of Grand Prix racing. A handsome wire-wheeled racer on orthodox lines, it was built in Aigle for Swiss driver Maurice Caillet. Brothers Claude and Georges Gachnang were its creators, combining their initials with their hometown to give it the acronymic name of 'Cegga'. Powering it was a 150 S Maserati engine, spruced up to Type 6 status with a new cylinder head and exhaust from Modena. The Cegga-

By 1962 improvement in the British cars was such that Phil Hill could only qualify eighth fastest for the 150-mile race at Aintree on 29 April. With radiator blanking plate in place he took his Dino 156 F1 to third place at the finish.

In 1961 Maserati's Giulio Alfieri began work on a new engine, his Type 8, for Formula 1. It was a 60-degree V12 with induction ports between its camshafts, fed by fuel injectors and controlled by motorcycle-type slide throttles.

Lifting one cylinder head from the Maserati Type 8 V12 revealed its finger-type cam followers and hairpin valve springs. Gearbox and final drive, in the foreground, were transverse and integral with the dry sump.

Trident exponents had every reason to remain loyal to their engines, for something was brewing back at the Viale Ciro Menotti. There the late-1961 efflux from Ferrari hadn't resulted in a corresponding influx. Giulio Alfieri already had his team in place and, if still constrained in finance, no shortage of new ideas. Mediocre initial results for his Type 6 four only encouraged him to get to work on a new engine that would offer better chances to his clients. He would build a good Grand Prix engine and the customers would come.

Alfieri's first inspiration was to base a new 1.5-litre engine on the 2.5-litre vee-twelve that he'd introduced in 1957. In his Type 7 project he reduced its bore only slightly, from 68.7 to 67.0mm, and its stroke drastically from 57 to 35mm to bring capacity down to 1,481mm. This would have produced an engine capable of extremely high revolutions if its ignition and valve gear could cope. Judging it too long and heavy to be an effective competitor, however, Giulio Alfieri gave up this compromised Type 7 idea.

Maserati used a Modena-built five-speed gearbox, but from Maserati, not Colotti.

The Gachnangs entered their creation for Caillet at Pau in April and Naples in May but he qualified for neither. This seems to have discouraged the little team for they made no further Grand Prix entries. Instead the Cegga-Maserati regrouped as a competitor in Swiss hillclimbing. There it was re-engined to 2.9-litre 'Birdcage' size and ultimately driven by co-creator Georges Gachnang.

Instead Alfieri started from scratch to design a new twelve that would be ideal for the 1.5-litre Formula 1. With a team of three draftsmen led by Ennio Ascari, he started his Type 8 project in October 1961 and completed its drawings by year's end. It was a 60° V12 designed to be placed

transversely in the chassis and angled forward, so much so that its forward cylinder bank was almost horizontal.

Given symmetrical 80° inclination of its two valves per cylinder, with their overhead cams and finger-type followers, the Type 8 was like its 12-cylinder Maserati predecessor in having downdraft inlet ports between the two camshafts of each bank. Each was topped by a Dell'Orto carburettor body serving as a slide throttle for Lucas port-type fuel injection.

Closed by hairpin springs, the valves were opened by cams driven by gear trains upward from two gears near the centre of the crankshaft. The two gears also took the drive to a transverse drum containing an 11-disc wet clutch. Each crankshaft gear initiated the camshaft drive to one of the cylinder banks. The crankshaft of chrome-molybdenum-vanadium alloy steel was carried in seven main bearings, the outer ones being rollers and the rest plain bearings.

The Type 8's dimensions were 55.2 x 52mm (1,493cc). Wet steel cylinder liners were carried in an aluminium casting that comprised the cylinder block, gearbox housing and half the enclosure for its final-drive gears. A large light-alloy sump enclosed the machinery and supported an ultra-compact transverse six-speed gearbox, all the components being lubricated by the same oil. Manifolding from a single water pump, driven from the left side of the gearbox, took coolant to both the blocks and heads.

Maserati's continuing financial constraints were such that the engine was only assembled in April 1963. Given four hours of testing, with a compression ratio of 11.5:1 it was producing 170bhp at 12,000rpm against a planned peak of 14,000 and at least 225bhp. Weighing 315lb, Alfieri's complete package would have fitted neatly in the

back of a small Grand Prix car. In fact it was given a desultory outing in a Lotus 18 chassis, almost certainly from Centro-Sud's garages.

Ultimately quixotic, this costly experiment had no issue at a time when a still-struggling Maserati had to watch its lire with care. With the introduction of a new Formula 1, however, the Trident would return to Grand Prix racing in 1966 with a powerful effort. Its hometown rivalry with Ferrari would again flame red-hot.

CHAPTER FIFTEEN

246 SP, 250 P and 275 P vs 63, 151 and 65

Wild and wonderful creations appeared as the mid-engine mania swept the rival camps in the early 1960s. While Ferrari's were the more successful, Maserati's were gloriously fantastical.

Only one motivation can explain Maserati's decision to build a new mid-engined sports-racing car for the 1961 season: sheer creative chutzpah on the part of the Modena company's leader, engineer Giulio Alfieri. As Omer Orsi's son Adolfo remarked, 'Engineer Alfieri was a

For Le Mans in 1961 Maserati installed its 3.0-litre V12 engine in three Type 63 chassis. On 6 August 1961 Walt Hansgen won the 71-mile feature race at Bridgehampton with a Cunningham entry, still wearing its Le Mans windscreen.

During practice for the 'Ring 1,000-kilometre race on 18 May 1961, Phil Hill tried the Ferrari Dino 246 SP assigned to Richie Ginther and Olivier Gendebien to check that its windscreen notch for visibility was adequate. It was the first of a new generation of mid-engined sports-racing Ferraris.

mixed blessing. He was very creative, but often too much so with fantastic ideas. These could have been very expensive for Maserati at a critical time.'

Alfieri's decision was bold, bordering on reckless, in view of the stunning performance in 1960 of his highly personal creation, the Type 61 'Birdcage'. This brilliant sports-racer had led every race in which it competed and either won or retired – the latter all too often. The 1961 season was the last under which sports-prototypes raced to a displacement limit of 3.0-litres. A rational view of the year's prospects would have favoured an overhaul of its weak points and the installation of a less compromised engine. Alfieri had a new V8 of 2,930cc on the drawing board that would have been ideal. Add some serious testing in advance of 1961's calendar and such a car would have been unbeatable.

But mid-engine mania was sweeping Modena and its environs. The new 1½-litre Grand Prix Formula for 1961 was concentrating minds. Demanding the ultimate in compactness and lightness to meet the minimum weight of 450kg, or 992lb, their creation virtually ruled out front-engined designs.[1] The lessons taught by Cooper and Lotus were all too compelling. In addition to their successful Formula 1 cars both had produced effective mid-engined sports-racers.

Early in 1960 all Modena was abuzz with the news that Ferrari was building a mid-engined single-seater. In May it first broke cover at the Aerautodromo and at the end of the month it was racing at Monte Carlo. If Ferrari had taken this bold step, could arch-rival Maserati afford to lag behind? Wouldn't such key Maserati customers as Camoradi, Cunningham and Count Volpi be demanding mid-engined cars?

This was the logic that found the Orsis approving Giulio Alfieri's audacious plan to leap ahead of his still-immature Type 61 to build a new mid-engined sports-racer for the 1961 season. In taking this step, said Maserati historians Luigi Orsini and Franco Zagari, 'Maserati dedicated themselves with possibly excessive enthusiasm to the new theories.'

Starting in the late summer of 1960 the new car was created as the Type 63.[2] Budget constraints ruled out the proposed V8 engine so Alfieri ingeniously adapted some components from the Type 61. Among them was its 2.9-litre four-cylinder engine, inclined more steeply at 58° to the right. It was credited with 260bhp at 6,800rpm.

Through a special bell housing enclosing its hydraulically actuated multiple-disc clutch, the engine drove directly to a transverse-shaft five-speed transaxle inherited from the Type 61, which in turn had acquired it from the 250 F and 300 S. Also borrowed from the front-engined car were its

---

1 Only one front-engined car competed under the new rules: the four-wheel-drive Ferguson P99. Built originally with a 2.5-litre Climax four, it had a 1.5-litre unit installed in 1961. At the end of that season Stirling Moss drove it to a sensational victory in a wet Oulton Park Gold Cup race.

2 Historian and author Willem Oosthoek advises that Type 62 had already been assigned to a 6.5-litre engine for speedboats.

parallel-wishbone front suspension and rack-and-pinion steering gear. Disc brakes made by Maserati under Girling patents were inherited from the front-engined 'Birdcage' as well.

The new car could also be called a 'Birdcage' for its frame was a similar three-dimensional structure of many small steel tubes, positioned to provide maximum strength for minimum weight. With its suspension brackets the frame weighed only 75lb. This was weightier than the frame of the 2.0-litre 'Birdcage' at 66lb, but the latter figure had risen with the reinforcements needed for the 2.9-litre version.

Rear suspension was completely new, by parallel wishbones and – as at the front – coil springs and adjustable Koni tubular dampers. This was the first Maserati since the V8RI Grand Prix car of 1935–36 to have completely independent rear-wheel suspension. Its driver sat enmeshed in tubing with a shift lever on the right and a small triangular panel with three gauges at his left. In unpainted aluminium, even where a deep windscreen was to be substituted, the Type 63 prototype was a slap in the face to the tradition of beautiful Maserati racing cars.

On 15 December 1960 Guerino Bertocchi turned the first laps of Modena's Aerautodromo in the Type 63 prototype, followed later by Giorgio Scarlatti. With 60 per cent of its weight on its rear wheels the car immediately declared that it wanted attention to its rear suspension, a diagnosis confirmed by the experienced Umberto Maglioli. Lengthening the wheelbase to 90.2in, up from the Type 61's 86.6in, improved both weight distribution and stability.

Based on the findings with the Type 63 prototype the Viale Ciro Menotti workshops built four definitive cars for the early races of the 1961 season. The Camoradi and Cunningham teams had one Type 63 apiece in time for the 12-hour race at Sebring on 25 March 1961. Too new and untested to do more than lead the early laps, both retired. With more time to prepare, Volpi's Scuderia Serenissima saw its two cars place fourth and fifth in the Targa Florio at the end of April.

In these two races Maserati and its customers were dismayed by the pace shown by a new Ferrari. The Trident had been first out of the starting gates with a mid-engined sports-racer, but the Prancing Horse had caught up fast. At Maranello chief engineer Carlo Chiti was now well into his stride with ideas that were both practical and innovative – a rare combination.

Accepting the modest risk that with 2.4-litres it would be well short of the category's 3.0-litre limit, Chiti specified the now-redundant 246 F1 V6

For his Type 63 of 1961 Giulio Alfieri adapted the 2.9-litre four-cylinder engine of the Maserati Type 61. Steeply inclined at 58 degrees to the right, it was fed by 48 IDM downdraft Weber carburettors.

as the power unit for his first sports-racing car with the engine behind the driver. It was credited with 270bhp at 8,000rpm from its 2,417cc (85 x 71mm). Though many of the Grand Prix components could be recycled for the sports car, the installation required new cylinder-block castings and new crankshafts.

For his new car, the 246 SP, Carlo Chiti used the same five-speed transaxle with overhung clutch at

A glimpse inside the Type 63 Maserati's combustion chambers showed their hemispherical contours and plug apertures for dual ignition. Drive to the overhead camshafts was by helical gears.

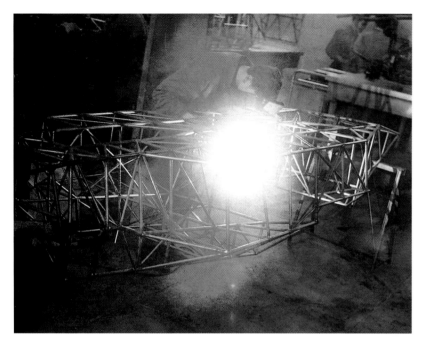

of the contemporary Grand Prix Ferrari. It was clothed by Medardo Fantuzzi in striking aluminium bodywork from its twin-oval grille to its truncated tail. To match the high windscreen required by the rules the tail was high as well, creating a Targa-like look with matching sidescreens.

Two days after its first showing to the press on 13 February 1961 the 246 SP was put through its paces on the Modena track for the first time. Rebuilt after it turned turtle when a brake disc broke while Wolfgang von Trips was driving, its testing resumed at the much faster Monza circuit on 14 March with Richie Ginther at the wheel. Ginther had rushed from his California home in response to an urgent request from Ferrari. His testing skills were both needed and respected at Maranello.

'We thought that the car would turn pretty much the same times as the [2½-litre] F1,' Carlo Chiti recalled, 'losing something on curves because of its extra 260lb but recovering on the straights thanks to its body design. Instead we realised that it lost much more on curves than expected and recovered less on the straights despite its speed advantage of 10–15mph.' The 246 SP was anything but stable, reported Modena resident Pete Coltrin: 'It was skating on the straight after the Vialone Curve and dancing past the pits on the way to the Curva Grande.'

Chiti conferred with Ginther, whose qualifications included an apprenticeship at a California aircraft manufacturer and a stint in Korea

Placing it upside-down on trestles, a Trident artisan completed welding of the Type 63's 75-pound 'Birdcage' frame. Its rigid yet light structure was a further progression from that of the front-engined Type 60/61.

A Sergio Baratto drawing showed the layout of Maserati's ambitious mid-engined Type 63 for 1961. At all four corners its suspension was by parallel wishbones with concentric coils and dampers.

the extreme rear that was fitted to his 1961 Grand Prix cars. A robust space frame of conventional design joined together front and rear parallel-wishbone suspensions with their concentric coil/damper units. As in the Maserati the main fuel tankage was along deep sills at both sides of the cockpit. The latter was handsomely finished in hammertone grey.

The sports car's wheelbase was 91.3in, an inch more than that of the Type 63 and the same as that

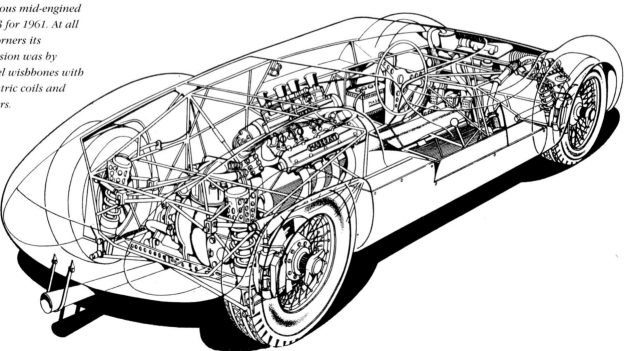

as a helicopter crew chief. 'We felt this was the fault of lift effect,' Chiti continued. 'In the past, when I was at Alfa Romeo, I had sensed something of the kind because both Consalvo Sanesi and Zanardi had seemingly mysterious accidents at Monza on the Ascari Bend.'

Another factor could have been instability caused by the more forward centre of pressure of the fully enclosed body. The 246 SP was equipped with a single small fin to counter this. With Medardo Fantuzzi present, the car was tested with added fins but these offered little help. When its tail was completely removed the 246 SP was slower on the straights but much faster through Monza's bends. What was the answer?

Success, as we know, has many fathers. Chiti and Ginther both contributed to the solution. 'I thought of applying some spoiling devices,' said Chiti, 'which in this particular case were pieces of sheet metal in appropriate positions. The improvement, which was enormous, became even greater when the spoiler was placed at the rear.' The latter position, Pete Coltrin wrote, was suggested by Ginther: 'Fantuzzi and his artisans fashioned a strip of aluminium as an air foil and attached it to the trailing edge of the rear deck. It worked from the start and with modifications worked even better.'[3]

Functioning as their name suggested, the devices tested were intended to 'spoil' or break up the airflow that seemed to be generating lift over the rear panels of the body. Although perfectly well understood today, this was a revolutionary idea in 1961. In fact the final design adopted for the 246 SP and other sports-racing Ferraris was less a spoiler than a flap that reduced lift at the rear of the body and, in spite of its appearance, brought a reduction in drag as well.

At Sebring the 246 SP demonstrated convincingly that this aerodynamic tweak was just what it needed. After its gearing was adjusted it turned the fastest lap in practice, several seconds within the record standing to the Type 61 Maserati. After a slow start it led the race in the hands of Richie Ginther and Wolfgang von Trips, only being tripped up when the latter bent a tie rod and wishbone on an off-course excursion. The new car's agility was ideal for the Targa Florio, which one 246 SP won after its sister crashed off the circuit.

---

3 Mauro Forghieri states that Vittorio Jano was also present, and that he drew upon his knowledge of the pre-war aerodynamic studies of Prof. Wunibald Kamm at Stuttgart to suggest the spoiler. Pete Coltrin's contemporary account makes no mention of Jano, however.

Between Sebring and the Targa the Le Mans circuit held its pre-race test weekend. Short-changed on displacement though it was, the 246 SP was one of the stars. The record set in 1957 by a Ferrari 335 S was undercut by two seconds thanks to Richie Ginther's knowledge of the new car; Phil Hill was two seconds quicker still in a 250 TRI 61, well suited to this fast circuit. Third and fifth fastest times were set by two four-cylinder Type 63s from the Viale Ciro Menotti.

For his first mid-engined sports-racer of 1961 Carlo Chiti used this 65-degree vee-six, as raced in the 1958–60 Grand Prix Ferraris. Instead of the magneto shown, the Type 246 SP had coil ignition with two Marelli distributors.

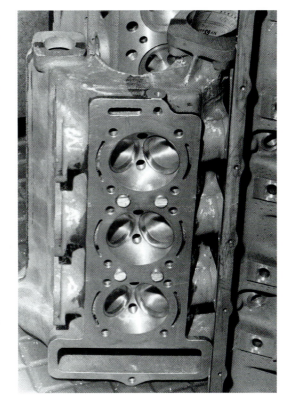

The 2.4-litre vee-six of the 246 SP placed its twin spark plugs as close to the centre of the chamber as its valve-seat inserts permitted. Drive to the overhead camshafts was by a pair of double-roller chains.

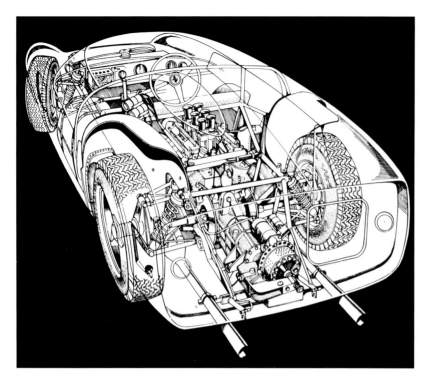

In his drawing of Ferrari's Type 246 SP, Sergio Baratto emphasised its high tail while revealing the transaxle, with clutch outboard at the rear, and parallel-wishbone suspension at all four wheels.

Fourth fastest, in the hands of Giorgio Scarlatti, was a new kind of Type 63 that Giulio Alfieri considered to be the car's definitive version. Visible through the tubing under its rear deck were six twin-throat Weber 38 IDM carburettors feeding a 3.0-litre version of the V12 that Maserati had built in 2.5-litre form to power its 250 F in 1957. Based on the original prototype, this car had a 12-cylinder engine because Briggs Cunningham's technical major domo Alfred Momo had questioned the car's ability to survive a long race with a rough four-cylinder engine shaking it apart.

This was the second of the three lives of Maserati's V12, which we first saw being used in the 250 F chassis in 1957. It was indeed much smoother than the four and accordingly kinder to the countless welds in the Type 63's multi-tube frame, whose wheelbase was extended by 2.5in to 93.7in – and some legroom deleted from the cockpit – to make room for it. The twelve also offered far greater power potential. With a 10.0:1 compression ratio it was rated at 320bhp at 8,200rpm.

In its V12 version the Type 63 was recognisable by its larger cooling-air inlet and its four megaphone exhausts protruding from the rear deck. Disappointment in the Sebring 12 Hours having ruptured relations between Camoradi and Maserati, Briggs Cunningham's team took two such cars to Le Mans in June while Serenissima fielded a singleton. Prepared by Alfred Momo, the two Cunningham Maseratis scaled 1,705lb at the Sarthe circuit's scrutineering. The lone 246 SP entered weighed only 1,619lb.

Apparently on the assumption that one was bound to be right, each of the three Maserati V12s had different cylinder dimensions: 68.3 x 68mm, 70.4 x 64mm and 75.2 x 56mm. All, however, suffered from overheating. One Type 63, a Cunningham entry driven by Dick Thompson and Augie Pabst, survived to finish fourth, the best position yet for a Maserati at Le Mans. Also troubled by high engine temperatures, Ferrari's 246 SP was among the leaders when a pit-management miscalculation stranded it on the circuit without fuel.

Post-Le Mans outings of the Type 63 showed considerable promise. Driving a four-cylinder Serenissima entry, Nino Vaccarella held second at Pescara in August before retiring. Cunningham's two V12 cars went to America, where Walt Hansgen won two major events in 1961, one at Bridgehampton in August and another at Elkhart Lake in September. In his talented hands and with the ministrations of Alfred Momo the developed Type 63 finally proved decisively faster than a well-driven Type 61.

However, by virtue of its victory in the Targa Florio the laurels in this first clash of mid-engined machinery went to Ferrari. Though Chiti started late, Ferrari's resources helped him catch up quickly. But Maserati had scored a coup by introducing mid-placed twelves in this class of car, a step Ferrari had hitherto abjured. Although unable to match the 246 SP's pace, the Type 63s performed well enough before they broke down to show that a lengthy V12 power unit behind the driver need not handicap handling, thanks to advances in both tyres and suspensions.

In another way the decks were cleared for the arrival of the rear-engined V12 at Ferrari. The exodus of a group of engineers and technicians from Maranello took place in November 1961. Although the new V8 sports-car engine left behind by Carlo Chiti was shown in both a 248 SP and 268 SP at Ferrari's February 1962 press conference, it wasn't subsequently viewed with favour by Enzo Ferrari, especially since Chiti made a very similar engine for new employer ATS. An equally powerful alternative was needed. The cars themselves looked little different apart from a lowering of their screens and rear decks thanks to new rules for windshield heights.

Further, a realignment of championships for 1962 posed new challenges. While the FIA placed the main emphasis on GT cars, the Le Mans organisers led the way in presenting an alternative points system for prototypes of up to 4.0-litres. They were joined by Sebring, the Targa Florio and the 'Ring 1,000 Kilometres to create the *Challenge*

In its first early-1961 tests the Type 246 SP Ferrari had a finned headrest extension. More and bigger fins were tried in order to improve its cornering in tests at Modena, here, and at Monza, but to no avail.

After experiments at Monza, with Richie Ginther as tester, the final aerodynamic solution for the Type 246 SP Ferrari of 1961 was a duck-tail spoiler at the extreme rear. This was an innovative breakthrough for the men of Maranello.

Mondial de Vitesse et Endurance, a championship that remained in effect through to 1974.

With the existing 3.0-litre sports-category cars also being accommodated, Maserati chose this as one of two options to offer new cars to its customers for 1962. Giulio Alfieri completely overhauled the frame design from that of the Type 63, increasing the number of smaller 10mm tubes. While front suspension was carried over, the rear wheels had a radical new guidance system.

Each rear hub was controlled by a pair of trailing radius rods and sprung by a longitudinal torsion bar. The hubs were carried by radius arms that swung forward from pivots at the ends of a transverse de Dion member, from which tension coil springs controlled the relative movements of the arms. The de Dion member, which was in fact a multi-tube cage in its own right, was controlled laterally by a guide sliding in a channel in the back of the transaxle. High-placed tubular dampers were anchored to the forward-facing arms close to their pivots. It looked as exotic as it sounds.

More compact than its predecessor, with a lower cowl and upswept haunches, the new Type 64 Maserati for 1962 proffered a modicum of style on its first appearance at the Modena track in mid-January. The quad exhausts for its V12 engine now swept down and emerged, in megaphones, under the tail. Cast-magnesium Amadori wheels were used for the first time. While Cunningham

accepted the factory's bodywork for his lone Type 64, Count Volpi's team commissioned a special design from veteran stylist Franco Scaglione for their single car.

In neither design were the latest thoughts on aerodynamics employed. Although Ferrari propagated the fiction that the purpose of its tail spoiler was to keep exhaust gases out of the cockpit and/or to keep fuel from spilling on the exhaust pipes, the device clearly worked. In retrospect it's evident that many of the handling problems that troubled the Type 63 and its 1962 successor were attributable to high aerodynamic lift from its rounded body forms, especially at the rear. Though a spoiler would have made all the difference – and this was doubtless known to Alfieri – in view of their rivalry there would have been great pressure at the Trident not to follow the lead of the Prancing Horse.

While Ferrari regrouped under new young technical chief Mauro Forghieri, the 1962 season saw the 12-cylinder Maseratis first into the lists. At Sebring in March the Type 64s of both Cunningham and Volpi appeared. While the latter's Testa Rossa Ferrari won the 12-hour race, both Maseratis were out within two hours, Cunningham's with problems with the new rear suspension and Volpi's with gearbox maladies. Their speed had been as inadequate as their appetite for rear tyres was excessive. Overheating was also a bugbear.

As extensively revised by Maserati for the 1962 season, the V12-powered Type 64 had cast-magnesium wheels, lower lines and a radical new rear suspension. One such car with the factory's body design went to Briggs Cunningham's stable.

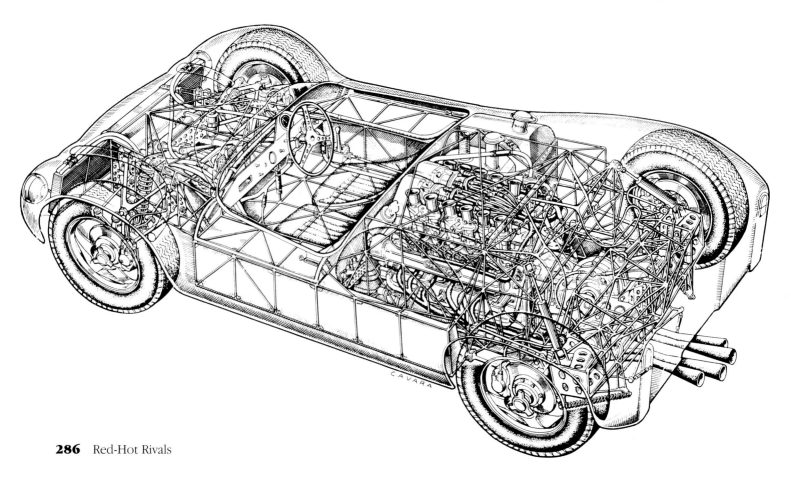

Hopes for the new car in 1962 had been high; Briggs Cunningham was expected to field three Type 64s at Le Mans. In the event the sole appearance in a major race after Sebring was Volpi's car in the Targa Florio, from which it retired with a steering breakage. The winner in Sicily, as the year before, was the nimble Ferrari 246 SP. Cunningham kept his Maserati in America, where it failed to finish in two 1962 races and for the 1963 season suffered the mortification of being fitted with a 4.7-litre Ford engine. The Type 64's season petered out in the most embarrassing way possible for the Trident.

Had Maserati thrown in the towel? Had the chaotic career of the mid-engined 'Birdcages' exhausted the patience and pocketbooks of Adolfo and Omer Orsi? Far from it! In fact in 1962 long-suffering Maserati backer Cunningham *did* have two Maseratis at Le Mans. They were joined by a third entry by John Horace Simone, who handled Maserati sales in France. The Paris-born son of an American diplomat, 'Colonel Johnny' Simone aided US Air Force intelligence in France during the Second World War and left the service as a lieutenant-colonel in 1946. The French awarded the handsome Simone the Legion d'Honneur for his wartime exploits.

After the halfway point in the 1962 24-hour race all three Maseratis were out. Co-driven by Walt Hansgen and Bruce McLaren, one of Briggs's cars had been fastest of all entries on the straight at 177mph and was in a strong second place at the third hour. These were completely new cars built to the new 1962 rules for the *Challenge Mondial de Vitesse et Endurance*, which allowed prototypes to have engines of up to 4.0-litres. In fact as well as in spirit the Type 151, as the new model was known, was a direct descendant of the 450 S of 1957, a lower and lighter version of that great car.

To bring the four-cam eight down to the smaller size Giulio Alfieri used the 4.2-litre Indianapolis stroke, 75.8mm, and a smaller bore of 91mm. Displacement was 3,944cc and output 360bhp at 7,000rpm. Ignition was dual with one distributor and one magneto. Oiling was dry-sump, with two big radiators set into the rear body surfaces and a 4.6-gallon reservoir capacity.

The 450 S was also the source for the five-speed transaxle of the Type 151. Bulky and heavy at 200lb, the mass of the gearbox had a powerful effect on the car's handling. As in the 450 S, a drop gear set behind the clutch lowered the propeller shaft on the Type 151. Holding the Type 151 together was a rambling frame of 1¼in steel tubes. Though the original drawing showed no

triangulated cross-bracing, some was later added in the course of construction.

Carried by the frame was a front suspension of conventional design, with tubular wishbones and rack-and-pinion steering, and a rear suspension that was anything but conventional. At a glance it was of de Dion type, with an axle crosstube guided in a central slot and hubs located by trailing arms. But a second look showed pivots and restraining

Rear suspension of the 1962 Type 64 Maserati was by this de Dion axle, welded of many small tubes. From each end of the axle a sprung arm went forward to the wheel hub, giving compound articulation.

While wife Laura checked the qualifying times, Briggs Cunningham prepared to race his Type 64 with 4.7-litre Ford V8 power at Bridgehampton on 15 September 1963. In the 500-kilometre race Briggs retired the Maserati-Ford after a mid-field run.

tension springs between the hubs and the main tube. It was a flexible de Dion suspension like that of the ill-fated Type 64.

Bodied as coupés, these Maseratis were brutal-looking cars with their bulging hoods, recessed tails and high doors extending deeply into the roof. They were kept remarkably small, with a 90.5in wheelbase and front and rear tracks on both sides of 50in, at considerable sacrifice of interior room. In fact Roy Salvadori, who was down to drive one of Briggs's Type 151s at Le Mans, had to give up the ride because he couldn't get into the car. All the final teams that year – McLaren/Hansgen, Thompson/Kimberly and Trintignant/Bianchi – were on the modest-stature side. The cars were light, however, under 2,160lb at the weigh-in, so the effort of compacting them paid off.

At Le Mans in 1962 the flexible de Dion proved to be *too* flexible. The cars wore their rear tyres at a terrific rate from friction against both the road and the body, occasionally throwing a tread at over 170mph on the Mulsanne Straight. So scanty was the supply of new tyres for the Simone car that a squad of mechanics was sent out to strip the near-new covers from one of the Cunningham Maseratis that had crashed after making a pit stop, having

been fitted with the wrong brake pads. Simone's entry finally retired when the rear radius rods tore away from its chassis after nine hours' racing.[4]

In terms of sheer pace the Maseratis were well in the hunt at Le Mans. Two joined the fastest Ferrari – the race-winning 4.0-litre Testa Rossa – in setting fastest laps in less than four minutes. After two hours they were second, fifth and eighth; one was running second in the third hour behind the leading Ferrari Dino 246 SP of the Rodriguez brothers. But the battle between the Red-Hot Rivals, looking and sounding so promising with the bellowing exhausts of the Trident eights, faded to Ferrari domination by the finish.[5]

After Le Mans, John Simone entered his impressive new Maserati in two more French events: the Reims 12-hour in July and the 1,000 Kilometres of Montlhéry in October. It failed to finish either race.

---

4 Prudently, Cunningham himself shared an E-Type Jaguar with Roy Salvadori to drive to a fourth-place finish.

5 Briggs Cunningham took his two coupés to race in America, where one was fitted with a 5.6-litre marine-racing version of the V8 engine. They had little success against the new generation of mid-engined cars.

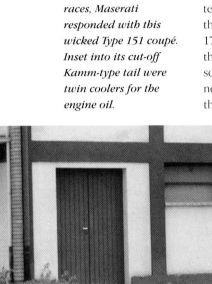

With new rules for 1962 allowing 4.0-litre prototypes in the major races, Maserati responded with this wicked Type 151 coupé. Inset into its cut-off Kamm-type tail were twin coolers for the engine oil.

Meanwhile at Maranello further development of the veteran 3.0-litre Colombo-designed V12 was continuing, based on the six-inlet-port heads that had been introduced in 1957. The need to enhance the twelve to power the 250 GTO for the now-vital GT Championship also played a role in bringing this engine up to the latest standard. In sports-racing tune it developed 310bhp at 7,500rpm. This was some 50 horsepower more than was offered by the 2.6-litre V8 with which the mid-engined 268 SP competed during 1962.

Late in 1962 a V12 was installed in a 268 SP body and chassis, the latter stretched from 91.3 to 94.5in in wheelbase through the engine bay. A dry-sump version of the twelve was chosen, fitted with a shorter exhaust system which to everyone's surprise produced five more horsepower instead of the expected reduction.

In November 1962 this experimental car appeared at the Modena circuit where Englishman Michael Parkes undertook its development. Engineer as well as driver, Parkes's suspension knowledge helped make the new combination work without major alteration to the straightforward parallel-wishbone suspension that dated from the Chiti era.

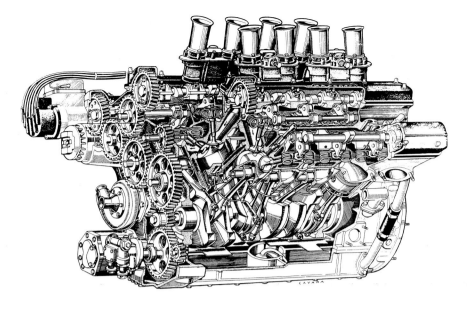

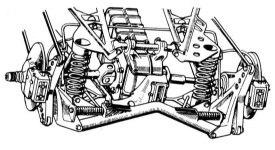

The resulting 250 P gained a reputation for remarkably good handling. John Surtees, who set a new Monza sports-car lap record with it, said that it was 'certainly a simpatico car to handle. Light throttle gives understeer characteristics and the suspension is designed to use tyres that allow changeover from understeer to oversteer. The car is a little heavy on a slow corner, so you go to the apex of the corner in understeer and change to oversteer. It is very stable at high speed but does tend to weave a little when there is a cross wind.' Its stability was specially evident at Le Mans where the 250 P was timed at 180mph, generally without drama.

Dry weight of the 250 P was up to 1,670lb from the 1,450 of the 246 SP, not only because the engine was heavier but also because Ferrari made this a genuine prototype with a fully carpeted and trimmed interior, curved-glass windscreen and deep, full-width instrument panel including a

To power his Type 151 of 1962 Giulio Alfieri produced a 3.9-litre version of the 450 S vee-eight. It continued to employ hairpin-type valve springs and a train of helical gears to its overhead camshafts.

Maserati drew upon Type 450 S drive-line componentry for 1962's Type 151, which had fuel tankage along its high sills. Suspension was new, including a version of Alfieri's compound de Dion rear axle, as shown in an inset.

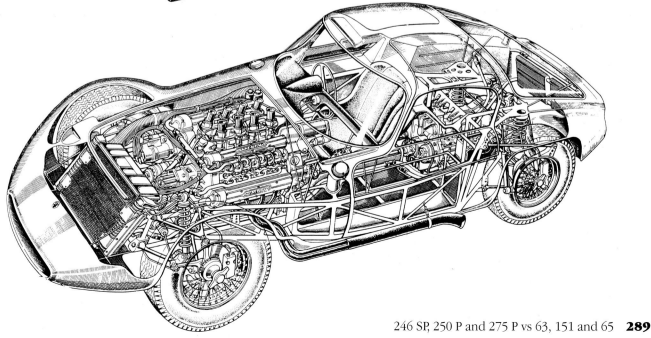

Briggs Cunningham took his two Type 151 coupés to America, where this one was acquired by Team Meridian. Skip Hudson drove it at Bridgehampton on 15 September 1963, but the car succumbed to gearbox and bodywork maladies.

In the Type 250 P, Ferrari successfully married one of its highly tuned V12s with the mid-engined chassis pioneered by the 246 P. Driven by Surtees and Mairesse, this car won the 'Ring 1,000-kilometre race from pole position on 19 May 1963.

proper glove compartment. 'Ferrari designed it from the start as a true prototype of a Gran Turismo car,' said John Surtees, newcomer to the Maranello team in 1963, 'and therefore the whole thing was made far more robust so that it could take a lot of wear and tear when it got into the customer's hands.

'It was no lightweight by racing standards,' champion motorcyclist Surtees continued, 'and called for a more manual effort than I had been used to exerting in motor racing. There was also a lot more noise. The car is very comfortable to drive

although we had some trouble with fumes in the cockpit due to a high-pressure area. Once I got the hang of that very willing V12 engine, I began to get a big kick out of driving the Ferrari prototypes.'

Turin's Pininfarina was again responsible for shaping the sports-racing Ferraris. A few well-placed scoops replaced the earlier multiple slots and vents, while the double-nostril air entry gave way to a single rectangular scoop flanked by built-in driving lights. Behind the cockpit a hoop-shaped airfoil helped redirect air spilling rearward off the high windshield. The cars ran both with and

without Plexiglas fairings over the doors, depending on how torrid conditions were in the hot, poorly ventilated cockpits.[6]

At Monza early in March 1963 the 250 P was given its first static display. Later in the month it showed to good effect dynamically when two examples placed first and second at Sebring. The first prototype used the Jano-designed transmission with its multiple-disc clutch exposed at the rear. When the 250 P was introduced, however, its clutch was a normal single-disc mounted at the engine flywheel. That's the way they ran at Sebring, but one of the three cars at the Nürburgring later in the year had the outboard clutch and two out of three had it by Le Mans time.

At the April Le Mans test session Surtees shattered all potential opposition by lapping at over 133mph, slashing 11.6 seconds from the track record. In the 24-hour race proper 250 Ps placed first and third, getting between seven and eight miles per gallon while winning at over 118mph and taking the Index of Performance award as well. Yet it had not been an all-Ferrari show. In what was virtually a works entry, Colonel Simone returned with a much-modified Type 151/1 Maserati that one report called 'frighteningly fast'.

Under the bulge in its hood was a new V8. Late in 1961 Maserati had begun to assemble the first of

a new breed of touring V8 engines with a much simpler layout than the 450 S. With cup-type tappets instead of roller fingers, coil valve springs instead of hairpins, a short block instead of a deep one with cross-bolted mains, chain drive to the cams instead of gears, one water pump instead of two and a normal oil pan instead of dry-sump lubrication, this was a design for production.

At Le Mans in 1963 the engine was run with its wet-sump oiling system. It dispensed with the rear radiators, which critics said only served to lubricate the following cars. Bore and stroke were 94 x 89mm for 4,941cc and an output of about 390bhp. Single-plug coil ignition was deemed adequate. The engine's only exotic feature was Lucas port-type fuel injection that Maserati was then developing for its production cars.

Maserati claimed that its 151/1 was 75lb lighter but the Le Mans weigh-in showed it 130lb heavier than its predecessor. To nobody's surprise it reverted to a normal de Dion rear suspension. Between the April test day and the race in June its

---

6 Phil Hill remarked with considerable frustration that after Ferrari moved its engines behind its drivers, its technicians paid little attention to isolating the cockpits from heat, assuming that the main source of calories had been removed but forgetting that the front-mounted radiators generated plenty of temperature.

The all-Italian team of Lorenzo Bandini and Lodovico Scarfiotti won the 24 Hours of Le Mans on 15–16 June 1963, driving this 250 P Ferrari. Their average speed of 118.105 mph was a new record, as was Surtees's fastest lap of 129.067 mph.

Ferrari opened its 1964 Challenge Mondial account with its 3.3-litre Type 275 P models in first and second places at Sebring on 21 March. This was the winning car of Mike Parkes and Umberto Maglioli.

body was smoothed, flattening the bulge above the engine and enclosing the exhaust pipes along the sills. Painted red with blue and white striping it was as striking as it was fast.

Veteran André Simon qualified the Maserati fifth fastest and astonished the crowd by leading the race's first lap. That this was no fluke he demonstrated through the first hour and the second, keeping the lead even after the handover

to co-driver Lucky Casner of Camoradi fame. Thereafter, however, it was slowed by transaxle ailments that retired it after the third hour. Later in 1963, in August at Brands Hatch, the Type 151/1 scored one of its rare finishes. Lucien Bianchi brought it home 13th, almost brakeless.

Based on this showing Ferrari had little to fear from Maserati, but Enzo was all too aware of Ford's interest in the GT and prototype categories. He

With prototypes allowed up to 4.0-litres in the Challenge Mondial, Ferrari fielded its Type 330 P with a V12 of 3,967cc (77 x 71mm). Graham Hill drove this British entry to victory in the Tourist Trophy at Goodwood on 29 August 1964.

armed himself for 1964 accordingly. Still roadsters – Ferraris were in fact the only open cars entered at Le Mans in 1964 – the body shapes of his prototypes were cleaned up further over 1963 and their ductwork improved, while their chassis were basically unchanged.

When powered by a 3.3-litre version of the V12 some prototypes were designated 275 P, while others, Ferrari's counter-Cobra weapons, had the 4.0-litre V12s and were named 330 P. This combination was first tried in public at Reims in June 1963, when Mike Parkes cooked the clutch at the start of a sports-car race but came back to set successive lap records. In Reims practice this first 330 P recorded the same lap speed, 132mph, as Jim Clark's pole-sitting Grand Prix Lotus-Climax.

As used in the first 330 Ps, the early Ferrari 4.0-litre engine was based on the familiar 3.0-litre V12 with a lowered crankshaft centreline. A new longer cylinder block, with dry cylinder liners and four-bolt caps for all main bearings, was used in later editions. This engine's new cylinder heads had more open hemispherical combustion chambers than the older twelve, providing improved breathing to match its added displacement. Output was 370bhp at 7,200rpm.

These uprated Ferrari prototypes had a storming start to the 1964 season. First and second at Sebring were filled by the 275 P with a 330 P third. At the Nürburgring a 275 P won. One of each type appeared for the mostly wet Le Mans test weekend, turning the expected 133+mph laps and,

in the case of the 330 P, just reaching 190mph on the Mulsanne Straight.

Another entrant for the April Le Mans tests was a new Maserati, the Type 151/3. This brute of a car arrived unpainted, its hand-hammered aluminium dully glistening. It embodied a new conception of frame and body, an ultimate realisation of the classic front-engined GT car layout. Its wheelbase was extended to 94.5in and its tracks widened by 4 to 5in. The super-squat body was an extreme interpretation of the coupé idea with a pure oval rear section and a mail-slot rear window, modified before the race with some added upward glazing.

The Type 151/3 Maserati of 1964 had a strikingly low hood line thanks to two measures. A dry-sump lubrication system was developed (later used on the same engine in production for the Ghibli) while its fuel-injection manifolding was revised to lower it well within the V8's central vee. Its output was up slightly to 410bhp at 5,800rpm.

Between April and the race the 151/3 survived a Monza testing accident to come to Le Mans fully painted for Simon and Trintignant to drive under John Simone's aegis. Its weight as measured at the track was up to 2,395lb – still by no means excessive. Though slowed at the start by throttle-cable binding the Maserati roared back, clocking a record high speed of 192.6mph on the Mulsanne Straight as it climbed up to third place after five hours. A blend of brake, gearbox and battery troubles halted it during the ninth hour.

Maserati's 1964 response to the challenge of Ferrari's 330 P was its formidable Type 151/3, which arrived unpainted at the Le Mans test weekend. Special manifolding and dry-sump oiling made its ultra-low bonnet possible.

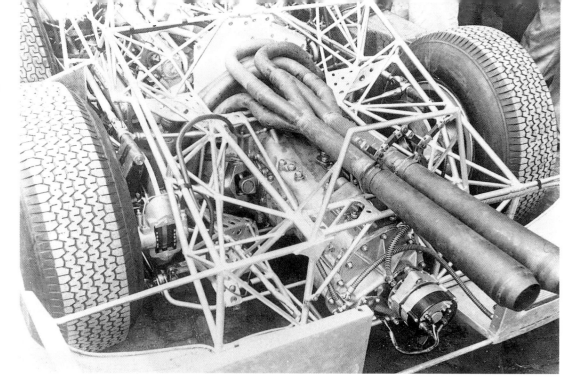

In 1965 an existing Type 63 Maserati chassis served as the starting point for the hasty construction of the V8-powered Type 65, with independent rear suspension, brakes in the air stream and transaxle extending well to the rear.

First tested on the Modena Aerautodromo on 8 June 1965, Colonel John Simone's Type 65 Maserati was white with red, blue and red striping. Its speed at Le Mans disappointed, as did its retirement after only three laps with its radiator damaged in a crash.

Unlike Maserati, Ferrari had prepared for Le Mans with unusual diligence. It obtained the use of Alfa Romeo's test track at Balocco, west of Milan, to carry out a full-dress simulation of the 24 Hours of Le Mans. They also tested the team cars thoroughly at Monza. Small wonder that the Le Mans finishing order showed a 275 P first, 330 P second and another 330 P third. The winning car averaged eight miles per gallon at a blistering record average of 121.6mph (up almost 4mph from the previous year), and again added the Index of Performance trophy to its haul.

Frustrated though their efforts had been, Giulio Alfieri and French patriot John Simone agreed that they'd created cars in the Type 151 family that had the speed potential to do well at Le Mans. They were back for 1965 with an uprated version of their radical 1964 contender, now the Type 151/4.

Alfieri decided to extract more power from his V8 by enlarging its bore by one millimetre for 95 x 89mm, increasing displacement to 5,047cc. Ports and combustion chambers were redesigned and dual ignition was adopted. Two engines were

built. One, to be used for the April practice weekend and June practice, developed 430bhp at 6,400rpm. The other, intended for the 24-hour race proper, produced 450bhp at 6,500rpm. Both could be revved safely to 7,000rpm.

While the more powerful engines were prepared Alfieri carried out some suspension changes. A new layout at the front with 'live' front hubs was created to carry the brake discs inboard of the uprights, away from the wheel. This allowed the use of a very large brake disc: 13.2in in diameter, much bigger than they could have inserted, with the caliper, within the 15in wire wheels.

Back in Simone's team for 1965 was Lucky Casner, who by then was racing only infrequently. Before he went out on the rain-swept track on 10 April he told Simone: 'I'll drive for two or three laps to get the feel of it and then see what the car can do.' Braking into the Mulsanne Hairpin the massive white car slewed off the track, cannoning off two trees and hurling its driver out. Four hours later, Casner died.

With the loss of both his car and his friend a lesser man would have given up, but John Simone was determined to see the Trident take the start at Le Mans in 1965. He commissioned Maserati to build a new car for the race on June 19–20, then just ten weeks away. For this important customer the Orsis, Alfieri and Bertocchi pulled out all the stops. They reverted to the general configuration of the mid-engined Types 63 and 64, designating the new car Type 65. Thus it was an open car with a multi-tubular 'Birdcage'-type space frame. Its general-arrangement drawing was signed off on 20 May 1965.

The Type 65's transmission was repositioned behind its rear axle. From a twin-disc clutch a shaft ran to a quick-change gear set at the extreme rear of the transaxle, whence the drive entered the five-speed transmission. Engine and gearbox were offset 1.9in to the left of the car's centreline. Using the same track and wheelbase dimensions as the 151/4 coupé, the 65 adopted its placement of the brake discs inboard of the suspension uprights at both front and rear.

Suspension at both front and rear of the Type 65 was independent. At first rear springing was by longitudinal torsion bars. After initial testing these were supplemented by coil springs around the tubular dampers. Front suspension used parallel wishbones braced by rearward-facing radius rods, with springing by concentric coils and dampers. Room was found for three fuel tanks whose capacity added up to 42 gallons. Back in the Maserati fold, Medardo Fantuzzi fashioned a purposeful open-cockpit body with a flat rear deck and chopped-off tail through which twin exhausts protruded.

Thus within the scant two months available Maserati designed, built and tested the Type 65 for Simone. Haste in the new car's construction could

The 4.0-litre Type 330 P Ferraris soldiered on into 1965 entered, like this one, by private teams. Bob Grossman and Skip Hudson had to retire William McKelvy's entry with differential problems at Sebring on 27 March 1965.

be blamed for its weight, which was 2,095lb dry and 2,635lb fuelled on the Le Mans scales. This was about the same as the GT40 Fords with 7.0-litre engines and a stout 400lb more than the mid-engined Ferraris.

That the power was there was shown by Guerino Bertocchi's test speed of 205mph on an Italian Autostrada. Umberto Maglioli was down to drive, and indeed tested the Type 65 at the Modena Aerautodromo, but its pilots at Le Mans were Jo Siffert and Jochen Neerpasch. In qualifying it was little faster than the six-cylinder Porsche 904s and on only the third lap of the 1965 race Siffert scrubbed its nose against the wattles lining the Tertre Rouge corner, damaging its radiator beyond repair.

Victory at Le Mans in 1965 went not to one of the open Ferrari prototypes but to a car that was essentially a closed version of the 275 P, the 250 LM. Maranello's prototypes were cars of a new Mauro Forghieri generation, led by the 275 P2 and 330 P2. For the first time the mid-engined twelves from Maranello had twin-cam cylinder heads of a design recognisably based on the Fraschetti/Jano twelves of the 1957 season. The smaller engine of 3,285cc produced 350bhp at 8,500rpm and the 330 P2's 3,967cc delivered 410bhp at 8,200rpm. A single-cam 4.4-litre twelve was also offered for private teams in the 365 P.

The P2-family chassis was of new lighter design, its space frame selectively stiffened by riveted-on

aluminium sheet. A major suspension change took place at the rear, where the suspension system became the same as that of the Grand Prix Ferrari. This included long parallel radius rods forward and much larger and deeper hub carriers. Borranis were replaced by aluminium wheels with wider rims to take the latest Dunlop racing tyres.

By far the sleekest sports Ferrari to date, the P2's shape was developed in model form in the small wind tunnel at Maranello. It was low, simple and shapely with a minimum of sheet metal, its side fuel tanks visible below the waistline. In its early tests it had only a low sports windscreen but Ferrari fitted it with an almost completely enclosed cockpit fairing that looked like a squat coupé with a sunroof over the driver's head.

This was the state of Ferrari's art in 1965, advancing rapidly to cope with the onslaught from Dearborn. Maranello's speed of development outstripped the best efforts of the Viale Ciro Menotti. After Le Mans the Type 65 was repaired and improved. A new nose overcame the overheating that had required the cutting of holes in its panelling at Le Mans. The suspension was reworked to solve the handling problems that marred its debut, eliminating the rear torsion bars and relying solely on coil springs. In spite of a wheelbase increase of 1.2in its weight was reduced by 200lb.

By September 1965 Maserati had completely rebuilt the Type 65 to track-readiness. However,

John Simone's resources to race it had been depleted. It was parked in the back of the company's temporary museum to wait for its time to come. That seemed to have arrived in the summer of 1967 when the Type 65 appeared at the Aerautodromo with a radical facelift.

Wheels were light-alloy with wider rims and tyres, especially at the rear. These were accommodated by grafted-on additions to the body, which carried quadruple headlamps. Incongruously wearing a Tennessee licence plate, the 65 was tested at Modena by Egon Hofer, a Philadelphia-born Austrian who was considering racing it either at Montlhéry or in the American Can-Am series. Neither came to pass. The Type 65 Maserati stood down after a racing career that was as abbreviated as its astonishingly brief gestation.

Mike Parkes, standing by the cockpit, and Jean Guichet won the 1,000 Kilometres of Monza on 25 April 1965 with this 275 P2. The race was run over the full circuit including the steep and bumpy banked oval.

Based on the chassis technology of its new four-cam works cars, Ferrari produced the 365 P for private teams powered by a two-cam V12 of 4,390 cc (81 x 71 mm). It had inboard rear disc brakes and an exposed rear-mounted clutch.

CHAPTER SIXTEEN

312 F1 vs Cooper-Maserati

While Ferrari seemed well-prepared for the 3.0-litre Formula 1 of 1966 with its armoury of vee-twelves, Maserati rashly teamed with Britain's Cooper, whose last Grand Prix victory dated from 1962. Which was destined to enjoy the greater success?

Excitement bordering on hysteria followed the announcement at the end of 1963 of a 3.0-litre capacity limit for Formula 1 cars from 1966. Fevered speculation was triggered by the accompaniment of a 1.5-litre limit for supercharged engines, easily the most favourable ratio for blown power units since 1939. Would drivers be able to cope with the much-ballyhooed

Qualifying fourth fastest for the Italian GP on 10 September 1967, Chris Amon was Maranello's sole entry. He was fourth at mid-race but fell to seventh at the finish after this pit stop to check failing rear dampers.

Emblematic of the 'Return to Power', an exciting doubling of displacement and output for Grand Prix cars for 1966, John Cooper conferred with American racer Richie Ginther in their new Maserati-powered T81 Cooper early in the season.

When a recuperating John Surtees visited Maranello in January of 1966 the first Type 312 F1, still unpainted, had progressed little since its press showing on 18 December. Ferrari's sports-prototypes enjoyed priority.

'Return to Power'? Would four-wheel drive be needed to handle twice the horses of the previous 1.5-litre cars? Prospects for the 1966 season were seen as sensational.

The new Formula 1 was widely viewed as a gift to Ferrari. Here was a company known for its engine expertise, much of which was dedicated to the extraction of power from 3.0-litre vee-twelves. Maranello's cars were forecast to walk the new season, especially as Coventry Climax had withdrawn from racing and left the Cooper and Lotus teams – despised by the Continentals as the '*garagistes*' who didn't make their own engines – high and dry.

Including BRM, which had an elaborate new H16 in the works, the British teams started the 1966 season with compromised cars using chassis from the 1.5-litre era fitted with the biggest engines they could conjure from available parts. Such cars were also eligible to compete in the first months of the year in the races in Australia and New Zealand that constituted the popular Tasman Series. It carried over the 2.5-litre size limit that had been abandoned internationally in 1961.

With the enthusiastic encouragement of team leader John Surtees, Ferrari too built a car to race down under. It used one of the 1965 158 F1 chassis motivated by a 246 F1 Dino V6 of 2.4-litres. Light and agile with responsive power, it was just the job for the Tasman races. Ready in good time for the Antipodean season, it was to be raced by John's own team. These plans imploded when a left front upright broke on his Lola T70 at Mosport in Canada, tripping Surtees into the worst crash of his career. Nevertheless, the shakedown of the Tasman hybrid continued at Alfa Romeo's Balocco test track in the hands of Lorenzo Bandini.

Enzo Ferrari stood staunchly behind Surtees during his long winter of recovery. Already a hero on two wheels in Italy for his MV Agusta exploits, *Il Grande* John had gained even more popularity after his 1964 World Championship for Ferrari. He was still hospitalised and undergoing physiotherapy on 18 December 1965 when Enzo summoned correspondents to Modena for his annual press conference. After lunch they decamped to the courtyard of the works at Maranello where mechanics lifted a dark cover from the 312 F1, the car that Ferrari planned to race in 1966.

Glistening in unpainted aluminium, the single-seater looked to be fresh from the erection shop. In spite of the installation of a substantial V12 engine its wheelbase of 94.5in was up less than an inch from that of its predecessors of half the capacity, helped by angling its drive shafts forward

Impressive-looking though it certainly was, with its swirling exhausts, the engine of Ferrari's 312 F1 was derived from the Jano/Fraschetti designs of 1957. Not until Spa in mid-1966 was it tweaked to give fully competitive power.

Having competed in sports-racing Maseratis and also in the Gilby Engineering 250 F, as here at Goodwood in 1954, Roy Salvadori was well placed to manage Cooper's 1966 team with its Trident-supplied vee-twelves.

As first tested in a Cooper chassis, the Type 9 Maserati V12 was fed by six twin-throat Weber carburettors. Its provisional ignition system had a massed array of 24 coils, one for each spark plug of the dual-ignition engine.

in plan view from the gearbox to the hubs. Suspension all around was on conventional Formula 1 lines with inboard springing units at the front, operated by upper wishbones acting as rocker arms. New-look wheels of five-star design were destined to be seen on many future Ferraris.

With dimensions of 77 x 53.5mm (2,990cc) the first Ferrari engine for the new Formula 1 was a short-stroke version of the contemporary 330 P3 four-cam sports-racing twelve with two valves per cylinder. 'Its power was announced at 310bhp,'

Front suspension of the T81 Cooper had upper rocker arms to inboard springs and offset of its brake discs into the air stream. In 1967 its high-pressure Lucas fuel-injection pump was nose-mounted to keep it cool.

John Surtees recalled, 'but I saw the test sheets and the reality was about 280bhp.' The twelve was recognisably on the same basis as the engines of the 1965 275 P2 and 330 P2 prototypes, whose top-end design dated from the 1957 season. The five-speed transaxle was also prototype-derived.

Strikingly, almost inexplicably, the technical team under Mauro Forghieri gave up an engineering advantage that it had enjoyed for the two previous years. From 1964 its V8 and flat-twelve engines were designed to serve as the rear portion of the frame. Attached to the monocoque, they carried all the stresses of the rear portion of the car, in torsion and bending, imposed by the rear suspension and driving wheels. Although not credited at the time by many in the Anglophile racing press, this was in fact an architectural and conceptual breakthrough by Ferrari.

The proximate reason for reversion to a conventional frame was that the engine, regarded as provisional, wasn't designed to serve structurally. Another reason was that the frame members extending back alongside the engine to the rear-suspension mountings helped hold the more than 10 gallons of fuel added to the 32 gallons of the 1.5-litre cars to feed the big twelve's appetite. The monocoque was of mixed construction with a framework of steel tubes braced by riveted-on aluminium sheets. Frame tubes on both sides linked the engine and front-mounted radiators, carrying oil on the left and water on the right.

Still on crutches, John Surtees had his first look at the new car early in January 1966. 'Suffice it to say that it was a familiar story,' he said of his look round the racing department. 'The F1 project was a long way behind schedule. The pressure of competition from Ford in endurance racing meant that priority was given to the prototypes. So the F1, despite the fact that it held out hopes of a renaissance for Ferrari, took second place.' Not until mid-March did the first 312 F1 have its baptism on the Modena circuit in the hands of Lorenzo Bandini.

Ford wasn't the only rival pressuring Ferrari. With the launch of the new Formula 1 the Red-Hot Rivalry with Maserati again clicked into gear. Ford's challenge in prototypes and GT cars was matched by a fresh attack in Formula 1 by the Trident, whose Giulio Alfieri was eager to see the marque back in Grand Prix racing. He had in fact been anything but idle, following up his aborted work on a 12-cylinder 1.5-litre engine with his mid-engined Type 65, built in record time for Le Mans in 1965.

In the latter part of that year Alfieri had been contacted by Mario Tozzi-Condivi, principal and

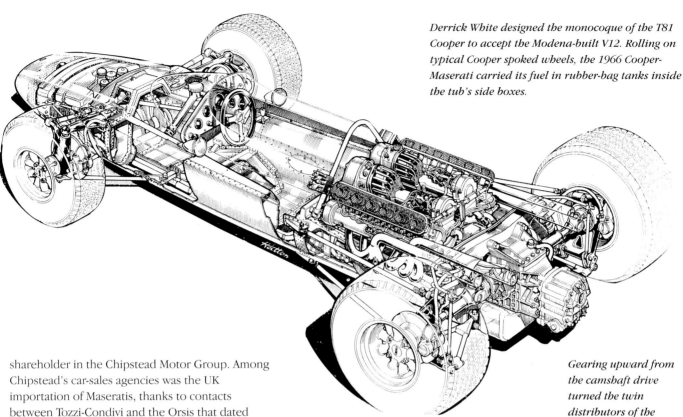

shareholder in the Chipstead Motor Group. Among Chipstead's car-sales agencies was the UK importation of Maseratis, thanks to contacts between Tozzi-Condivi and the Orsis that dated back to 1947. Also involved in Chipstead was racing-mad Jonathan Sieff, a member of the Sieff dynasty that had founded the Marks & Spencer chain of stores.

In 1960 Chipstead had acquired the retail dealership owned by racing driver Roy Salvadori, whom we recall for his Formula 1 exploits in Cooper-Maseratis in 1959. Another acquisition, in the spring of 1965, was the Cooper Car Company, in the wake of the 1964 death of the company's business brain, John Cooper's father Charles. John had been well aware that the forthcoming 1966 Formula 1 would place financial strains on a company whose Grand Prix efforts had been struggling, at best, over the last couple of years. And he knew that Chipstead-linked Maserati could solve his problem of an engine for the new formula.

For Roy Salvadori the new alliance offered not only a directorship at Cooper but also a role as the company's racing manager.[1] With Tozzi-Condivi, Sieff and John Cooper he commuted to Modena in 1965 to arrange a source of engines. Alfieri was eager, said Salvadori, while 'the Orsis were not so keen, but Mario traded on his friendship with them and was his usual persuasive self. Soon they agreed to go along with our ideas and we won over the Bertocchis, father and son. Guerino Bertocchi was nominally only chief mechanic, but his influence at Maserati was far more powerful than his title and it was vital to win him over to our side.'

1 In 1964, Salvadori's last season in the cockpit, he raced an exotic Cooper-Maserati, a Monaco sports-racer powered by a 4.9-litre Trident V8 rated at 430bhp at 7,000rpm. Like the Grand Prix Cooper-Maserati that Salvadori had raced in 1959 it was created by Harry Pearce for the Tommy Atkins stable. It was less successful than its 1963 predecessor, a Monaco with 2.7-litre FPF Climax power.

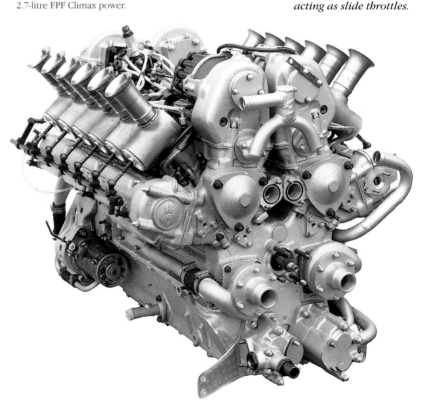

Cylinder heads being machined for the Type 9 V12 at Maserati showed their exhaust ports, on the right, and inlet ports on the left-hand example. Combustion chambers were pure hemispheres.

Decades of Maserati expertise showed in the rods and pistons of the Type 9 V12. Pistons had narrow slipper-type thrust surfaces and three rings, two for compression and one for oil control.

Maserati received an advance from Cooper to kick-start the programme, which committed the Italians to supply engines for three works cars and to shoulder all development costs. Chipstead contracted with Maserati as the Trident's exclusive Grand Prix agent, selling on the engines for Cooper's customer cars as well as securing a supply for its own works cars. Ultimately the latter would require a float of a dozen engines. Cooper was to

pay Maserati a flat fee of £750, around $2,100, for each engine rebuild regardless of the degree of disaster suffered.

'Heaped in a corner of the Maserati workshops were a number of the old 1957 Formula 1 2.5-litre V12 engines with twin overhead camshafts,' recalled Roy Salvadori. 'These formed the basis for Giulio Alfieri's development work.' Having already built his twelves in sizes of 2.5, 3.0 and 3.5-litres, the engineer had no problem settling on the dimensions of his 1966 Type 9 engine. He chose the 70.4 x 64.0mm measurements of one of the engines he raced in the Type 63 at Le Mans in 1961 – the median between two extremes of proportions entered there – for 2,989cc. With its clutch his twelve weighed 420lb.

By relocating the distributors to suit the mid-engined installation in his Type 63 and 64 sports-racers Alfieri had already taken the first step toward adapting his twelve to a mid-placed installation in the T81 Cooper, whose monocoque chassis was designed by former Jaguar man Derrick White. He was assisted by Tony Robinson, who had built successful monocoques for both Grand Prix and Indy cars in the early 1960s. Riveted and bonded of duraluminium sheet, with steel sheet facing the engine, the tub contained space for 50 gallons' worth of rubber-bag fuel tanks along its flanks.

Suspension was conventional, like Ferrari with an upper rocker-type wishbone operating inboard springs and dampers, but with a novel tweak. The front hubs were 'live', rotating within the uprights, to carry the brake discs inboard of the uprights, away from the wheel and well out in the air stream. This allowed the use of a large brake disc, 10.75in in diameter, bigger than could have been inserted, with its caliper, within 14in wheels and especially the 13in wheels that some tyre companies were now offering.

As we saw, Giulio Alfieri had used a similar layout for the front brakes of his Type 151/4 coupé, as it was modified for Le Mans in 1965, and for the discs at all four corners of the mid-engined Type 65 of the same year. The conclusion is inescapable that Derrick White was influenced to consider this layout by the Maseratis he saw during his factory visits. Wheels were to Cooper's characteristic spoked design.

Driving through a ZF five-speed gearbox, the Maserati V12 as supplied to Cooper was the company's Type 9. The Trident thrust ahead of the Prancing Horse with its first tests in a car in November of 1965. Employed as test mule was Cooper's T80, a space-frame chassis prepared for tests of an aborted Climax 16-cylinder engine for the previous formula, given the new front suspension with inboard-offset discs. While Roy Salvadori himself conducted most of its testing at Goodwood and Silverstone, Cooper team driver Jochen Rindt also tested the new Cooper-Maserati.

Though the first trials were made with carburettors, for 1966 the Type 9 was fed by Lucas fuel injection. Used initially were two six-cylinder metering units in the central vee, driven by gears from the tails of the inlet camshafts.[2] Dell'Orto carburettor bodies, initially used as throttles, were soon replaced by bespoke rotary throttles for each cylinder. While the twin water pumps of the earlier engine were carried over initially, some were cooled by a larger single pump driven from the crank nose.

'Initially the engines were not producing much over 300bhp,' wrote Roy Salvadori, 'but by the middle of 1966 Maserati were claiming 360bhp at 9,200rpm' for the injected engines, with a 10.0:1 compression ratio. However, a check on the test bench of engine maker Coventry Climax showed 30bhp less than this. Salvadori was convinced that the Modena dynamometer operator, Guerino Bertocchi, 'relied on flash, rather than consistent, readings.' In their favour, added Salvadori, 'these engines proved reasonably reliable during two seasons' racing.'[3]

Both Cooper-Maserati and Ferrari were well over the new Formula 1's minimum weight of 500kg, 1,102lb. Of his new racer Roy Salvadori said that it 'was heavier and bulkier than we had hoped and the engine bay seemed to be crammed with complicated machinery.' This attracted all the cameras at London's Racing Car Show in January, where the first complete new T81 Cooper-Maserati was the star.

'Heavy and bulky' also described the 312 F1 Ferrari. Before trying it John Surtees used the 'Tasman' Dino V6 to complete his recovery, turning many laps of Modena's little circuit. Then, he wrote, 'the 312 V12 was wheeled out and it looked absolutely enormous alongside the Tasman Dino, my "convalescence car". I took this thing out and it was two and a half seconds slower round Modena than the 2.4-litre V6. It just didn't want to go. It was

The Type 9 V12's installation in Jo Bonnier's private T81 used the rotary throttles that were Alfieri's final choice for 1966. Power went through a German ZF transaxle, giving five forward speeds.

The Cooper-Maserati's rear suspension had a reversed lower wishbone and trailing radius rods. A rubber boot encased the sliding splines that allowed half-shaft length to change with wheel movement.

2 One mid-engined racing car of 1966 did use the Maserati V12, in 2½-litre form, with carburettors. This was a Brabham prepared for Frank Gardner to drive in the Australia-New Zealand Tasman series. The Brabham-Maserati had such inconsistent throttle response – not unlike Maserati's own 1957 experience – that it practised but was never raced.

3 It must have helped that Heini Mader, a Swiss engine builder, was engaged by Cooper to oversee the maintenance and supply of the engines. He was at the beginning of gaining an excellent reputation in this field.

Pictured at the Viale Ciro Menotti, this factory-fresh Cooper-Maserati was ready for delivery to Rob Walker's private stable. Its nosepiece had a detachable extension for use when maximum cooling wasn't required.

very driveable but it was heavy and didn't have the power,' scaling 150lb more than the 246 Dino. This set the scene for conflict between Surtees and Ferrari team manager Eugenio Dragoni, an independent industrialist and enthusiast who was nurturing the Ferrari career of relative newcomer – and appealingly Italian – Lorenzo Bandini.

In England, meanwhile, a sign of what *Motoring News* called the 'Cooper Revival' was the team's move in February into spacious new quarters at Byfleet in Surrey, formerly the home of renowned Brooklands engineers Thomson & Taylor. 'There is a lot of machinery installed and Cooper do all their own machining and welding,' the weekly reported. 'There is room for more than a dozen cars to be worked on at once without crowding and the whole place is clean and well lit. The offices and design department are on the first floor.'

Roy Salvadori was sorting his Cooper-Maserati team for 1966. Thrusting but raw Austrian Jochen Rindt, in his second season with Cooper, was joined by freckled American Richie Ginther until the latter's Honda GP car was ready. Talented New Zealander Chris Amon was on standby for the team.

Thanks in no small measure to early availability of the space-framed test car, T81 Cooper-Maseratis were sold to Rob Walker's team for Jo Siffert to

drive and to privateers Guy Ligier in France and Jo Bonnier, a Swede living in Switzerland. 'The price of the F.1 car is £12,000,' said *Motoring News*, 'but even at that price Cooper lose about £3,000 on each! We imagine that Chipstead Group are subsidising this in an effort to put Cooper back on the map.'

The private teams of Walker and Ligier represented the Trident in the first clash of the season with the Prancing Horse at Syracuse on May Day. The new Cooper-Maseratis were 'quite spectacular in the hands of Siffert,' wrote Paul Sheldon, 'and satisfyingly noisy.' Jo Siffert put his Walker car on the grid's front row but his time was bettered by both pole-sitter Surtees, in the 312 F1, and Bandini in the 'Tasman' vee-six. Suffering from ignition problems, both Coopers fell back in the 195-mile race, Siffert's retiring with a universal-joint failure, while Surtees went through to win, although he 'had to row it along like mad to beat Lorenzo in the little V6.'

Two weeks later the rivals faced off again, this time with two works Coopers, for Silverstone's 102-mile International Trophy. Only Surtees was present with the V12 Ferrari, but he was able to outpace the best T81, Bonnier's in third place. Rindt had been third but handling problems, already evident in practice on this fast circuit, dropped him to fifth a lap back. Not until later in the season did the team discover that instead of the ZF differential, which it thought to be responsible, its Dunlop tyres were letting the cars down on the oily track surfaces that developed during a race.

The real surprise at Silverstone was that John Surtees was unable to match the speed of Jack Brabham's Repco-Brabham, which won from pole position and set fastest lap. This foreshadowed trouble for the season, thought Surtees, who back at Maranello emphasised to Mauro Forghieri and engine designer Franco Rocchi 'just how hard I had had to wind the thing up in order to finish second at Silverstone. They admitted that the team couldn't really afford the time or, I believe, the money to build a totally new engine and had to streamline the technical operation, making components which were interchangeable with the sports-car programme.'

At Syracuse Surtees had been at pains to point out to the press that the 312 F1 as it stood was 'only an interim development'. Further developments, however, were taking longer as they always seemed to do in the run-up to Le Mans, when all Maranello's efforts were dedicated to the 24-hour race. With the 312 F1 still two seconds slower around Modena than the 246-powered Dino, Surtees told Enzo Ferrari that he felt the latter car was a far better bet for the tight Monaco circuit and went to the Principality with every expectation of racing it on 22 May.

The 1964 champion's hopes were dashed. Team manager Dragoni took the line that 'we make 12-cylinder road cars so you've got to race the V12.' Surtees duly did so, sharing the front row of the grid with Jim Clark, and led the race until his gearbox, under stress from the pressured drive, failed after only 14 of the 100 laps. 'I don't believe it had sufficient fuel capacity to last us through to the finish,' the Englishman reflected afterward. Lorenzo Bandini's second place with the 246 Dino – and his fastest race lap – only strengthened Surtees's belief that he could have won with it.

Early in the Monaco going that second place was occupied by Jochen Rindt in the works Cooper T81, but overheating was affecting the Maserati-powered cars. The Austrian faded to fifth, from which he retired. Ginther was out with half-shaft problems while the privateers were still running at the finish but so far in arrears, after various problems, that they weren't classified as finishers. For both vaunted new twelves from Emilia the Monaco result was a disaster.

For the fast Spa circuit on 13 June both teams made an extra effort. Dynamometers in Modena and Maranello howled overtime with Alfieri uprating his Type 9 and Franco Rocchi tweaking the Ferrari's top end to lift its power above the 300 mark. The results were evident on the grid with Surtees on pole and Rindt second fastest. Although another 312 F1 was available Bandini continued in the 246 Dino, thought by some to be a stratagem used by Dragoni to prevent direct comparison between his Italian favourite and established star Surtees.

The second clash of 1966 between the Red-Hot Rivals at Silverstone on 14 May saw John Surtees come out ahead of Trident-powered cars, albeit behind Jack Brabham's Brabham-Repco, the surprise combination of the season.

Dramatically filmed for the movie *Grand Prix*, rain hit the Belgian race hard. In stormy conditions Jochen Rindt forged into the lead on the fourth of 28 laps and looked well set to give a Cooper-Maserati its first victory. But as the track dried towards the end his Dunlops played their usual tricks, making the car 'almost uncontrollable' in Rindt's words. Though also on Dunlops, John Surtees held second in his 312 F1 and in a shrewd drive accelerated into the lead near the end of the 245-mile race. Instead of hearty congratulation on his victory, team manager Dragoni criticised John for spending too much time behind a Maserati-powered car! The rivalry was alive and well in Belgium.

In Ferrari's highly politicised atmosphere John Surtees was certain that one of Eugenio Dragoni's motives for constantly doing him down was his aim of helping Ferrari achieve an all-Italian team with Bandini and Ludovico Scarfiotti, a descendant of one of the men who joined the original Gianni Agnelli to found the Fiat auto company. Knowing that a new three-valve engine was in the works, Dragoni went so far as to state publicly that 'with the power we will have, we won't need Surtees'. This seemed to *Il Grande* John an insulting as well as strange way to run a racing team.

When at Le Mans Dragoni told Surtees that he wanted Scarfiotti to take the first stint in the 330 P3

The weather was cool enough at Silverstone in May 1966 for Jo Bonnier to race with his red and white Cooper-Maserati's nose cone in place. The Swede finished third behind the Ferrari of Surtees, 77 seconds adrift.

Ferrari found space for an oil reservoir behind the radiator of its 1966 Type 312 F1. Suspension used tubular lower wishbones and upper rocker arms operating inboard coil/damper units.

they were to share, the car designated to go fast enough to break the Fords, this was the final straw for the frustrated Briton. Having worked hard to regain his fitness after 1965's severe injuries, having also delivered two Grand Prix wins in 1966 in the Ferrari he didn't want to be racing, Surtees told Dragoni that he was 'tired of being constantly sabotaged in my efforts to win by decisions that made no sense.' He left the circuit and drove to Maranello, where in an emotional meeting with Enzo Ferrari their 'divorce' was agreed.

The news that a driver of Surtees's calibre was on the loose was phoned straight through at 3:00am from a contact in Modena to Mario Tozzi-Condivi at the Chipstead Group. Roy Salvadori, who had been a Grand Prix team-mate of John's in 1961 and '62, was eager to sign him to replace Ginther, whose GP Honda was nearly ready. 'He was a brilliant driver and just the man we needed in the Cooper team,' wrote Salvadori. It was an added benefit, he said, that 'his main aim seemed to be to get back into racing and beat the Ferraris!' This lit an even hotter fire under the Red-Hot Rivalry.

With two headstrong drivers in Surtees and Rindt, Roy Salvadori set up separate in-house teams: 'Each driver had his own chassis, engines and mechanics. The arrangement was cumbersome, but operated well and prevented either driver from complaining that the other was receiving preferential treatment.' While Salvadori

managed the team, John Cooper had overall responsibility for car preparation.

At Maranello the team regrouped, building a new long-chassis 312 F1 to suit the lanky Mike Parkes – contrary to Dragoni's aim of an all-Italian squad. Bandini and Scarfiotti were also on the strength. Bandini was the star at Reims in early July, qualifying on pole in his 312 F1 and leading the race easily until breaking a throttle cable. Next to him the Surtees Cooper-Maserati surged at the start but soon fell back with fuel-vaporisation problems in the champagne district's hot weather. Best-placed Trident-powered car was Rindt in fourth.

At Byfleet the technically savvy Surtees was already having an impact. One of his first acts, he recalled, was 'to get Maserati to change to Marelli ignition, which made the V12 a little less prone to oiling its plugs. We made detail changes to the suspension which improved the Cooper's traction but, although the Maserati had about the same power as the two-valve Ferrari I had driven at Spa, it was bulky and lacked refinement.' The ZF differential was still being blamed for problems which were, in fact, attributable to the Dunlops, Ferrari already having changed over to Firestones at the suggestion of Surtees.

The British and Dutch Grands Prix were washouts for the British-based team, plagued with handling and electrical gremlins. Strikes were the problem for Ferrari, which failed to send cars to

Denied the V6-powered car that he really wanted to race, at Monaco in 1966 John Surtees pedalled his Type 312 F1 Ferrari in the lead for the first 14 laps until – as he forecast – its transmission wilted under the strain.

Running minus his nose cone, Jochen Rindt showed the Cooper-Maserati's potential by holding second in the early going at Monaco on 22 May 1966. His engine fading, he fell to fifth before retiring on the 56th of 100 laps.

Brands Hatch. Entries for Parkes and Bandini at Zandvoort a week later were muted, the best result a fifth for the Italian. Rindt spun off the circuit in his Cooper, which was struck eight laps later by a spinning Parkes. Both races were won by Jack Brabham, whose shrewdly effective new cars were the season's surprise package.

Brabham won again in the German GP on a damp Nürburgring but he was kept honest in the best performance so far by the Cooper-Maseratis. Called 'brilliantly swift and smooth' by Salvadori, Surtees finished second in spite of losing clutch control. He also set fastest lap while Rindt was third. Great satisfaction was taken in a dismal performance by Ferrari, whose best placing was Bandini in sixth. For the second race in a row Parkes left the track while Scarfiotti, in the Dino 246, retired.

On 4 September loomed the Italian Grand Prix at Monza, for which Italian teams traditionally made an extra effort. 'All the Orsi family, Alfieri and the Maserati mechanics turned up to support the Cooper team at Monza,' said Salvadori, 'and were hoping to see us defeat Ferrari.' They'd made a contribution in the metal as well as morale in the form of one Type 9 with a top-end overhaul that tidied up its central vee to allow its 12 throttle bodies and ram pipes to be sloped inward, where they were less obstructive to the air stream. Rindt put this in the third row of the grid while Surtees qualified in the second row with a conventional Type 9 V12 behind him.

Mike Parkes was on pole with Scarfiotti next to him in their Ferraris, enjoying their 36-valve engines at last. The new unit's inlet ports, now serving two valves apiece, moved from the central vee to positions between its camshafts in Maserati fashion, while its exhaust pipes remained outboard. Though Ferrari was well aware of the advantage offered by four valves per cylinder, a technology whose time had returned, it deliberately chose three valves. This was, said Mauro Forghieri, because the engine's bottom end was still the old sports-car design, not well suited to high crankshaft speeds and loads. Though piecemeal engineering was still dictating the pace of Formula 1 progress at Maranello, the new engine did give a rousing 370 horsepower.

Now running on Firestones, the Cooper-Maseratis were pacey on the fast Monza circuit. Surtees had a glimpse of the lead early on and was disputing second with Mike Parkes when a fuel-bladder leak – of which the team had been aware just before the start – became severe enough to force retirement. Ferrari finished one-two with 'Lulu' Scarfiotti scoring the biggest win of his career. Jochen Rindt was fourth for the Trident. The fuel-tank fiasco led to a shake-up in the Byfleet organisation that placed preparation as well as management under Roy Salvadori.

With Jack Brabham having clinched the championship at Monza, Ferrari took a desultory attitude to the season's remaining races, sending one car for Bandini to America and none to Mexico. Lorenzo's Watkins Glen appearance saw him leading the race until his engine broke at one-third distance. Surtees, who found himself leading eventual winner Jim Clark, was now in with an excellent chance of a victory. When he and another

driver collided on the track, however, the pumped-up Surtees spent so much time in the pits in a tirade against inattentive drivers that he couldn't make it up and finished third behind Rindt, who coasted home with empty fuel bladders.

Maserati took special care over preparation of its twelves for the race at Mexico City's heady altitude of 7,300ft. This paid off with pole position for John Surtees and fifth fastest for Jochen Rindt, a second slower. At mid-distance on 23 October the latter

retired with a broken suspension ball joint. After a faltering start with a fresh engine John Surtees swept into a lead which he held to the finish ahead of two Repco-Brabhams to score the first victory for a Cooper-Maserati and the first GP win for a Cooper since 1962. This was a popular success in part because, as Paul Sheldon wrote, 'The cars were not the fastest ever built but they were held in great affection for they looked and sounded just like a Grand Prix car should.'

French building contractor Guy Ligier was denied finishes in the points in the 1966 season with his private blue Cooper-Maserati. His best results were ninth in the Dutch Grand Prix and tenth in Britain.

For the 1966 Italian GP on 4 September Giulio Alfieri produced a new version of his Type 9 V12 with its inlet stacks curved inward to offer less aerodynamic resistance. Jochen Rindt drove it to fourth place a lap behind the winning Ferrari.

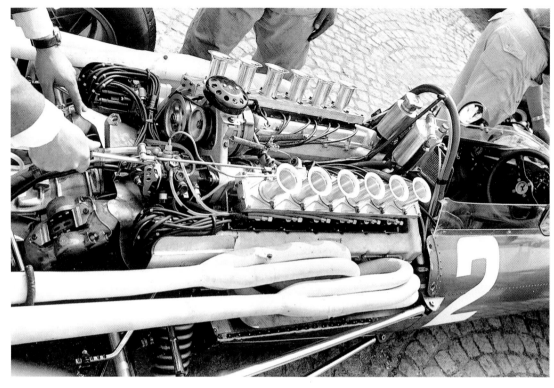

Lodovico Scarfiotti was a popular winner in the 1966 Italian Grand Prix with his version of Ferrari's new 36-valve V12, which had its inlet ports between the camshafts Maserati-style. This photograph shows the engine of his team-mate Bandini's car.

For 1967 Forghieri and Rocchi readied another version of their 36-valve V12 with its exhaust in the central vee. The Ferrari's cylinder block and transaxle still had much in common with Maranello's sports-racers.

This had been a year of high drama for our rivals. At its centre was John Surtees, the first man since Juan Fangio in 1954 to win championship Grands Prix for two different teams in a single season. Though Ferrari had two wins to Cooper-Maserati's one, the rivals finished with 32 gross championship points apiece. With the best five scores counting, both had to drop points and so finished the year with 31 for Ferrari and 30 for Cooper-Maserati. Having scored nine points for

Ferrari and 19 for Cooper, John Surtees ranked second behind champion Brabham. His team-mate Rindt was third on points. As a result it was as good as a draw with a wafer-thin margin for Maranello.

After his Mexican victory, 'a tremendously satisfying way to finish the season,' John Surtees could well have been minded to carry on with Cooper in 1967. In the close season, however, the British team was unable to guarantee to the driver that it would continue to have a supply of Maserati

engines. By the time this was resolved Surtees had already transferred his affections to Honda, for whom he set up a UK-based team. This was a regrettable loss for both parties, for the brief liaison between Surtees and the Trident-powered Cooper had been impressively productive.

To fill the gap Salvadori drafted in the Mexican driver Pedro Rodriguez, who carried on racing after his brother Ricardo's death during practice for his home Grand Prix in 1962. Although a proven winner in sports cars during his Ferrari years, Pedro had driven indifferent machinery in nine Grands Prix since 1963. Disappearing into the cockpit of the Cooper-Maserati for the South African GP on 2 January, Pedro put it on the second row and survived an eventful race – in spite of the loss of third and fourth gears – to score a debut victory.

The unheralded Mexican's shock arrival atop a Formula 1 podium was bitter gall for the resident Austrian, who saw himself as cock of the walk after Surtees's departure. 'For some reason Jochen Rindt took an instant dislike to Pedro,' said Roy Salvadori, 'and was terribly rude to him all the time.' Matters didn't improve when Rodriguez 'slaughtered' Rindt in a high-stakes game of gin rummy. At this early stage of his career Rindt was hard on his cars, with heavy tyre wear, while Rodriguez was the opposite, smooth yet impressively fast.

Eugenio Dragoni was still Ferrari's team manager through the 24 hours of Daytona in February, which Maranello won against the might of Ford's Mark II GTs with an historic one-two-three finish. Thereafter former journalist Franco Lini was assigned the reins by Enzo Ferrari. He had a driver cadre which, although talented and promising, was relatively untested at racing's top level. Lorenzo Bandini and Ludovico Scarfiotti were still on board, joined by British engineer Mike Parkes and a driver whom Cooper had used once in 1966, New Zealander Chris Amon. Asked about Amon, Dragoni termed him '*una bomba*' – which requires no translation.

Although the Prancing Horse's emphasis continued to be on sports-racers through Le Mans, Forghieri and Rocchi managed to find time and money to improve the 312 F1 as well. First fruits of their efforts were on view at Brands Hatch on 12 March for the Race of Champions, run in two 26-mile heats and a 106-mile final. While Scarfiotti had his 36-valve Monza winner, Bandini drove a new version of that car. Its cylinder heads were mirror-imaged so that the exhaust pipes were all in the engine's central vee. Much neater, this made room for more fuel in the monocoque limbs flanking the engine. Quoted power was now 375bhp at 10,000rpm.

This was 1967's first joust for the Red-Hot Rivalry, with Cooper fielding two Type 81s for its squabbling drivers. Rindt's was dubbed an 81B, its tub reskinned in lighter aluminium and wearing a more compact Hewland transaxle. The fastest of the two rivals, Scarfiotti and Rindt, had identical times on the third row of the first heat's grid, two

Seen at Brands Hatch on 12 March, Byfleet's initial response for 1967 was the new T81B Cooper, reskinned for lightness and equipped with a Hewland transaxle. Rear brakes were now in the air stream and rubber couplings accommodated drive-shaft plunge.

First used in Monaco practice in May 1967, Maserati's Type 10 V12 was a commendably compact unit with its inlet ports in the central vee. Accessories were driven by cogged-rubber belts.

seconds off Dan Gurney's pole in his Eagle V12. It was Gurney's day but Bandini made a race of it in the final to finish second ahead of Jo Siffert's private Cooper-Maserati. Rodriguez was fourth and Scarfiotti fifth, separated by just over a second. For the Italian twelves the rivalry was warming globally.

Only private Cooper-Maseratis faced a lone works Ferrari in Silverstone's 152-mile International Trophy at the end of April. It was Mike Parkes's day

in his long-wheelbase 312 F1 with the latest 36-valve engine, setting joint pole and winning from Jack Brabham. The plucky Siffert was third in Rob Walker's Cooper. Byfleet had been preparing for the Monaco GP a week later, including the presentation in practice of a completely new engine from the Viale Ciro Menotti.

'Alfieri was always full of enthusiasm and friendly co-operation,' Roy Salvadori recalled of Maserati's chief, 'completely dedicated to his work and prepared to talk about his engines at any time, even if I telephoned him in the middle of the night.' His Type 10 V12 kept the Type 9's bottom end but cast in magnesium to reduce its weight. It had three valves per cylinder with the twin inlets fed by individual ports in the central vee. The valves were all dead vertical in relation to the cylinder, opened by close-spaced twin camshafts running in ball bearings. Combustion chambers were recessed in the tops of the pistons in the manner associated with British engineer Sam Heron, thus the 'Heron head'.

A notable feature of the Type 10 was its provision for three spark plugs per cylinder, two flanking the single exhaust valve and one between the inlet valves. This was no small challenge to the ignition department, which sometimes threatened to overwhelm the engine. And if Cosworth's Keith Duckworth did say that an engine that needs more than one spark plug per cylinder must have something wrong with it, he could feel justified in his view. The Type 10 first raced at Silverstone in July and its triple-plug

version made its debut at Watkins Glen at the beginning of October.

The Cooper squad was lucky to be guaranteed two starting places among the 16 at Monaco, for its cars didn't behave well at all in the principality. Starting from the back of the grid and lacking two cylinders Rodriguez eked out a fifth place with Chris Amon's Ferrari two laps ahead in third. For Ferrari the race was an unmitigated disaster. Chasing leader and ultimate winner Denny Hulme, Lorenzo Bandini crashed, suffering injuries in the resulting fire that cost him his life three days later. Many mooted that he may have been overdriving, pressured prematurely into a team-leading role by Enzo Ferrari.

The Trident thrust back at Zandvoort for the Dutch GP, filling the grid's second row while the Prancing Horses of Amon and Parkes were back in the fourth row. It didn't pay off, however, with both Coopers falling out. Best Ferrari was Amon's in fourth place. The devastating pace of the Ford-V8-powered Lotus 49s at this, their first appearance, boded ill for future victory opportunities.

High-speed racing resumed in mid-June at Spa, where the fast qualifiers lapped at better than 145mph. This suited both Amon and Rindt, who occupied the grid's second row with identical times in their rival machines. In the race the New Zealander just outpaced the Austrian to place third to the latter's fourth. Another tragedy for Ferrari was a first-lap crash by Parkes, whose top-line career was ended by breaks to both leg and wrist.

Scarfiotti too was lost to the Maranello cause, withdrawing in dismay at the death of his friend Bandini and Parkes's accident.

From the sublime to the ridiculous, the circus moved on to the tight 2.75-mile Bugatti circuit at Le Mans. There Chris Amon was the sole Ferrari protagonist, a state of affairs that continued until the season's final race in Mexico. He and Rindt were seventh and eighth fastest qualifiers but neither finished. Siffert and Rodriguez scored points for Cooper in fourth and sixth places.

Britain's Grand Prix at Silverstone on 15 July witnessed a riposte from Cooper. Rindt had Derrick White's new creation, the T86. Aiming for lowness and lightness it had a gaping maw for its radiator and magnesium skinning for its monocoque. It was fractionally faster in qualifying than Rodriguez's T81 but not on the pace of Amon's Ferrari. The latter finished a respectable third while Pedro was fifth, a lap down.

With six races down and five to go, the FIA took stock of the points, all of which were awarded to the constructors – with no deductions – in 1967. Thanks in no small measure to its South African victory, Cooper-Maserati led Ferrari with 19 points to 15. Ferrari gained at the German GP, where Chris Amon totted up four points for third place against Jo Bonnier's two for fifth place in his private Cooper-Maser, his best finish of the year.

A dash to Mosport in Canada saw Amon add a point for Ferrari with a sixth-place finish in heavy rain that shorted out Rindt's ignition. This was

For his Type 10 V12, Maserati's Giulio Alfieri adopted bowl-in-piston combustion chambers with flat-faced cylinder heads and three valves per cylinder. Individual cylinder-head inserts carried its cup-type tappets.

G. CAVARA

Slimmer than its predecessor and fitted with new yo-yo-style wheels, the T86 Cooper had the triple-ignition version of the Type 10 V12 for Watkins Glen. Roy Salvadori stood behind its roll bar while Nina Rindt was being briefed in the pit.

destined to be the last points haul of 1967 for Maranello. In the Italian Grand Prix Chris Amon had a brand-new 48-valve engine, still with central exhausts, that was Rocchi's most potent offering yet. Ferrari claimed 410bhp at 10,600rpm for this Lucas-injected twelve.

It took Amon to fourth on the grid, less than a second in arrears of Jim Clark's pole and two seconds quicker than Rindt's best in the T86. In the race Chris's twelve went off tune and the best he could manage was seventh. The result was thrilling for Maserati's fans and staff because Jochen Rindt

was fourth, on the same lap as winner John Surtees in his Lola-chassis Honda. This was rated a big success in the relentless rivalry.

At Monza all competitors were weighed with oil, water and a minimum of fuel to check their conformity with the required weight of just over 1,100lb. Thanks to its increased use of magnesium in mid-season in both chassis and engine Ferrari had done extremely well with its 312 F1-67, which scaled 1,158lb. The lightest Cooper-Maserati was a T81B at 1,246lb while the T86 weighed 1,268lb. Coopers built for the 1966 season scaled in excess

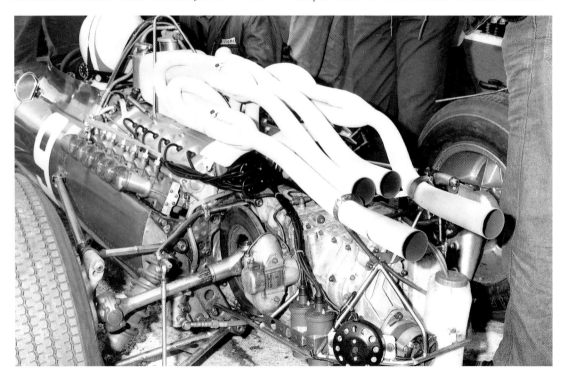

For Monza in 1967 Ferrari moved its 312 F1 V12 into the modern era with narrow-angle four-valve heads. Inlet ports were outboard and exhausts in the central vee. That year it was too new to be reliable, however.

of 1,300lb. Only the H16-powered BRMs weighed more – a lot more.

Roy Salvadori had his own driver problems after Pedro Rodriguez was injured in a crash in a Formula 2 race in Sicily. From Monza his place was taken by Jacky Ickx, who finished sixth in spite of a deflating tyre on his final laps. This was the Belgian's first of many drives in full 3.0-litre Formula 1 cars. He joined Rindt at Watkins Glen, where both versions of the Type 10 Maserati V12 blew up in the race. Amon's Ferrari blew as well when he was a worthy second.

Jochen Rindt having worn out his welcome at Cooper, a now-healthy Pedro Rodriguez was the sole factory Cooper-Maserati exponent in his hometown Grand Prix at Mexico City on 22 October. Franco Lini helmed a last-gasp effort from Maranello with two cars for Amon and British Formula 3 ace Jonathan Williams. The newcomer was ninth just behind Amon, who fell from second place with an embarrassing shortage of fuel. The plucky Rodriguez finished sixth to claim a final point for Cooper.

In 1967 there was no doubt about the rivals' relative standing. Cooper was third in manufacturers' points with 28 while Ferrari was equal fourth with Honda with 20 points. Ferrari had experienced a hecatomb of its drivers and a slow start to its technology thanks to its concentration on the magnificent 330 P4, while Cooper and Maserati had struggled with updates to both chassis and engine that failed to yield the desired advantages. Nevertheless, it was the Anglo-Italian effort that delivered the superior result.

For 1968 Ickx left Cooper to join Amon at Ferrari. Apart from Forghieri's pioneering

experimentation with wings the Prancing Horses were little changed in '68, the main development effort going into the new flat-twelve 312 B F1. At Byfleet the Cooper team no longer had the backing of Mario Tozzi-Condivi, who had left, so Maserati's twelves were replaced by BRM's. This proved such a dismal combination that 1968 was Cooper's last season in Grand Prix racing. The announcement came in May 1969.

A last hurrah for the Maserati-powered works Coopers was the South African Grand Prix at Kyalami on New Year's Day 1968. None other than Lulu Scarfiotti joined Brian Redman in the works team. Both, however, suffered retirements, as did Jo Bonnier's private entry. The only Trident finisher was Jo Siffert in Rob Walker's veteran 1966 car, now nicknamed the 'Torrey Canyon' for its propensity to leak oil in all directions. He was just out of the points in seventh while Chris Amon – still on the Ferrari strength – was fourth.

This wasn't quite the end. The unique T86-Maserati appeared at Monaco in 1969 in the hands of Colin Crabbe's private team. Though he started from the back of the grid, Vic Elford kept it between the walls of Monte Carlo to finish seventh and last, six laps behind winner Graham Hill. Not a single Ferrari finished ahead of him in this, the last-ever appearance of a Maserati power unit in a championship Formula 1 race.[4] With its 312 B F1, however, Ferrari would go on to sublime greatness.

Privateer Jo Bonnier soldiered on through 1967 in his T81 Cooper with its Type 9 Maserati V12. He used it effectively to pick up points at both the German and, here, American Grands Prix.

---

4 The authoritative website resource Forix counts this as the 596th appearance of a Maserati engine in a championship Formula 1 Grand Prix since 1950.

CHAPTER SEVENTEEN

Coda to a rivalry

U nder the auspices of Shell the Ferrari-Maserati rivalry was reborn in 1999. At four circuits, Spa, the Nürburgring, Vallelunga and Montchier, it was again Monza versus 300 S, Mondial versus A6GCS/2000, 250 F versus 625 and 'Birdcage' versus Testarossa. Joining the existing Ferrari Challenge for historic cars, a Maserati Challenge in parallel attracted enthusiasts for these great cars who were ready and able to ride them hard and put them away wet.

Though the rivalry on the track was as heated as ever, it came about because the commercial rivalry between the two marques was neutered. In 1993 Fiat transformed a minority interest in Maserati into full control. Fiat-owned Ferrari acquired half its former rival in 1997 and in 1999 took the balance to gain full authority and responsibility for Maserati. It was news that rocked Modena. In an ultimate irony of the world of cars the Prancing Horse had subsumed the Trident. Somewhere Enzo Ferrari and Alfieri Maserati were grimacing.

Just at the time their racing rivalry ended both companies had seen dramatic changes in their ownership. The change at Maserati resulted from an enquiry from Paris's Citroën: could the Italians make an engine for an exotic new model? Yes, came the answer, but it would cost us a lot to tool up for the production volumes required. This led

One of Italy's most flamboyant motoring personalities, émigré Argentinean Alejandro de Tomaso built a Ford-powered Formula 1 car in 1970 to be driven by Piers Courage. In 1975 he took effective control of a Maserati made bankrupt by Citroën.

Engineered to race in the International Grand Touring category, Maserati's MC12 was granted the privilege of premiering a completely new V12 engine that later powered Ferrari's Enzo. The former Red-Hot Rivals now made a formidable team.

to an investment in Maserati by Citroën that saw the latter acquiring 60 per cent of its shares in 1968. The French company bought 15 per cent more in 1970 and the rest the year after that. Citroën in turn was owned by tyre-maker Michelin.

In retrospect the timing was good for the Orsis, who could not have foreseen the Energy Crisis and troublesome regulatory times just ahead. Giulio Alfieri carried on, producing the new 90° vee-six that powered both Citroën's SM and Maserati's mid-engined Merak. The V8-powered Bora was launched as well, but a racing version failed to take

to the track. Omer Orsi's son Adolfo noted that as part of the Citroën deal a subvention of one billion lire for competition activities was provided. No competition eventuated, however. 'On what was it spent?' he had every right to ask.

In 1969 Fiat acquired effective control of Ferrari's road-car operations, leaving racing in the hands of Enzo. Thus both Modena companies were in the hands of larger auto makers. This seemed to offer both firms much-needed protection when the Energy Crisis of 1973 cut swathes through the ranks of makers of costly and

fuel-hungry exotic cars. Maserati's parent had problems as well. A short-lived attempt by Citroën to ally with Fiat saw the French company falling into Peugeot's orbit instead.

The new external circumstances took their toll at Maserati. Its French proprietor had neither the answers nor the willingness to let the Viale Ciro Menotti respond, as it had so often in the past. The Trident's legendary flexibility and resourcefulness were 'suffocated by the clumsy presence of the new bureaucratic and pragmatic ownership,' regretfully related Luigi Orsini and Franco Zagari. The 1974 blood-red balance sheet for Maserati caused Peugeot-Citroën to put it into liquidation in May 1975.

Thus in 1975, the year in which Ferrari won both the constructors' and drivers' championships in Formula 1, Maserati entered its most problematic phase. Dramatic negotiations that summer found Maserati in the possession of Rome's GEPI, a state holding company, and under the control of Alejandro de Tomaso. A man of iron whims, Argentinean de Tomaso had attracted controversy since his arrival in Italy in 1955. Maker of dc Tomaso cars and owner of the Ghia and Vignale coachbuilders, he had a predilection for creating interesting prototypes that seldom matured.

A former racing driver, sometimes for the Maserati brothers, Alejandro de Tomaso had successfully deployed state funding to gain working control of failing motorcycle companies Benelli and Moto Guzzi. He exercised the same technique at Maserati. Joining him on the Maserati board were GEPI's Romano Prodi and, representing the Trident's heritage, Omer Orsi. Orsi's presence was in fact vital, for he had the credibility to persuade Maserati's suppliers and dealers to stand by the company at a time of crisis.

De Tomaso gradually built up his personal holding in the company to 51 per cent. Through his friend Lee Iacocca he inveigled Chrysler into buying 17 per cent of Maserati's shares, while a reluctant GEPI retained 32 per cent. After two years Omer Orsi left the board, tiring of de Tomaso's mercurial management style.

Alejandro de Tomaso sought to revive Maserati by giving Italy its own equivalent of BMW. 'Scepticism and incredulity', said one commentator, attended the December 1981 launch of the Biturbo, visually close kin to the 3-Series BMW. Its all-independent suspension was also on 3-Series lines. Under its bonnet was a 90° V6 evolved from the engine of the SM and Merak, ingeniously fitted with twin Japanese turbochargers and new three-valve cylinder heads.

Omer Orsi could afford to smile. In selling full control of Maserati to Citroën in 1971 his family's timing neatly anticipated the motor industry's looming challenges of energy crises and emissions constraints.

Thanks to the attractive pricing of this new interpretation of the Trident and the use of the Innocenti facility in Milan for assembly, Maserati production soared from 528 in 1981 to 5,333 in 1983. The Quattroporte was revived, a reminder that Maserati had been willing to make the four-door model that Ferrari expressly abjured, while the Biturbo spawned variants and successors with up to five valves per cylinder. Chrysler's involvement led to production in Milan of the

To meet Citroën's requirements Maserati designed and built an ingenious 90-degree V6 of 2,670cc. It featured two-stage chain drive to its four overhead cams and main-bearing caps integral with its bolted-on lower block.

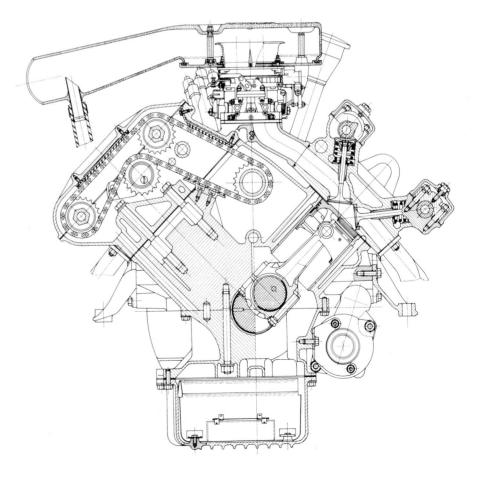

Left: In 1972 Citroën-owned Maserati introduced its mid-engined Merak, sharing its V6 with the front-drive SM. The capacity of the six was enlarged to 2,965cc to deliver 208bhp at 5,800rpm in its SS version from 1975.

Below left: De Tomaso made no secret of his desire to turn the Trident into an Italian version of BMW, as betrayed by the shape of his Biturbo. This was a 1987 Type 228 version with its twin-turbo vee-six producing 250bhp.

anodyne TC by Maserati, powered by a four-cylinder engine whose only noteworthy feature was its high cost.

In 1989 speculation that Maserati would return to racing swirled around the appointment at Viale Ciro Menotti of Giacomo Caliri, a former aerodynamic specialist at Ferrari who had been technical director of the Minardi team. De Tomaso, however, scoffed that his responsibilities were more banal. A tentative return to competition was Maserati's production of a handful of Barchetta models, open glass-fibre-bodied spyders powered by twin-turbo 2.0-litre vee-sixes. For these a one-make racing series, the Grantrofeo Barchetta, was organised in 1992 and '93.

Ferrari, meanwhile, was flourishing. By introducing first its V6 Dino and then the V8 308 range the Maranello company fashioned enhanced access to its products. Sales topped the 2,000 mark in 1979, 3,000 in 1985 and 4,000 – by a single unit – in 1988. Its last championships in Formula 1, however, dated from 1979. In spite of numerous technical advances the Prancing Horse failed to get

into its stride in the turbocharged era of Grand Prix racing. Nor was it immune from dilettantish if well-meaning 'guidance' from its masters in Turin in these final years of the life of Enzo Ferrari. Having outlived his contemporary Ernesto Maserati by 13 years, Ferrari died in August 1988.

The familial links remained strong with the appointment of Enzo's son Piero as Ferrari's vice chairman. At the end of 1991 Luca di Montezemolo took over as chairman from Piero Fusaro. Racing director for Maranello in 1974 and '75, di Montezemolo paid tribute to the founder:

Above: Preservation of the Ferrari patrimony during its transition to Fiat ownership was ensured by the continuing role of Enzo's son Piero (centre), here with the author (left), and Rodolfo Mailander at an exhibition of the latter's photography.

Far left: From 1990 Maserati came under the firm control of Ferrari's Luca di Montezemolo, at right with Italy's President Carlo Azeglia Ciampi and a Quattroporte at a presentation in Rome in 2004.

Left: Pictured with his father Ernesto, Alfieri Maserati successfully established AM Engineering to produce high-quality gearing for both OEM and aftermarket use. He also blessed an attempt to revive the OSCA marque.

The Maserati works on the Viale Ciro Menotti was unrecognisable after its transformation under Ferrari's aegis. Its spectacular new presentation honoured the Trident's storied past.

'He was a man who always looked forward, a spirit that I have worked hard to restore to the company after some difficult years. I try to remember and to use what I learned from him. We are determined to maintain the traditions and the standards that he established.'

Enzo's patrimony was powerful, added di Montezemolo: 'Whether intuitively or calculatedly, Enzo Ferrari gave Ferrari a laser-like intensity of precise marketing. He believed in firm prices, requiring payment in full before any car left the works – sometimes *before* it was built. The Ferrari logo and prancing-horse emblem became some of the world's best-known trademarks. Our cars in Italian racing red and the sharp graphic contrast of a bold yellow created an unforgettable visual impact.' Ownership of Ferrari was exercised at the level of the Fiat Group, offering a less meddlesome partner than Fiat Auto, which controlled Fiat, Alfa Romeo and Lancia.

Getting to grips in the early 1990s with a struggling Ferrari on the race track and an inherited product line that had more than a few bugs, Luca di Montezemolo was handed yet another challenge in April 1997. Faults in Ferraris paled in comparison

with those suffered by Maserati, whose product problems overtaxed its ability to service them, especially in the far-flung markets that had boosted its volume. The de Tomaso regime proved unequal to the demanding task of combining high production with high quality.

In 1990 Fiat acquired the 49 per cent of a faltering Maserati not owned by de Tomaso. The other shoe dropped in 1993, when the rest of both Maserati and Innocenti fell into Fiat's hands. Progress with Maserati was hesitant until 1997, when the company came under the management control of Ferrari, together with a 50 per cent shareholding. Ferrari acquired the other half in 1999 to become sole owner of its one-time Red-Hot Rival.

Thus began a new relationship that confounded the historically intense competition between the two Modenese rivals. That none of the founders was still living can only be considered a blessing. Members of the next generation were active in the industry, Ernesto's son Alfieri as the owner of an engineering firm and Enzo's son Piero as a holder of ten per cent of Ferrari, involved in many of the company's projects. Both could only be gratified

that the lives of the respective firms had been prolonged through Fiat's intervention.

Questions were raised about Ferrari's ability and indeed desire to lend a helping hand to an important commercial competitor. In fact the Maranello company could only qualify by virtue of the strong growth and profitability that it had achieved under di Montezemolo. 'We plan to bring to Maserati some of the techniques for improving quality and streamlining production that we have implemented successfully at Ferrari in order to achieve these advances,' he explained 'We have made changes – and here I am quoting the opinion of outside observers – that many said would be impossible in Italy.'

Drastically, Ferrari shut down Maserati's production altogether for six months to revitalise its factory. A new era began in 1999 with the launch of the 3200 GT with a twin-turbo V8 engine. Di Montezemolo ensured that Ferrari's engineers were not mean with their technology. For example, the new-generation V12 created for the Ferrari Enzo of 2002 was shared with Maserati's GT racing car, the MC12, which scored its first victory in 2004. The MC12 reintroduced Maserati to international

competition, albeit calculatedly in a category that threatened no direct clash with Ferrari.

Thanks to Ferrari's stewardship of both product and distribution, Maserati flourished. Its Quattroporte was revived to general acclaim. In June 2005 the Viale Ciro Menotti built its 20,000th car since Ferrari took full charge of its former rival. Ironically, by then the company was no longer Ferrari's.

In February 2005, in the wake of the settlement that ruptured the short-lived partnership between General Motors and Fiat, the latter announced that Maserati was to return to Fiat's direct ownership. In a transition period some of its synergies with Ferrari remained, but the new focus was to be an alliance with Alfa Romeo. Said Fiat's CEO Sergio Marchionne, 'The technical and commercial collaboration between Maserati and Alfa Romeo will give the latter the necessary impetus to re-establish itself as a leading contender in its segment and to expand its presence in international markets, as has occurred for Maserati.' The little Modena firm was to educate the far bigger Milan marque in the ways of the world.

Both the model range and the manufacturing facilities of Maserati were dramatically updated during the years from 1999 to 2005 when it was under Ferrari's direct ownership.

By then Luca di Montezemolo surveyed the scene from the lofty position of chairman of the Fiat Group in addition to his continuing role at Ferrari. 'The synergies between the two marques will bring benefits to both,' he said of the link between Alfa and Maserati, 'and will allow us to strengthen our portfolio in the sports-car market.' Observers speculated that the hiving off of Maserati would make it easier for Fiat to raise funds by a stock-market float of a Prancing Horse no longer harnessed to the Trident. In the first decade of the 21st century Fiat Auto's cheering revival made that scenario less plausible.

Co-ordination from the top of Fiat ensures that we'll not experience a revival of the memorable clashes between Ferrari and Maserati that enlivened so many years of racing in the mid-20th century. Many of their battles could be traced back to tests and races on the 1.4-mile perimeter track of Modena's Aerautodromo. Its sweeping turn and wriggling chicane were the yardsticks of performance for the latest and best products of the Red-Hot Rivals.

Until 1954, thanks to Fangio, Maserati held the Modena lap record. In tests in the spring of 1957 a record lap time of 59.0 seconds was shared between Eugenio Castellotti on Ferrari and Jean Behra on Maserati. In spite of a slight lengthening of the track in 1960 a new testing record of 57.0 seconds was set on 30 July of that year by Phil Hill in a Dino 246 F1 Grand Prix car. It remains the official absolute record in perpetuity. The race lap record of 57.8 seconds is to the credit of the Lotus-Climax of Stirling Moss, set on 3 September 1961. The new wave was not to be denied.

From 1962 auto racing was banned at the Aerautodromo, whose safety provisions were unequal to rising car speeds. Indeed we recall that in the 1950s it took the lives of a talented Ferrari engineer, Andrea Fraschetti, and star driver Eugenio Castellotti. After the 1961 race the circuit was declared unsafe for car racing, although motorcycle races persisted to 1976. Nevertheless, car testing by both Ferrari and Maserati continued on the perimeter track into the early 1970s. With the advances being made in racing cars its layout was clearly outdated; Ferrari last tested there in 1971.

Finally the Aerautodromo was closed and retired to wooded parkland with facilities for expositions. Although it was named the Parco Enzo Ferrari, which is appropriate enough, a dedication could well have been made that offered a tribute to the compelling rivalry between Modena's racing-car builders that transfixed not only the city's passionate residents but also the world for two dramatic decades.

While its diagonal served as an airstrip, the perimeter road of Modena's historic Aerautodromo was both test and race circuit. It was the venue for many epic battles between Ferrari and Maserati, both virtual and actual.

BIBLIOGRAPHY

Benatti, Giancarlo, and Pedroni, Piero. *Il Romanzo dei Bolidi Rossi*, Edizioni Il Fiorino, Modena, 1996.

Bertett, Luigi. *Monza Yearbook 1960, 1961, 1962, 1963, 1964, 1965, 1966*, SIAS, Milan, 1960, 1961, 1962, 1963, 1964, 1965, 1966.

Cancellieri, Gianni. *Maserati – Catalogue raisonné 1926–1990*, Automobilia, Milan, 1990.

— and De Agostini, Cesare. *Polvere e Gloria, La Coppa d'Oro delle Dolomiti 1947–1956*, Giorgio Nada, Milan, 2000.

Canestrini, Giovanni. *Mille Miglia*, L'Editrice dell'Automobile, Milan, 1967.

Carli, Emanuale Alberto. *Settant'anni di gare automobilistiche in Italia*, L'Editrice dell'Automobile, Milan, 1967.

Casucci, Piero. *Rivista Maserati 1*, Automobilia, Milan, 1985.

— *Ferrari F1 1948–1963*, Editoriale Domus, Milan, 1984.

— *Ferrari F1 1964–1976*, Editoriale Domus, Milan, 1965.

Colombo, Gioachino. *Origins of the Ferrari Legend*, Haynes, Sparkford, 1987.

Curami, Andrea, and Vergnano, Piero. *La 'Sport' ei suoi artigiani 1937–1965*, Giorgio Nada, Milan, 2001.

Cutter, Robert, and Fendell, Bob. *The Encyclopaedia of Auto Racing Greats*, Prentice-Hall, Englewood Cliffs, 1973.

Fangio, Juan Manuel, with Carozzo, Roberto. *Fangio, My Racing Life*, Patrick Stephens, Wellingborough, 1990.

Ferrari, Enzo. *Piloti, Che Gente …* Conti Editore, Bologna, 1985.

Finn, Joel E. *Ferrari Testa Rossa V-12*, Motorbooks, St Paul, 2003.

— *Maserati: The Postwar Sportsracing Cars*, John W. Barnes Jr, Scarsdale, 1977.

— *Maserati Birdcage – The marvellous Tipo 60 and 61 sports racing cars*, Osprey, London, 1980.

Fitzgerald, Warren, and Merritt, Richard. *Ferrari, The Sports and Gran Turismo Cars*, Bond, Newport Beach, 1968.

Fondi, Pino. *Il mitico Giro di Sicilia*, Giorgio Nada, Milan, 1996.

Frère, Paul. *On the Starting Grid*, B.T. Batsford, London, 1957.

— *Sports Car and Competition Driving*, Robert Bentley, Cambridge, 1963.

Fusi, Luigi. *Alfa Romeo – All Cars From 1910*, Emmeti Grafica, Milan, 1978.

Gauld, Graham. *Modena Racing Memories*, MBI Publishing, Osceola, 1999.

Georgano, G.N. (editor). *The Beaulieu Encyclopedia of the Automobile*, The Stationery Office, London, 2000.

— (editor). *The New Encyclopedia of Automobiles – 1885 to the Present*, Crescent Books, New York, 1986.

— with Bochroch, Albert R. *The Encyclopedia of Motor Sport*, Viking Press, New York, 1971.

Godfrey, John. *Ferrari Dino SPs*, Patrick Stephens, Wellingborough, 1990.

Gozzi, Franco. *Memoirs of Enzo Ferrari's Lieutenant*, Giorgio Nada, Milan, 2002.

Grayson, Stan (editor). *Ferrari – The Man, The Machines*, Automobile Quarterly, Princeton, 1975.

Guichard, Ami (editor). *Annual Automobile Review*, Edita, Lausanne, Editions 1953 to 1968.

Hawthorn, Mike. *Challenge Me the Race*, William Kimber, London, 1958.

Hodges, David. *A–Z of Formula Racing Cars*, Bay View, Bideford, 1990.

— *The French Grand Prix, 1906–1966*, Temple Press, London, 1967.

— *The Le Mans 24-Hour Race*, Temple Press, London, 1963.

— *The Monaco Grand Prix*, Temple Press, London, 1964.

Huet, Christian. *Gordini – Un Sorcier Une Equipe*, Editions Christian Huet, Paris, 1984.

Jarnaud, Robert. *Les Gordini*, Editions de l'Automobiliste, Paris, 1983.

Jenkinson, Denis. *A Story of Formula 1 – 1954–60*, Grenville, London, 1960.

— *Racing Car Review*. Grenville, London, Editions 1948 to 1958.

Lewis, Peter. *Alf Francis – Racing Mechanic,* G.T. Foulis, London, 1957.

Ludvigsen, Karl. *Alberto Ascari*, Haynes, Sparkford, 2000.

— *Classic Grand Prix Cars – The Front-Engined Era 1906–1960*, Haynes, Sparkford, 2006.

— *Classic Racing Engines*, Haynes, Sparkford, 2001.

— 'Duel of the Decade: Moss vs. Fangio,' *Speed Age*, May 1956.

— *Ferrari – The Factory*, Ludvigsen Library Series, Iconografix, Hudson, 2002.

— *Ferrari: 50 Years of Innovations in Technology*, Ferrari SpA, Modena, 1997.

— *Juan Manuel Fangio*, Haynes, Sparkford, 1999.

— *The V12 Engine*, Haynes, Sparkford, 2005.

McDonough, Ed. *Ferrari 156 Sharknose*, Sutton, Stroud, 2001.

Moss, Stirling, with Nye, Doug. *Stirling Moss – My Cars, My Career*, Patrick Stephens, Wellingborough, 1987.

Nye, Doug. *The Autocourse History of the Grand Prix Car – 1945–65*, Hazleton, Richmond, 1993.

— *Cooper Cars*, Osprey, London, 1983.

— *Dino – the Little Ferrari*, Osprey, London, 1979.

Oosthoek, Willem. *Birdcage to Supercage*, Dalton Watson, Deerfield, 2004.

Orsini, Luigi, and Zagari, Franco. *Maserati*, Libreria dell'Automobile, Milan, 1980.

— *OSCA – La Rivincita dei Maserati*, Giorgio Nada, Milan, 1989.

Pascal, Dominique. *Ferrari au Mans*, Editions EPA, Paris, 1984.

Pellegrini, Daniele P.M. (editor). *Rivista Maserati*, Giorgio Nada, Milan, 1998–9.

Pirazzini, Ezio. *L'Autodromo di Ferrari*, Marabini, Imola, 1992.

Pomeroy, Laurence. *The Evolution of the Racing Car*, William Kimber, London, 1966.

— *The Grand Prix Car*, Motor Racing Publications, Abingdon-on-Thames, 1949.

— *The Grand Prix Car, Volume Two*, Motor Racing Publications, London, 1954.

Posthumus, Cyril. *The German Grand Prix*, Temple Press, London, 1966.

— *World Sports Car Championship*, MacGibbon & Kee, London, 1961.

Prunet, Antoine. *Ferrari Sport et Prototypes*, Editions EPA, Paris, 1978.

Rogliatti, Gianni. *All Ferrari Engines*, Ferrari SpA, Modena, 2002.

Rolofson, Bob. 'How Moss Chose Maserati,' *Sports Cars Illustrated*, April 1956.

Salvadori, Roy, and Pritchard, Anthony. *Roy Salvadori – Racing Driver*, Patrick Stephens, Wellingborough, 1985.

Sculati, Eraldo. *Ferrari 1956*, Scuderia Ferrari Editions, Modena, 1956.

Sheldon, Paul, with Rabagliati, Duncan. *A Record of Grand Prix and Voiturette Racing*, Volume 4 1937–1949, Volume 5 1950–1953, Volume 6 1954–1959, Volume 7 1960–1964 and Volume 8 1965–1969, St Leonards, Bradford, 1993, 1988, 1987, 1991 and 1994.

Small, Steve. *Grand Prix Who's Who*, 3rd Edition, Travel Publishing, Reading, 2000.

Starkey, John; Renwick, Christopher; and Olczyk, Philippe. *Ferrari – Fifty Years on the Track*, Renwick & Starkey, San Diego, 1998.

Surtees, John, with Henry, Alan. *John Surtees – World Champion*, Hazleton, Richmond, 1991.

Tanner, Hans. *Maserati Owner's Handbook*, Floyd Clymer, Los Angeles, 1959.

Taruffi, Piero. *Works Driver*, Temple Press, London, 1964.

Thompson, Jonathan. *The Ferrari Formula One Cars – 1948–1976*, Aztex, Tucson, 1976.

Tragatsch, Erwin. *Das grosse Rennfahrerbuch*, Hallwag, Bern, 1970.

Wimpffen, János L. *Time and Two Seats – Five Decades of Long Distance Racing*, Motorsport Research Group, Redmond, 1999.

Yates, Brock. *Enzo Ferrari*, Doubleday, London, 1991.

In addition to books, many contemporary periodicals were consulted in the Ludvigsen Library in Suffolk during the research; where relevant they and the respective authors are referenced in the text. Of particular value to the work were *The Autocar, Automobile Quarterly, Cavallino, Autosport, The Motor, Ferrarissima, Speed Age, Settimo Giorno, Il Giorno, Auto Italiana, Auto Moto Sport, Interauto, Motor Sport, Forza* and *Road & Track*. The annuals *Autocourse* and *Automobile Year* have also been of value.

PHOTO CREDITS

The principal source for images for this book has been the Ludvigsen Library, www. ludvigsen.com. Where indicated below, with respect to the photographer, the images are the copyright property of the Library. Its holdings have benefited from the acquisition of the Cyril Posthumus archive, invaluable for the early years, and the Dalton Watson archive. Credited photographers are listed below. Any failure to identify photographers of specific images is unintentional and regretted.

Jesse Alexander
www.jessealexander.com
159 top, 180, 216, 222 bottom, 223 bottom, 227, 231 top, 232 bottom, 233.

Marcus Chambers, Ludvigsen Library
121, 209, 210 top.

Edward Eves, Ludvigsen Library
167, 215 bottom, 217, 245, 246, 247 both, 248 both, 252, 255, 274, 276 both, 277 both, 281 both, 282 top, 301 top, 302 top, 304 both, 305 both, 311 bottom, 312 top, 314 top.

Ferrari SpA
285 both, 290 bottom, 291, 292 both, 296, 297 top.

Walter Gotschke Picture Library
www.gotschke-art.com
Endpapers.

Pete Hagenbuch
214 top.

Indianapolis Motor Speedway
16 top, 198, 234, 235.

Peter Keen, Ludvigsen Library
190 bottom, 191, 192, 193 top.

Max LeGrand, Ludvigsen Library
122 top, 257 bottom, 261, 262 bottom, 263, 264 top, 267, 268, 270 both, 272, 275, 298, 307, 308 top, 309, 310.

Karl Ludvigsen, Ludvigsen Library
46 top, 50 both, 51 top two, 52 both, 53 both, 54, 55, 62 right, 63 all, 95 bottom, 96 bottom, 97 both, 104 both, 115 top, 122 bottom, 123 top, 124, 126 top, 127, 128, 138, 139 bottom, 146 bottom, 147, 148 both, 149 bottom, 159 bottom, 160 top & bottom, 161 all, 162 both, 163, 166 top, 168 both, 169, 171, 185, 193 bottom, 194, 197, 199 both, 200 bottom, 202, 203 top, 205 both, 206 both, 207, 208, 210 bottom, 211, 212 bottom, 213 both, 214 centre, 215 top, 218, 219 bottom, 222 top, 224 bottom, 226 both, 228, 229 both, 230 both, 231 bottom, 232 top, 239, 240, 241 top, 243, 254 bottom, 265 both, 269 both, 283 both, 302 bottom, 308 bottom, 313, 316 both, 317, 320.

Rodolfo Mailander, Ludvigsen Library
17 bottom, 19, 25, 32 bottom, 34, 38 top, 59 both, 62 left, 64 both, 65 both, 66 top, 69 both, 70 both, 71 both, 76, 77 top, 78 bottom, 79 top, 80, 81 both, 82 top, 83 bottom, 84 both, 85 top, 86, 87, 88 top, 90 both, 91, 96 top, 98, 99 bottom, 100, 101 both, 102 both, 103 bottom, 105, 109 bottom, 110 top, 113, 115 bottom, 116 top, 117, 120, 129, 130 both, 131, 133 both, 134 top, 139 top, 140 bottom, 142 both, 146 top, 150, 152, 156, 157 both, 176 bottom, 196 top, 258 bottom right.

Maserati SpA
51 bottom, 56 all, 123 bottom, 170, 258 top, 259 bottom, 288, 293, 294 both, 303 bottom, 314 bottom, 318, 322 both, 324, 325.

Gabriela Noris
266 centre and bottom.

Adolfo Orsi, Historica Selecta
14 bottom, 18 bottom, 112 bottom, 151, 174, 321.

Stanley Rosenthall, Ludvigsen Library
49 top, 251, 266 top, 271, 278, 287 both, 290 top, 295, 297 bottom.

Bill Stahl
49 bottom, 212 top, 214 bottom.

Julius Weitmann
238, 280.

Stephen F. Wilder, Ludvigsen Library
250 both.

INDEX